Causal Inference for Data Science

Causal Inference for Data Science

ALEIX RUIZ DE VILLA ROBERT

MANNING

SHELTER ISLAND

Manning Publications Co.
20 Baldwin Road
PO Box 761
Shelter Island, NY 11964

Development editor:	Frances Lefkowitz
Technical development editor:	Frances Buontempo
Review editor:	Dunja Nikitovic
Production editor:	Keri Hales
Copy editor:	Tiffany Taylor
Proofreader:	Jason Everett
Technical proofreader:	Timothy Lin
Typesetter and cover designer:	Marija Tudor

ISBN 9781633439658
Printed in the United States of America

Get the eBook FREE!

(PDF, ePub, Kindle, and liveBook all included)

We believe that once you buy a book from us, you should be able to read it in any format we have available. To get electronic versions of this book at no additional cost to you, purchase and then register this book at the Manning website.

Go to https://www.manning.com/freebook and follow the instructions to complete your pBook registration.

That's it!
Thanks from Manning!

Dedicated to my son Aran

brief contents

PART 1 INFERENCE AND THE ROLE OF CONFOUNDERS 1

    1 ▪ Introducing causality 3
    2 ▪ First steps: Working with confounders 30
    3 ▪ Applying causal inference 67
    4 ▪ How machine learning and causal inference can help each other 85

PART 2 THE ADJUSTMENT FORMULA IN PRACTICE 117

    5 ▪ Finding comparable cases with propensity scores 119
    6 ▪ Direct and indirect effects with linear models 150
    7 ▪ Dealing with complex graphs 178
    8 ▪ Advanced tools with the DoubleML library 221

PART 3 OTHER STRATEGIES BEYOND THE ADJUSTMENT FORMULA 247

    9 ▪ Instrumental variables 249
    10 ▪ Potential outcomes framework 272
    11 ▪ The effect of a time-related event 288

contents

preface   xiii
acknowledgments   xv
about this book   xvii
about the author   xxiii
about the cover illustration   xxiv

PART 1   INFERENCE AND THE ROLE OF CONFOUNDERS .. 1

1   **Introducing causality   3**

   1.1   How causal inference works   5

     *Step 1: Determine the type of data   5 ▪ Step 2: Understand your
problem   6 ▪ Step 3: Create a model   6 ▪ Step 4: Share your
model   6 ▪ Step 5: Apply causal inference techniques   7*

   1.2   Contrasts between causal models and the predictive
models of machine learning   8

   1.3   Experimental studies   10

     *Motivating example: Deploying a new website   10 ▪ A/B
testing   12 ▪ Randomized controlled trials   13 ▪ Steps to perform
an A/B test   14 ▪ Limitations of A/B testing and RCTs   16*

   1.4   Observational studies   16

     *Simulating synthetic data   18 ▪ Causal effects under
confounding   20*

1.5   Reviewing basic statistical concepts   21

    Empirical distributions and data-generating distributions   21
    A refresher on conditional probabilities and expectations   23

1.6   Further reading   27

1.7   Chapter quiz   28

2   **First steps: Working with confounders   30**

2.1   Learning the basic elements of causal inference through
        Simpson's paradox   32

    *What's the problem?   33 ▪ Develop your intuition: How to
    approach the problem   35 ▪ Solving Simpson's paradox   36*

2.2   Generalizing to other problems   38

    *Describing the problem with a graph   39 ▪ Articulating what we
    would like to know   39 ▪ Finding the way to calculate the causal
    effect   40 ▪ Articulating what we would like to know: The language
    of interventions   40 ▪ Finding the way to calculate the causal effect:
    The adjustment formula   42 ▪ How does the treatment work in each
    situation? The positivity assumption   44*

2.3   Interventions and RCTs   46

2.4   First contact with the structural approach   47

    *Simulating the kidney stone example   49 ▪ Interventions in the
    structural approach   51*

2.5   When to apply the adjustment formula   53

    *RCT or A/B test   54 ▪ Confounders   55 ▪ Unobserved
    confounders   55 ▪ Mediators   56 ▪ Many confounders   57
    Outcome predictive variables   57 ▪ Treatment predictive
    variables   59 ▪ Conditional Intervention   60 ▪ Combining all
    the previous situations   61 ▪ Summarizing the differences between
    intervening and applying the adjustment formula   62*

2.6   So, what's the plan?   63

2.7   Lessons learned   65

2.8   Chapter quiz   65

3   **Applying causal inference   67**

3.1   When and why to use graphs in causal inference analysis   68

3.2   Steps to formulate your problem using graphs   70

    *List all the variables   70 ▪ Create your graph   72 ▪ State your
    assumptions   75 ▪ State your objectives   76 ▪ Check the positivity
    assumption   77*

3.3 Other examples 78

    Recommender systems 78 ▪ Pricing 80 ▪ Simulations 81

3.4 Further reading 83

3.5 Chapter quiz 83

4 **How machine learning and causal inference can help each other 85**

4.1 What does supervised learning do? 87

    When should causal inference be used vs. supervised learning? 89
    The goal of data fitting 90 ▪ When the future and the past behave
    the same way 92 ▪ When do causal inference and supervised
    learning coincide? 93 ▪ Predictive error is a false friend 94
    Validation of interventions 100

4.2 How does supervised learning participate in causal inference? 101

    Empirical and generating distributions in the adjustment
    formula 103 ▪ The flexibility of the adjustment formula 104
    The adjustment formula for continuous distributions 104
    Algorithms for calculating the adjustment formula 104 ▪ Cross–
    fitting: Avoiding overfitting 108

4.3 Other applications of causal inference in machine learning 112

    Reinforcement learning 112 ▪ Fairness 113 ▪ Spurious
    correlations 113 ▪ Natural language processing 114
    Explainability 114

4.4 Further reading 114

4.5 Chapter quiz 115

PART 2 THE ADJUSTMENT FORMULA IN PRACTICE 117

5 **Finding comparable cases with propensity scores 119**

5.1 Developing your intuition about the propensity scores 121

    Finding matches for estimating causal effects 122 ▪ But is there a
    match? 124 ▪ Why matching can be hard 124 ▪ How
    propensity scores can be used to calculate the ATE 126

5.2 Basic notions of propensity scores 127

    Which cases are we working with? 128 ▪ What are the propensity
    scores? 130 ▪ The positivity assumption is … an
    assumption 130

5.3   Propensity scores in practice   131

*Data preparation   131 ▪ Calculating the propensity scores   132
Assess the positivity assumption   134 ▪ Calculating ATEs drawn
from the propensity scores   140*

5.4   Calculating propensity score adjustment:
An exercise   147

Exercise steps   147

5.5   Further reading   148

5.6   Chapter quiz   149

6   *Direct and indirect effects with linear models*   150

6.1   Estimating causal effects with linear models   153

*Simulating a pricing problem: A walkthrough   153 ▪ Direct
and indirect effects   159*

6.2   Understanding causal dynamics through linear
models   165

*The analogy of a gas flowing through pipes   165 ▪ How correlation
flows through a graph   166 ▪ Calculating causation and
correlation from the arrows' coefficients   171 ▪ Linear models
and the "do" operator   173*

6.3   Chapter quiz   176

7   *Dealing with complex graphs*   178

7.1   Altering the correlation between two variables
conditioning on a third one   182

*Arrival time example of conditional independence   183
Mathematical example of conditional independence   183
Breaking a causal model into independent modules   185
The bricks of DAGs: Factorizing probability distributions   188
What's the d-separation about?   195 ▪ Defining
d-separation   199*

7.2   Back-door criterion   201

The importance of the back-door criterion   205

7.3   Good and bad controls   207

Good controls   208 ▪ Neutral controls   208 ▪ Bad controls   209

7.4   Revisiting previous chapters   210

*Efficient controls   210 ▪ Propensity score   215 ▪ Again: Don't
include variables in your model just because they make the model*

more accurate   216 ▪ *Should you adjust for income?   216*
Linear models   217

7.5 An advanced tool for identifying causal effects:
       The do-calculus   218

7.6 Further reading   219

7.7 Chapter quiz   220

8 Advanced tools with the DoubleML library   221

8.1 Double machine learning   224

FWL theorem: The predecessor of DML   225 ▪ *Nonlinear models
with DML   229* ▪ *DML in practice   233* ▪ *Heterogeneous
treatment effects   238*

8.2 Confidence intervals   239

Simulating new datasets with bootstrapping   240 ▪ *Analytical
formulas for confidence intervals   241*

8.3 Doubly robust estimators   243

AIPW in practice   244

8.4 Further reading   245

8.5 Chapter quiz   245

PART 3   OTHER STRATEGIES BEYOND THE ADJUSTMENT
FORMULA 247

9 Instrumental variables   249

9.1 Understanding IVs through an example   251

The example's DAG   253 ▪ *IV assumptions   254* ▪ *IVs in
RCTs   255*

9.2 Estimating the causal effect with IVs   256

Applying IVs with linear models   256 ▪ *Applying IVs for partially
linear models   258* ▪ *An alternative formula for the IV
method   260* ▪ *The lack of a general formula for the general IV
graph   261*

9.3 Instrumental variables in practice   261

Two-stage least squares (2SLS) algorithm   263 ▪ *Weak
instruments   265* ▪ *IVs with DoubleML   268*

9.4 References   270

9.5 Chapter quiz   271

10 **Potential outcomes framework   272**

10.1   What is a potential outcome?   273

Individual outcomes   273 ▪ *Population outcomes   276*
Causal effects   276 ▪ *PO assumptions   277*

10.2   How do POs relate to DAGs?   278

The first law of causal inference   278 ▪ *Expressing PO assumptions
with DAGs   279* ▪ *Counterfactuals   280*

10.3   Adjustment formula with potential outcomes   282

10.4   IVs with potential outcomes   285

10.5   Chapter quiz   287

11 **The effect of a time-related event   288**

11.1   Which types of data will we use?   291

11.2   Regression discontinuity design   292

Data simulation   294 ▪ *RDD terminology   295*
Assumptions   297 ▪ *Effect estimation   298* ▪ *RDD in
practice   298*

11.3   Synthetic controls   310

Data simulation   312 ▪ *Synthetic controls terminology   313*
Assumptions   314 ▪ *Effect estimation   315* ▪ *Synthetic
controls in practice   315* ▪ *Selecting training and predicting
time periods   316*

11.4   Differences in differences   321

Data simulation   323 ▪ *DiD terminology   324*
Assumptions   327 ▪ *Effect estimation   329* ▪ *In practice   330*

11.5   Chapter quiz   335

11.6   Method comparison   335

11.7   References   336

appendix A   *The math behind the adjustment formula   337*

appendix B   *Solutions to exercises in chapter 2   341*

appendix C   *Technical lemma for the propensity scores   350*

appendix D   *Proof for doubly robust $\widehat{\text{ATE}}_{aipw}$ estimator   354*

appendix E   *Technical lemma for the alternative instrumental variable
estimator   357*

appendix F   *Proof of the instrumental variable formula for imperfect
compliance   358*

index   361

preface

The first time causal inference caught my attention was when I read a paper in 2016. It talked about causality, and I understood absolutely none of it. Curious about this exotic topic, I read Judea Pearl's works. Initially, I didn't expect much could be done with mathematical and statistical tools to model causality. But as I kept reading, I realized a lot can be done with causality from an applied perspective.

Back in 2016, I had been working as a data scientist for a few years. I enjoyed learning machine learning techniques; it was a new world, and my technical background was an advantage. Machine learning opened the doors to a variety of industries and companies, allowing me to enjoy my work and be productive.

Between 2016 and 2018, I began to sense that much of machine learning's progress was achieved through trial and error, without a deep understanding of its inner workings, and deep learning played a major role in this approach. The focus was on computing power and programming rather than on modeling the world. I was not against this approach, but it didn't fully satisfy me. At the same time, I was delving into causal inference. Each day, I found myself more aligned with its goals—uncovering the "why"—and its methods, which place a greater emphasis on statistics and mathematics while still incorporating programming.

At the end of 2018, I decided to take a year off to dive deeper into causal inference. I realized that companies often struggle to accurately assess the effect of their decisions, and it seemed inevitable that they would soon recognize the need for causal inference and create job opportunities in the process. When I discussed work problems with my data scientist colleagues, I noticed that I could understand and analyze their issues more quickly and thoroughly than before. And on a personal level, learning about causal inference fundamentally changed how I view the world: I began to find causal problems in many areas of society, including healthcare, economics, journalism, politics, and more.

It is satisfying to spend my time on a technique that can provide me with income and also help me better understand the world we live in. Since 2018, I have explained the basics of causal inference in many seminars, classes, blog posts, and now this book! Every time I teach this topic, I experience the same excitement as when I first discovered it.

acknowledgments

When I started writing this book, I thought it would take about a year. What a fool I was! It's taken three years, and I'm very proud and satisfied with the result. I think I've struck a neat balance between theory and practice and between intuition and formalism, which isn't always easy to do.

I thank my wife, Teresa, for supporting all my crazy ideas and projects. I love you (for better reasons than your support for this book!). I also thank my mother, Ana; father, Quique; and sister, Julia, for their constant support throughout my life. My need to understand why things are the way they are and what we can do to change them comes from them.

Next, a huge thanks to Manning for investing the time, effort, patience, and money to make this book possible. Among the Manning team, Frances Lefkowitz deserves a special mention. Without her, the book would be completely different. But not only that: she also made this long journey of writing rewarding in its own right. Her teachings and perspective have changed how I communicate with others in my daily work. (She is probably thinking about how these same sentences should be rephrased!) It has been a real pleasure to work with you, Frances. I would also like to thank the Manning production team who worked diligently behind the scenes to shepherd this book into its final format.

I can't forget my friends and colleagues who made extensive corrections and comments to improve the book: Llorenç Badiella, Carlos Ochoa, Bartek Skorulski, María José Peláez, and Jesús Cerquides. Thanks a lot! I also appreciate the reviewers whose suggestions helped make this a better book: Adi Shavit, Alexey Agarkov, Ayush Bihani, Benedikt Stemmler, Brian Cocolicchio, Carlos Aya-Moreno, Edgar Hassler, Ezra

Schroeder, Gregorio Piccoli, Jillian Morrison, Kali Kaneko, Karan Gupta, Kay Engelhardt, Kim Falk Jørgensen, Lara Thompson, Maxim Volgin, Mikael Dautrey, Peter Henstock, Peter Rabinovitch, Salil Athalye, Sergio Govoni, Shantanu Neema, Simone Sguazza, Sudipta Mukherjee, Thomas Joseph Heiman, Timothy Lin, Tony Dubitsky, and Tymoteusz Wołodźko. Thanks also to Sean Taylor, Matheus Facure, Philipp Bach, and Paul Hünermund for their support.

A special thanks to Ramon Navarro and Eudald Camprubí—the founders of Nuclia, a startup in Manresa, Catalonia—for understanding my passion for causal inference while keeping me on their team. Ramon and Eduald, deep down, you know that your startup would have been better off in Gracia, Barcelona, but, hey, nothing is perfect in this life!

Finally, I acknowledge the many researchers who have dedicated decades to advancing causal inference and bringing it to the forefront for the rest of us to build on. I want to thank Judea Pearl in a way he'd appreciate: through a counterfactual. If it weren't for him, I might never have ventured into the world of causal inference. The list of researchers contributing to causal inference is large. Among them, E. Bareinboim has expanded the area of graphical models in causal inference. Causal inference with a more statistical and econometrical flavor has been developed thanks to people like J. Robins, D. Rubin, V. Chernozhukov, G. Imbens, J. Angrist, MJ van der Laan, A. Rotnitzky, and E.H. Kennedy. Then there are B. Schölkopf and his colleagues, who have delved into the connections between causal inference and machine learning. And that's just scratching the surface—there are many more.

about this book

This book is designed for beginner or experienced data scientists, machine learning practitioners and researchers, data analysts, economists, and statisticians who want to improve their decision-making using observational data. It aims to give you a strong foundation in applying causal inference in your everyday tasks. It offers an intuitive guide to understanding which tools to use and, coupled with a more formal approach, ensures that you're confident in your actions.

Prerequisites

To follow along with the book, you will need a basic background in the following:

- Probability
  - Basic probability formulas such as the law of total probability and conditional probabilities
  - Basic probability distributions such as gaussians and binomials
  - How to generate random numbers with a computer
- Statistics
  - Linear and logistic regression
  - Confidence intervals
  - Recommended: basic knowledge of A/B testing and randomized controlled trials (how group assignment is done and hypothesis testing)
- Programming
  - Basic coding skills (reading/writing basic programs) with at least one programming language such as Python, R, or Julia

- Machine learning
  - Cross-validation and hyperparameter tuning
  - Recommended: Experience with machine learning models such as kNN, random forests, boosting, and deep learning

How this book is organized: A road map

This book is divided into three parts. Part 1 is all about the starting points of understanding cause and effect. You'll learn when to apply causal inference; the way certain variables, known as confounders, can twist your analysis; and how to estimate causal impacts by removing their influence using a method called the adjustment formula:

- Chapter 1 explains the two ways to infer causality from data: with experiments (called A/B tests or randomized controlled trials) or without them. It also explains the risks of analyzing nonexperimental data in the presence of confounders.
- Chapter 2 introduces the adjustment formula, which estimates the causal impact in nonexperimental data by removing the influence of confounders.
- Chapter 3 uses examples to show how to model your analysis using graphs.
- Chapter 4 explains how machine learning is used to calculate the adjustment formula and how causal inference can improve some aspects of machine learning.

Part 2 covers real-world issues you may face when using the adjustment formula from part 1:

- Chapter 5 discusses how to detect the lack of data in a treatment or decision you are evaluating.
- Chapter 6 explains how to estimate the causal effects of continuous variables using linear models.
- Chapter 7 covers how to know which variables you need to include in your analysis when your causal graph is complex by using the back-door criterion.
- Chapter 8 teaches the double machine learning technique (an advanced method to estimate causal effects) and confidence intervals. The chapter also explains how to calculate them with the DoubleML package.

Part 3 shows methods besides the adjustment formula for studying causes and effects:

- Chapter 9 introduces the instrumental variables technique, a method that uses an independent source of variation to estimate the causal effect that does not require knowing any confounders.
- Chapter 10 discusses the potential outcomes framework, an alternative to graphical causal models.
- Chapter 11 explains time-related techniques often used in economics, such as synthetic controls, regression discontinuity designs, and differences in differences.

The learning path and philosophy of this book

You will start by learning how to identify when you have a causal problem. Not every question is causal; sometimes we just want to describe what's happening now or predict what will happen in the future.

Next, the book guides you through the steps of making sense of causal questions, including these important ideas:

- When you need an experiment, when to use causal inference, and when to use machine learning
- Using causal diagrams to represent what's happening in the real world
- Using these diagrams to clearly share your goals, what you assume is true, the risks you're taking, and what your data can and cannot tell you
- Checking whether you have all the information (variables) you need for your analysis and, if not, how to figure out what's missing
- Estimating causal effects using statistical and machine learning techniques

Different learning styles

Learning does not follow a single path: some prefer *examples*, others lean toward *code*, and some find clarity in *math*. I've incorporated all three aspects in this book. Although you may have a preferred method, I suggest stepping out of your comfort zone to explore the others, as well. If you're at ease with math, try applying the techniques using synthetic datasets. Conversely, if you're more inclined toward coding, give the mathematical proofs a shot. The more points of view you have on this material, the better you will understand it.

When learning something new, I follow a "Think first, read next" approach. Here's how that approach plays out, in case you want to try learning this way:

- When I see a technical word, I try to remember its definition on my own before looking at the book.
- If the book states a fact, such as how confounders cause spurious correlations, I think about whether it makes sense to me before the book explains it.
- When the book talks about a math idea, such as linear regression, I come up with an example in my head. This way, what I'm thinking matches what I'm reading.

This approach may be a bit more difficult at first because I read more slowly, but it helps a lot in the long run. That's why you'll find "Think first, read next" sections in the book—they're to encourage thinking first.

How can you make sure you really get a concept?

- Instead of just asking whether you understand a concept, try asking yourself if you know what to do with it or how to use it. If those things aren't clear, you probably didn't understand the idea well.
- If part of you feels like going over it again, take a moment to reread it before moving forward.

- A great way to be sure you understand something is to explain it in simple words. So, in each chapter, you'll find a quiz section to practice this.
- Another good check is to see whether you can summarize the main ideas. That's why there's a "Summary" section at the end of each chapter.

What if you get stuck? Take your time, and go step by step. There is no rush.

Developing intuition and formal methodology

To begin using causal inference, you must get comfortable with its concepts and methods. This comfort, or intuition, comes from practicing the right kinds of problems.

Building your intuition

Causal inference is fascinating because it mixes ideas that feel both natural and surprisingly counterintuitive. In our daily lives, we often think about causes and effects. For example, we all agree that if it rains and the ground becomes wet, the rain is the reason the ground is wet. It is as simple as that. However, when we try to figure out how we know there's a cause-and-effect relationship, it's not so simple. We just observe that one event happens before another. As you read this book, you'll come across concepts that may be new or unexpected to you. You may have to look at familiar ideas, such as conditional probabilities, linear models, and even machine learning models, from a new angle. I'll introduce these fresh perspectives with examples and ideas that are easy to grasp. However, sticking to intuitive explanations means that sometimes we'll skip over detailed formalities. Don't get me wrong: definitions, theorems, and formulas have to be 100% correct. Being informal isn't an excuse for inaccuracies. But echoing George E.P. Box's idea that "All models are wrong, but some are useful," this book focuses on explaining helpful concepts in a straightforward way, often using metaphors and simplifications.

You will encounter some informality in this book when we discuss the distinctions between causal inference, machine learning, and statistics. For instance, I may say that causal inference is for finding causes, and machine learning is for predicting. This isn't an absolute statement but more of a generalization to guide you in identifying the kind of problem you're dealing with and the tools you need. As you delve deeper into causal inference, you'll find that, as in any field of knowledge, there's overlap between subjects and approaches, and the boundaries are somewhat blurry (if you're interested in the formal foundations of causal inference, I highly recommend reading Judea Pearl's book *Causality*, 2000, Cambridge University Press).

This book uses examples not just to explain what causal inference is but also to demonstrate how to use it. There's a balance to strike in how much detail to include with these examples. The more detailed they are, the more realistic they become. But if there's too much detail, you may not "see the forest for the trees," making the examples less helpful. I usually keep the examples simple so they're easier to understand and can be more easily adapted to your situation later.

Practicing the methodology

In addition to exercises, repetition is another tool I use to help you grasp causal inference techniques and make them part of your skill set. You'll learn how to figure out causal effects using binary variables, linear models, various algorithms that mix with machine learning models, and more. At first, each chapter may seem to tackle a different topic, but eventually you may notice that we're often doing similar things, just from different angles.

In causal inference, understanding what to do is important, but knowing what *not* to do can be even more crucial. There can be many potential causes we're not even aware of. These unknown unknowns are vital. Apart from understanding which formulas to use in different situations, it's also crucial to know which battles to fight and which to avoid. Being aware of what you know and what you don't know can help you avoid many problems. This knowledge lets you pick projects where you're more likely to succeed.

About the code

This book contains many examples of source code both in numbered listings and in line with normal text. In both cases, source code is formatted in a `fixed-width font like this` to separate it from ordinary text.

In some cases, the original source code has been reformatted; we've added line breaks and reworked indentation to accommodate the available page space in the book. Additionally, comments in the source code have been removed from the listings when the code is described in the text.

The code in the book was created with Quarto and turned into HTML (for R) and IPYNB (for Python) files. You can get executable snippets of code from the liveBook (online) version of this book at https://livebook.manning.com/book/causal-infer ence-for-data-science. All the code used in the examples, along with answers to the exercises, is available on the book's website at www.manning.com/books/causal-inference -for-data-science and on the GitHub repo at https://github.com/aleixrvr/CausalInfer ence4DataScience.

liveBook discussion forum

Purchase of *Causal Inference for Data Science* includes free access to liveBook, Manning's online reading platform. Using liveBook's exclusive discussion features, you can attach comments to the book globally or to specific sections or paragraphs. It's a snap to make notes for yourself, ask and answer technical questions, and receive help from the author and other users. To access the forum, go to https://livebook.manning .com/book/causal-inference-for-data-science/discussion. You can also learn more about Manning's forums and the rules of conduct at https://livebook.manning .com/discussion.

Manning's commitment to our readers is to provide a venue where a meaningful dialogue between individual readers and between readers and the author can take place. It is not a commitment to any specific amount of participation on the part of the author, whose contribution to the forum remains voluntary (and unpaid). We suggest you try asking the author some challenging questions lest his interest stray! The forum and the archives of previous discussions will be accessible from the publisher's website as long as the book is in print.

about the author

ALEIX RUIZ DE VILLA ROBERT has over 15 years of experience as a data scientist. He earned his PhD in mathematics and a master's in financial mathematics from Universitat Autònoma de Barcelona. He was the head of data science at LaVanguardia.com and SCRM (Lidl International Hub) and chief data scientist at Onna.

Since 2019, he has been working independently as a freelancer, focusing on research projects and teaching at various universities and business schools. He also advises the startup Nuclia.

Aleix is very active in organizing open events related to data science. He helped run the Barcelona R Users Group from 2011 to 2017 and founded and co-organized the Barcelona Data Science and Machine Learning meetup from 2014 to 2021.

about the cover illustration

The figure on the cover of *Causal Inference for Data Science* is "Femme Grecque," or "Greek Woman," taken from a collection by Jacques Grasset de Saint-Sauveur, published in 1788. Each illustration is finely drawn and colored by hand.

In those days, it was easy to identify where people lived and what their trade or station in life was just by their dress. Manning celebrates the inventiveness and initiative of the computer business with book covers based on the rich diversity of regional culture centuries ago, brought back to life by pictures from collections such as this one.

Part 1

Inference and the role of Confounders

You've probably heard the saying "Correlation is not causation." But what does it really mean? Is correlation helpful in understanding causation? For example, you may want to know how changing the price of a product affects sales. This part of the book explains that the best way to figure out if one thing causes another is to do experiments. However, you can't always do experiments. That's where causal inference comes into play.

One big reason just looking at correlation may not help (or may even lead you in the wrong direction) when you don't have experimental data is *confounders*. Confounders are factors that influence both the decision we're evaluating and the outcome we're interested in. They play a major role in causal inference. In chapter 2, you'll learn how much a confounder can twist your analysis and how to estimate the effect on your decision by removing the influence of confounders using the *adjustment formula*.

Chapter 3 will teach you how to use graphs to model your analysis. Graphs help you clearly state your objectives, lay out your assumptions, and figure out which causes and effects you can estimate from your data.

Finally, Chapter 4 will show you how to use machine learning to work out the adjustment formula when you're dealing with many confounders.

Introducing causality

This chapter covers

- Why and when we need causal inference
- How causal inference works
- The difference between observational data and experimental data
- Reviewing relevant statistical concepts

In many businesses and organizations, when we use machine learning, our goal is to make educated guesses about what will happen in the future. For example, a hospital may want to guess which patients will become very sick soon so doctors can treat those patients first. Often, just being able to make such guesses is enough; understanding *why* things happen isn't always necessary.

Causal inference is about figuring out *why* something happens. More than that, it's about asking what can be done to change an outcome. For instance, a hospital may want to understand which factors cause a certain illness. If it knows these causes, it can take steps like advising on public health policies or supporting

3

research to develop drugs that prevent the illness, aiming to reduce the number of people who get sick.

Why is causality important for anyone working with data? As data scientists or analysts, the questions we're most interested in often involve understanding cause and effect. We say that *X* causes *Y* if, when we change *X*, *Y* also changes. For example, if your goal is to keep your customers, you may want to know what actions will make them stay. This is a causal question: you're trying to find out what's behind your customer retention rates so you can improve them. This idea applies to many areas, such as designing marketing strategies, setting prices, adding new features to an app, making changes in an organization, introducing new policies, and developing medications. Understanding causality helps us see the effects of our decisions and identify which factors influence the outcomes we care about.

Ask yourself

Think about the kinds of questions you're interested in when you look at data. How many of these questions are about causality? Hint: Many causal questions involve looking at the effects of decisions or identifying factors (especially ones you can change) that influence your outcomes.

Understanding causality isn't straightforward. For example, imagine that you're trying to figure out why some people get sick more often than others. When looking at the data, you notice that people living in the country seem to get sick more often than city dwellers. Does this mean living in the country makes people sick? If that were true, moving to a city should mean you get sick less often. But is that the whole story? Living in a city has its own challenges, such as more pollution, lack of fresh food, and stress. So, the fact that city dwellers get sick less may be because city folks usually have higher incomes and can afford better healthcare, more nutritious food, and gym memberships. If this is what's really happening, moving from the country to a city may not actually make you healthier. In fact, without the income to afford healthcare or mitigate new city-based health risks, you may even get sicker.

This example demonstrates a common challenge in understanding cause and effect. Just because living in the city and being healthier often go hand in hand does not mean living in the city is what makes people healthier. This type of situation is why we often say "Correlation is not causation." Just because two things occur together doesn't prove that one causes the other. There may be other, more important reasons for the difference, such as how much money people have, which was the case in our example.

This is why learning about causal inference is so important for data scientists: it gives us tools to estimate causal effects. That is, it helps us discern mere coincidences (correlations) from true causes (causation), allowing us to identify the actual factors that lead to certain outcomes.

1.1 How causal inference works

Let's keep going with our example of trying to figure out what causes a certain illness. Let's say you have a collection of data that includes details on your patients (age, how many times they've been to the hospital, and other similar information) and the treatments they have received. What would you do to understand what's causing the illness? Let's explore how to determine the causes with five steps we typically use to solve causal problems. We will use these steps, shown in figure 1.1, and explore them in more detail throughout this book.

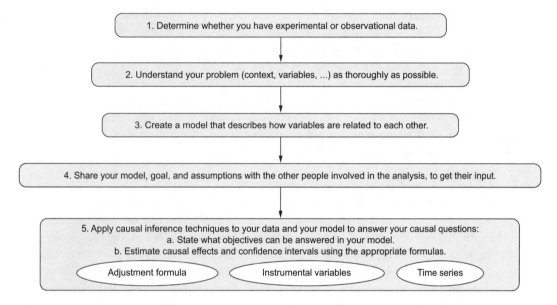

Figure 1.1 Five steps in the typical process of causal inference

1.1.1 Step 1: Determine the type of data

The first thing to understand is how your data has been created. Sometimes we can set up and run an experiment before we collect data. This lets us control the environment so we can be sure about the effects of something we're interested in. When we do this, we're working with *experimental data*. However, we can't always run experiments. For example, if we want to see how smoking affects teenagers and we know smoking can cause cancer, we can't ethically make some teenagers smoke. Or if we're looking at old data, we can't go back in time to set up an experiment. When we can't use experiments to get our data, we have what's called *observational data*. These two types of data are very different. Generally, we trust results from experimental data more than those from observational data.

When we can't run experiments, this is where causal inference comes in. If you're asking causal questions but can't use experimental data, you need causal inference. In   our city–country example, no experiment was set up; we just collected data as it came to us. The same is true for our example about determining the cause of certain ailments.

1.1.2 Step 2: Understand your problem

If you want to figure out what causes people to get sick, you have to collect all the possible reasons for the illness. Beyond basic details like age, gender, and location, you also need patients' medical history. Although the saying "The more information, the better" may remind you of a Big Data mantra, it holds particular importance here. In machine learning, you can build accurate predictive models without having all the variables; but in causal inference, missing a relevant variable can lead to a failure.

For instance, for certain illnesses, knowing about comorbidities (other illnesses besides the one you're interested in) can be very important. Let's say that for some reason you don't have access to information about patients' comorbidities. In causal inference, you won't be able to determine the cause of the illness you're studying. However, you may be able to create a successful predictive model with machine learning. This is because comorbidities lead to more frequent hospital visits. So even without details on patients' comorbidities, you may have highly correlated information in the form of the frequency of patients' visits. This information may be sufficient for machine learning to predict the likelihood of patients getting sick.

1.1.3 Step 3: Create a model

Once you have all the important factors, you create a causal model that attempts to isolate the true causal effect by accounting for potential confounding variables that might influence both the "cause" and "effect" variables. Causal models are conceptual frameworks often represented using Directed Acyclic Graphs (DAGs) which visually depict the causal relationships between variables, including potential mediating variables and confounders. In a causal DAG, variables are represented as nodes and causal relationships between them as arrows. You'll learn more about causal modeling with DAGs in chapter 3, and we will use them throughout most of this book. Another approach to causal modeling is to use equations, which we'll talk about in chapter 10.

You can go for simpler models with fewer factors and fewer assumptions. But if the model is too simple, it may not work well in the real world and won't help you make accurate predictions. On the other hand, more complex models can be hard to handle in terms of mathematical formulas, computational methods, or checking whether complex assumptions hold in reality.

In the end, the way to know whether a model is good enough is to determine whether it's useful for your goal. It depends on what you want to achieve. For example, if you make a model for a personal app to find objects in pictures, some mistakes may be okay. But if the model is for a self-driving car, a small mistake could cause an accident. In that case, you need a super-accurate model so it is reliable and useful.

1.1.4 Step 4: Share your model

You have your model, which is shaped by certain assumptions, and a clear goal in mind (typically to estimate a causal effect). It's crucial to lay out these assumptions and goals explicitly and collaborate with experts and others involved in the analysis. This step is vital because you may have overlooked important variables or misunderstood how variables are connected. In the example, you may share your model with physicians and biologists to get their input.

Engaging in communication with others is a good practice to ensure that you're asking the right questions, aligning on overall goals, and identifying possible variables and their relationships accurately. This collaborative process helps in minimizing blind spots and enhancing the robustness of your analysis.

1.1.5 *Step 5: Apply causal inference techniques*

In this final step, it's time to apply causal inference techniques to your dataset and use your model to address your causal questions. Remember, just because two variables are correlated doesn't necessarily mean one causes the other. Often, when there's a correlation but no direct causation, it's because of a third factor that influences both. These third-factor variables are known as *confounders* and will be explained in detail in this chapter.

Informally speaking, in causal inference, the presence of confounders is the root of all evil because they can lead to misleading conclusions. Luckily, causal inference provides a set of formulas, algorithms, and methodologies to handle them. This involves a series of steps:

1 Ask yourself what you can answer with the information you have and ascertain which of your causal questions can be answered using your model and your data. Sometimes the lack of information about confounders becomes a problem. Identify which cases can be overcome, and consider alternatives for the rest, such as gathering new data or finding surrogate variables.

2 Discern correlation from causation using your data to estimate causal effects. This is done using a specific set of formulas. Most of this book is devoted to explaining how, when, and why to employ these formulas; how to select the appropriate formulas for different kinds of problems; and how to apply them efficiently using statistical and machine learning techniques.

In this book, you will see three different techniques for estimating causal effects. We will discuss when and how each technique can be applied:

- *Adjustment formula*—The adjustment formula is a mathematical formula designed to remove the effect of confounders: that is, factors that affect the treatment or decision variable and the outcome at the same time. This formula and its applications take up a big part of this book. The main formula is explained in chapter 2, and its variations are explained in chapters 4–8.

- *Instrumental variables*—Some methods use an extra variable called an *instrument*. An instrument is a variable that is not related to any confounders and only directly influences the treatment, not the outcome. It serves as an independent source of variation. There are many versions of this technique, but in this book, we will cover the basic form. This method will be explained in chapter 10.

- *Time series-related techniques*—These techniques were discovered by econometricians and work very well with time series data; they include differences in differences, regression discontinuity design, and synthetic controls. Like instrumental variables, there are many versions of these techniques. In this book, we will only focus on their time series applications, which will be explained in chapter 11.

Besides getting causal estimates, you also need to calculate *confidence intervals*, as covered in chapter 8. To estimate confidence intervals, there are general methods like bootstrapping as well as specific methods for each of the three techniques, often included in their respective software packages.

As I've said, there are two frameworks to work with causal inference. One framework popularized primarily by Turing award-winning Judea Pearl, uses DAGs. The other is based on *potential outcomes* (POs); this approach is closer to the way of thinking used in statistics and econometrics and was developed and popularized by, among others, Donald Rubin, James Robins, Guido Imbens, and Nobel winner Joshua Angrist. In parts 1 and 2 of this book, we will use the language of DAGs; in part 3, we will work with POs. Each framework uses different notations and basic concepts, but they are inherently similar. Both will give you the same results for many problems, but in some cases, one or the other is more appropriate to use.

1.2 Contrasts between causal models and the predictive models of machine learning

The main principle guiding this book is simple: *the better you understand the tools of causal inference and the context of your problem, the more reliable your conclusions from causal analysis will be.* The goal is to equip you with a solid understanding so you can confidently apply causal inference in your daily work. Therefore, we will go deeply into the math, including algorithms and statistical calculations. If you come from the machine learning world, you may find these details a bit overwhelming at first and wonder why you need to learn them. In some senses, causal inference is closer to statistics than machine learning. In short, you need to know the theoretical underpinnings of causal inference because in contrast to the predictive models of machine learning, *it is difficult to determine whether causal conclusions are accurate.* So, to assess their conclusions, causal inference practitioners need a deeper understanding of what is going on in their models.

For instance, knowing the intricacies of model design or having domain knowledge is not a prerequisite for successfully building predictive machine-learning models. It is possible, for instance, to win Kaggle competitions without any domain knowledge at all. It is also possible to use support vector machines (SVMs) to create successful predictive models without understanding the complex math behind the model. Similarly, you can make very accurate text classifiers using a set of embeddings without knowing how these embeddings are created. You can also train reliable neural networks without understanding the mathematical differences between the different gradient descent strategies.

Of course, building a trustworthy product on top of a predictive model does require an understanding of how the model operates. Without that understanding, your model may introduce biases or, in more serious cases, cause harm to society. This is why we are concerned with fairness and explainability in machine learning—they help us tackle these problems and ensure responsible and ethical use of the technology.

In contrast with predictive modeling, causal inference requires a solid understanding of four key areas of the problem:

- *Definitions*—Concepts like spurious correlations, confounders, interventions, etc., are intricate but reflect aspects of reality. Without a clear grasp, your causal models may be flawed.
- *Assumptions*—Knowing when to apply specific techniques is guided by assumptions. In this book, many assumptions are inherently embedded in the directed acyclic graph (DAG).
- *Risks and limitations*—Recognizing what can be inferred from data and what cannot, as well as understanding the consequences of overlooking a relevant variable, is vital in causal inference. These considerations can significantly affect your conclusions.
- *Goals*—Clearly defining what you are trying to estimate is essential. Defining the goals helps you to guide the entire causal inference process.

Let's illustrate this difference between the two types of models with an example. When you construct a house using plans from an architect, you can inspect the finished house to ensure that every detail (walls, ceilings, doors) aligns with the plans. So, you can know whether the house is correctly built. Similarly, in machine learning, you can know whether a trained model will work as expected by evaluating your model on a test dataset using cross-validation. Essentially, once your model is complete, assuming future data behaves similarly to the past, you can assess how well your model is likely to perform.

But suppose you want to ensure that your house can withstand earthquakes. How can you assess whether the house is earthquake resistant? This is a causal question (what effect will an earthquake have on the structural integrity of this house?) and requires a causal approach. Waiting for a real earthquake isn't practical, so you explore other ways to boost your confidence:

- *Determining the correct building process for earthquake safety*—You rely on a theory about how earthquakes affect houses, and you construct your house in alignment with this theory. This assures you that the resulting house is correctly built as you meticulously supervise each step of the construction process to ensure its adherence.
- *Simulating scenarios*—If the theory isn't a perfect fit or you want additional assurance, you can create a model and simulate small earthquakes to observe how your house responds. In causal inference, this is comparable to creating synthetic data to test the effectiveness of the technique you plan to use.

Although ensuring correct building processes and simulating scenarios boost confidence, they aren't definitive solutions. Still, they enhance your confidence in the results. Even if your findings are correct, if you don't trust them, you won't act on your conclusions.

You may be wondering if there's a tool like cross-validation for causal inference problems. Unfortunately, as we'll discuss in the book, *such a tool doesn't exist.* The only way to know whether your conclusions are right is to test them in the real world or conduct an experiment like an A/B test or a randomized controlled trial. In essence, the goal of causal inference—to understand what would happen in a different scenario than what actually occurred—means that without testing, achieving 100% certainty about the accuracy of your conclusions is nearly impossible.

1.3 Experimental studies

As we've talked about before, whether we have experimental data determines whether we need causal inference. In this section, we'll introduce A/B tests, also known as randomized controlled trials (RCTs), and explore why they are considered the gold standard for establishing causal relationships. Even though this book doesn't focus on them, many causal inference methods try to mimic what A/B tests do. That's why understanding A/B tests is important.

1.3.1 Motivating example: Deploying a new website

Imagine that you're working for an online business, such as an e-commerce site. The website is crucial for the company because a good-quality site makes users feel comfortable, providing a better experience and leading to more sales. Over the last two years, regular customers have told you what they don't like about the site, so you have a clear idea of what needs to be improved. The company decides to overhaul the website, incorporating all the new features customers have been asking for. After six months of hard work by the IT department, the updated website is launched.

Now you start to question whether all the effort was worthwhile. Has the new website increased user engagement and sales? You based the updates on feedback from your most loyal customers, which seemed reliable. But what works for one group of customers may not appeal to everyone. Your regular customers have specific needs that may not represent the majority of your users. So, you realize it's essential to monitor your website's performance metrics to determine whether the new version is successful.

A month into tracking, you review the data and see the graph shown in figure 1.2 of website visits over time. At first glance, it looks like the website was losing visitors until the new version was launched, after which visits started to increase. It seems as though your efforts have paid off!

You launched the new website right after a holiday, and you realize that this timing may explain the initial drop and subsequent increase in site visits. The decrease may simply be due to the holiday lull, and the uptick may be a normal post-holiday surge, not necessarily a result of the new site features. But you have a hunch that without the

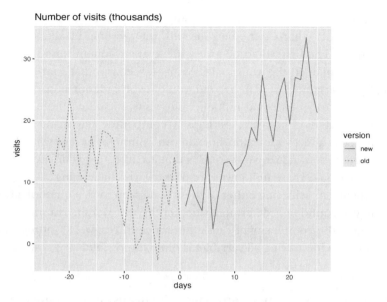

Figure 1.2   Comparison of website traffic before and after launching the new version. You want to figure out whether creating the new website was beneficial in terms of attracting more visitors.

new site, this increase might have been smaller. To truly understand the effect of the website overhaul, you think about comparing current visitor numbers to those from the same period last year.

But the complexity doesn't end with accounting for seasonality. Other factors may also be affecting site traffic. For example, a recent marketing campaign may have played a significant role in drawing more visitors. This layer of complexity suggests that evaluating the new website's success involves considering a variety of potential influences, not just the timing of its launch.

Think first, read next
What other factors may affect web views?

More than seasonality may be influencing the numbers. Other factors may be at play:

- A marketing campaign may have boosted site traffic.
- Maybe your competitors made a mistake, sending their customers your way.
- New regulations (for example, the General Data Protection Regulation [GDPR] in the European Union) may have affected customer trust and website usability.
- Successful new hires may be making a big difference.
- The overall socioeconomic situation may have improved compared to last year.

As you delve deeper, it becomes clear that assessing the effect of the new website isn't straightforward. To truly compare the new site with the old one, ideally, you'd need one of two situations. The first would be a very stable environment where everything except the website remained the same as last year—a scenario that's rare in today's ever-changing business landscape. The second would involve identifying and accounting for all possible factors that could influence site visits, including those you might not even be aware of. For instance, perhaps a competitor has made significant changes that indirectly affect your traffic, but you can't pinpoint exactly what they did. And then there are unknown factors—variables that are affecting your site traffic but to which you're oblivious. These unknowns are particularly challenging.

Given the difficulty in achieving either of these ideal scenarios, a question arises: is there another way to confidently determine whether the new website is a success? This challenge highlights the complexity of causal inference in real-world settings, where controlling for or even identifying all variables is often impossible.

1.3.2   A/B testing

The most effective way to sidestep the problems we've discussed is to conduct an A/B test: a special kind of experiment designed to provide the clarity we need. Before diving into A/B testing, however, it's crucial to understand what it really means for one event to cause another. This foundational understanding sets the stage for appreciating how A/B testing can isolate the effect of changing one variable (like a website design) on an outcome (such as site visits or sales), giving us a clearer picture of cause and effect.

> **Develop your intuition**
>
> Our main goal is to figure out which of the two versions gets more visits. To do this, we'll first look at the challenges of examining the data from figure 1.2. Then, we'll suggest various solutions and improve them step by step. This process will naturally lead us to explain what A/B tests are.

We've loosely said that X causes Y if changing X leads to a change in Y. In our scenario, X is the website version, and Y is the number of visits to the site. To empirically measure X's effect on Y, based on this definition, you'd have to change X and see if Y changes. But the challenge you face is altering X without also changing other factors that may influence Y. For example, if you launch a new website at the same time as a new marketing campaign, it's unclear whether any change in Y is due to the website or the campaign.

In an ideal world, to accurately assess the new website's effect on visit numbers, you'd need two identical universes: one with the old website and one with the new one. Then, any difference in visits could be directly attributed to the website version.

Unfortunately, creating such parallel universes isn't feasible, so you must find another approach.

Generally speaking, two main factors can influence a website's visitor numbers at any given time: the surrounding environment or context and the type of users visiting the site. For a fair comparison between the old and new website versions, you want these factors to be the same for both as much as possible.

One way to ensure that both versions experience the same environmental conditions is to run an experiment where both websites are live simultaneously. This setup means any external changes, such as new laws or competitive strategies, will affect both versions equally.

The challenge now is deciding which users see which version of the website. Technically, users can be identified by cookies, allowing you to direct traffic to a specific version based on this identifier. From a business standpoint, it may seem logical to direct your most frequent visitors to the new site because their feedback inspired the changes. Although this makes business sense, it complicates the experiment. If only frequent users see the new version, it's hard to tell whether any change in overall site visits is due to the website's improvements or happens because these particular users are more inclined to visit more often.

This highlights a critical point: *whatever characteristic you use to assign versions of the website will cast doubt on the results of your experiment.* It raises the question of whether changes in visit numbers are truly due to the website's modifications or a result of the specific behaviors of the user group you selected.

The only way you can ensure that you don't introduce any kind of bias with the assignment is to decide who sees what totally at random. Imagine that for each person (each has a unique ID), you're doing a virtual coin toss to decide if they'll use version A or B. Because of the ID, they'll stick to one version—they won't switch versions each time they visit your site. This procedure ensures that if you have lots of users, group A and group B will have the same distribution of population characteristics. So, things like how often they visit your site, their age, where they come from, and other important details that may influence how they use your site will be evenly split between the two groups.

An *A/B test* is an experiment to test two different options, A and B, to see which one works better for a specific goal you have in mind. Both options are tested at the same time, and users are randomly assigned to option A or B without consideration of their personal traits. This method ensures that both options are tested under the same conditions, and if you have enough users, both groups will be similar in terms of the important characteristics of the people who visit your website.

1.3.3 *Randomized controlled trials*

A/B tests have been used for a very long time. In healthcare, they are known as *randomized controlled trials* (RCTs) and have been around for hundreds of years. The earliest one we know of was in 1747, when James Lind was looking for a way to cure scurvy.

The basic idea is the same. Suppose you have a new *treatment* that you think may cure a certain illness. You want to test if it works. So, you set up two groups: one (the *intervention* group) gets the new medicine, and the other (the *control* group) gets something else to compare it against, such as an old medicine or a placebo (a treatment that does nothing). These are your A and B groups. It's important that people aren't assigned to either group based on things like age because then you wouldn't know whether the treatment worked on its own or because of who was in the group. Instead, the treatment assignment is done at random, just as in an A/B test. Officially, A/B tests are a type of RCT. But although *RCT* is a term often used in healthcare, *A/B test* is more commonly used by companies, especially those online. For this book, we'll use both terms to mean the same thing: we have a treatment or decision to make, and we want to see how it affects a particular outcome.

1.3.4   *Steps to perform an A/B test*

The way an A/B test is conducted is similar to the scientific method itself. The main goal is to come up with a hypothesis and then carry out an experiment to see whether it's true. For more detailed explanations, check out the "Further reading" section. Here, we're just providing a brief overview.

STEP 1: HYPOTHESIS AND EXPERIMENT DESIGN
The experiment begins with a hypothesis, which should outline the cause-and-effect relationship you're interested in between the treatment or decision and our primary outcome of interest. For instance, if there's a new way to treat a disease, your starting hypothesis may be that this new method works just as well as the old one (meaning the new method isn't necessarily better). This assumption suggests that switching to the new method won't offer any extra benefits. However, if the new treatment is truly superior, the experiment should provide enough evidence to refute this hypothesis.

After setting your hypothesis, you plan the experiment. The design can vary significantly, especially between A/B testing on websites and RCTs for new medical treatments. RCTs tend to be more complex because they deal with people's health (which involves following lots of rules and international standards and respecting privacy). They also have to consider the psychological effects of using placebos and finding volunteers for the study. On the other hand, A/B tests on digital platforms can be simpler. Often there are no ethical concerns, and users may participate in the test without even realizing it.

STEP 2: EXECUTION
This is when you carry out the experiment, being very careful not to make any mistakes, especially with the randomization process. Mistakes here may lead to incorrect conclusions.

STEP 3: ANALYSIS
After the experiment is done, you end up with data showing how each group responded. For example, you might find that 80% of patients treated with the new

method got better, whereas only 70% improved with the old method. This data could look like this in a very simplified form:

- Old treatment: 1, 0, 0, 1, 1, 1, 1, 0, 1, 1
- New treatment: 1, 1, 1, 0, 1, 1, 1, 1, 1, 0

Here, "1" means a patient got better, and "0" means they didn't. You can look at other outcomes, too, if needed. Now, the big question is, "Is the new treatment better than the old one?" With a 10% higher recovery rate, it seems as though it may be.

The difference in the average results between the two groups is known as the *average treatment effect* (ATE). It tells us how much effect the treatments have compared to each other. The ATE is very important in causal inference and will be explained in detail in chapter 2.

Important interpretation

Because you assign people to groups randomly, if your sample is big enough, both groups will have similar characteristics, such as age. This means that when you calculate the average result for a group, you're estimating what would happen if everyone got that treatment. So, calculating the ATE is an estimation of the difference between the effectiveness of the new treatment if it were given to the whole population and the effectiveness of the old treatment if it were given to the whole population.

Once you have calculated the ATE, the next question is, "If you did the experiment again the same way, would you get the same results?" If you think the answer is "No," you can't fully trust the results.

Indeed, you cannot expect to get the same results if you repeat the experiment. Every time you run the experiment, each person's situation may change a bit, which may change their results. This leads you to wonder how many of your results are due to chance. Separating signal from noise is a key part of statistics. Typically, the randomness of A/B tests is analyzed using hypothesis testing and *p*-values. Some people prefer Bayesian hypothesis testing, instead. We won't dive into those methods here, but you can find more information in the "Further reading" section if you're interested.

It's important to note that RCTs (and A/B tests) can tell us whether two options lead to different outcomes, but they don't explain why. For example, if a new website design has many changes from the old one and you see a difference in the number of visits, you can't say for sure what specific change made the difference. On the other hand, if your test changes something small, and it doesn't have a big effect, you may need a really large group of people to see any difference. So, you have to find a balance.

CHECKPOINT

Let's emphasize how important A/B tests or RCTs are in establishing a causal relationship with statistical confidence. They're not optional; they're the most reliable method to confirm causality. If you're unsure about this, we recommend revisiting section 1.4.2.

As you go through each step, consider what you might do differently. Hold onto your questions and reflections for the upcoming sections to see if things become clearer.

1.3.5   Limitations of A/B testing and RCTs

A/B tests and RCTs are the gold standard for detecting causality: whenever possible, you should always run an A/B test or RCT. However, like any tools, they also have limitations. Causal inference can be used in situations like the following, where an A/B test or RCT is not feasible:

- *Experimenting is infeasible.* For instance, if you want to know how a new product of your competition affected your sales, good luck asking your competition to randomize which customers they show the new product to and sending you their sales stats.
- *Experimenting is unethical.* If you want to see whether smoking produces cancer in children, it is not ethical to make some children smoke because they are in the intervention group.
- *Experimenting is timely or costly.* If you want to safely know whether a treatment has long-term side effects, the experiment needs to have a long duration.
- *There is a lack of external validity.* Usually, RCTs need to recruit people for the experiment. This set of people may have a particular interest in participating in the experiment (money, potential recovery of an illness, and so on). Thus, they may not be representative of the general distribution of people who would potentially use the treatment. In this case, we say that there is a lack of external validity.

> **Question**
> Which experiments can you run in your organization to answer causal questions of interest? How would you design them?
>
> Hint: you can try to design experiments related to the answers you gave in this chapter's introduction.

1.4   Observational studies

Experiments are great because they clearly reveal the causal nature between two variables. But you can't always do experiments. When you can't, you fall into the realm of observational data: data that has not been obtained through an A/B test or RCT. This section talks about what can go wrong without A/B tests. Observational data seems to encompass most of the data we usually work with.

> **Ask yourself**
> What kinds of observational data does your organization use?

Some examples of observational data are as follows:

- A customer database that links your marketing efforts to customer actions
- Tracking sales changes based on decisions your company makes
- Data on how different countries handled COVID-19 and the effects of the spreading virus

Generally, most data is used to evaluate social policies without doing experiments. We're used to drawing conclusions from observational data (sometimes right, sometimes not so right). Next we'll explore why observational data can be tricky to work with.

When do you need causal inference?

You need causal inference whenever you want to make decisions based on observational data. If you continue your journey through causal inference, at some point you will find that causal inference is also useful for extracting information from RCTs or A/B tests that cannot be extracted otherwise. However, for the sake of simplicity, we will start by considering causal inference only for observational data.

As mentioned previously, "Correlation is not causation" is a famous saying in statistics. Here, *correlation* means two things happening together, not just the math formula. But how misleading can it be? Consider a chart (figure 1.3) showing the link between arcade revenue and computer science PhDs. They have a mathematical correlation of 0.98, which is very high. This may make it seem as though one causes the other. But if you stop to think about it, you'll realize that idea doesn't make sense.

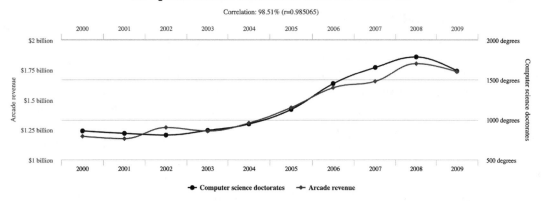

Figure 1.3   Link between arcade earnings and computer science doctorates. Although there's a strong correlation, it's possible to question whether there is actually a cause-and-effect connection. Source: www.tylervigen.com/spurious-correlations.

Above and beyond

Check out Tyler Vigen's awesome Spurious Corrections web page (www.tylervigen .com/spurious-correlations) and the correlations in the site's charts. Note that in some cases, you can give a plausible explanation, but others seem nonsensical.

Just because two things are correlated doesn't mean one causes the other. But why are they correlated? There's usually a reason! Often it's because of a common cause. For example, an increase in population may explain why both arcade revenue and the number of computer science PhDs are going up. More people may mean more arcade customers and more students pursuing higher education.

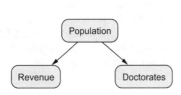

Figure 1.4   Both arcade revenue and computer science doctorates increase when the population increases, so the population is a potential common cause between the two.

Humans often think that if two things happen together, there must be a common reason. This isn't always the case, but thinking this way can be helpful at times. The idea of a common cause affecting both things can be shown with a graph, such as in figure 1.4.

We can say that just finding a correlation isn't enough to prove cause and effect. This is mainly because causation has a direction. For example, when you light a fire under a pot of water, you understand that the fire causes the water to boil. In causal inference, we express this as *fire → boiling*.

This relationship doesn't work the other way around; it is not symmetric. Obviously, boiling water in a microwave, for instance, doesn't cause a fire on the stove. So although correlation treats two things as if they may influence each other equally ($\mathrm{corr}(x, y) = \mathrm{corr}(y, x)$), causation doesn't work that way. Correlation is blind with respect to causal directionality.

1.4.1 *Simulating synthetic data*

In the previous section, you found out that a factor can link two other factors together. This makes sense, right? But can you check whether this idea is correct? Absolutely. You can do this by making *synthetic datasets* and trying your ideas on them.

We will use made-up data to demonstrate how two things may appear connected when actually they are not. In this case, we'll create a number for the US population, naming it `population`. Then, we will create two new variables, `revenue` and `doctorates`. Their values will be based only on `population`, without taking any information from each other. In the end, you'll notice that `doctorates` and `revenue` look like they're linked. This is a coded example of what we call a *spurious correlation*.

The code in listings 1.1 and 1.2 shows that the correlation between `doctorates` and `revenue` is 0.95. This example doesn't prove that the population is the actual reason for the link between arcade revenue and computer science doctorates. It just suggests that the reason for their connection may be a third factor, such as population, that affects both of them.

Listing 1.1 (R) Building a synthetic dataset that creates spurious correlations

```
set.seed(1234)

time <- 2000:2009
population <- 280 + 3 * (time - 2000) +
    rnorm(n=length(time), sd=0.1)
revenue <- 1.25 + (population - 280) * 0.015 +
    rnorm(n=length(time), sd=0.05)
)
doctorates <- 700 + (population - 280) * 30 +
    rnorm(n=length(time), sd=10)

cor(doctorates, revenue)
```

In millions of people

In billions of dollars

In number of people

Listing 1.2 (Python) Building a synthetic dataset that creates spurious correlations

```
from numpy.random import uniform, seed, normal
from numpy import arange, corrcoef
import pandas as pd

seed(1234)

time = arange(2000, 2010)
population = 280 + 3 * (time - 2000) + \
    normal(size=len(time), scale=0.1)
revenue = 1.25 + (population - 280) * 0.015 + \
    normal(size=len(time), scale=0.05)
doctorates = 700 + (population - 280) * 30 + \
    normal(size=len(time), scale=10)
corrcoef(doctorates, revenue)[0][1]
```

In millions of people

In billions of dollars

In number of people

In this book, we will use a lot of synthetic datasets. The reason is that when we work with data as analysts, our main goal is to create a model of how things work in the real world using this data. There's a process that creates the data, such as the laws of physics or how things really work. We're trying to reverse-engineer to figure out how reality operates based on the data we have.

But here's the tricky part: we don't have a direct way to see these rules. We can only guess them based on data and experiments. So even if we do a really good job, we can't be certain that our conclusions match exactly how things work in reality. There's always some uncertainty. Figure 1.5 shows how we use data to depict reality.

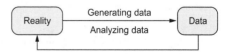

Figure 1.5 Standard steps in data analysis: we collect some data generated by our environment. The data-generating process is hidden from us. Our goal is to study this data to figure out how things really operate. Think of it as reverse engineering.

When we're learning about a new scientific topic, it's important to know whether we're doing it right. In our case, when we work with real data, as we've mentioned before, we can't always be sure our results are correct. We need a process to validate our methodology.

Here's a way to deal with this challenge: instead of using real data, we make our data, and then we use the methods we believe are the best for the job to analyze it. Because we know exactly how we created this data, it's like having the "truth" or the correct answers. This helps us be certain that our conclusions are accurate.

Think of it like learning to swim. At first, you start in a safe, shallow swimming pool where you can touch the bottom. This is similar to analyzing data when you know the correct answers. Once you've learned and practiced in this safe environment, you can move on to more challenging and unfamiliar situations, such as swimming in the open sea. This is similar to analyzing real data without knowing the correct answers in advance.

1.4.2 *Causal effects under confounding*

This section introduces a basic graph you'll see often in this book. It's the simplest example where causal inference is needed: estimating the effect of one variable on another when a third variable influences both of them. This third factor can create correlations among variables that confound the main effect, leading to the classic "Correlation is not causation" problem. The first big step in this book is learning how to separate this bias, called *confounding bias*, using something called the *adjustment formula*, which we'll cover in chapter 2.

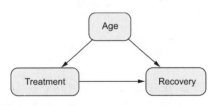

Figure 1.6 Apart from how treatment may affect recovery, there's a third element affecting both simultaneously. These elements are called confounders. For instance, in this example, age is a confounder.

Here's a scenario to think about. You're a doctor, and there's a new medication for a certain illness. Initial studies suggest it's more effective than the current treatment. You've been giving this new drug a try for almost a year, focusing on older patients because they're more at risk. However, not all older patients get the new drug, and some younger ones do. Now you want to figure out whether the new drug really is as effective as the studies say, based on your own experience. The situation can be visualized with the graph shown in figure 1.6.

Age influences the choice of medication (treatment) because you consider the patient's age before deciding on a specific drug. Additionally, age affects recovery because older individuals usually recover more slowly than younger ones. When you aim to understand the effect of a treatment or a decision on a result, and another factor affects both, we call that factor a *confounder*. In this scenario, age is a confounder. Often we encounter not just one but several confounders at the same time. The factor whose effect we're trying to measure is often referred to as the *treatment* or *decision variable.* The result we're interested in, or what we want to see the treatment's effect on, is known as the *outcome.* Refer to figure 1.7.

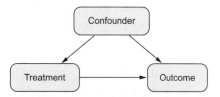

The term *confounder* is used because this factor can make your data difficult to analyze. It's hard to tell whether changes in the result come from the treatment itself or the confounder. In the example, the new drug was mostly given to older people, so you can't be sure if the better recovery rates are because of the drug or because of the patient's age. This situation means the ATE

Figure 1.7   This graph is particularly important in causal inference, and you'll encounter it frequently. When analyzing the effect of a treatment on an outcome, you may have factors that affect them both. These factors are known as confounders, and they can change the relationship between the treatment and the outcome.

formula, which you use to measure how effective a new treatment is for everyone, doesn't work in this case.

Think first, read next

If you run an RCT or A/B test, which confounders will there be?

To understand this, let's revisit what a confounder is: it's a factor that affects both the treatment choice and the outcome. But in experiments, the treatment choice is based only on chance (because treatments are assigned randomly). This randomness doesn't change the outcome, so we can say there are *no confounders in experimental data.* This is a key reason data from experiments is more reliable than observational data.

Causal inference gives us tools to use when we have data from observations, not experiments. Figure 1.7, whether it has one or many factors, is something you'll see a lot. The first few chapters of this book focus on this scenario. Specifically, you'll learn how to obtain unbiased estimates of the ATE whenever possible.

1.5   *Reviewing basic statistical concepts*

In this section, we'll go over some statistical ideas that are important for this book. You may have learned about these in a basic statistics class. If you're already comfortable with these concepts, you can skip this section. However, it's important to thoroughly understand *conditional probabilities* and *expectations,* because we'll use these concepts a lot in the book, and they're very important for understanding causal inference.

1.5.1   *Empirical distributions and data-generating distributions*

In all the problems we tackle, there are typically two different distributions. The first is the distribution that generates the data. In reality, a physical mechanism is responsible for creating our data. This is what we have been calling the *data-generation process.* This process may have some uncertainty and thus an inherent probability distribution, which we will call the *data-generating distribution.* Except for exceptional cases, we don't know this distribution. The laws that create our data are usually determined by nature, and we don't have access to this information.

Take a coin toss as an example. If we toss a coin n times, with a probability of heads $P(H) = p$, we expect that in the long run, as n tends to infinity, we will obtain a proportion p of heads and a proportion $1 - p$ of tails. The thing is, we don't know the exact value of p. Even though the coin has been carefully crafted, there may still be some imprecision in the process. We usually assume that $p = 1/2$, but we would need an infinite sample to guarantee this conclusion. So, in reality, we don't know the true value of p.

The other distribution is what we call the *empirical distribution* obtained from a sample. Suppose we toss a coin five times, and we get H, H, T, T, T. We can summarize the results as shown in table 1.1. We expect that if instead of five times, we toss the coin a large number of times, the probability of obtaining H in our sample will be close to p.

Table 1.1   Empirical distribution from a sample of H, H, T, T, T

Outcome	Probability
H	2/5
T	3/5

From the formal point of view, we can do that because *the sample itself is a distribution on its own*: the empirical distribution. If we assume that every observation has the same weight and we have a sample size of n, each observation has a probability of $1/n$. In our case, each observation has a weight of $1/5$, and the probability distribution is precisely the one shown in table 1.1. The expectation of this distribution then coincides with the sample average:

$$1 \times \frac{2}{5} + 0 \times \frac{3}{5} = \tilde{x}$$

There is a close relationship between the empirical distribution and the data-generating distribution. As n tends to infinity, the empirical distribution tends to the data-generating distribution. This result is known as the Glivenko–Cantelli theorem, which is technical and out of the scope of this book. This theorem also holds for a variety of situations such as whether the variable is continuous or if we have a random vector instead of a random variable.

Suppose we want heads to win; we can denote success (heads) by 1 and tails by 0. Denote by x_i the toss number i; thus the prior sample (H, H, T, T, T) turns into 1, 1, 1, 0, 0. Then the proportion of times we get H coincides with the mean of x_i, denoted by $\tilde{x} = 2/5$. At the same time, this average can be calculated as

$$\tilde{x} = 1 \times \frac{2}{5} + 0 \times \left(1 - \frac{2}{5}\right) = 1 \times \frac{2}{5} + 0 \times \frac{3}{5}$$

The analog of the average for the data-generating distribution, called *expectation*, is calculated using the fact that $P(H) = p$. For a given binary random variable X, the expectation is calculated as

$$E[X] = 1 \times p + 0 \times (1 - p) = p$$

So, we get a probability of heads of $\tilde{x} = 2/5$, but if we had a very large sample, this probability should be close to p.

Notice the notation we use to distinguish between the samples ($\tilde{x}$) and the data-generating distribution or expectation ($E[X]$). In statistics, we are interested in answering questions related to the differences between our sample and the underlying process that generated the data, such as whether we have a large enough sample size to be confident about the result we have obtained from our sample.

> **Keep in mind**
>
> When figuring out causal effects, the first step is identifying the correct formula to use. After that, you can consider the best statistical approach. Chapter 8 delves into the discussion of optimal statistical methods and how to infer confidence intervals.
>
> For this reason, when it comes to selecting a formula, we focus on the data-generating distribution. The discussion shifts to the empirical distribution when we're exploring statistical approaches.

1.5.2 *A refresher on conditional probabilities and expectations*

To read this book, you need a solid understanding of conditional probabilities and conditional expectations. If you are already familiar with them, you can skip this section. However, in my experience, conditional probabilities are harder to understand than they may seem. I was taught them in the first year of my mathematics degree, but it wasn't until years later that I felt comfortable with them. So, if either of these concepts is not absolutely clear to you, follow along with me in this section.

CONDITIONAL PROBABILITIES

Let's start by assuming that we have some data as in table 1.2 with variables X, Y, and Z. The value of a is used on purpose to get used to the abstract notation of conditional probabilities.

Table 1.2 Simulated data

X	Y	Z
3	0.03	A
6	−24.08	A
a	7.01	A

Table 1.2   Simulated data (continued)

X	Y	Z
–2	–3.00	B
a	10.89	B

In this case, conditioning to $X = a$ means obtaining a new table and selecting those cases where the variable X equals a. If you think about this from the perspective of programming, we would be filtering the data or selecting those rows, as in table 1.3. The variables Y and Z, under the constraint that $X = a$, are denoted as $Y|X = a$ and $Z|X = a$, respectively. Conditioning on $X = a$, the distribution of Y and Z may change. For instance, whereas in table 1.2, Z takes the value of A 3/5 of the time, in table 1.3, Z takes the value A 1/2 of the time. In terms of notation, we write these quantities $P(Z = A) = 3/5$ and $P(Z = A|X = a) = 1/2$.

Table 1.3   Simulated data conditioned on X = a

X	Y	Z
a	7.01	A
a	10.89	B

You may have been introduced to conditional probabilities in the past via a mathematical formula

$$P(Z = A|X = a) = \frac{P(Z = A, X = a)}{P(X = a)}$$

where the comma (,) stands for *and*: $P(Z = A, X = a)$ means the probability that $Z = A$ and $X = a$. The advantage of this formula is that it tells you how these conditional probabilities can be calculated from the original table 1.2 and the frequencies (probabilities) with which the events $Z = A$ and $X = a$ appear there. The formula comes from the steps we have followed to calculate $P(Z = A|X = a) = 1/2$, dividing the following quantities:

$$P(Z = A|X = a) = \frac{1}{2}$$
$$= \frac{\# \text{ times } Z = A \text{ in table 1.3}}{\# \text{ rows in table 1.3}}$$
$$= \frac{\# \text{ times } Z = A \text{ and } X = a \text{ in table 1.1}}{\# X = a \text{ in table 1.1}}$$

The expression remains unchanged when dividing the numerator and denominator by 5 (the number of rows in table 1.1), so we arrive at the expression

$$P(Z = A|X = a) = \frac{P(Z = A, X = a)}{P(X = a)}$$

We can condition on two or more variables at the same time. For instance, conditioning on $X = a$ and $Z = B$, we get table 1.4. The variable Y under the constraints $X = a$ and $Z = B$ is denoted as $Y|X = a, Z = B$. In the same way as before, we can calculate $P(Y = 10.89|X = a, Z = B) = 1$, because 10.89 is the unique value that Y takes under the constraints $X = a$ and $Z = B$.

Table 1.4 Simulated data conditioned on X = a and Z = B

X	Y	Z
a	10.89	B

In general, whenever you have two variables X and Y, conditioning on $X = x$ will probably change the behavior of Y, and the frequency with which Y takes its values will be different than before conditioning:

$$P(Y = y|X = x)$$

Sometimes, to make the notation easier to read, we will make a slight abuse of notation and write $P(Y|X)$ or even $P(Y|X = x)$ instead of the full correct expression $P(Y = y|X = x)$. The conditional probability can be calculated from the original probability P with the formula

$$P(Y = y|X = x) = \frac{P(Y = y, X = x)}{P(X = x)}$$

CONDITIONAL EXPECTATIONS

Now that, through conditioning, we have a new variable, following the previous example $Y|X = a$, we can calculate some typical quantities from it, such as $P(Y = 7.01|x = a) = 1/2$ (because we have only two observations) or $P(Y = 1|X = a) = 0$. In particular, we can calculate the expectation of this new variable called *conditional expectation*: $E[Y|X = a]$. In this example, because for $Y|X = a$ each observation weighs $1/2$, $E[Y|X = a] = 7.01 \times 1/2 + 10.89 \times 1/2 = 8.95$. Notice that if a variable Y is binary, $E[Y|X] = P(Y|X)$. To see this, you just need to apply the definition of conditional expectation. Because Y is categorical, it takes only two values: 0 and 1. So,

$$E[Y|X] = 1 \times P(X = 1|X) + 0 \times P(X = 0|X) = P(X = 1|X)$$

In figure 1.8, we have simulated data to show, through another example, the difference between the distribution of a variable and its conditional distribution and expectation. On the left, we have the sample of a variable Y, which is the combination of the sample of two different Gaussian distributions with the same: one based on a value $x = 0$ with an expectation of 0, and the other based on $x = 2$ with an expectation of 2. As you can see, the mean of the sample of the unconditional distribution is 1. But on the right, the same values of y are separated into two groups, each for its corresponding value of x: the left group is the distribution of $Y|X = 0$, and the right group is the conditional distribution $Y|X = 2$. The black dots represent the expectation $E[Y|X = 0]$ and $E[Y|X = 2]$. The points have been jittered on the x axis to improve visualization and avoid overlapping.

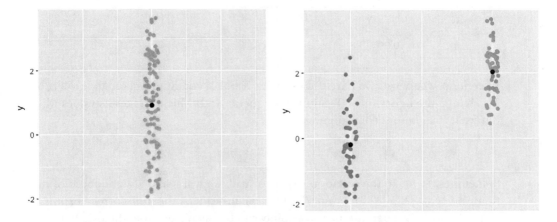

Figure 1.8   On the left is a sample of a variable x. On the right, the same data is split by two different values of x, giving the conditional distributions for different xs. The central black dots are the means for each group, so on the left is the unconditional expectation and on the right are the two conditional expectations.

Throughout the book, we may need to talk about $E[Y|X]$ as an abstract quantity, which means it's detached from any particular dataset or problem we are dealing with. In machine learning or causal inference, we are interested in the relationship between some variable X and an outcome Y. So, how can you imagine $E[Y|X]$ in general? The mathematical notation $E[Y|X]$ is just a recipe:

1   $E[Y|X]$ is shorthand notation for choosing particular values x and y: that is, we are actually talking about $E[Y|X = x]$.
2   Select those cases in your data where $X = x$.
3   Calculate the mean of the variable Y for this particular group.

In general, because the expression $E[Y|X = x]$ only depends on the value of x, $E[Y|X = x]$ can be seen as a function of x.

So far, we have talked about calculations of conditional expectations using numerical examples (table 1.4) and visual examples (figure 1.8). To ease the use of the abstract quantity $E[Y|X = x]$, let's now describe an example where you need to imagine conditional expectations based on the description given here. Pick a population of your choice. Mentally, make two groups: people younger than 30, called group *A*, and those older than 30, called group *B*. The group variable will be called *X*. So, *X* = *A* denotes the group of people younger than 30, and *X* = *B* is the group of people older than 30. Suppose you are interested in studying population heights, denoted by variable *Y*. You can imagine the process of calculating the mean height of group *A*. This quantity has a name in mathematical terms. As you have just seen, selecting group *A* and then calculating their mean height is denoted by $E[Y|X=A]$. Respectively, the process of selecting group *B* and calculating their heights is denoted by $E[Y|X=B]$. Note that we are talking about abstract quantities, even though we have no data whatsoever.

Another situation where you may be interested in calculating conditional probabilities and expectations is when you have an explicit functional relationship between variables. Suppose that instead of data, you have this linear model

$$Y = 1 + 2X + \varepsilon$$

where ε is a centered Gaussian distribution. This means *X* may vary in its own way, and *Y* depends on *X* and a random factor. Conditioning to *X* = *x* just means the value of *X* will be set to *x*, whereas the variable *Y* may still vary due to the randomness of ε. In general, if *Y*, *X*, and ε are related by some function $Y = \mathrm{f}(X, \varepsilon)$, conditioning on *X* = *x* means that now *Y* will vary with *X* fixed:

$$Y = f(X = x, \varepsilon)$$

So, the *conditional expectation* $E[Y|X = x]$ has to be calculated only taking into account the randomness of ε because *x* is a fixed value.

In chapter 2, you will see that in the presence of confounding factors, calculating conditional probabilities does not always give a good answer to causal problems. You will need to find a formula to remove the effect of confounders from your calculations.

Note that the notion of conditional probability is a statistical or probabilistic notion, *not a causal one*. The conditional probability $P(Y|X)$ just means calculating how often an event *Y* happens among those cases where the event *X* is also happening. So, it describes frequencies or probabilities of events.

1.6   *Further reading*

- A/B testing:
  - "Refuted Causal Claims from Observational Studies": https://experiment guide.com/refuted_observational_studies
  - *Controlled Experiments on the Web: Survey and Practical Guide* by Ron Kohavi, Roger Longbotham, Dan Sommerfield, and Randal M. Henne (Springer, 2009): www.robotics.stanford.edu/~ronnyk/2009controlledExperimentsOn TheWebSurvey.pdf
  - The chapter "A/B Testing" in David Sweet's *Experimentation for Engineers* (Manning, 2023): www.manning.com/books/experimentation-for-engineers

- *Experimentation Works: The Surprising Power of Business Experiments* by Stefan Thomke (Harvard Business Review Press, 2020): https://store.hbr.org/prod uct/experimentation-works-the-surprising-power-of-business-experiments/ 10248
- *Trustworthy Online Controlled Experiments: A Practical Guide to A/B Testing* by Ron Kohavi, Diane Tang, and Ya Xu (Cambridge University Press, 2020): https://experimentguide.com

- Causal inference:
    - *The Book of Why: The New Science of Cause and Effect* by Judea Pearl and Dana Mackenzie (Basic Books, 2018). Here you will find the basic philosophy of causal inference, but not formulas or tools that you can directly apply to problems.
    - *Causal Inference In Statistics: A Primer* by Judea Pearl, Madelyn Glymour, and Nicholas P. Jewell (Wiley, 2016). This is a technical introductory book, more technical than the one you are reading now.
    - *Causality: Models, Reasoning, and Inference* by Judea Pearl (Cambridge University Press, 2020) is an awesome book but difficult to read.
    - *Mostly Harmless Econometrics* by Joshua Angrist and Jörn-Steffen Pischke (Princeton University Press, 2009) is a classic in econometrics. They also wrote a more introductory version called *Mastering 'Metrics: The Path from Cause to Effect* (Princeton University Press, 2014).
    - *Causal Inference for Statistics, Social, and Biomedical Sciences: An Introduction* by Guido Imbens and Donald Rubin (Cambridge University Press, 2015) focuses on the boundary between RCTs and causal inference.

1.7   *Chapter quiz*

As we conclude the chapter, it's important to ensure that you have a solid understanding of the key concepts. Here are the essential questions you should be able to answer clearly and concisely. If you can't, I suggest rereading the corresponding references:

1 What is the difference between observational and experimental data?
   Answer in section 1.1.1
2 When should you run an A/B test or RCT?
   Answer in section 1.3.5
3 When running an A/B test, if your sample is large enough, both groups will have the same population characteristics. Why?
   Answer in section 1.3.4, "Step 3: Analysis"
4 Give one reason correlations do not always provide the right evidence for causation.
   Answer in section 1.4
5 Which confounders can you find in an A/B test?
   Answer in section 1.4.2

Summary

- Causal inference uses methods and tools to uncover causal relationships between a treatment and an outcome using data.
- Confounding factors influence both the treatment and the outcome, complicating the identification of causal relationships from correlations alone. Identifying confounders in your analysis is crucial.
- Always conduct an experiment (RCT or A/B test) when possible. Random treatment assignment eliminates confounding, yielding the clearest estimates.
- When experiments are not feasible, you deal with observational data. Causal inference is essential for making informed decisions using such data.
- Directed acyclic graphs (DAGs) help illustrate the relationships between variables and identify possible paths of confounding.
- The average treatment effect (ATE) quantifies the causal effect of one variable on another. The computation of ATE is affected by confounding and will be detailed in upcoming chapters.

First steps: Working with confounders

Imagine that you have a causal question, such as wanting to assess the consequences of a past decision, or deciding which of two treatments is better, or determining which of two marketing strategies is more effective. You are comparing two options, called A and B. These may be past decisions, medical treatments, or marketing campaigns, and you want to know their effects on a specific result.

You may think that the best approach is to see what happens when A is used, see what happens with B, and compare the two outcomes to decide if A is better than B. However, as we will explore in this chapter, this intuitive method can often lead to wrong conclusions, especially when dealing with observational data. This is a critical point to consider! Think about how often you or others have made decisions this way.

In chapter 1, we discussed that when dealing with observational data (which isn't collected from a controlled experiment), we often encounter confounding variables. These confounders are factors that influence both the treatment (or action) and the outcome. This means confounders can cause changes in both the treatment and the outcome, and we may not even know they exist or have any details about them.

Confounding

A confounder is a variable that affects the decision/treatment variable and also affects the outcome of interest at the same time.

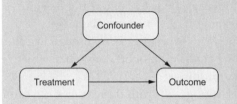

A confounder is a shared cause affecting both the treatment and the outcome. When a confounder is present, it prevents us from accurately measuring the treatment's effect by comparing averages.

When you see a positive correlation between two variables in your data analysis, you may wonder if it suggests a causal relationship between them. Even if you're aware that confounders are affecting the data, shouldn't a positive correlation still imply some form of causal link? The answer is no. In the next section, we will look at Simpson's paradox, which illustrates why interpreting correlation as causation is problematic. It shows that confounders can flip a positive causal relationship into a negative correlation or vice versa. Therefore, relying solely on correlations can lead you to completely incorrect conclusions.

However, it is possible to eliminate the influence of confounders in some cases, which allows us to get unbiased estimates. In this chapter, through an example of Simpson's paradox, you will learn to recognize these situations. Then we'll use a mathematical method known as the *adjustment formula* to calculate causal effects.

We'll also formally define the average treatment effect (ATE), introduced in chapter 2. The ATE measures the overall difference in effects between two treatments, helping you determine which option, A or B, is more effective. In a randomized controlled trial (RCT) or A/B test, you can directly calculate the ATE by calculating the *difference in means* of the outcomes between the two alternatives. However, when using observational data, the difference in means may not always represent the ATE accurately.

This chapter establishes the foundation for the rest of the book. You will get a good understanding of how confounders can complicate your analysis and how to effectively address them. This knowledge will help you

- Be cautious when making direct comparisons between options in observational data.
- Identify situations where confounding factors can be managed.
- Apply a specific formula to distinguish between correlations and causation.

> **Why use the adjustment formula?**
> The adjustment formula is a tool that helps us find the real cause-and-effect connection between two variables. It removes the influence of confounding factors that may hide the true causal relationship.

The first objective of this chapter is to learn the adjustment formula, which lets us remove the effects of confounding to estimate causal effects. The second objective is to identify situations where we need to apply the adjustment formula. In chapter 4, we will explore how the adjustment formula can be calculated using machine learning techniques. And part 2 of the book is dedicated to various adaptations of the adjustment formula, such as propensity scores, which are extensively used in healthcare, linear models for analyzing trends, and the application of off-the-shelf machine learning models for dealing with nonlinear relationships.

In this chapter, we will mainly work with graphs with three nodes: a treatment, an outcome, and a confounder. Chapter 7 will tackle the challenge of dealing with numerous confounders that have complex interactions, described as complex graphs. In that chapter, we will discuss when the adjustment formula is appropriate to use and when it is not.

2.1   Learning the basic elements of causal inference through Simpson's paradox

Imagine that you work at a hospital that treats kidney stones using two different treatments, treatment A and treatment B. We will explore a real dataset from a 1986 study (www.ncbi.nlm.nih.gov/pmc/articles/PMC1339981; the numbers have been slightly adjusted for educational purposes) in table 2.1. In the study, 350 patients received treatment A and 350 patients received treatment B. The study was not an RCT, so the data is observational. The variable Size in the dataset indicates the pretreatment size of the kidney stones.

Table 2.1   Kidney stone dataset

Treatment	Size	Patients	Recovered
A	Small	87	81
B	Small	270	234
A	Large	263	192
B	Large	80	50

The hospital has to choose between the two treatments, treatment A and treatment B. It can only select one treatment for patients, so it wants to determine which treatment is more effective.

Think first, read next
Main problem: If the hospital must stick to just one of the treatments, which should it choose?

To answer this question, we need to calculate recovery rates. Should we also stratify by kidney stone size? Let's start without stratification. Recovery rates are described in table 2.2.

Table 2.2   Recovery rates by treatment

	Treatment A	**Treatment B**
Recovery rate	78% (273/350)	**81% (284/350)**

It's evident that treatment B has better recovery rates, so it seems like the preferred choice at first glance. Because we also have information about the size of the kidney stones, we can enhance our initial analysis by taking this variable into account. The data is broken down by size in table 2.3.

Table 2.3   Recovery rates by treatment and size

	Treatment A	**Treatment B**
Small stones	**93% (81/87)**	87% (234/270)
Large stones	**73% (192/263)**	63% (50/80)

For small stones, treatment A is better. For large stones, treatment A is also better. But as we saw in table 2.2, the overall data suggests that B is better. This is an example of the so-called *Simpson's paradox*: if we analyze only treatment and outcome variables, we get the opposite result than if we include the size of the stone in the analysis.

Simpson's paradox
Simpson's paradox is the situation in which a trend appears in different groups of data but disappears or reverses when these groups are combined.

2.1.1   *What's the problem?*

Let's analyze this data from another perspective. Figure 2.1 shows the distribution of stones that received each treatment.

It appears we have an imbalance in how treatments are assigned based on the size of the kidney stones, which complicates the comparison of treatment outcomes. Treatment A involves open surgical procedures, which are riskier but can be more effective

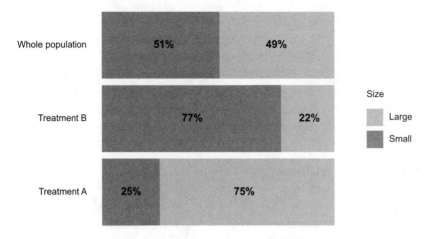

Figure 2.1   The sizes of kidney stones vary between treatments. Larger stones, which are more challenging cases, tend to receive treatment A, whereas smaller, easier cases are often assigned to treatment B. In both scenarios, the distribution of stone sizes differs significantly from the overall distribution.

for larger stones; treatment B does not involve open surgery. Among all patients, 51% have small stones. Among those who receive treatment B, 77% have small stones; and among those who received treatment A, the proportion with small stones is 25%.

It turns out that doctors likely assign treatment based on the stone's size, with larger stones more often handled by open surgery. This means treatment A is given to a higher proportion of more challenging cases, whereas treatment B is applied more frequently to less-severe cases. This sets up an unfair comparison between the two treatments.

Think first, read next
Before continuing, can you come up with a graph describing the relationship between the variables involved in this problem?

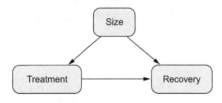

Figure 2.2   Representation of the kidney stone's dynamics, including age as a confounder

Figure 2.2 illustrates the dynamics of how the data was generated, highlighting the relationships between stone size, treatment choice, and recovery outcomes. Doctors determined the treatment based on the size of the kidney stone, indicated by an arrow from Size to Treatment in the diagram. Larger stones, being more challenging to treat, also have a direct effect on recovery outcomes, leading us to draw another arrow from Size to Recovery. Finally, the primary effect we are interested in measuring is how the treatment influences recovery, represented by an arrow from Treatment to Recovery. This diagram helps visualize the relationships and potential confounding effects in the data.

Think first, read next

Can you think of a situation where the arrow from Size to Treatment is reversed? That is, when would the treatment affect the size of a kidney stone?

Consider a treatment that, for some reason, makes a kidney stone bigger. Obviously, a treatment aimed at removing kidney stones shouldn't increase their size—it's counterproductive. Later in this chapter, we'll discuss how the direction of this effect determines whether to use the adjustment formula.

The importance of domain knowledge

Figure 2.2 shows that the distribution of sizes varies between different treatments. We know from the background information that doctors choose the treatment based on the size of the stones. Without expertise in this area, we wouldn't know whether size influences the choice of treatment or if it's the other way around. This direction is determined by domain knowledge; and as we'll see, understanding the context of a problem can drastically affect the results.

2.1.2 *Develop your intuition: How to approach the problem*

In the previous section, we identified the root of the paradox: treatments have unequal proportions of large stones, which are tougher to treat. Therefore, directly comparing treatments is not fair because treatment A faces more challenging cases than treatment B. This section prepares you to understand how to calculate a solution that fairly compares both treatments.

THE SOURCE OF THE PROBLEM IS CONFOUNDING

Let's discuss what confounding is and how it complicates understanding cause and effect. Confounding occurs when two things, such as large stones and treatment A, often occur together. If we only look at data from treatment A to see the recovery rate, we can't tell if the treatment's success is because of the treatment itself or because it often deals with severe cases (large stones). This makes it hard to separate the treatment's effect from the effect of the stone size. We observe things happening together (correlations), but it's unclear whether one causes the other. On the other hand, A/B tests don't have confounders. This allows us to measure the effect on each group accurately without any misleading factors.

CONDITIONING IS PART OF THE SOLUTION

In causality, we are interested in measuring when a variable changes and how it causally affects the rest of the variables. How does conditioning affect causality? When we condition on a variable, we keep its value constant so it does not vary. So, intuitively speaking, we no longer need to consider its effect. Let me explain.

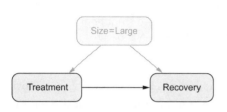

Figure 2.3   Conditioning on Size = Large means selecting the subset of data where Size is Large. When we condition on a variable, that variable holds constant, so it does not affect any other variables.

Remember that *conditioning* means selecting all the cases with a specific value of a specific variable. When we condition on a variable, we freeze its value. For example, if we condition on Size = Large, we select those patients with large stones in our dataset. Within this group, size no longer varies; it affects all patients uniformly. The value of the variable Size remains fixed, so, informally speaking, the effect of size disappears (see figure 2.3).

This means that when we focus only on the group with large stones, there's no more confounding between treatment and recovery, so we can measure the effect without any bias. As shown in table 2.2, the success rate of treatment A for large stones is 73%, compared to 63% for treatment B—a difference of 11%. For small stones, treatment A is 93% effective, whereas treatment B is 87%, a difference of 6%. Because both the 11% and 6% are measured without bias, and treatment A performs better in both groups, at this point we can safely argue that treatment A is better than B. However, our analysis doesn't stop here; we still need to determine by how much treatment A is better. We have two unbiased estimates (11% and 6%), and the next section will explain how we combine them to find the overall effect.

2.1.3   Solving Simpson's paradox

Let's start by revisiting the problem we want to solve: if the hospital can use only one treatment, which should it be?

> **Think first, read next**
> We have seen that the distribution of stone sizes differs between treatments. What would be the proportion of large stones among those given treatment A if everyone received that treatment?

As shown in figure 2.2, if everyone received treatment A, the group treated with A would represent the entire population, which includes 49% large stones. This is a crucial point. There are two different scenarios: the historical data shows that 77% of large stones received treatment A, but a new, hypothetical scenario has treatment A given to a population with 49% large stones. The challenge now is to adapt our historical data to this new hypothetical scenario.

Refresher on the law of total probability

The law of total probability provides an alternative formula to calculate a conditional probability by stratifying in groups. In our example, we can write

$$P(\text{Recovery=1}|\text{Treatment} = A) =$$
$$P(\text{Recovery=1}|\text{Size=Large, Treatment} = A)P(\text{Size=Large, Treatment} = A)+$$
$$P(\text{Recovery=1}|\text{Size=Small, Treatment} = A)P(\text{Size=Small, Treatment} = A)$$

In words, this formula can be read as

Total Efficacy = Efficacy Large × Frequency Large + Efficacy Small × Frequency Small

---

Remember that the efficacy of treatment A for the whole population is 78% (table 2.4, repeated here for easier reading). This value can be computed as the ratio recovered/total for those who received treatment A. But it can be calculated another way, using the total probability theorem (see the sidebar "Refresher on the law of total probability"): calculate the efficacy for those receiving treatment A who have large stones (73%), multiply the result by the frequency with which that happened (100% − 25% = 75%), repeat for small stones, and add the results:

$$78\% = 73\% \times 75\% + 93\% \times 25\%$$

Table 2.4 Recovery rates by treatment and size (repeated here for easier reading)

	Treatment A	Treatment B
Small stones	**93% (81/87)**	87% (234/270)
Large stones	**73% (192/263)**	63% (50/80)

Now we are in a position to answer the main question. If we applied treatment A to everyone, the proportion of large/small stones would no longer be 75%/25% but 49%/51%. In this hypothetical new situation, we could apply the same formula but reweight using the 49%/51% ratio. The efficacy of treatment A in large stones would still be 73%, but treatment A would be used on large stones only 49% of the time. Applying the same argument to small stones, the formula would be

$$83\% = 73\% \times 49\% + 93\% \times 51\%$$

Let's put both formulas together to highlight the differences:

$$78\% = 73\% \times 75\% + 93\% \times 25\%$$
$$83\% = 73\% \times 49\% + 93\% \times 51\%$$

So if we applied treatment A to everyone, we would expect a recovery rate of 83%. This is greater than the previous 78%, as we would expect: in this new, hypothetical situation, A would receive fewer difficult cases (large stones), so its success rate would be higher.

Now that we know the expected efficacy of treatment A, we should repeat the process for treatment B. Finally, the hospital should choose the treatment with a higher recovery rate when given to everyone. (Spoiler alert: treatment A is best.) I strongly suggest that you try this on your own; you will find the solution at the end of the chapter.

> **Exercise 2.1**
>
> What would be the efficacy of treatment B if it were given to everyone? Which treatment would be better?

This new formula we have discovered is called the *adjustment formula*. But what are we calculating? In the following section, we will explain what it is and give it a name.

2.2 *Generalizing to other problems*

In the previous section, we explored an example of Simpson's paradox and learned an intuitive solution. How can we apply what we've learned to other situations? Should we use a similar method of adjusting proportions (the adjustment formula) for similar situations? First, let's define what "similar situations" means. We'll revisit the kidney stone example, focusing on the general steps and key principles that can guide us in addressing other problems:

- *About the problem*
  - We're dealing with two treatments and their effect on an outcome, specifically the recovery rate.
  - A third factor, a confounder, influences both the choice of treatment and the outcome itself.

- *About the solution*
  1 We described the problem using a graph.
  2 We defined our goal: to know what would happen in a situation different from the current one. We formed this goal into a question: what would the outcome be if everyone received one specific treatment?
  3 We devised a method to answer this question: calculate what the outcome would be if everyone received treatment A, do the same for treatment B, and then compare the results to see the difference.

To use the solution across various contexts, we need to embrace the concept of *abstraction*. Abstraction may seem like a hard wall that blocks you from deeper understanding, but let's look at its more approachable side: flexibility. An abstract concept is a common idea that appears in many different scenarios. Typically, when entering a new field, it takes time to familiarize yourself with its fundamental concepts, terminology, and rules. This requires specialization. However, if you can apply knowledge from other areas, your onboarding becomes easier (and if you are lucky, you may bring something new to the table). This is feasible as long as there are commonalities across these fields. Thus, mastering abstract concepts offers a competitive edge, enabling you to adapt quickly to new situations. Machine learning exemplifies this approach by using a general method to find relationships between features and outcomes applicable across various industries and domains. Let's go back to our kidney stone example to identify the abstract elements involved.

2.2.1   Describing the problem with a graph

The initial step toward abstraction involves creating a graph that describes the interactions among variables. In this graph, the variables (*nodes*) represent physical quantities or metrics, and the arrows depict the relationships between these variables. When we draw a simple arrow that may represent a complex relationship, we lose a lot of information: the specifics of this relationship. For example, we may think the size of a kidney stone influences the recovery rate, but we can't describe mathematically how size affects recovery. However, the underlying relationship is often embedded within the data collected, and if needed, we may be able to elucidate this relationship through methods such as supervised learning.

What *is* drawn in the graph is as important as what is *not* drawn. When we draw a graph with just three nodes, we're basically saying those are the only elements we need to solve the problem. But keep in mind that the kidney stone example is just a simplification to help you understand the basics of causal inference. Usually you'll run into many more factors in real situations.

The toughest part comes after we draw the graph. At that point, we step back from the real world and focus only on the model we've built—the graph. All the analysis and conclusions about Simpson's paradox were made from just the graph and the data we had; we didn't need any further information. *That's why it's very important to be comfortable with the graph you're using. If the graph itself does not fully convince you, you won't trust the conclusions it leads you to!*

2.2.2   Articulating what we would like to know

We set out to determine which of the two treatments is better. Before diving into which treatment is better, we need to define what "better" means. Ideally, we want to know what would happen if everyone got treatment A and then everyone got treatment B and compare which one helps more people. So, our objective is to simulate what would happen if everyone received a particular treatment (a situation that has not happened), using data from a situation where both treatments were assigned to patients (reality). This is a huge jump toward abstraction.

Think of it this way. Say a hospital has to choose between different treatments for an illness. The hospital wants to know which treatment works best. If we want to answer similar questions for other problems, we need to define what it means for "everyone to receive the same treatment" in each case. And remember, we may have different graphs representing different scenarios. So, we need a solution that can be figured out from both the graph and the data. That's why we need a formal definition of our key measurement for any graph. Fair warning, though—it's going to be pretty abstract!

2.2.3   *Finding the way to calculate the causal effect*

We've found out that by reweighting the efficacy of the treatments with the adjustment formula, we can simulate the scenario of giving one treatment to every patient. The kidney stone problem serves as a clear example of causal inference basics. But there's a catch: it may give you the wrong impression that the adjustment formula always simulates what would happen if everyone received the same treatment. That's not always the case. For this reason, we need a theory to guide us, based on the graph, about when to apply the adjustment formula and when not to.

In every causal inference problem you tackle, you'll need to tailor these three abstract concepts to your specific situation, as shown in figure 2.4. In this section, we'll focus on steps 2 and 3 from this diagram.

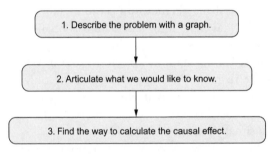

Figure 2.4   **Abstract concepts that need to be adapted in each causal problem**

2.2.4   *Articulating what we would like to know: The language of interventions*

Let's define what an *intervention* is so that it can be used for many different problems. Our example of Simpson's paradox involves the following situation. Historically, there have been some dynamics, or *data-generating processes*, where doctors have made an initial guess about size of kidney stones and used this information to decide which treatment to give. In this way, events are generated with a particular frequency, such as that 49% of the stones are large. The probability distribution that generates these frequencies (the probabilities we would observe if we had infinite data) will be denoted by P. We say then that $P(\text{Size} = \text{Large}) = 49\%$. The data-generating process for the kidney stone example is shown in figure 2.5 (where Size is renamed S, Treatment is T, and Recovery is R).

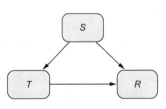

Figure 2.5   **Data-generation process producing observed probability distribution *P*. *S* stands for Size, *T* for Treatment, and *R* for Recovery.**

At some point, we consider what would happen if we
gave treatment A to everyone. That is, we *intervene* with
the system. The system will no longer behave as before;
we are changing its dynamics so that we will observe
different frequencies. The probability distribution in
this new scenario is denoted by $P|\text{do}(T = A)$. (The
word *do* is used to express the fact that we are intervening with the system—we are doing something.)

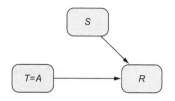

**Figure 2.6   Data-generation
process producing the intervened
probability distribution
$P|\text{do}(T = A)$, which models what
would happen if we gave
treatment A to every patient**

   Because treatment A will be given to everyone,
Treatment no longer depends on Size; the graph generating this distribution is shown in figure 2.6.

In short

$P|T = A$ refers to the probability distribution of selecting the data for those who were
treated with treatment A. On the other hand, $P|\text{do}(T = A)$ refers to the probability dis-
tribution if everyone was treated with treatment A. In other words, $P|T = A$ is what hap-
pened in our dataset, and $P|\text{do}(T = A)$ and $P|\text{do}(T = B)$ are what we need to know to
decide which treatment is better.

Let's now give a formal definition of what an intervention is in any general graph.
This mathematical formalism will let us clearly express our objective.

Formally speaking, what is an intervention?

In a graph, intervening a node *T* with the value *A* means creating a new graph where
all the arrows pointing to *T* are removed and the value of *T* is fixed to *A*.

An intervened graph derives a new set of frequencies that, as we said before, we are
calling $P|\text{do}(T = A)$. This abstract definition represents what would happen in a hypo-
thetical intervention. If we carried out the intervention in our example hospital, the
result probably wouldn't be exactly as the model represents. For starters, in practice,
there are always exceptions, but this definition does not consider any. However, this
simplistic definition translates the effects of an intervention in reality into our mathematical model so that we can emulate our quantity of interest in the graph.

   This definition of an intervention is a key ingredient in causal inference theory. It
may strike you as surprising, but you should be able to see that it is useful because it
describes an ideal situation that would answer our problem question: what is the effect
of a particular treatment? How and when we can simulate this scenario from other
data and other causal questions is what the rest of the book is about.

   Note that intervening and conditioning are two different concepts with different
meanings. *Conditioning*, in historical data, is concerned with what we have seen,

whereas *intervening* is about a situation where we do something potentially different from how things have been so far.

Test your knowledge

Is intervening the same as observing? For instance, in the Simpson's paradox example, is it the same thing to calculate $P(R = 1|T = A)$ and $P(R = 1|do(T = A))$?

To answer this question, we need to ask what the definition of each quantity is. The quantity $P(R = 1|T = A)$ refers to the observed (historical) probability of recovering when treatment A was given. Formally speaking, this quantity is a conditional probability: we select the subpopulation of patients who take treatment A, and calculate the probability of recovering, which in our example is 78%. What about $P(R = 1|do(T = A))$? Well, this refers to the quantity found in section 2.1.3. If we gave treatment A to everyone, the distribution of sizes would change, and we would obtain a recovery rate of 83%:

$$P(R = 1|T = A) = 78\%$$
$$P(R = 1|do(T = A)) = 83\%$$

Remember, the quantity $P(R = 1|T = A)$ is what we observed, and the quantity $P(R = 1|do(T = A))$ answers the question *what would happen* if we gave treatment A to everyone. The main difference between the two quantities is that in $P|T = A$, the distribution of kidney stone sizes is the one specific for treatment A (25% small, 77% large), whereas in $P|do(T = A)$ the distribution of sizes corresponds to the entire population (51% small, 49% large).

Exercise 2.2

If you would like to play a little more with the differences between observing and intervening, check out the optional exercise "Observe and do are different things" in appendix B.

2.2.5 *Finding the way to calculate the causal effect: The adjustment formula*

We've finally arrived at the adjustment formula. This formula calculates the recovery rate in the intervened graph. Simplifying notation and writing 1 for "yes" and 0 for "no," we have

$$P(R = 1|do(T = A)) = 83\% = 73\% \times 49\% + 93\% \times 51\%$$
$$= P(R = 1|T = A, S = \text{Large}) \times P(S = \text{Large})$$
$$+ P(R = 1|T = A, S = \text{Small}) \times P(S = \text{Small})$$

The magic of this formula is that it lets you calculate something you haven't observed, $P(R = 1|\text{do}(T = A))$, in terms of data you *have* observed: probability P.

ADJUSTMENT FORMULA

In general, if we have figure 2.6 for any discrete variables S, R, and T, the adjustment formula calculates the probability under an intervention from observational data:

$$P(R = 1|\text{do}(T = A)) = \sum_s P(R = 1|S = s, T = A)P(S = s)$$

This formula is especially awesome because we made no assumptions whatsoever about the probability distribution P (well, besides being discrete, the formula can be easily adapted to the continuous case)! This means it works in a wide variety of situations. If you are curious about how the adjustment formula is derived mathematically, I strongly encourage you to look at "The math behind the adjustment formula" in appendix A.

ADJUSTMENT FORMULA FOR OUTCOMES WITH MANY VALUES

We can easily find situations where the outcome R is not a binary variable but has many possible values r_1, ..., r_k. For example, suppose the outcome R is the number of days a patient needs to recover. We may be interested in the probability that patients recover in a particular number of days r if the treatment is A for everyone: $P(R = r|\text{do}(T = A))$. But we may be more interested in the expected number of days that patients need to recover if the treatment is A for everyone, or, mathematically speaking, $E[R|\text{do}(T = A)]$.

The adjustment formula in this case is the following:

$$E[R|\text{do}(T = A)] = \sum_s E[R|T = A, S = s]P(S = s)$$

Let's see where this formula comes from. The first thing we need to know is the quantity $E[R|\text{do}(T = A)]$. We can apply the definition of the mathematical expectation of a variable:

$$E[R|\text{do}(T = A)] = \sum_k r_k P(R = r_k|\text{do}(T = A))$$

Now we can apply the adjustment formula to each of the terms, $P(R = r_k|\text{do}(T = A))$, obtaining

$$\sum_k r_k P(R = r_k|\text{do}(T = A)) = \sum_k r_k \sum_s P(R = r_k|T = A, S = s)P(S = s)$$

I once had a teacher who suggested that whenever you encounter a double summation, you should switch the order of summation because it often leads to interesting results. Following this advice, if we sum first over s and then over k, we arrive at an expression that can ultimately be simplified using conditional expectations, which was our objective:

$$\sum_{s}\sum_{k} r_k P(R = r_k | T = A, S = s)P(S = s) = \sum_{s} E[R|T = A, S = s]P(S = s)$$

For continuous variables, this formula should be expressed in terms of integrals. But this is rarely seen in practice because we will apply it directly to data, so we omit it for now.

ADJUSTMENT FORMULA AND OTHER GRAPHS

The adjustment formula gives us the quantity $P(R = 1 | do(T = A))$ as long as the data-generating process follows a graph like figure 2.6. In general, this is not valid. We may be interested in calculating $P|do(T = A)$ in a myriad of problems. In some of them, we will use the adjustment formula, and in others we won't. Chapter 7 is devoted to seeing which graphs we can use the adjustment formula for and which we cannot. Recall that our ultimate interest is knowing whether treatment A works better than treatment B.

AVERAGE TREATMENT EFFECT (ATE)

The ATE of two alternative values A and B of a variable T on a binary variable R is defined as the difference:

$$\text{ATE} = P(R = 1|do(T = A)) - P(R = 1|do(T = B))$$

If the variable R has many values,

$$\text{ATE} = E[R|do(T = A)] - E[R|do(T = B)]$$

Depending on whether this difference is positive or negative, we can pick the optimal treatment. In the kidney stone example, if the ATE is positive, it means the probability of recovery is greater if we give everyone treatment A than if we give everyone treatment B. So, if we want to stick to a single treatment, we should pick treatment A. If the ATE is negative, by a symmetrical argument, we should pick treatment B. The solution to exercise 1 tells us that $P(R = 1|do(T = A)) = 83\%$, whereas $P(R = 1|do(T = B)) = 74\%$, so ATE = 9%, and we should pick treatment A.

2.2.6 *How does the treatment work in each situation? The positivity assumption*

The adjustment formula implicitly requires an important assumption that we haven't talked about yet. Imagine an extreme case where treatment A has only been tested with large stones. This is unfortunate because we don't know how it will work with small stones. If something has not been tried, we don't have any information about it. Mathematically speaking, we cannot use the term that measures the efficacy of treatment A in small stones $P(R = 1|T = A, S = \text{small})$ because the event $(T = A, S = \text{small})$ has never happened: that is, $P(T = A|S = \text{small}) = 0$.

Let's now see in detail what the positivity assumption is. Let P_0 be the data-generation distribution (instead of the empirical distribution obtained from data). To apply the adjustment formula, we require that for each value of the confounding variable, it is possible for us to see both types of treatment: that is, for each value of the confounder $S = s$ that can occur $(P_0(S = s) > 0)$ and for each value of the treatment $T = t$,

$$0 < P_0(T = t|S = s) < 1$$

The same has to hold if instead of a variable, $S = (S_1, \ldots, Sp)$ is a vector. For any combination of values such that $P_0(S_1 = s_1, \ldots, Sp = s_p) > 0$,

$$0 < P_0(T = t|S_1 = s_1, \ldots, S_p = s_p) < 1$$

Definition of the positivity assumption

We say that the *positivity assumption* holds if for all the values confounders may take, $s = (s_1, \ldots, s_p)$, and for each treatment, $T = t$, we have that

$$0 < P_0(T = t|S = s) < 1$$

We furthermore require that the probability is not 1, because that would mean that for this particular value of the confounders, there is only one treatment in the data. Notice that we have written the assumption in terms of the data-generation distribution instead of the observed empirical distribution. Not having data for a treatment $T = t$ for a value $S = s$ $(P(T = t|S = s) = 0)$ is a problem that may be solved by gathering more data (increasing the sample size). However, the actual problem is that even with more data, we might never gather this information. This may happen when a treatment is purposely not given to a particular subset of patients. For instance, physicians may decide not to give a treatment to older people because it entails a higher risk. Whenever the problem is the design of the assignment policy, increasing the sample size will not solve it: there will always be a combination of confounders $S = s$ and treatment $T = t$ that will never happen, which is mathematically expressed in terms of the data-generation distribution as $P_0(T = t|S = s) = 0$.

This definition is easy to verify whenever there is only one covariate and it is categorical (as in the kidney stone example). If for each value of S (in this case, small and large) we have data about both treatments, the positivity assumption holds. However, if for a particular value of S we don't have data about, let's say, treatment A, theoretically speaking this doesn't mean the positivity assumption doesn't hold. It may be a matter of sampling size: if $P_0(T = A|S = s)$ is very small and we get more data, at some point we will get data about treatment A with confounder S. In practice, if we have only one or a few confounders, and for some value there is no data about a particular treatment, it raises a red flag. We either say that for these values of the confounder, we cannot estimate the intervened effect; or, if that is not enough (depending on the context), we conclude that we cannot estimate the causal effect at all.

You will frequently have many confounders, with some of them even being continuous. Unfortunately, in this case, it is not possible to check whether the positivity assumption holds. Consider the case of a single confounder S being continuous: the probability that S repeats a particular value s is exactly zero (because in a continuous variable, the probability of obtaining a particular value is always zero). So, unless some value repeats itself, we will never be able to check the positivity assumption from data. That's why in practice, this condition has to be assumed. A similar situation happens when there are many confounders and they are categorical. Imagine that we have a large set of confounders. Any particular combination of values $S = (S_1, \ldots, S_p)$ will appear very infrequently, so we will have very little data for them. For a particular combination $S = (S_1, \ldots, S_p)$, if we observe only one of the two treatments, we cannot be sure whether the problem is that for this combination we will never see both treatments, or that we don't have enough data.

In practice, depending on the type of problem you are dealing with, you will pay more or less attention to this assumption. For instance, in healthcare, when comparing different treatments, not having data about one treatment in a particular subgroup of the population is a problem that has to be dealt with (and we will talk about it in chapter 5).

2.3 *Interventions and RCTs*

We said that an intervention is a model for applying the same treatment to everyone in our population. Suppose that instead of using this definition, we used an alternative one: that an intervention is when you run an RCT—that is, the treatment assignment is randomized. It turns out that we would arrive at the same conclusions and, thus, the same adjustment formula. This is nice because we can think about interventions as applying the same treatment to everyone or applying an RCT, whatever fits best for each person and situation. Consider again the kidney stone data (figure 2.3).

> **Think first, read next**
>
> If we run an RCT randomizing treatment to measure its effect on recovery, which proportion of large stones would treatment A get? What is the expected recovery rate in an RCT for treatment A?

The argument is pretty similar to the one from section 2.1.3. If a treatment is assigned at random, 50% of the population will get treatment A. But more importantly, the representation of large/small stones in treatment A will be the same as the whole population, so once again, treatment A will get 49% of large stones. If we calculate the recovery rate for those receiving treatment A, it will be

$$83\% = 73\% \times 49\% + 93\% \times 51\%$$

which is exactly the same as when we defined $P(R = 1|\text{do}(T = A))$.

You may wonder what would happen if, departing from the observed data, we perform an RCT; which graph would represent the data-generating process? We should remove the arrow from Size to Treatment because kidney stone size no longer affects the treatment. We obtain figure 2.7.

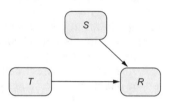

Figure 2.7   Graph depicting an RCT. In an RCT, various factors may influence the outcome, but none influence the treatment, as the treatment is assigned randomly. This means there are no confounders.

We are basically saying that to calculate the hypothetical recovery rate for an RCT, we would need to use the same formula and obtain the same graph (with the exception of the values for Treatment, which in this case may be both A and B).

Causal inference tries to mimic what would happen if we applied an RCT

The intervened distribution $P|\text{do}(T = A)$ derives the same quantity in two situations at the same time: running a hypothetical RCT and measuring the effect of treatment A or hypothetically giving treatment A to everyone. That's why we say that $P|\text{do}(T = A)$ solves a problem mimicking an RCT.

2.4   First contact with the structural approach

In this section, we'll explore a different way of representing interventions, known as the *structural* approach. Instead of using graphs, this approach relies on functions. It's a bit like writing code, which may make it easier for some readers to grasp. Structural equations are essentially just another way to express the same information found in the graph. We introduce them informally in the section "The math behind the adjustment formula" in appendix A and formally in chapter 7.

Let's explore how to represent basic graphs using the structural approach. Imagine the connection shown in figure 2.8, where Treatment influences a patient's chances of Recovery. The structural approach represents this connection using a function:

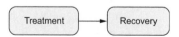

Figure 2.8   Graph modeling how Treatment affects patient's Recovery. Here, we assume that no other factors are relevant to the analysis, similar to the conditions in an RCT.

$$\text{Recovery} := f(\text{Treatment}, U)$$

The variable *U* represents a set of unknown factors unique to each patient—including things like age—that can affect the patient's recovery but are unrelated to the treatment. If we excluded the variable *U* and wrote Recovery = f(Treatment), we would essentially be claiming that Recovery solely depends on Treatment. This would imply that all patients receiving the same treatment would have identical responses, which is not the case.

The symbol :=

We use the symbol :=, known as the *assignment* or *walrus operator* (due to its resemblance to a walrus's teeth), instead of the regular equality symbol (=) because it signifies assignment, much like in programming. When we write $Y := 2X$, it means once you know the value of X, you set the value of Y to $2 \times X$. However, if you change the value of Y, the value of X remains the same. In contrast, in a mathematical equation like $Y = 2X$, a change in the value of X also changes the value of Y, and vice versa. This symbol may appear to be a minor detail, but it reflects the inherent causality direction, where changes in X influence Y. It encodes the direction of the causal arrow $X \rightarrow Y$.

In this specific case, the function *f* represents, among other factors, the intricate biology of the patient, which involves highly complex dynamics. *In practical situations, we rarely know the function f.* Nevertheless, as we'll see in chapters 4 and 8, we can approximate these functions using machine learning models.

In the structural approach, we need to model every variable. In this model, the Treatment variable does not depend on any other variable in the graph, so we say it is the result of a random variable:

$$T := U_0$$

Let's model the kidney stone example with the structural approach (see figure 2.9). We need to model every variable in the graph:

$$S := U_S$$
$$T := g(S, U_T)$$
$$R := f(S, T, U_R)$$

Each variable has its corresponding term *U* representing all the unknown factors that affect it.

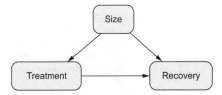

Figure 2.9   Graph modeling the dynamics of the kidney stone data

2.4.1   *Simulating the kidney stone example*

As discussed in section 1.5.1, one of the best ways to understand a new method is to try it on data we make ourselves. This helps us ensure that our results are correct. So, let's simulate the dynamics of the kidney stone example using code.

We don't know the real relationship between Treatment, Size, and Recovery. That's why, in this example, we'll rely on the relationship we estimate from data. For instance, we will assume that the probability of recovery for treatment A and small stones is 93%, obtained from table 2.3. In other words, we will use the empirical distribution (see section 1.6.1).

Listings 2.1 and 2.2 define the functions g and f and how they are used to create the dataset.

Listing 2.1   (R) Synthetic data generation for the kidney stone problem

```
library(data.table)
set.seed(1234)
patients_n <- 10000          Probabilities calculated with the
g <- function(size, u_1){    conditional probability formula:
                             P(T | S) = P(T, S)/P(S)

                    Total patients = 750

  prob_small <- 0.51
  prob_large <- 1 - prob_small
  prob_A <- ifelse(
    size == 'small',
    (87/750)/prob_small,
    (263/750)/prob_large
  )
  return(ifelse(u_1 < prob_A, "A", "B"))
}
f <- function(size, treatment, u_2){   Probabilities obtained
                                       from table 2.3

  if(size=='small'){
    prob <- ifelse(treatment == 'A', 0.93, 0.87)
  }else{
    prob <- ifelse(treatment == 'A', 0.73, 0.63)
  }
  return(ifelse(u_2 < prob, 1, 0))
}
kidney_data <- data.frame()
for(patient in 1:patients_n){
  u_0 <- runif(1)
  u_1 <- runif(1)
  u_2 <- runif(1)
  size <- ifelse(u_0 < 0.51, 'small', 'large')
  treatment <- g(size, u_1)
  recovery <- f(size, treatment, u_2)
  kidney_data <- rbind(
    kidney_data,
    data.frame(size=size, treatment=treatment, recovery=recovery)
  )
}
```

```
setDT(kidney_data)
kidney_data[, .(recovery_prob = mean(recovery)), treatment]
```

Listing 2.2 (Python) Synthetic data generation for the kidney stone problem

```
from numpy.random import uniform, seed
import pandas as pd
seed(1234)
patients_n = 10000                        Probabilities calculated with the
def g(size, u_1):                         conditional probability formula:
                                          P(T|S) = P(T, S)/P(S)

                          ◁─┤ Total patients = 750

    prob_small = 0.51
    prob_large = 1 - prob_small
    prob_A = (87 / 750) / prob_small if size == "small" else \
        (263 / 750) / prob_large
    return "A" if u_1 < prob_A else "B"
def f(size, treatment, u_2):              Probabilities obtained
                                  ◁─┤     from table 2.3

    if size == "small":
        prob = 0.93 if treatment == "A" else 0.87
    else:
        prob = 0.73 if treatment == "A" else 0.63
    return 1 if u_2 < prob else 0
sizes = []
treatments = []
recoveries = []
for patient in range(patients_n):
    u_0 = uniform(size=1)
    u_1 = uniform(size=1)
    u_2 = uniform(size=1)
    size = "small" if u_0 < 0.51 else "large"
    treatment = g(size, u_1)
    recovery = f(size, treatment, u_2)
    sizes.append(size)
    treatments.append(treatment)
    recoveries.append(recovery)
kidney_data = pd.DataFrame(
    {"size": sizes, "treatment": treatments, "recovery": recoveries}
)
kidney_data.groupby("treatment")["recovery"].mean()
```

The results (from R) are shown in table 2.5. We obtain recovery rates similar to those in table 2.2 (up to some degree of uncertainty): 81% for treatment A and 78% for treatment B.

Table 2.5 Results from listing XREF Generation_r_1_res

Treatment	Recovery rate
A	0.8
B	0.78

2.4.2 Interventions in the structural approach

Let's now see how an intervention is applied in code. In this case, we will simulate the operation $R|do(T = A)$. Remember that the definition of intervention tells us to remove all the incoming arrows from the variable T and set its value to A. In code, we give the value of treatment A to all the patients.

Listing 2.3 (R) Generating a dataset by intervening the treatment to *A*

```
kidney_data_A <- data.frame()
for(patient in 1:patients_n){
  u_0 <- runif(1)
  u_1 <- runif(1)
  u_2 <- runif(1)
  size <- ifelse(u_0 < 0.51, 'small', 'large')    Everyone receives
  treatment <- 'A'                                  treatment A.
  recovery <- f(size, treatment, u_2)
  kidney_data_A <- rbind(
    kidney_data_A,
    data.frame(size=size, treatment=treatment, recovery=recovery)
  )
}
setDT(kidney_data_A)
kidney_data_A[, .(recovery_prob = mean(recovery)), treatment]
```

Listing 2.4 (Python) Generating a dataset by intervening the treatment to *A*

```
sizes = []
treatments = []
recoveries = []
for patient in range(patients_n):
  u_0 = uniform(size=1)
  u_1 = uniform(size=1)
  u_2 = uniform(size=1)
  size = "small" if u_0 < 0.51 else "large"    Everyone receives
  treatment = "A"                               treatment A.
  recovery = f(size, treatment, u_2)
  sizes.append(size)
  treatments.append(treatment)
  recoveries.append(recovery)
kidney_data_A = pd.DataFrame({
  "size": sizes,
  "treatment": treatments,
  "recovery": recoveries}
)
kidney_data_A.groupby("treatment")["recovery"].mean()
```

Treatment	Recovery rate
A	0.83

We can see that the results are similar to the ones obtained from the adjustment formula (up to some degree of uncertainty) in section 2.1.3: 83% for treatment A. Let's now simulate the effect of running an RCT, selecting treatments at random.

Listing 2.5 (R) Simulating an RCT

```r
kidney_data_RCT <- data.frame()
for(patient in 1:patients_n){
  u_0 <- runif(1)
  u_1 <- runif(1)
  u_2 <- runif(1)
  size <- ifelse(u_0 < 0.51, 'small', 'large')
  treatment <- ifelse(u_1 < 0.5, 'A', 'B')
  recovery <- f(size, treatment, u_2)
  kidney_data_RCT <- rbind(
    kidney_data_RCT,
    data.frame(size=size, treatment=treatment, recovery=recovery)
  )
}
setDT(kidney_data_RCT)
kidney_data_RCT[, .(recovery_prob = mean(recovery)), treatment]
```

Listing 2.6 (Python) Simulating an RCT

```python
sizes = []
treatments = []
recoveries = []
for patient in range(patients_n):
    u_0 = uniform(size=1)
    u_1 = uniform(size=1)
    u_2 = uniform(size=1)
    size = "small" if u_0 < 0.51 else "large"
    treatment = "A" if u_1 < 0.5 else "B"
    recovery = f(size, treatment, u_2)
    sizes.append(size)
    treatments.append(treatment)
    recoveries.append(recovery)
kidney_data_RCT = pd.DataFrame({
    "size": sizes, "treatment": treatments,
    "recovery": recoveries
})
kidney_data_RCT.groupby("treatment")["recovery"].mean()
```

Treatment	Recovery rate
A	0.83
B	0.75

As expected, RCTs give us estimates similar to the ones obtained in listings 2.3 and 2.4, and from the adjustment formula, up to some degree of uncertainty. The solution of the adjustment formula for treatment B is calculated in the section "Solution to Simpson's paradox" in appendix B and is a 74% recovery rate.

2.5 *When to apply the adjustment formula*

Just to recap, the kidney stone example taught us two important things. First, we figured out *what* we want to find out: the effect of a hypothetical intervention. Second, we learned *how* to calculate it using the adjustment formula. However, this formula is far from a "one tool fits all" solution. So, let's now look at some simple graphs to understand when and how to correctly calculate the effect of an intervention.

To practice when to use the adjustment formula, we'll follow the same approach as before: create artificial datasets and see if the adjustment formula is the right method to estimate the ATE. To introduce the alternatives to the adjustment formula, we'll go through a series of exercises with a similar structure. *The objective in each scenario is to determine which formula to use for calculating the ATE.* Given the variables Treatment T and Outcome O, we will work through the following steps:

1 Check the structural equations and see how things change when you use different treatments in those equations. The approach is the same as in section 2.4.2 but with mathematical calculations instead of coding. This means you'll have to calculate what happens in the equations when the treatment changes:
   - Set $T = 1$, regardless of the rest of the variables, and calculate the expected value of O (which, mathematically speaking, is $E[O|\text{do}(T=1)]$).
   - Set $T = 0$, and calculate the expected value of O (mathematically speaking, $E[O|\text{do}(T=0)]$).
   - Calculate the difference $ATE = E[O|\text{do}(T=1)] - E[O|\text{do}(T=0)]$.

2 Estimate the difference in means from data: that is, $E[O|T=1] - E[O|T=0]$.
3 Apply the adjustment formula to the dataset.
4 Answer the following question: in the difference in means and the adjustment formula, is there any unbiased estimator of the true ATE?

Thus, in each exercise, I'll ask you to complete table 2.6, where adjustment(t) denotes the function that calculates the adjustment formula from data for treatment t.

Table 2.6 Exercise results

True ATE	
$E[O\|T = 1] - E[O\|T = 0]$	
adjustment(1) – adjustment(0)	
Estimation of ATE	

Once you have the results, you can verify that your estimation of the ATE is correct because it should be similar to the true ATE in step 1.

2.5.1   *RCT or A/B test*

The simplest graph ever is the one for an RCT, shown in figure 2.10. We have seen that other variables may affect O: for instance, in the kidney stone data, we can assume that age affects patients' recovery rate. In fact, we can expect that many variables affect the outcome O. However, in this case, they are not necessary for studying the relationship between T and O (check the case of predictive variables in section 2.5.6).

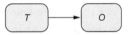

Figure 2.10   RCT or A/B test. T stands for Treatment and O for Outcome.

Test your knowledge

For figure 2.10, what is the corresponding intervened graph?

To answer this question, we need to remember the definition of an intervened graph. To intervene variable T with value t to see its effect on O, we need to create a new graph where we have removed all arrows coming from the confounding factor C and set T to value t. But in this case, there are no confounding factors! Thus for this model, the intervened and observed graphs are the same. In terms of formulas, we can write $P(O|\mathrm{do}(T=t)) = P(O|T=t)$.

This means the observed quantities $P(O|T=t)$ are already the quantities of interest $P(O|\mathrm{do}(T=t))$. This is to be expected. If you remember, in RCTs and A/B tests, there are no confounding factors because confounders are variables that affect T. However, in an RCT or A/B test, the only variable affecting T is randomness, because patients or groups A and B are assigned at random. This is why, in an RCT, the observed probabilities determine causality. And that's why, once again, when performing RCTs, we don't have to apply the adjustment formula; a direct calculation (difference in means) of the mean of the outcome O on each group will do the job.

RCT SIMULATION EXERCISE

Fill table 2.6 with the following data-generation process and a sample size of 10,000:

$$T := B(0.5)$$
$$R := B(0.3)T + B(0.5)(1-T)$$

Notice that T and R are binary variables, where $B(p)$ is drawn from the Bernoulli distribution with expectation p.

2.5.2   *Confounders*

We already know the confounder graph pretty well, as shown in figure 2.11, and we talked about the kidney stone example. In this case, to calculate the effect of an intervention, we need to apply the adjustment formula.

CONFOUNDER SIMULATION EXERCISE
Fill table 2.6 with the following data-generation process and a sample size of 10,000

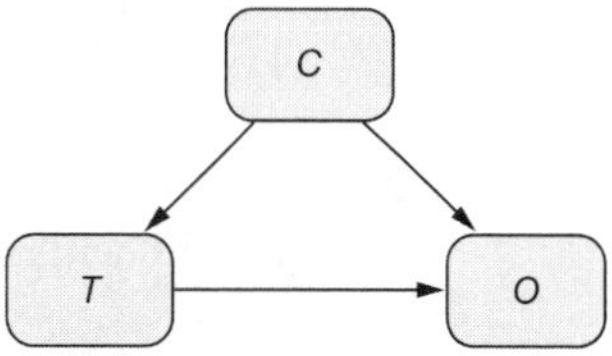

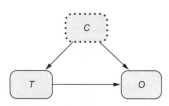

Figure 2.11   Graph with a confounder.

$$C := B(0.8)$$
$$T := B(0.6)C + B(0.2)(1 - C)$$
$$R := B(0.3)T + B(0.5)(1 - T) + C + \varepsilon$$

where $B(p)$ is drawn from the Bernoulli distribution with expectation p, and $\varepsilon \sim N(0,1)$.

2.5.3   *Unobserved confounders*

Imagine that in the kidney stone example, doctors tell us they have used stone sizes to decide which treatment to give, but unfortunately, they didn't store stone sizes because the software they were using was not designed to save that data. We will then use dashed lines in the graph to denote that this is an *unobserved* variable (see figure 2.12).

Figure 2.12   Graph with an unobserved confounder (we don't have data about this variable).

We know that we should apply the adjustment formula. However, we have no information about C at all. This means we cannot compute the quantity $P(O|T, C)$ or $P(C)$. This implies that we cannot estimate the causal effect of T into O.

Be very careful about missing confounders

Although we may be aware of many confounding factors in practice, we typically don't know all of them. Simpson's paradox has shown us that failing to use the adjustment formula can lead to choosing the wrong treatment. Therefore, the effect of not including a relevant confounder can be devastating.

Missing relevant confounders is the Achilles' heel of the adjustment formula. To address this, you should strive to include as many as possible. Unfortunately, in real-world scenarios, you may not have access to all of them. If this is unavoidable, it's crucial to explicitly state this assumption and communicate it to those interested in your analysis.

> *(continued)*
>
> There are tools to analyze the sensitivity of your results to unmeasured confounders. However, they are out of the scope of this book. If you're curious, look up more about this topic in specialized literature about sensitivity analysis in causal inference.

UNOBSERVED CONFOUNDERS SIMULATION EXERCISE

Fill table 2.6 with the following data-generation process and a sample size of 10,000

$$C := B(0.8)$$
$$T := B(0.6)C + B(0.2)(1 - C)$$
$$R := B(0.3)T + B(0.5)(1 - T) + C + \varepsilon$$

where $B(p)$ is drawn from the Bernoulli distribution with expectation p, and $\varepsilon \sim N(0,1)$.

2.5.4 *Mediators*

Imagine that in the kidney stone data, treatments are assigned at random, but for whatever reason, stone size post treatment is affected. Notice that even though we areusing the same word, *size*, we had a pretreatment size, and now we have a post-treatment size. Figure 2.13 illustrates this situation.

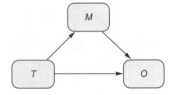

Intuitively, this means Treatment affects Recovery in two different ways: a direct one $(T \rightarrow O)$ and an indirect one $(T \rightarrow M \rightarrow O)$ modifying stones' sizes. Because part of the effect from T to O goes through M, the variable M is called a *mediator*. To estimate the overall effect from T to O, we don't care about the different ways in which the treatment produces a recovery. All these paths are the treatment's responsi-

Figure 2.13   Graph with a mediator. For example, post-treatment size is a mediator in the kidney stone example. Once a treatment is given to a patient, their kidney stone's size may change. *M* stands for Mediator, *T* for Treatment, and *O* for Outcome.

bility. Informally speaking, we don't need to intercept either of the two paths, so $P(O|\text{do}(T = t)) = P(O|T = t)$. The same conclusion can be derived from the formal point of view: the intervened graph and observed graph are the same. We will also have $P(O|\text{do}(T = t)) = P(O|T = t)$, so no adjustment formula is needed.

A CASE WHERE THE ADJUSTMENT FORMULA AND THE EFFECT OF INTERVENTION DO NOT COINCIDE

Even though the interventional quantity and the observed quantity are the same, you may wonder what would happen if we applied the adjustment formula in the mediator example. Well, it would generally give a different new quantity and, more importantly, an incorrect one. So, in this case, we don't have to apply the adjustment formula: if we do, we will introduce *bias*.

For some particular problems, we may be interested in distinguishing between direct and indirect effects. We will see some examples in chapters 6 and 7.

MEDIATOR SIMULATION EXERCISE

Fill table 2.6 with the following data-generation process and a sample size of 10,000

$$T := B(0.4)$$
$$M := B(0.6)T + B(0.2)(1-T)$$
$$R := B(0.4)T + B(0.5)(1-T) + M + \varepsilon$$

where $B(p)$ is drawn from the Bernoulli distribution with expectation p, and $\varepsilon \sim N(0,1)$.

2.5.5   *Many confounders*

We have explained how to apply the adjustment formula with just one confounder. In practice, we often have to deal with many. Imagine that you develop a new version of a mobile app, and you are interested in knowing the effect of the new version on engagement. You can expect that among your customers, younger people will be early adopters because they are more used to technology; at the same time, you can expect younger people to have different behaviors in engagement. Thus, in this case, age is a confounder. Typical confounders are age, location, and sex.

Many confounders can be represented as shown in figure 2.14. The solution is simple: the adjustment formula is the same with many confounders, using terms like $P(Y|X, Z_1, Z_2, ..., Z_n)$ or $P(Z_1, ..., Z_n)$. That is, Z is treated as a random vector. Statistically speaking, calculating these probabilities is not straightforward. Spoiler alert: we will use machine learning techniques to do so (see chapter 4).

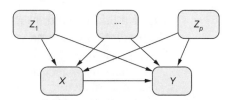

Figure 2.14   Graph with p different confounders. Usually, in practice, we don't have a single confounder; rather we have many of them.

In this situation, we also need to check the positivity assumption, which in this case is expressed with all confounding variables together:

$$P(T|Z_1, Z_2, ..., Z_n) > 0$$

This is read that all combinations of all values of all confounding factors have been tried at some point. This is a huge requirement, especially when we have a large number of confounders. The combinatorial explosion grows exponentially in the number of variables, which means the data sample should also grow exponentially fast. We will talk more about this in chapter 4 when we incorporate machine learning techniques in the adjustment formula.

2.5.6   *Outcome predictive variables*

Consider the situation explained previously, where we have predictive variables (one or more P) that do not affect the variable T (figure 2.15).

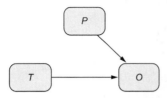

Figure 2.15 A predictive outcome variable predicts the outcome but not the treatment. In this case, there is no difference between applying the adjustment formula or just the difference of means from a bias point of view. However, adjusting for the predictive variable can be beneficial because it may decrease the variance of your estimations.

Test your knowledge

For figure 2.15, what is the corresponding intervened graph?

Again, the answer to this "Test your knowledge" question is that the intervened and observed graphs are the same, implying that

$$P(O|\text{do}(T = t)) = P(O|T = t)$$

Moreover, in this particular case, the adjustment formula and $P(O|T = t)$ coincide.

Above and beyond: Mathematical derivation of the adjustment formula for a predictive outcome variable (optional)

If you are curious to know why the adjustment formula gives the same result as $P(O|T = t)$, this sidebar provides a short proof. First, notice that in figure 2.15, P and T are independent, so $P(t, p) = P(t)P(p)$. Now, let's use this assumption in the calculation of the adjustment formula. By the definition of the adjustment formula, we have that

$$P(O|\text{do}(T = t)) = \sum_p P(O|T = t, p)P(p)$$

We can rearrange the earlier independence assumption, obtaining $P(p) = P(T = t, p)/P(T = t)$. Substituting this term in the previous equation, we have

$$\sum_p P(O|T = t, p)P(p) = \frac{1}{P(T = t)} \sum_p P(O|T = t, p)P(T = t, p)$$

Applying the definition of conditional expectation $P(O|T = t, p) = P(O, T = t, p)/P(T = t, p)$, the terms $P(T = t, p)$ cancel out, giving

$$\frac{1}{P(T = t)} \sum_p P(O|T = t, p)P(T = t, p) = \frac{1}{P(T = t)} \sum_p P(O, T = t, p)$$

But summing all the terms $P(O, T = t, p)$ with respect to p gives us $P(O, T = t)$. So finally,

$$\frac{1}{P(T = t)} \sum_p P(O, T = t, p) = \frac{P(O, T = t)}{P(T = t)} = P(O|T = t)$$

From the statistical point of view, $P(O|T = t)$ just uses the information of T and O, whereas when we use the adjustment formula, we involve all other variables P. Even though two quantities aim for the same value, it can be statistically helpful to use the adjustment formula because the variance of the estimation is potentially lower, which increases the accuracy of our estimates.

PREDICTOR SIMULATION EXERCISE
Fill table 2.6 with the following data-generation process and a sample size of 10,000

$$T := B(0.4)$$
$$P := B(0.4)$$
$$O := B(0.4)T + B(0.5)(1 - T) + P + \varepsilon$$

where $B(p)$ is drawn from the Bernoulli distribution with expectation p and $\varepsilon \sim N(0,1)$.

2.5.7 *Treatment predictive variables*

There is one case left: when we have treatment predictive variables that predict the treatment but not the outcome, as shown in figure 2.16.

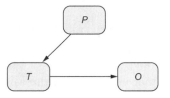

Figure 2.16 Again, in the case of a predictive treatment variable, there is no difference between applying the adjustment formula or just the difference of means from a bias point of view. However, adjusting for the predictive treatment variable can be harmful because it may increase the variance of your estimations.

Here, the intervened graph and the observed graph are different. However, we are in a situation where the adjustment formula and the direct calculation $P(O|T)$ again give the same result.

> **Above and beyond: Mathematical derivation of the adjustment formula for a predictive treatment variable (optional)**
>
> Because variables P only affect O though T, all the information necessary to predict O is contained in T (this will be explained in more detail in chapter 7), which leads to $P(O|T, P) = P(O|T)$:
>
> $$P(O|do(T = t)) = \sum_p P(O|T = t, p)P(p) = P(O|T = t) \sum_p P(p) = P(O|T = t)$$

Unlike the previous example, where adjusting for predictive variables can reduce the variance of your estimations, adjusting for treatment predictors can increase the variance. So, you're advised not to control for treatment predictors whenever you can.

2.5.8 *Conditional Intervention*

Imagine that we want to calculate the effect of an intervention for a particular value of a confounder Z. For instance, in the kidney stone example, if we choose the population of patients with small stones (figure 2.17), what would be the effect of giving everyone treatment A?

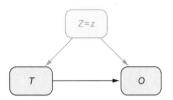

Figure 2.17 Sometimes we aim to measure the treatment's effect on a specific subgroup. In this graph, we can do this by first conditioning on the confounder and then comparing the average outcomes. Z stands for Confounder, T for Treatment, and O for Outcome.

Test your knowledge

For figure 2.17, what is the intervened graph corresponding to the intervention do($T = t$)?

In this case, if we condition on a particular value z, intuitively, the effect of variable Z disappears (this does not always happen, as we will see in chapter 7). That is, for this particular population, Z has no variation and thus does not affect T or O. This implies that the intervened graph (removing all arrows that end on T) is the same as the observed graph.

Formally speaking, the probability of O in the intervened graph for those with value z is expressed as $P(O|\text{do}(T = t), Z = z)$. This is called the *z-specific effect*. But because the intervened and observed graphs are the same, we have

$$P(O|\text{do}(T = t), Z = z) = P(O|T = t, Z = z)$$

The reasoning still holds, whether Z is a random variable or a random vector. This means if we have all the confounders, intervening for a particular set $Z = z$ can be computed just like the conditional probability. We will come back to this in chapter 4 when we talk about machine learning methods.

The definition of z-specific effects

The definition of $P(O|\text{do}(T = t), Z = z)$ is subtle, and we have to be careful about how to read it. We have introduced it like this: first we condition on the population of interest (those with $Z = z$), and then we intervene in the graph. If we always proceed like this, sooner or later we will get into trouble.

Consider the example in the following figure, where the size of the stone S acts as a mediator. If we first condition on S = Small, we are choosing those patients who, after receiving the treatment, have stones that are small. But if we set a particular treatment for everyone, we will enter a strange situation where some patients have small stones and then, if we change the treatment, have large stones. And then our mind explodes! It's like a weird time-dependent loop.

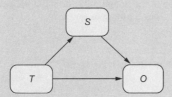

Clearly defining the effect of the intervention on a group defined by post-treatment stone size is challenging. It requires the use of Pearlian counterfactuals, as explained in chapter 10.

This kind of situation can be dealt with by using counterfactuals (you will find a short introduction to counterfactuals in chapter 10). To make everything easier, in general, $P(O|do(T = t), Z = z)$ means this: first we intervene, and then we select the population $Z = z$ of interest. If we have a confounder, it doesn't matter if we intervene first or second because the value will not change due to the treatment. That's why in this section, the order doesn't matter.

2.5.9 Combining all the previous situations

Let's summarize the types of variables we've discussed and their effect on your data analysis. As you work with your data, check whether any of the following kinds of variables appear in your study (see figure 2.18):

- Observed confounding factors (C_1) that may need adjustment. Unobserved confounding factors (C_2) pose the greatest risk in these analyses.
- Predictive variables (P) that do not require adjustment but can help reduce variance in your estimates.
- Pretreatment decision variables (PT) that affect decision-making but not the outcome (Y). Including these can increase the variance of the estimated ATE, so it's typically better to exclude them.

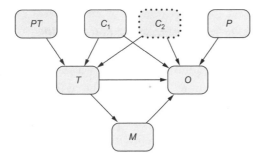

Figure 2.18 All of the previous situations in a single graph

- Mediators (*M*) are generally not included in the adjustment formula; specific cases are discussed in chapters 6 and 7.

Table 2.7 tells you, for each type of variable, whether the adjustment formula should be included.

Table 2.7 Types of variables to consider in the adjustment formula

Type of variable	Should it be included in the adjustment formula for calculating $P(Y = 1|do(X = x))$?
Confounder	Definitely.
Missing confounder	Definitely, but not possible. This is a problem!
Mediator	No: it will introduce bias.
Outcome predictive variable	It doesn't introduce bias; in general, it is recommended because it may improve statistical accuracy.
Treatment predictive variable	It doesn't introduce bias; in general, it is not recommended because it may hurt statistical accuracy.

Of course, this is still a simplified version of how complex the relationships between variables can be. For instance, observed and unobserved confounders can be related (see figure 2.19). In chapter 7, we will deal with the situation where we have any possible graph and develop a tool called a back-door criterion to assess whether we can estimate ATEs and which variables we should include in the adjustment formula.

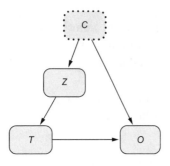

Figure 2.19   In real-world scenarios, things can get more complicated. For example, suppose you know a confounder is affecting your study, but you lack information about it. Can adjusting other variables help you get an unbiased estimate? We'll explore these kinds of situations in chapter 7.

2.5.10 *Summarizing the differences between intervening and applying the adjustment formula*

In section 2.2.5, we introduced the adjustment formula as a way to figure out the effect of an intervention. Then, in section 2.5, we learned that the adjustment formula doesn't always work for estimating the impact of an intervention (like when there's a mediator involved, see 2.5.4). In figure 2.20, we've put together a quick summary to help you visualize the differences between the conditional probability, the intervened probability, and the adjustment formula.

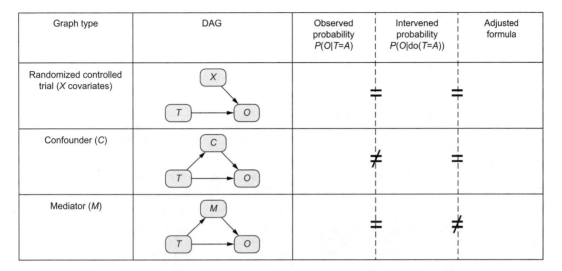

Graph type	DAG	Observed probability $P(O\|T=A)$	Intervened probability $P(O\|do(T=A))$	Adjusted formula
Randomized controlled trial (*X* covariates)		$=$	$=$	
Confounder (*C*)		$\neq$	$=$	
Mediator (*M*)		$=$	$\neq$	

Figure 2.20 Differences between the conditional probability, the intervened probability, and the adjustment formula for the cases of an RCT, a confounder, and a mediator. The equal and unequal signs determine whether the adjacent quantities agree. *T* stands for Treatment, *C* for Confounder, *M* for Mediator, and *X* for Covariates.

In the case of an RCT, the three values line up. This means that even if we consider characteristics like a patient's age (*X*), the adjustment formula still gives us an unbiased estimate of the effect after the intervention. However, when there's a confounder, the observed conditional and the intervened probabilities generally differ (think about something like Simpson's paradox). Here, we can use the adjustment formula to calculate the intervened probability. In situations involving a mediator, the observed and intervened probabilities are equal. But the adjustment formula tends to give a biased estimate.

2.6 So, what's the plan?

The adjustment formula is just one of the techniques that can be used in step 5 in the map of a causal analysis shown in chapter 1 and repeated in figure 2.21. But knowing the adjustment formula is just the beginning. Additional steps are required to apply it to a particular problem, as shown in figure 2.22.

First you need to be able to answer whether the adjustment formula is the proper tool for your directed acyclic graph (DAG) and, if it is, which variables you should adjust for (explained in chapter 7). Then you should check that the positivity assumption holds (described in chapter 5).

The second thing to do is obtain a numerical estimate. You will use a different method depending on the nature of your treatment variable. If your treatment variable is binary, you have two options. If you have a small number of confounding variables, you can apply the adjustment formula as it is (as described in this chapter). But if you have a large number relative to your sample size, as explained in chapter 4, you will need to use machine learning methods.

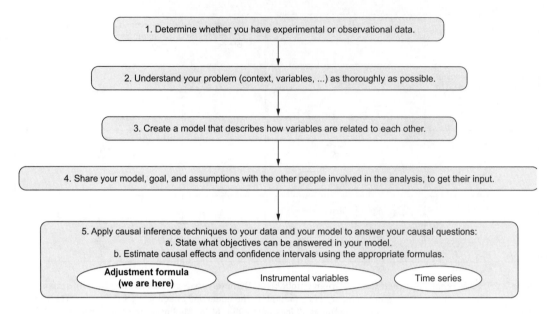

Figure 2.21   Five steps describing the typical process in causal inference

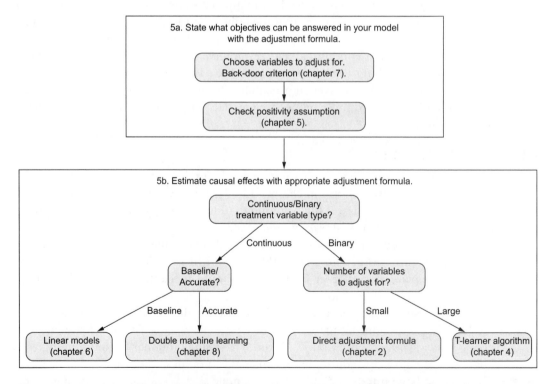

Figure 2.22   This diagram outlines the approach for parts 1 and 2 of the book, focusing on applying the adjustment formula across various scenarios using different techniques.

On the other hand, if your treatment variable is continuous, the adjustment formula explained in this chapter cannot be applied directly. In this case, you have two options. If you want a preliminary result that uses methods you can understand and that can be used as a baseline before further analysis, you should use linear methods (chapter 6). If instead you require an accurate method capable of handling nonlinear relationships, you should use double machine learning (chapter 8).

> **TIP**   Figure 2.22 is a useful mental map. Keep in mind that it is not entirely accurate, however. For example, the techniques used for continuous variables can also be used for binary variables. Formally speaking, the double machine learning technique is not an application of the adjustment formula. However, it can be applied under the same circumstances and does a similar job. That's why we include it here.

2.7   Lessons learned

The following points aim to clear up misunderstandings that may arise when attempting to answer causal questions without using the appropriate tools:

- We know correlation is not causation, but if there is some correlation, there must be some causation, too, in the same direction—right?!

  This idea is wrong, and we have Simpson's paradox to prove it: if you use only correlations, the decision may completely change depending on which variables you include in the analysis. Do not rely on correlations only.

- Data does not speak by itself.

  You have seen that in causal analysis, relying only on data is not enough. You need to model how data was generated, and this model will tell you which formulas to apply.

- More data does not solve the problem.

  One of the ways Big Data tries to address prediction problems is to gather more data (more variables or more sample size). For example, deep learning has specialized in creating more accurate models by increasing the volume of data and the size of the network. However, in causal matters, more data helps, but it is not enough. In the kidney stone example, we have only eight data points, and the way to solve it is not to obtain a larger sample size but rather to model the problem from a causal point of view.

- Correlation is not enough.

  Correlation is a symmetric function of your variables: $\text{corr}(x, y) = \text{corr}(y, x)$. But causality is not: if x causes y, changing y does not change x. So when analyzing causal relationships, we need a language that makes directionality explicit.

2.8   Chapter quiz

As we conclude the chapter, it's important to ensure that you have a solid understanding of the key concepts. Here are the essential questions you should be able to answer clearly and concisely. If you can't, I suggest rereading the corresponding references:

1   What is a confounder?
    Answer in the sidebar "Confounding"
2   Why do we need the adjustment formula?
    Answer in the section "Adjustment formula"
3   We shouldn't always apply the adjustment formula by default. Name an analysis comprising three variables in which we should not apply the adjustment formula. Answer in section 2.5.4
4   What are the potential consequences if we fail to use the adjustment formula when necessary or, conversely, if we apply it when it's not needed? Answer in section 2.5
5   What does the notion of causal intervention represent in the real world? Remember the formal definition of intervention in the sidebar "Formally speaking, what is an intervention?" Answer in section 2.3
6   What measures the average treatment effect (ATE)? Answer in section 2.2.5

Summary

- Before making a causal judgment, remember Simpson's paradox: it shows you how conclusions can differ depending on which sets of variables you include in the analysis. This fact should prevent you from making a simple comparison of two alternatives when dealing with observational data because the result may be flawed.
- You can use the adjustment formula to discern correlation from causation.
- Domain knowledge is crucial to causal inference because it will lead you to a graph that will tell you whether you should apply the adjustment formula.
- The main risk in any causal analysis is missing relevant confounders. So, you need to make explicit which confounders you have information about and which ones you don't.
- RCTs and A/B tests ensure that there are no confounders. That's why it is always recommended that they be run if possible.
- Before applying the adjustment formula, you need to assess the positivity assumption: to evaluate how the treatment works in a particular situation, it needs to have been tried at some time in the past.
- Use graphs to clarify and communicate with the rest of the team what the objective and assumptions of the analysis are.

Applying causal inference

In the previous chapter, we saw that we can model causal problems with graphs. We also learned that the graph is crucial for calculating the causal impact we are looking for. Depending on the geometry of the graph, we may need to apply the adjustment formula. Now we need to discuss how to create these graphs.

In this chapter, we explore some example scenarios where you can apply causal inference techniques. When tackling a specific problem with causal inference, there are two main steps. First you need to translate your problem description into causal language. Graphs are excellent tools for this—they help put into a model all the information you have about how data was generated. Creating the graph is crucial because it determines which formulas you'll use later, like the adjustment formula. Many people find this stage challenging and don't know where to start. That's why we'll use examples in this chapter to guide you through the graph creation process and offer tips to help you start your own graphs.

Once you're comfortable with the graph that represents your problem, the second phase is to use formulas, algorithms, or other methods to estimate causal effects. The following chapters in this book focus on this phase.

The examples in this chapter are simplified. The aim is to illustrate basic cases that can inspire you or be adapted to your specific case. We've avoided excessive detail to keep things easy to understand and adaptable to other situations.

When to use directed acyclic graphs (DAGs)

When you're working on a problem involving causal inference using the graphical approach, it's a recommended practice to begin by drawing a graph of your problem. This helps you clearly state your assumptions, find out which variables you need and which ones you don't, and set specific goals for your analysis.

3.1   *When and why to use graphs in causal inference analysis*

In chapter 1, we introduced figure 1.1, which we show again here as figure 3.1. This figure outlines the typical steps for conducting a causal inference analysis using graphs. (Remember, there's another approach called the potential outcomes framework, which we'll cover in part 3 of this book and which doesn't rely on graphs.) Graphs play a significant role in most of these steps. Let's delve into how they're involved in each step from 2 to 5 (points a and b). We're assuming that we're working with observational data, which is why we don't include step 1.

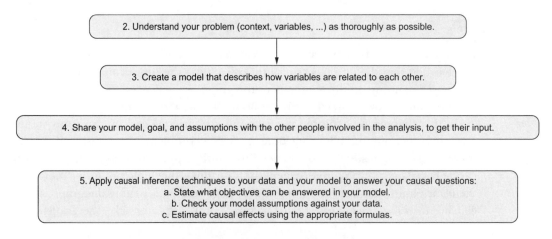

Figure 3.1   Steps to translate a causal problem into causal inference language

In this chapter, we will look in detail at step 5 from figure 3.1:

- What can we answer with the information we have? Use the graph to determine which goals can be achieved. For instance, if we hadn't measured stone size in our kidney stones example, we wouldn't be able to estimate treatment effects.
- Check whether the positivity assumption holds (see chapter 2). Other assumptions will be discussed in chapter 7 to assess a model with data.

Keep in mind that although domain knowledge is useful in machine learning, in casual inference it is vital. In chapter 2, we learned that doctors assess kidney-stone size before treatment, a detail we'd only know by asking them directly. This influences our model, setting the arrow from Size to Treatment. Consequently, to estimate the treatment's effect on recovery, we must use the adjustment formula. Remember, if the arrow pointed the other way (Treatment to Size), suggesting that treatment affected stone size afterward, we wouldn't need the adjustment formula. Thus, the model dictates the calculations needed later.

Graphs show which variables matter in our study and how they're connected. We'll primarily use DAGs in this book. *Directed* means arrows show causality (changing A affects B, but not vice versa). *Acyclic* means paths never loop back to the same node (this is more of a constraint than a feature). If you follow the arrows, you won't return to your starting point. Check out figures 3.2 and 3.3 for examples.

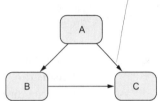

Figure 3.2 In an acyclic graph, there are no cycles.

Graphs play a crucial role as they bridge domain experts and analysts. With a graph, you can collaborate with experts to do the following:

- Ensure that all relevant variables are accounted for in the analysis, including those available and those not.
- Identify which variables are directly connected and which aren't (indicated by arrows).
- Clarify the objectives of your analysis, such as which causal effects you aim to estimate (represented by arrows).

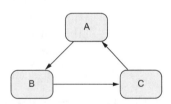

Figure 3.3 A cyclic graph contains a path that starts from A and ends at A: A → B → C → A.

Our conclusions will mainly stem from the graph, which should contain all the necessary information. Therefore, it's critical to create it accurately. The next section provides guidelines to avoid drawing incorrect conclusions. Fortunately, graphs are intuitive and straightforward, facilitating communication between domain experts and analysts, as well as among analysts themselves.

Getting in the habit of creating a graph for your problem may require some effort in the beginning. It's a technique that needs to be exercised: every time you face a causal problem, the first thing to do is to ask yourself what the graph will look like, even in the simplest cases. By repeating this strategy, you will get used to framing causal questions into graphs.

As you start creating your graph, you will see that some parts are very clear and others are fuzzy. Or perhaps you don't know where to start. The tips proposed in this chapter should ease the way. At some point, you will need to deal with complex graphs (more arrows, nodes, and so on). A good recommendation, even in these cases, is to start simple with the parts of the graph you understand the best; later you can increase the complexity, adding more nodes and arrows.

After creating a graph proposal, it's a good idea to share it with others. This way, you can ensure that it meets the analysis's purpose and get feedback in case you've overlooked something important.

3.2 Steps to formulate your problem using graphs

Let's follow a series of steps to guide you through creating the graph:

1 List all relevant variables that may have a role in the data generation process. Consult with domain experts if needed. Remember, listing all variables is crucial to avoid missing confounding factors, which is a significant risk in causal inference.
2 Create the graph by examining each pair of variables to determine whether there's a direct causal effect and, if so, its direction.
3 Clearly state the main assumptions and limitations of your model. Be sure everyone on the team understands them.
4 Confirm that everyone involved agrees on the analysis objectives.
5 Validate whether there's enough variability in the data to answer the causal questions of interest. For example, check the positivity assumption, which states that for each value of the confounders, there is data on the different types of treatments.

The following sections walk you through these steps.

3.2.1 List all the variables

Imagine that you work on a media platform in the area of sports and culture. Posts are written daily and published on the internet through the site and also on social media platforms. In your role, you're tasked with analyzing data to assist in content decisions. The head of the writing team wants to know which topic, sports or culture, garners more reader engagement. This is a common need in many industries: comparing performance.

One approach is an A/B test: for each new post, choose at random whether it should be about sports or culture; then, after some time, measure which of the two has more views. However, this may not be feasible for your project. First, in some situations, the A/B test forces you to write about a particular topic, but there may not be relevant news to write about it. These posts will not arouse interest as usual, so pageviews will be lower than expected. Second, the time needed to measure effectiveness depends on the number of readers. With a large audience, you'd gather data quickly, but a smaller audience could prolong the test for weeks or months, potentially harming your business by not delivering expected content promptly.

You first need to understand the context to analyze this problem using causal inference with historical data. Here's the company's process:

1 The writing team decides on the topic for each post.
2 The marketing team selects the advertising platform for each post. Typically, sports posts are advertised on Facebook because marketing believes they are more shareable there. Culture posts are often advertised using Google AdWords because people searching for cultural information may come across the posts while browsing Google (e.g., for venue or schedule details).

The number of pageviews for each topic cannot be directly measured to draw conclusions because the choice of platform can influence pageviews. Some platforms may be more effective than others.

Ask yourself

Which variables have something to say about this problem? They may serve different roles:

- What is the treatment or decision variable?
- What is the outcome variable?
- Which variables influence the outcome?
- What are the contextual variables, such as a country's socioeconomic status?

Identify variables with direct, indirect, or no impact on the outcome. For example, you can't directly control topic popularity, but you can promote a topic; you can't directly change cholesterol levels, but you can through diets or medication; weather may have no direct impact.

It's vital to list all variables that can play a role in your problem: those you have data for, those you don't, and even those you're unsure how to describe. As seen in the previous chapters, missing relevant confounding factors is a major risk in causal inference: they can completely alter conclusions, as with Simpson's paradox. Sometimes we're aware of a relevant confounder but lack information about it. For example, in the kidney stone scenario, if doctors mention using kidney stone size to decide on treatment but don't have individual size data, we must acknowledge that causal analysis isn't feasible. We must list all the confounding factors because if we are not careful enough, we may limit ourselves and not make explicit unobserved confounding factors for fear of concluding that our problem has no solution. Chapter 7 will explore potential workarounds for missing variables in some cases.

For our example, the critical variables to consider are as follows:

- The decision variable is the post topic.

- The outcome can be post pageviews, although other outcomes of interest may include long-term or short-term pageviews or pageviews divided by the effort required to write a post of this type.
- You also need to account for the specific advertising platform chosen for each post (Facebook ads, Google AdWords, etc.).

Your historical dataset consists of three columns: Topic, Platform, and Number of Visits. Each row represents a post and describes the topic, the platform used for advertising, and the number of visits it received.

The variables selected so far are those explicitly specified by the writing team. However, other factors may influence the model, such as these:

- *Seasonality*—Sports seasons affect engagement, so seasonality is important.
- *Year*—Significant events like the Olympics, new stadium constructions, and team changes can impact engagement.
- *Popularity of the topic*—You may write more about a pop band because everyone is listening to them at the moment. Measuring popularity can be challenging and will be discussed later in this chapter.

This list of variables may evolve with better context and more details. Additionally, some advertising platforms provide information about visits from specific ads, which can simplify analysis. However, a particular ad may have been shown many times to a user until the user finally clicked it. If we don't have this information, we will attribute all the merit to the last ad shown and clicked, which will not give us the correct picture. This doesn't happen when we use a causal model. Because page visits happen after the post has been advertised, a click is attributed to the fact it has been advertised (one or more times), not only to the last time it was advertised.

3.2.2 *Create your graph*

Once you have the list of variables, you need to model the relationship between each pair of variables. For any pair X and Y, we may find

- No direct causal relationship between them (although there can be an indirect relationship through other variables)
- A direct causal relationship, where either X causes Y or Y causes X

THE MEANING OF AN ARROW

We will put an arrow $X \rightarrow Y$ whenever we think there is a potential effect from X to Y. That is, we will put an arrow when we are sure there is an effect and also when we are unsure. We will not put an arrow when we are sure X and Y have no direct causal relationship.

Formally speaking (we will look more deeply at this in chapter 7), we say Y can be calculated as a function of X and potentially some other variables or effects expressed via a random variable U:

$$Y := f(X, U)$$

In other words, *Y* depends on *X*. But just knowing *X*, we cannot determine the exact value of *Y*, because other unknown factors *U* also affect *Y*. That is why, even if we know *X*, the variable *Y*|*X* is still a random variable (where randomness comes from *U*).

Remember that we use the walrus symbol (:=) to express the direction of the arrow *X* → *Y*. Typically, the variable *U* may encode other *unobserved* variables that may affect the process. If other variables *Z* are observed and affect *Y*, we will write *Y* := *f*(*X*, *Z*, *U*). For simplicity, because the meaning of the arrow is the same, let's consider the case without other variables. This formula has to be read as in coding: when you know the value of *X*, you can calculate the value of *Y* through whatever form the function *f* takes. But if you change *Y*, the value of *X* will remain the same.

Writing that *Y* is a function of *X* is a very general statement. It includes a particularly strange case: when the dependency through *f* doesn't actually depend on X, such as *f*(*X*, *U*) = *U*. We would like to avoid this kind of degenerate case. The problem is that from a formal perspective, it is difficult to impose a restriction on *f*, saying that it truly depends on *X*. So, when we put an arrow *X* → *Y*, we are saying that *X* may potentially affect *Y*, including the case where it doesn't.

STATING ASSUMPTIONS BY THE LACK OF ARROWS

It is when we say there is no arrow (direct causal relationship) between *X* and *Y* that we are actually saying something! That is, we make assumptions about our model precisely when we *do not* draw an arrow between two nodes. For example, compare figure 3.4, where all nodes are connected, with figure 3.5. In the latter, if we want to study the causal effect from A to C, from A to D, or from C to D, our intuition tells us that B plays no role in this model. B can be safely removed so we have a simpler model. This is because we are making assumptions represented by the lack of arrows connecting B to other nodes. On the other hand, figure 3.4 is a graph of four nodes, which, among directed graphs of four nodes, is as general as possible (all nodes are connected). For now, we cannot simplify it any further.

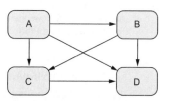

Figure 3.4 Example involving four variables, each connected with a complete set of arrows. The only assumptions made here concern the directions of the arrows.

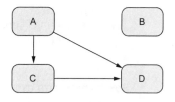

Figure 3.5 Example with four variables, assuming no causal effects among certain variables. The assumptions are represented by the absence of arrows in the graph.

One tip that usually helps with setting the direction of an arrow is *using time*: what precedes what. If that is not enough, you can use Judea Pearl's listening metaphor:

X is a cause of Y if Y listens to X and decides its value in response to what it hears.

—Listening metaphor; Judea Pearl

Let's revisit our example of topic relevance introduced in section 3.2.1. The objective is to calculate the causal effect of Topic on Pageviews, represented by an arrow from Topic to Pageviews, which we aim to estimate. We'll consider Seasonality and Popularity as confounding variables (for simplicity, we'll exclude Year, which is also a confounder). The choice of platform follows the topic decision, so Topic influences Platform. Additionally, the platform choice may impact the number of pageviews, reflecting its role in advertising. Furthermore, it's reasonable to assume that platforms consider seasonality and topic popularity when deciding when and to whom to display ads. Thus, we include arrows from Seasonality and Popularity to Platform. If there's any uncertainty, we err on the side of caution and include arrows (remember, we remove arrows only when we're confident there's no direct effect). The resulting graph is shown in figure 3.6.

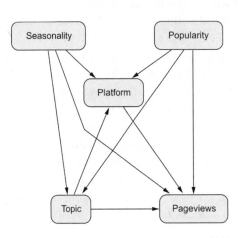

Figure 3.6   Graph showing the effect of Topic on Pageviews. Seasonality and Popularity are confounders, and Platform is a mediator.

Above and beyond

Causal inference includes a field called *causal discovery*, which focuses on automatically deriving the causal graph from data. Generally, recovering the graph solely from data is impossible without additional assumptions. You don't need to delve into this for using causal inference, but here's a brief explanation for curious readers.

Consider a scenario with only two variables, X and Y. Although we can measure their correlation, which is symmetric (corr(X, Y) = corr(Y, X)), it doesn't indicate the direction of a potential arrow: $X \rightarrow Y$ or $Y \rightarrow X$. It's been demonstrated (see chapter 7) that for any data distribution of pairs (X, Y), two causal models produce this data, but with arrows pointing in opposite directions. Therefore, the joint probability of (X, Y) doesn't uniquely determine the arrow's direction; we can't determine it solely from the data.

HOW TO DEAL WITH CYCLIC GRAPHS

When faced with cyclic graphs, such as when A causes B and B causes A simultaneously, we encounter a challenge because acyclic graphs can't represent these situations. In such cases, we will have arrows A → B and B → A, forming a loop (A → B → A). This is a limitation of DAGs. However, we can address this problem with time series data collected over different periods. In the next section, we'll explain how to use time series to unfold a graph over time. Unfortunately, there isn't yet a fully developed theory to guide us in dealing with directed graphs that cannot be unfolded over time. Therefore, if you don't have time series data, applying the theory explained in this book may be challenging.

Consider a store where you increase the price of a specific item. This change will likely affect demand, which in turn influences your decision to adjust the price again. However, on closer examination, you realize that the price doesn't immediately impact demand and vice versa. It takes time for price changes to affect demand and time for you to reassess prices. To represent this in a graph, you create a cyclic graph where price affects demand and demand affects price simultaneously.

But this isn't entirely accurate. Today's prices influence today's demand, subsequently affecting tomorrow's prices. You can address this issue by unfolding this process over time and considering each variable at its specific time point. For instance, if P_t represents the price at time t and D_t represents the demand at time t, you can write $P_t \to D_t \to P_{(t+1)}$. This way, you avoid a cyclic graph, as illustrated in figure 3.7.

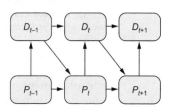

Figure 3.7 Graph representing pricing discounts based on historical purchasing frequency. Price and demand affect future prices and demands.

Moreover, you can assume that $t-1$ prices affect the decision of t prices made by the company. At the same time, those who couldn't buy the item at time $t-1$ will be willing to buy it at time t, so D_{t-1} also affects Dt.

3.2.3 State your assumptions

Most of the assumptions you have made are embedded in the construction of the graph: the choice of variables, the placement of arrows, and the direction of those arrows. It's good practice to have other team members review the initial version of the graph and provide feedback. During this process, you can discuss which arrows to add or remove.

For example, in figure 3.6, there may be a discussion about whether it's necessary to include an arrow from Seasonality to Platform. Someone may argue that the platform's decision about which ad to show is based on the topic's popularity rather than the time of year. This implies that Seasonality has no direct effect on Platform, only an indirect effect through Popularity. If you're convinced of this (backed by additional information), you can remove the arrow from Seasonality to Platform and add another from Seasonality to Popularity. However, if there's uncertainty about whether Seasonality directly affects Platform, you will leave the arrow as is.

There's a challenge with measuring Popularity. You aren't sure what it entails or how to calculate it. One approach can be tracking how often the topic appears across various media sources, but that can be expensive. Alternatively, you can use a *proxy*, like Google Trends, which may not be an exact measure but captures most of the needed information. If you go for proxies, it's important to communicate this to the rest of the team.

Let's consider a simple example involving a company with multiple teams working on various projects, where we want to measure each team's effectiveness in terms of hours per project. We need to collect data on the variables Team and Efficacy. Because projects may vary in difficulty, we also need to include Project as a variable to account for this.

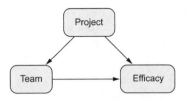

Figure 3.8   Graph representing the situation in which groups do not choose which project they will work on

To summarize, we have three variables: Team, Project, and Efficacy. Clearly, Team and Project both influence Efficacy: some teams are more efficient than others, and some projects are harder than others, impacting Efficacy accordingly. However, determining whether Project influences Team or vice versa is not straightforward without additional information. If a manager assigns projects, we will have a situation similar to the kidney stones problem discussed in the previous chapter, as shown in figure 3.8.

We cannot measure each team's efficacy directly because some teams may be assigned more difficult tasks, leading to an unfair comparison. However, if teams have the autonomy to choose which projects to work on, the situation changes. The total time

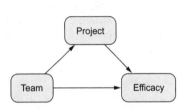

Figure 3.9   Graph representing the situation in which groups choose which project they will work on

spent on a project already accounts for the project selection, which becomes the team's responsibility. Essentially, how the choice of project influences their performance becomes their concern. The direction of the arrow will be as shown in figure 3.9.

A similar scenario can arise when measuring a musician's performance. Even though the quality of their instrument may affect their play, it's often considered part of their music.

3.2.4   State your objectives

When initiating a causal inference project, we have specific objectives in mind, and various stakeholders may have different expectations about the results. It's critical to specify precisely what we want from the analysis to avoid what statisticians call a *type III error*: providing a correct answer to the wrong question. Fortunately, objectives can be translated into arrows in graphs, ensuring alignment and clarity among all stakeholders.

In the topic preference example, you want to find the topic's impact on the total number of pageviews. In the model, the topic has two possible ways to affect pageviews: a *direct effect* (interest from users about the topic) and an *indirect effect* (through the platform chosen to advertise the post). The *total effect* is the effect through all the paths at the same time. When you think about the topic's impact per se, you do not consider the total effect because it also contains the platform's effect on pageviews. You are actually interested in the direct effect, isolated from the platform effect. Figure 3.10 shows this effect as a thicker arrow. Currently you don't have tools to measure this effect. Using Seasonality and Popularity as confounders, the adjustment formula will give you the total effect of the Topic on Pageviews, the aggregated effect for the two paths, but not the direct effect. Direct and indirect effects will be fully defined and explained in chapter 7.

The analysis doesn't necessarily end with evaluating the topic's impact. Another aspect of interest can be assessing the effectiveness of the platform. Using the same data and model, the objective will be to understand the effect of Platform on Pageviews. This entails calculating the effect of the thicker arrow shown in figure 3.11. To achieve this, you can apply the adjustment formula, including Seasonality, Popularity, and Topic as confounders.

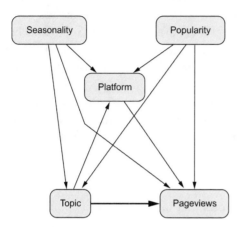

Figure 3.10 Direct effect of Topic on total Pageviews

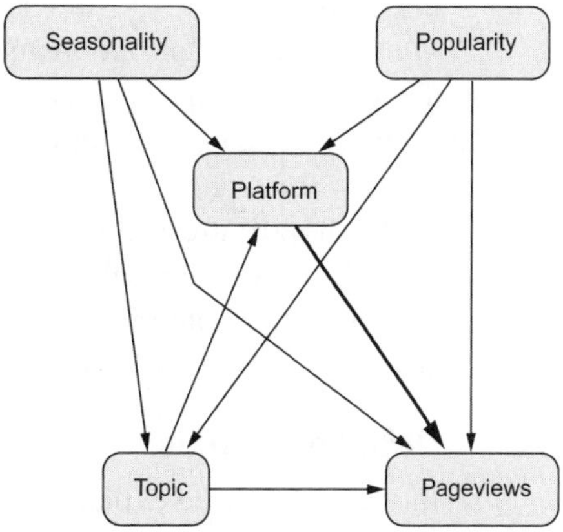

Figure 3.11 Effect of Platform on total Pageviews

3.2.5 *Check the positivity assumption*

In our example, if cultural articles are only advertised on Google but sports articles are advertised on both Google and Facebook, this presents a limitation (see table 3.1). Because we don't have data about how culture will perform on Facebook's platform (as it has never occurred), we cannot accurately estimate the platform's impact on pageviews. In this case, Topic acts as a confounder. Therefore, it wouldn't be fair to compare the platform's impact across topics.

At most, we can measure the difference in interest when Google is used for both topics or compare the efficacy of Google and Facebook when advertising sports. Directly estimating the platform's impact on pageviews across topics will be challenging due to the lack of data for one of the platforms.

Table 3.1 In which combinations do we have data?

	Culture	**Sports**
Facebook	No	Yes
Google	Yes	Yes

> **Reminder of the definition of the positivity assumption**
> We say that the *positivity assumption* holds if for all the values confounders may take, $s = (s_1, ..., s_p)$, and for each treatment, $T = t$, we have that
>
> $$0 < P_0(T = t | S = s) < 1$$

In general, it's essential to verify that the positivity assumption holds. This means we can only measure the difference in impact between two alternatives in situations where we have information about both. If there are contexts where we only have information about one alternative, we cannot accurately estimate causal effects for it. Therefore, we need to limit our analysis to the portion of the data that includes both alternatives.

It's important to note that the lack of positivity is not reflected in the graph. An arrow indicates a causal relationship, not whether we have data for all possible combinations of variable values. Thus, we must ensure that our data includes information about both alternatives to estimate causal effects accurately.

3.3 *Other examples*

In this section, we explain some examples that may inspire you about analysis where you can apply causal inference techniques.

3.3.1 *Recommender systems*

We're all familiar with recommender systems, which suggest TV series on streaming platforms or items on e-commerce sites. These systems typically use supervised learning techniques to predict which items customers may purchase next.

Consider a scenario where you enter a large e-commerce platform that sells a vast array of products. After you view or purchase an item, the recommender system suggests similar products or items that complement your recent purchase. The sheer volume of available products means without the recommender, you may not even consider many of them. This process is akin to how autocomplete functions in text, suggesting what may come next.

However, there are situations where the available item list is small, and predicting the next item isn't enough for the recommender to make a meaningful impact. For instance, imagine owning a supermarket where a customer consistently buys bread every Monday, Wednesday, and Friday morning without fail. You can accurately predict that they will buy bread next Monday morning. If you train a recommender system as a predictive model, it will recommend buying bread next Monday, achieving 100% accuracy. But the fact that the customer bought bread is not due to the recommender; they would have done so anyway. In this scenario, there's no arrow from Recommendation to Buy in the graph because the recommender system doesn't affect whether the customer buys the item (see figure 3.12).

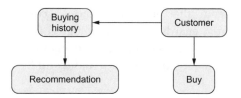

Figure 3.12 **Graph of a pure recommender system that does not influence the customer. This system may predict customer behavior accurately, but it does not affect their actions.**

Test your knowledge

Let's consider an extreme scenario where the previous situation happens for all items and clients. Imagine that you have a mobile app with a recommender system that predicts very well (accuracy 100%) what clients will buy, but they would have bought those things anyway, regardless of the recommendation. Suppose you want to measure the efficacy of the recommender: do customers buy more due to the recommender? To do so, you run an A/B test. One group gets recommendations from your recommender system, and the other uses the app without the recommender. In this scenario, what is the average treatment effect (ATE) of using the recommender system versus not using it?

If figure 3.12 holds true for all customers and products, the ATE is zero because the recommender system has no impact on sales. However, this doesn't imply that training recommender systems as predictive models are not useful. Instead, it illustrates that you can train a recommender system that accurately predicts customer behavior without influencing their actions.

The key takeaway is that the predictive accuracy obtained from training a recommender system using techniques like cross-validation may not accurately reflect its real-world impact. Therefore, once you've trained a recommender system, it's important to validate its effectiveness by conducting an A/B test, as described earlier. This allows you to assess whether the recommender system influences customer behavior and leads to increased sales.

Looking at this situation through the lens of causal inference offers a different perspective. Here, recommendations serve as treatments, similar to interventions in a medical study. You can view each recommendation as a potential treatment, and your goal is to understand how users of your recommender system react when a specific item is recommended compared to when it is not.

Ultimately, your objective is to identify which recommendations have the most significant impact on users. This impact can be measured by assessing the probability of a user making a purchase when an item is recommended versus when it is not. In essence, you aim to calculate the effect of recommendations on purchasing behavior.

In the scenario where you already have a recommender system in operation and have been making recommendations based on historical purchases, you can outline how the data is generated at a specific point in time. Your data includes each customer's historical purchases and may incorporate demographic information such as gender, age, and location.

However, it's essential to acknowledge that our dataset lacks a comprehensive description of each customer, particularly regarding the psychological traits influencing their purchase decisions. Therefore, you must consider Personality as an unobserved variable acting as a confounder between Historical Purchases and Purchases, as shown in figure 3.13.

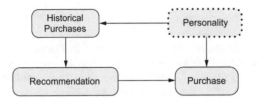

Figure 3.13   Standard graph of a recommender system. The key feature here is the arrow from Historical Purchases to Recommendations, representing the recommender's function.

In practice, additional factors may influence recommendations, such as seasonality and weather. We are excluding these factors from our current analysis for simplicity, but they should be carefully considered in each recommender system as relevant external influences.

Under the framework of causal inference, our focus lies on estimating the impact of recommending an item compared to not recommending it. This corresponds to calculating the ATE of Recommendations on Purchases, as shown in figure 3.13. Despite not aligning precisely with the scenarios outlined in chapter 2 due to unobserved factors, we'll explore in chapter 7 how to compute the ATE using the adjustment formula while adjusting for the variable (or variables) of Historical Purchases. Check out section 3.4 for reading suggestions about causal inference in recommender systems.

3.3.2   Pricing

Pricing problems revolve around finding the ideal price for an item that maximizes a company's profit. This entails experimenting with various prices to gauge how many items are sold. Typically, as the price increases, the quantity sold decreases. Our goal is to pinpoint the price that maximizes revenue, calculated as the price multiplied by the quantity sold.

Let's consider a scenario involving a digital platform. Ideally, we'd conduct an A/B test with two or more prices to ensure fair comparisons. However, in some countries, displaying different prices to different customers is illegal due to potential discrimination concerns. Even if legal, such practices can harm a company's reputation if customers become aware of price discrepancies. Therefore, A/B testing for pricing can be a delicate matter. This is where causal inference may offer valuable assistance.

Imagine that you're giving discounts to customers based on how often they make purchases: the more frequent the purchases, the bigger the discount. It's important to avoid a complete separation, where significant discounts are only given to frequent customers and small discounts to infrequent customers. If you do this, you'll encounter a problem later because the positivity assumption won't hold. To address this, it's necessary to randomly assign both large and small discounts to both frequent and infrequent customers.

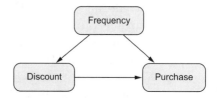

Figure 3.14   Graph representing pricing discounts based on historical purchasing frequency

After gathering data, you want to know the optimal discount you should offer. Frequent customers have higher discounts, and at the same time, they are more likely to buy more. So, historical purchase frequency acts as a confounder in calculating the effect of the discount on purchasing (see figure 3.14).

3.3.3   *Simulations*

In this section, we'll explore some simplified examples where causal inference tools can substitute for computer simulators. Simulators are often intricate, and fully replacing them with causal inference tools isn't feasible. So, this section serves as a thought experiment for readers interested in diving deeper. If this isn't your cup of tea, feel free to skip ahead.

There's a category of problems typically addressed using simulator tools. These tools serve various purposes: predicting outcomes, forecasting under conditions different than those historically seen, and generating data for scenarios that are impossible to observe directly. Simulators operate differently from machine learning or causal inference. They create a physical model of reality and then simulate data under diverse conditions as needed. For instance, consider traffic simulation, where you aim to model traffic dynamics to inform decisions like rerouting or lane closures. Similarly, simulating patient flows in hospitals helps identify departments where additional resources can significantly enhance hospital operations. Although we'll focus on traffic simulation, the principles apply to other scenarios. Traffic simulators strive to closely mimic reality, requiring intricate details such as traffic signals, car types, and driver behavior. However, we can simplify this with causal inference, creating a model that learns from existing data, where traffic policies serve as interventions in the model.

Imagine a city with detectors on its streets. These detectors measure two quantities: flow and occupancy. Flow is how many cars pass through a detector in, let's say, an hour. Flow is not enough to describe the state of a street. We may have a low flow rate because currently fewer cars are travelling on that street or there are so many that they are stuck in a traffic jam. To complement flow, we need occupancy, which is how often a detector has a car over it. Occupancy measures the density of cars. An occupancy of 100% means all cars are stopped, whereas an occupancy close to 0% means there is free flow: that is, cars travelling at maximum speed. For a particular detector, D, there are two types of roles for other detectors: upstream detectors send flow to D, and downstream detectors receive flow from D. The higher the flow in upstream detectors, the more cars will arrive at our selected detector. On the other hand, the more congested downstream detectors are, the more congested our detector will be. Congestion always travels upstream.

Figure 3.15 shows traffic flow regarding detector D. We can put a direct arrow from upstream to downstream whenever cars can go from one detector to another via streets without detector D. Cars drive in the direction of the arrows, so flow also goes in that direction. However, if we want to draw a graph describing how congestion works, the arrows should be reversed: congestion downstream will cause congestion on our detector D and other detectors upstream, as shown in figure 3.16.

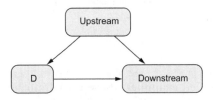

Figure 3.15   Example where D receives flow from upstream detectors. Arrows describe the flow.

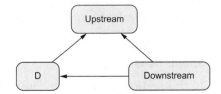

Figure 3.16   Example where D gets congested from downstream detectors. Arrows describe how congestion propagates.

Imagine that D is located on a small street, whereas its upstream and downstream detectors are placed on streets with lots of traffic. If there is an accident at D, its upstream detectors will be affected. But by how much? Because D has low traffic, its impact on upstream detectors may also be low. If we try to answer this question directly from data, we may come up with a wrong answer.

Historically, when downstream detectors are congested, the congestion propagates up to D and its upstream detectors. So if we look at the data for days where D was congested, we will see that its upstream detectors are also congested. But not because of D—because of downstream detectors!

Now that we've seen some causal inference, we know, looking at the graph, that downstream detectors act as confounders to calculate the effect of D on upstream detectors. To calculate the effect of D on upstream detectors, we will need to apply the adjustment formula.

We can even elaborate on this example. It is odd to have two graphs explaining the same system. This can be solved as we did in section 3.2.2 "How to deal with cyclic graphs," by unfolding the graph through time, obtaining figure 3.17. When we include time in our model, we implicitly say that we need more data. We need different measurements of flow and occupancy through each period of time.

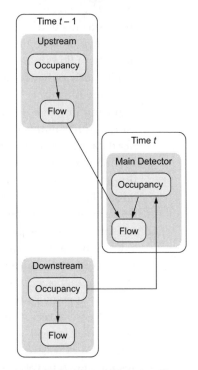

Figure 3.17   Description of traffic behavior unfolded in time

3.4   *Further reading*

If you want to learn more about causal inference and recommender systems, check out the following references:

- "Recommendations as Treatments: Debiasing Learning and Evaluation" by Tobias Schnabel, Adith Swaminathan, Ashudeep Singh, Navin Chandak, and Thorsten Joachims (Proceedings of the 33rd International Conference on Machine Learning, 2016): https://proceedings.mlr.press/v48/schnabel16.pdf
- SIGIR 2016 Tutorial on Counterfactual Evaluation and Learning for Search, Recommendation and Ad Placement (https://www.cs.cornell.edu/~adith/CfactSIGIR2016/)
- "The Simpson's Paradox in the Offline Evaluation of Recommendation Systems" by Amir H. Jadidinejad, Craig Macdonald, and Iadh Ounis (https://arxiv.org/pdf/2104.08912.pdf)
- "Causal Embeddings for Recommendation" by Stephen Bonner and Flavian Vasile (https://arxiv.org/abs/1706.07639)

3.5   *Chapter quiz*

As we conclude the chapter, it's important to ensure that you have a solid understanding of the key concepts. Here are the essential questions you should be able to answer clearly and concisely. If you can't, I suggest rereading the corresponding references:

1 When should you put an arrow in your DAG?
  Answer in section "The meaning of an arrow"
2 What is the difference between total, direct, and indirect effects?
  Answer in section 3.2.4
3 How can you deal with situations in which an event A affects B, and later, B affects A?
  Answer in section "How to deal with cyclic graphs"

Summary

- Creating graphs requires practice. To get into the habit, each time you face a causal problem, begin by thinking about what the graph will look like. Always start simple.
- The presence of an arrow is not an assumption but the lack of it.
- It is a good practice to work hand in hand with the domain experts to create the graph.
- There are five steps to create a graph:
  1 List all the variables that may affect how data was generated. Remember to list them all; missing confounders is one of the most important risks in causal inference.
  2 Create the graph, inspecting each pair of variables to see whether there is some direct causal effect and, if there is any, in which direction. You can turn

cyclic graphs into acyclic ones, unfolding them through time and paying the price of needing more data: a collection of it for each time point.

3 Make explicit the main assumptions and limitations of your model. Ensure that the rest of the team is on the same page about them.

4 Make sure everyone involved agrees on the objectives of the analysis.

5 Check the positivity assumption. If doesn't hold, restrict the problem to those cases where it holds.

How machine learning and causal inference can help each other

This chapter covers

- What we are estimating when we use machine learning models
- When to use causal inference and when to use machine learning
- Using machine learning models in the adjustment formula

In recent years, machine learning has experienced explosive growth across various domains, revolutionizing fields like image recognition, language translation, and autonomous vehicles. These advancements have been remarkable, often giving the impression that machine learning is the ultimate solution to replicate human intelligence. However, like any tool, machine learning has its limitations. As we'll explore in this chapter, one notable limitation is its struggle to effectively handle causality. AI must incorporate causal inference techniques alongside machine learning methods to unlock its full potential.

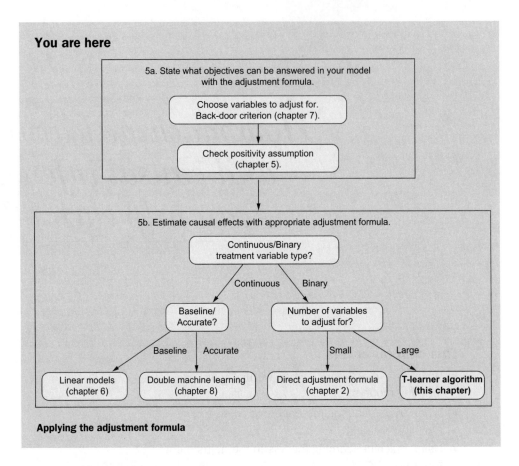

You are here

5a. State what objectives can be answered in your model with the adjustment formula.

Choose variables to adjust for.
Back-door criterion (chapter 7).

Check positivity assumption
(chapter 5).

5b. Estimate causal effects with appropriate adjustment formula.

Continuous/Binary
treatment variable type?

Continuous   Binary

Baseline/
Accurate?

Number of variables
to adjust for?

Baseline   Accurate   Small   Large

Linear models
(chapter 6)

Double machine learning
(chapter 8)

Direct adjustment formula
(chapter 2)

**T-learner algorithm
(this chapter)**

Applying the adjustment formula

Supervised learning, the most prevalent form of machine learning, focuses on making predictions based on historical data. It aims to create predictive models to anticipate outcomes (*y*) given input variables (*x*). These models are commonly used for forecasting, such as predicting future sales, or for automating tasks, such as identifying spam emails. In supervised learning, the emphasis is on accurate predictions, often leading to models perceived as black boxes, as we're generally less concerned about how they arrive at their predictions.

Causal inference, on the other hand, operates differently. It aims to ascertain the causal relationships between variables, particularly identifying which factors influence an outcome (*y*) and to what extent. Although this may sound to you very much like a linear regression, it primarily deals with correlations, not causation. We'll delve into how linear regression fits into causal inference in chapter 6. However, it's essential to recognize that causal inference and supervised learning have distinct goals and methodologies. Both involve modeling the relationship between *x* and *y*, but their objectives and approaches differ significantly.

This chapter aims to clarify when to use machine learning and when causal inference is more appropriate. We'll also explore situations where these two methodologies can complement each other for optimal results. To achieve this, we must grasp the fundamental goals and limitations of both methodologies and the statistical quantities they estimate.

The first part of this chapter is devoted to exploring the nature of supervised learning. As we will see, its main aim is to estimate a conditional expectation—which, in the case of categorical variables, is just a conditional probability. However, as we've learned from causal inference, conditional probabilities differ significantly from intervened probabilities. In chapter 2, for instance, when addressing the kidney stones problem, conditional probabilities told us what we observed, in contrast to intervened distributions, which explained what would happen if we gave the same treatment to everyone.

Once a supervised learning model accurately estimates conditional probabilities, we can infer the most probable outcome. This method, which relies on past data to forecast future events, is effective for prediction. However, it's only reliable if future events behave similarly to past events. This represents the first limitation of supervised learning that we'll explore in this chapter. In contrast, interventional quantities estimate what would happen in a different scenario. A clear understanding of this distinction will guide us in determining when to apply machine learning and when to employ causal inference.

Although machine learning and causal inference serve distinct purposes, they can complement each other. For instance, machine learning can aid causal inference by providing an effective way to implement the adjustment formula. As you may recall, the adjustment formula relies on conditional probabilities. Because estimating these probabilities is the objective of supervised learning, we can use supervised learning models to implement the adjustment formula more accurately. There are several alternative methods to accomplish this, which we'll introduce in the second part of this chapter and elaborate on in subsequent chapters.

> **When should you use machine learning in causal inference?**
> When dealing with many confounders, you should use supervised learning methods to implement the adjustment formula.

4.1   What does supervised learning do?

In one sentence, supervised learning is all about prediction; it learns by interpolating what happened in the past. We will explain this statement next.

> **NOTE** The following discussion assumes that you are familiar with basic statistical modeling with linear models and logistic regression. We also assume that you know a little about machine learning modeling techniques (decision trees, *k*-nearest neighbors, neural networks) and how cross-validation works. The chapter uses a few basic machine learning concepts, and we will go over them in case they're new to you.

From a formal point of view, to create a supervised learning model, we need a set of historical data $D = \{(x_i, y_i)\}$, where x_i is a vector and y_i is a variable (and sometimes a vector, depending on the problem you are working on). For example, x can be an image, and y can be a category of animals; or x can be the number of sales of a product until today, and y can be the sales prediction for tomorrow. Whenever the outcome variable y is categorical, we say it is a *classification problem*; when it is continuous, we call it a *regression*. The objective is to create a function f from data D such that for each x, we can compute an outcome $f(x)$ that we will use as a prediction of the true value y. Of course, we assume that at the moment of the prediction $f(x)$, we will not know the true value y; otherwise we wouldn't need the prediction.

The function f cannot be built out of nowhere, so we need to give it some structure or make assumptions about its form. For instance, it may be a linear model, a decision tree (derived models such as random forests or boosted trees), k-nearest neighbors, or a deep learning model. We express such a structure by saying that the function f belongs to a family F (the family of linear models or decision trees). In practice, we select the type of model (family of functions) that is best suited (in terms of accuracy, computational resources, and so on) for each particular problem.

To find the optimal predictive function, we use the historical dataset D. We look for the function that best predicts (fits) the past. Mathematically, we want to find or create the function f that best fits data D. This means that what the function predicts is as close as possible to what happened. Of course, we need to define what "close" means. To make it simple, we will focus on the regression problem where Y is continuous and the notion of distance between two points a and b is the *square loss* $(a-b)^2$. For every observation x_i in our dataset, we want our predictive function f to be as close as possible to the corresponding value y_i, so we make the loss $(y_i - f(x_i))^2$ as small as possible. Averaging over all the observations, we conclude that we are looking for the function in the particular family of functions F that minimizes the *empirical loss*:

$$\min_{f \in F} \frac{1}{n} \sum_i (f(x_i) - y_i)^2$$

Depending on the types of functions (the family F) we have chosen, this minimization is done or approximated in one way or another. For instance, the algorithm to fit a decision tree to data by minimizing the empirical loss is very different from the algorithms used to fit neural networks. With this process, we can find the function that predicts the past the best. But will this function predict the future as well? Not necessarily. If the family of functions is too flexible—for instance, if has a lot of parameters—it may adjust so well to the past that it cannot discriminate between what is signal and what is noise and and thus will make bad predictions for the future. This is called *overfitting*.

To avoid overfitting, we can apply a strategy pretty similar to one that some people use to study for exams. We could study all the available solved exams from earlier years, but then we would not be sure whether we understood the concepts or had just memorized the answers to the problems. Instead, we can select a subset of exams and set them aside. We study with the rest, and whenever we feel confident about what we have learned, we test ourselves on the subset we haven't read yet. This will tell us how well we will perform in the final exam. In machine learning, this strategy is called *train-test splitting*, a form of *cross-validation*. To see if the model we have found is too attached to the particularities of the past, we set aside a subset of data called *test*. The rest of the data is called *train* and will be used to fit the model. The obtained model trained on the train set is used to make predictions on the test set. These predictions are checked against what happened in reality (we know what happened in the test set). The differences between predictions and reality on the test set give us an estimate of how well the model will perform in the future when we use it in production with new data. From the different families of functions and configurations, the final model we select to make predictions is the one that minimizes the error when applied in the test set.

4.1.1 When should causal inference be used vs. supervised learning?

Both causal inference and supervised learning involve creating a model that links an input variable *x* with an output variable *y*. It may seem like they do the same thing, but they don't. As we'll explore in this section, the key difference isn't in the models themselves but rather in how these models are used after they're made. To illustrate, let's look at a scenario where both causal inference and supervised learning may produce the same model but use it differently.

At the start of the COVID-19 pandemic, some hospitals wanted to figure out which positive patients to treat first. They developed a predictive model that used patient information like age and existing health conditions to estimate how many days it might be before a patient needed to be in the intensive care unit (ICU). This model helped hospitals prioritize patients who were more likely to need ICU care soon. The value of the model lay in its accurate predictions. When making these predictions, a hospital didn't worry about what factors led to the patient being hospitalized or the details of how the model was constructed. The focus was solely on whether the model correctly predicted the number of days a patient could stay out of the ICU, allowing the hospital to manage priorities based on these predictions.

On the other hand, if a statistician had access to the same dataset, they would likely create a model linking the same input variables with the same output—but their goal would be to understand which factors caused a patient to need the ICU. Instead of using the model to decide which patients to treat first, the statistician would use their findings to support healthcare policies that helped prevent patients from needing intensive care. For example, if the analysis showed that older people were at higher risk for severe COVID, the statistician might recommend that they stay home and limit their social interactions.

For many years, statisticians have been identifying factors that influence outcomes. Causal inference enhances this process by adding a new layer of formalism, methodology, and tools specifically tailored to handle causal questions. Essentially, the role of a causal analyst mirrors that of a statistician: determining which factors increase the likelihood of someone needing to go to the ICU. Causal inference equips us with more specialized tools to tackle these problems effectively.

The interesting part is that predictive and causal models may look similar. It's common for both to use linear models, for example. The key difference is how these models are used, influencing how they are created and validated. For instance, in supervised learning, models are often validated using cross-validation to help choose which variables to include. In contrast, selecting variables for causal inference is a careful process involving identifying confounders. Also, as we'll explore later in this chapter, cross-validation alone isn't sufficient to validate causal inference models. Whenever possible, these models should be validated using A/B tests.

The diagram in figure 4.1 illustrates when to use each technique. If you're unsure, ask yourself, "Do I want to affect the input variables or the output variables?"

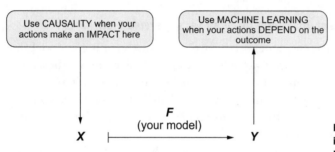

Figure 4.1   **When to use causal inference or machine learning. Model input is denoted by *X* and the outcome by *Y*.**

4.1.2   *The goal of data fitting*

We have seen how to train a machine learning model by minimizing the difference between what the model predicts and the data, minimizing the empirical risk. The question is, what is the model aiming to estimate? The answer is, a conditional expectation. But let's not rush things; let's start with a very simple example.

Imagine that you have n different values $a_1, \ldots, a_n$ (say, peoples' heights) generated by some probability distribution. Let's say you want to make a prediction with only one quantity. The prediction should be as close as possible to each number a_i. So, you can set the problem as finding a number that minimizes the distance with respect to all a_is. We'll choose the *sum of squared errors* for convenience:

$$\min_{\mu} \sum_i (a_i - \mu)^2$$

It turns out that this optimal μ that minimizes all the distances is the mean of the values $a_1, \ldots, a_n$:

$$\mu = \frac{1}{n} \sum_i a_i$$

You may already know that the mean minimizes the sum of squared errors. The following sidebar shows a simple proof. I'm sharing this proof because it gives you a clue about why this happens. Interestingly, similar logic applies to determining the best predictor among machine learning models when using the square loss function.

Above and beyond: Why the mean is the best predictor for a set of values

We can prove that the mean is the best predictor, in terms of minimizing the sum of squared errors, with a little algebra. Suppose we think there is a value a that does a better job than the mean. Is it possible? Well, no. We need to compare the sum of squared errors using this particular value a

$$\frac{1}{n}\sum_{i}(a_i - a)^2$$

with the sum of squared errors using the mean μ. To do that, we can use a mathematical trick, adding and subtracting μ simultaneously, and develop this expression:

$$\sum_{i}(a_i - a)^2 = \frac{1}{n}\sum_{i}(a_i - \mu + \mu - a)^2 =$$

$$\frac{1}{n}\sum_{i}(a_i - \mu)^2 + (\mu - a)^2 + \frac{2}{n}\sum_{i}(a_i - \mu)(\mu - a)$$

Notice that the term $(\mu - a)^2$ may seem to lack the $1/n$ term. But this is not the case because $(\mu - a)^2$ is constant (it does not depend on i) and we are adding it n times. Rearranging terms and taking into account that by the definition of μ, the last term is zero,

$$\frac{1}{n}\sum_{i}(a_i - \mu)^2 + (\mu - a)^2 + \frac{2(\mu - a)}{n}\sum_{i}(a_i - \mu) =$$

$$\frac{1}{n}\sum_{i}(a_i - \mu)^2 + (\mu - a)^2 \geq \frac{1}{n}\sum_{i}(a_i - \mu)^2$$

In summary, we have seen that for any quantity a, the mean distance to the set of as $(a_1, ..., a_n)$ is greater than the mean distance from the mean

$$\sum_{i}(a_i - a)^2 \geq \frac{1}{n}\sum_{i}(a_i - \mu)^2$$

So, the mean is the best predictor when using the squared loss as distance.

Let's translate this knowledge into the problem of training a machine learning model. Consider a regression problem where we want to create a model to predict some outcome variable Y using covariates X_1, ..., X_m. For example, let's say we're trying to make a model that guesses how many days a person may spend in the ICU. We're looking at their age and whether they have any other health problems. We'll use Y for the number of days, X_1 for age, and X_2 for comorbidities. Even if people have the same age and comorbidities, some may stay in the ICU longer than others.

Mathematically speaking, this is expressed by saying that for those having the set of values $(x_1, ..., x_m)$, we can consider the outcome conditional variable $Y|x_1, ..., x_m$. If we want to predict the distribution $Y|x_1, ..., x_m$, what will be the best value if we use the square loss function? Arguing based on the proof in the previous sidebar, the best predictor will be the mean of $Y|x_1, ..., x_m$: that is, $E[Y|x_1, ..., x_m]$.

What does a supervised learning model aim to do?

The best predictor of Y, given values $x_1, ..., x_m$ and the square loss function, is the conditional expectation $E[Y|x_1, ..., x_m]$. For the case of classification, there is not much difference because for a binary variable Y, $E[Y|x_1, ..., x_m] = P(Y = 1|x_1, ..., x_m)$. So, any supervised learning model trained for maximizing the accuracy (classification) or minimizing the mean square loss (regression) aims to estimate the value $E[Y|x_1, ..., x_m]$.

4.1.3   *When the future and the past behave the same way*

Now that we have seen what supervised learning tries to estimate, you may wonder when it is correct to use it. Intuition tells us that *supervised learning works as long as the future behaves like the past.* In fact, more than intuition is behind this statement. Basic machine learning theory, such as Vapnik–Chervonenkis (VC) dimension and probably approximately correct (PAC) learning, starts with the assumption that we have a dataset of pairs (x_i, y_i), x_i being features and y_i being outcomes, that are independent and identically distributed (i.i.d. for short). That is, all pairs (x_i, y_i) are generated by the same distribution (have been generated under the same dynamics), and each pair (x_i, y_i) is independent of the others. Such an assumption is not only for data obtained in the past but also for *data that will be obtained in the future,* which we will make a prediction on. This is the formal way to express that data from the past and the future behaves the same way.

But if predictive models are useful when the future behaves like the past, what position does this leave us in when we are interested in intervening in the system and changing its behavior? We have to proceed cautiously, because if we intervene in the system, its dynamics will change, the distribution of outcomes will also change, and the predictive model will no longer predict accurately. For instance, at the beginning of COVID-19, epidemiologists created models that predicted an exponential growth of infections. These predictions convinced societies to take measures against COVID. And some of these measures worked, slowing the number of infections. Paradoxically, the models that initially helped countries decide what to do will not predict well anymore. We created a predictive model (that worked) that pushed us to take actions, and those actions made the initial predictions fail. But even though they failed, the model was very helpful! This example tells us that if we are going to use a predictive model to make decisions, we need to know what we expect from these predictions and understand how they will affect the future.

> **When do we need a model of how nature works?**
> Knowing how nature works isn't necessary for making accurate predictions. For instance, predicting the sunrise time tomorrow on Earth can be done effectively by assuming it will be the same as today—something our ancestors did for centuries without astronomy knowledge. However, predicting the sunrise time tomorrow on Mars at a specific location requires a physical model of the solar system. In other words, if the situation doesn't change much, machine learning works fine. But if you want to predict what will happen in new situations, you'll need causal inference.

4.1.4 When do causal inference and supervised learning coincide?

Can a predictive model replace a causal model? Sometimes; each situation needs to be looked at individually. For example, imagine that you work for an online shopping site, and you're trying to figure out the best prices for your products. So far, you've mainly given discounts to loyal customers rather than occasional shoppers. Your main goal is determining how the price affects whether a customer decides to buy a product.

> **Think first, read next**
> Imagine that you're creating a graph to show these ideas: what would it look like? Picture two different scenarios for making a predictive model. One uses just the price as an input, and the other uses both price and loyalty as inputs. How will each model respond if you change the discount strategy?

With the data you have, you can build a model that shows the likelihood of a customer buying a product at a certain price. This model, which we can call *purchase = f(price)*, uses only the price as an input and the purchase decision as an output. If you keep your discount policy the same, this model can sometimes predict purchase chances accurately without needing any other information. Because discounts are usually given to loyal customers, the price itself tells you a lot about the customer's loyalty. This means the price alone carries enough information to indicate whether the customer is likely loyal.

But what happens if you start offering discounts to everyone, to keep more customers? Then your predictions will probably fail. Because you're now giving discounts to infrequent customers as well, a model that only looks at price may mistakenly think these customers are loyal. In the past, the data used to train the model usually saw discounts given to loyal clients. So, the model will likely predict a high chance of purchase for these infrequent customers, even though many of them may just be trying out your business. Your new pricing strategy doesn't match the historical data. The probability of being infrequent and having a discount has changed and now is different from the historical distribution of newcomers having discounts.

The obvious solution is to include the variable *loyalty* in your model, creating a model *purchase* = *f*(*price*, *loyalty*). Is that enough to make better predictions? The answer is yes. Loyalty is a confounder, as shown in figure 4.2. As we saw in chapter 2 (recall the *z*-specific effects), in this case the intervened and observed distributions for a particular degree of loyalty are the same:

$$P(Purchase \mid \mathrm{do}(discount), loyalty) = P(Purchase \mid discount, loyalty)$$

So, the predictive model and the interventional quantity coincide. But they do so only if we include *all possible confounders*. This conclusion holds in other problems that involve predictions with confounders (we would need to follow the same argument). In the same way that missing the *loyalty* variable can lead to wrong predictions, missing other confounders will also mean predicting incorrectly.

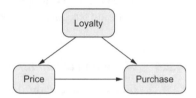

Figure 4.2   **Loyal customers receive discounts, which at the same time affect purchases.**

Ask yourself
Can you think of any other examples where predictive models and interventions coincide?

4.1.5   *Predictive error is a false friend*

What happens with the predictive ability of a model? Will it guide our causal journey the same way it helps us choose the best machine learning model? Unfortunately, the predictive capability is a false friend. It may seem helpful, but generally it is not reliable for assessing causal matters. To see how and why this is so, as in the previous section, let's create two models with nearly the same predictive capability but very different performance in situations where we want to do something different than we did in the past.

Imagine that you are a video game designer in charge of designing levels for a new version of Pac-Man. As the player's game progresses, they need to reach harder levels; but if the difficulty is too much for them, players will get frustrated and stop playing. So, you need to keep a balance in the level of difficulty. To know how difficult a new level is, you usually need a beta tester to play it and give you feedback. However, repeating this process to keep improving the design may be slow. Ideally, you would like to have a tool that tells you how difficult the level you are creating is. Let's say you have access to the historical database for the existing levels. You also have the total time each user had to play each level to pass it. Can you create a predictive model from this data that tells you the game's difficulty in real time as you design it? That would reduce the number of reviews you need from your beta testers.

When creating a new level, designers generally have three elements: the number of ghosts, the number of fruit bonuses, and the layout.

Test your knowledge
How will the graph explain these dynamics?

For simplicity, we will only consider the number of ghosts and bonuses. Both directly affect the game's difficulty, which we will measure as the total time spent on that level. We want to express level-difficulty data in a graph. The graph will have at least three nodes:

- Number of ghosts
- Number of bonuses
- Time, in minutes, required to finish the level

The number of ghosts and bonuses will affect the time needed to finish the level. Is there any relationship between ghosts and bonuses? Yes, there is. These two weren't selected at random. A designer chose them with some intent in mind. For instance, maybe when the designer wanted to increase the difficulty, they simultaneously increased the number of ghosts and decreased the number of bonuses. Whatever the designer's intent, it determines how the level is designed, so it must be included in the graph as an unobserved variable. We don't have access to this variable because even if we could ask the designer what they had in mind when they designed the level, it would be difficult to translate in a way that could be included in our model. Figure 4.3 shows that the designer's intent is an important confounder, which we unfortunately don't have access to.

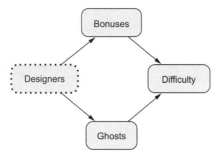

Figure 4.3   Design process for Pac-Man levels. The designer's creativity shapes how many bonuses and ghosts appear on each level. This process is intricate, making it challenging to describe in full detail.

What if we want to create a predictive model for level difficulty using only the number of bonuses? Is there any difference between this model and the one that includes the number of ghosts? We suspect there is. Let's create and analyze a synthetic dataset as an example to see how different it may be. Because we are creating the data, we will see if the conclusions are correct in each case. To create the dataset, we will assume that when the designer wanted to increase the difficulty level, they increased the number of ghosts and simultaneously reduced the number of bonuses. Ghosts and bonuses are negatively correlated. We also use a simple linear model to describe the time (in minutes) spent on the level

$$time = 20 + 1.5 \times ghosts - 2 \times bonuses + error$$

where *error*, which represents the inherent variation each time someone finishes the level, follows a normal distribution centered at 0 and with a standard deviation of 0.1. The following R and Python code listings generate this data. The number of ghosts is set randomly between two and six, and the number of bonuses decreases with respect to the number of ghosts. In this way, they are negatively correlated.

Listing 4.1   (R) Creating synthetic data for a new level design

```
set.seed(2023)
n <- 100
ghosts <- sample(2:6, n, replace = TRUE)
bonuses <- 8 - ghosts +
    0.2 * sample(c(-1, 0, 1), n, replace = TRUE)
error <- rnorm(n, sd=0.1)
time <- 20 + 1.5 * ghosts -2 * bonuses + error
```

Listing 4.2   (Python) Creating synthetic data for a new level design

```
from numpy.random import choice, normal
import pandas as pd
n = 100
ghosts = choice(range(2, 7), n)
bonuses = 8 - ghosts + 0.2 * choice([-1, 0, 1], n)
error = normal(n, scale=0.1)
time = 20 + 1.5 * ghosts -2 * bonuses + error
df = pd.DataFrame({
    'time': time, 'bonuses': bonuses, 'ghosts': ghosts
})
```

Figure 4.4 shows how the number of bonuses decreases with respect to the number of ghosts in this dataset.

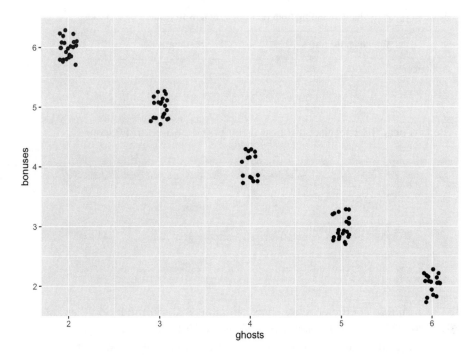

Figure 4.4   Number of ghosts versus number of bonuses. There is a strong correlation between them because they have a variable in common: the designer's creative process. Points have been slightly perturbed to avoid point overlap.

Now let's see the differences between using only bonuses to predict the time spent on a level and using both bonuses and ghosts. First we create a linear model regressing time with respect to bonuses.

Listing 4.3   (R) Obtaining a linear model of bonuses and time

```
summary(lm(time~bonuses))
```

Listing 4.4   (Python) Obtaining a linear model of bonuses and time

```
import statsmodels.formula.api as smf
mod = smf.ols(formula='time ~ bonuses', data=df)
mod.fit().summary()
```

The resulting coefficients are shown in table 4.1. R squared turns out to be 0.9969, which seems high. In principle, we should have used cross-validation to get a reliable estimate of the goodness of fit. However, this example is so simple (a linear regression with only one regressor) that there is no overfitting, so having a high R squared means we will have low predictive error in cross-validation. To make the example simple, we didn't perform the cross-validation.

Table 4.1 Coefficients resulting from regressing time with respect to bonuses

Coefficients	Estimate
(Intercept)	31.90
bonuses	-3.49

Let's repeat the exercise, but now using both bonuses and ghosts.

Listing 4.5   (R) Obtaining a linear model of bonuses and ghosts

```
summary(lm(time~ghosts + bonuses))
```

Listing 4.6   (Python) Obtaining a linear model of bonuses and ghosts

```
import statsmodels.formula.api as smf
mod = smf.ols(formula='time ~ ghosts + bonuses', data=df)
mod.fit().summary()
```

The resulting coefficients are shown in table 4.2, and the model has an R squared of 0.9996. This is even higher than before, which is not surprising because we are now including all the information. However, the difference between the R squared of the two models is pretty small. Because R squared expresses how well the model will perform when predicting (in this case, because the model is so simple that there will be no overfitting), we can expect that the two models will have similar prediction ability.

Table 4.2   Resulting coefficients from regressing time with respect to bonuses and ghosts

Coefficients	Estimate
(Intercept)	19.44
ghosts	1.56
bonuses	-1.92

The question now is, are both models equally useful for our task at hand? Of course not. If they were, we wouldn't spend an entire section looking at them. A problem arises when the designer breaks the dynamics of historical data and wants to design in a new way. For instance, now they try to keep a balance between ghosts and bonuses: whenever they increase the former, they also increase the latter so that the level remains stable. In this situation, the two models will disagree. Say we want to know what would happen if we simultaneously added six ghosts and six bonuses. The model with only bonuses, using the estimated coefficients in table 4.1, will predict an estimated time of 31.90 – 3.48 × 6 = 11.02 minutes, whereas the other one, using the coefficients from table 4.2 will predict $19.44 - 1.92 \times 6 + 1.56 \times 6 = 17.28$. Of course, the latter one is correct.

The problem is that historically, bonuses and ghosts have been highly correlated. So, when the model with only bonuses has to predict with six bonuses, it assumes that the number of ghosts will be very low. This is how it has always been until now! It makes sense. But the designer has changed their style, and now the model faces a situation that has rarely happened (in this dataset, it has *never* happened): a large number of bonuses and a large number of ghosts. That is what makes the first model fail miserably with its predictions.

The results are summarized in table 4.3. Although R squared tells us there is only a 0.3% difference between the two models, due to a change in the design strategy, the error in predicting six ghosts and six bonuses is approximately 36%, which is huge compared to the differences in R squared. This tells us once again that cross-validation is useful as long as nothing new happens, but if we want to predict a new situation, it is not a good indicator of what will happen.

Table 4.3   Resulting coefficients from regressing time with respect to bonuses and ghosts

	Model with only bonuses	Model with bonuses and ghosts	Percentage difference
R squared	0.9969	0.9996	0.3%
Prediction with 6 ghosts and 6 bonuses	11.52	17.03	36%

Let's outline the concept we've covered. We have an outcome variable Y (time) influenced by two other variables, x_1 (bonuses) and X_2 (ghosts), so we can express this as $Y = f(X_1, X_2)$. Simultaneously, the bonuses variable depends on ghosts, so $x_1 = g(X_2)$. For simplicity, let's set aside the random term. In machine learning, the goal is to approximate the function f. Because $f(X_1, X_2) = f(g(X_2), X_2)$, the approximation works perfectly by using only X_2 as input (and ignoring x_1 completely). However, when we intervene, the approximation of f using only X_2 fails to make accurate predictions.

What do we do with other confounding variables, such as the layout design of the game? We can make a similar argument, saying that the designer may have opted for geometry that makes the game more difficult, and these may be correlated with other relevant variables. If we don't include the layout geometry, we are omitting some confounders, and the conclusions can be wrong once again. To properly estimate the difficulty, we should describe the game layout through some variables and include them in the model (for instance, as images, as is done in image recognition).

In general, which variables you need to include will depend on the graph that describes your problem. We have seen a selection of simple cases; in chapter 7, we will learn about new tools to deal with any type of graph.

Why can't we select causal inference models based on their cross-validation error?

Supervised learning models are validated using cross-validation, which estimates the error we will make when using predictive models in unseen data. However, we cannot rely on cross-validation to assess whether a causal model is valid. We've seen the example of two predictive models with almost the same cross-validation error (the *R* squared, in this case) that predict very differently in situations unlike our historical data. Missing an important confounder may change our results significantly. That's why we need to be very careful and include all confounding factors. To do so, it is necessary to understand the problem fully by asking the domain experts for all its details.

4.1.6 *Validation of interventions*

The example in the previous section leads to an interesting question. If the predictive capability is not good enough to measure the validity of a causal inference model, what is good enough to do this? As we explained, cross-validation gives us a good estimate of how accurate our model will be in the future, as long as the system behaves as in the past. However, causal questions are about what would happen if the system behaved differently. We analysts try to answer this question by creating a causal model of reality and then, using causal tools as the adjustment formula, drawing conclusions. Unlike in machine learning, where we can directly observe how the system is currently working, when we ask causal questions, we want to know what would have happened if the system behaved differently. Yes, we are using a model to answer this question, but at the end of the day, it is just a model. We may have made bad assumptions or errors in the process. So, our conclusions may not be true. The only way to see if our model works is to try it in real life—that is, to perform an A/B test. Unfortunately, we want to use causal inference precisely when we *can't* run an A/B test! That's why it is so important to follow the best practices we have been discussing in chapters 1–4 whenever you work with causal inference:

- Understand the problem at hand very well.
- Make assumptions only when you are certain about them.
- Validate your model with domain experts.
- Validate your model with not just one but several studies; the more independent, the better.

Conclusion

The only way to see if a causal model is valid is to perform an A/B test. In situations where A/B tests are not available, we need to make sure the model represents reality as well as we can, with the fewest assumptions and the best argumentation possible, because we may not be able to check its validity directly.

4.2 How does supervised learning participate in causal inference?

So far, we have been talking about the differences between supervised learning and causal inference. Now we will see how supervised learning can help us calculate the adjustment formula that we use in causal inference. The strategy is simple. Remember that the adjustment formula contains terms with conditional probabilities $P(Y = y | X = x, Z = z)$. We have seen that the job of supervised learning is to precisely estimate these quantities. So, we will train a supervised learning model to predict Y using covariates X and Z and then substitute the predicted outcomes in the following adjustment formula. This technique is called the *plug-in* estimate:

$$P(Y = y | do(X = x)) = \sum_x P(Y = y | X = x, Z = z) P(Z = z)$$

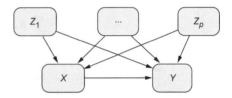

The idea is simple, but there are problems we need to be aware of. In the second part of this chapter, we will walk through the details of how to train and use machine learning models to evaluate the adjustment formula.

In practice, you can expect to have not one but a bunch of different confounders, as in figure 4.5. Remember from chapter 2 that for a variable X, outcome Y, and p confounders $Z_1, \ldots, Z_p$, the adjustment formula is the following:

Figure 4.5 In practice, it is normal to have many confounders. On these occasions, we will need to apply machine learning techniques.

$$P(Y = y | do(X = x)) = \sum_z P(Y = y | X = x, Z_1 = z_1, \ldots, Z_p = z_p) P(Z_1 = z_1, \ldots, Z_p = z_p)$$

For instance, X can be a treatment, Y may be recovery, and $Z_1, \ldots, Z_p$ may refer to variables such as age, gender, location, comorbidities, and so on. In the kidney stone example from in chapter 2, we had only one confounder—the size of the stone—and we can easily calculate the quantities $P(Y = y | X = x, Z = z)$. Of the cases where we had some treatment and a particular size, we just count the proportion of patients who recovered.

The problem is that when we have a larger set of confounders $Z_1, \ldots, Z_p$, there may be a combination of values $z_1, \ldots, z_p$ that never or hardly ever appears in our dataset. These are possible combinations, but we don't have a large enough sample size to see them. For example, if we consider (condition on) the cases where age = young, we will have some number of observations. When we look for the cases where age = young and gender = female, we will have fewer cases. Every time we condition on an additional variable, we will decrease the number of observations, and we will often run out of observations. If we try to use the same counting technique, we will have a hard time calculating $P(Y|X, Z_1, ..., Z_p)$ because we will have very few observations. And smaller sample size implies larger variance. Thus, the estimation of the quantity $P(Y|X, Z_1, ..., Z_p)$ will have a large variance.

This problem cannot be addressed by reducing the number of covariates. Remember, they are confounders, and missing a relevant confounder may lead to wrong conclusions.

We talked about the case when Y may take different real values $y_1, ..., y_k$. With only one confounder Z, the expected intervened value $E[Y|do(X = x)]$ is

$$E[Y = y|do(X = x)] = \sum_z E[Y = y|X = x, Z = z]P(Z = z)$$

When we have many confounders instead of one, the formula becomes

$$E[Y = y|do(X = x)] = \sum_z E[Y = y|X = x, Z_1 = z_1, ..., Z_p = z_p]P(Z_1 = z_1, ..., Z_p = z_p)$$

This formula is similar to our binary outcomes for variable Y. We only need to change one thing: instead of using $P(Y|X, Z_1, ..., Z_p)$, we now use $E(Y|X, Z_1, ..., Z_p)$. Fortunately, when Y takes many possible values, the quantity $E(Y|X, Z_1, ..., Z_p)$ is precisely what a supervised learning model estimates! Moreover, because for binary variables the conditional probabilities and expectation coincide, $P(Y|X, Z) = E[Y|X, Z]$, the adjustment formula as written here is valid for both situations:

$$E[Y = y|do(X = x)] = \sum_z E[Y = y|X = x, Z_1 = z_1, ..., Z_p = z_p]P(Z_1 = z_1, ..., Z_p = z_p)$$

The adjustment formula for binary Y and when Y takes many values is the same as this one. Because supervised learning techniques target conditional expectation $E[Y|X, Z]$, we can use them to evaluate the adjustment formula. The idea is to train a machine learning model from data and substitute its predictions in the corresponding place in the formula.

> **NOTE** Supervised learning models for evaluating the adjustment formula are known as *meta-learners*. We'll soon cover the S-learner and T-learner. These algorithms are useful for applying the adjustment formula when you have many confounders. However, it is usually better to use double machine learning methods, as detailed in chapter 8. We discuss meta-learners because they are occasionally used, and understanding them will help you better grasp the methods in chapter 8.

4.2.1   *Empirical and generating distributions in the adjustment formula*

So far, when discussing the adjustment formula, we have talked about a probability distribution *P*. But except for a few cases, we haven't clarified which probability distribution we're talking about. There are two protagonist distributions in our problem. As we introduced in chapter 1, the process that generated the data, which we don't have access to, has a *data-generating distribution*. On the other hand, the data we will be working with will be a sample of this distribution that can be regarded as another probability distribution, called the *empirical distribution*. This section explains how both are related, which will help us correctly apply the adjustment formula.

In practice, when we have a dataset with variables *x*, *y*, and *z*, our data will look like table 4.4. If we have sample size *n*, the empirical distribution assigns the same weight to every observation: that is, it gives a weight of $1/n$ to each row.

Table 4.4   Empirical distribution in a case with multiple confounders

Y	X	Z_1	...	Z_p	Empirical probability
y^1	x^1	z_1^1	...	z_p^1	$1/n$
y^2	x^2	z_1^2	...	z_p^2	...
y^3	x^3	z_1^3	...	z_p^3	$1/n$

Recall that the adjustment formula talks about a probability distribution. The question is, of the two, which should we apply it to? Ideally, we would like to apply the adjustment formula to the data-generating distribution because it is the one that determines the system. But there is the small problem that we need an infinite sample to have access to it ... That sounds a bit impractical, so we will go for option two and apply the formula using the empirical distribution. Fortunately, we can sleep at night because we know that as the sample size increases, the empirical distribution converges to the data-generating distribution. Thus, our calculations will be closer to the real value of the adjustment formula. In chapter 8, we will come back to this discussion.

Here is the point this adds up to: if we apply the adjustment formula to our data—the empirical distribution P_E—we will always have that $P_E(Z_1 = z_1, ..., Z_p = z_p) = 1/n$. So the adjustment formula, with data $\{(x^i, y^i, z_1^i, ..., z_p^i)\}$ for $i = 1, ..., n$, as in table 4.4, becomes

$$P_E(Y = y | \mathrm{do}(X = x)) = \sum_{z^i} P_E\left(Y = y | X = x, z_1^i, ..., z_p^i\right) P_E\left(z_1^i, ..., z_p^i\right) =$$

$$\frac{1}{n} \sum_{z^i} P_E\left(Y = y | X = x, z_1^i, ..., z_p^i\right)$$

because for the empirical distribution, we have that $PE(z_1^i, ..., z_p^i) = 1/n$.

In practice, we do a little abuse of notation: even though we apply the formula to the empirical distribution PE, we drop the subindex and just write P. The same reasoning applies when the variable Y can take many different values $y_1, \ldots, y_k$. In this case, the formula would be

$$E[Y = y|\mathrm{do}(X = x)] = \frac{1}{n} \sum_{z^i} E\left[Y = y|X = x, z^i_1, \ldots, z^i_p\right]$$

4.2.2   *The flexibility of the adjustment formula*

Notice that we don't make any assumptions about the particular form that $P(Y|X, Z_1, \ldots, Z_p)$ may take. We don't assume a binomial distribution, or a linear function in the continuous case. This is good because the formula is very general and works for many situations. In particular, it gives us a lot of flexibility, letting us use any suitable machine learning model to estimate the quantity $P(Y|X, Z_1, \ldots, Z_p)$.

4.2.3   *The adjustment formula for continuous distributions*

Until now, we have avoided talking about continuous variables. That's because there is nothing special about them that affects how we work with them. We need to substitute sums with integrals, and everything will work fine. Some people may feel uncomfortable with integrals because they haven't used them for a while. The good news is that you don't need them. We will apply the adjustment formula to the empirical distribution, and because we have a sample of size n, this distribution will have at most n different values for the outcome Y. So, it can be dealt with like the earlier case where Y has $y_1, \ldots, y_k$ different values.

If you're curious what the intervened quantity will look like in the case of continuous Y, X, and Z, the reasoning in deriving $E[Y|\mathrm{do}(X = x)]$ still holds as when Y takes a discrete set of real values: we only need to substitute the summation with respect to values of Zs with an integral where f is the density function for variables Z, obtaining

$$E[Y|\mathrm{do}(X = x)] = \int_z E[Y|x, z_1, \ldots, z_p] f(z_1, \ldots, z_p) dz_1 \ldots dz_p$$

4.2.4   *Algorithms for calculating the adjustment formula*

Next we will look at two different approaches to using machine learning in the adjustment formula. We will also calculate the average treatment effect (ATE) for the binary X case: $E[Y|\mathrm{do}(X = 1)] - E[Y|\mathrm{do}(X = 0)]$.

THE S-LEARNER ALGORITHM: A SIMPLE APPROACH FOR EVALUATING THE ADJUSTMENT FORMULA

The S-learner algorithm (S is short for *single*) is a naive approach: we train a machine learning model and plug its predictions into the adjustment formula. It's nice, but depending on your data, you may get unrealistic results. The T-learner (T is short for *two*) solves this problem by separating it into two parts. The last approach, called cross-fitting, splits data in a way that may remind you of cross-validation and complements the T-learner to avoid overfitting the machine learning models.

The S-learner is the simplest form for applying the adjustment formula with a machine learning algorithm. We need to estimate the quantities $P(Y|X, Z_1, ..., Z_p)$ or $E(Y|X, Z_1, ..., Z_p)$ with a machine learning technique and apply the formula from the previous section. The algorithm does the following. To estimate the intervened quantity at a particular value of $X = x$ for either categorical Y, $P(Y = y|\text{do}(X = x))$, or continuous Y, $E[Y|\text{do}(X = x)]$, we apply the following steps:

1   Use the historical data $\{(x^i, y^i, z_1^i, ..., z_p^i)\}$ with $i = 1, ..., n$ (superindex i expresses the observation number) to train a machine learning model f with covariates x and all confounders $Z_1, ..., Z_p$. When Y is categorical, run a classifier (to estimate the probability of $Y = 1$ conditioned on the covariates); and when Y is continuous, run a regressor.

2   For each observation $i = 1, ..., n$ (or corresponding row in table 4.4), make a prediction, which we call $f(x, z_1^i, ..., z_p^i)$ for data i, but instead of using the historical value x^i, set the value to the current x we are interested in for calculating the ATE: first 1 and then 0.

Then estimate the ATE (remember that this formula is also valid for the case where Y is binary):

$$\text{ATE} = E[Y|\text{do}(X = 1)] - E[Y|\text{do}(X = 0)] \approx \frac{1}{n} \sum_i \left[f\left(1, z_1^i, ..., z_p^i\right) - f\left(0, z_1^i, ..., z_p^i\right) \right]$$

And that's it—simple! There are some important points to keep in mind. First, when we talk about training a machine learning model, we implicitly assume the whole process: trying different models (like boosted trees, linear models, and even deep learning), hyperparameter tuning, and selecting the best model through cross-validation.

The second point is about which variables the model should include. Unlike in machine learning, where we can play with which variables to include and which to remove, typically through cross-validation, this is not the case in causal inference. Variables Z are selected because they are confounders. Removing one from the model can be dangerous because we may fall into a situation like Simpson's paradox, where including/excluding the variable changes the results of the estimation. And cross-validation will not detect this problem, as we saw in chapter 3. The selection of variables Z is made before training any machine learning on the grounds of modeling the data-generating process and creating the graph. In some cases, it is not necessary to include all confounder factors (we will talk about this in chapter 7), but this has to be decided based on the graph, not on the cross-validation.

THE T-LEARNER ALGORITHM: SPLITTING DATA TO IMPROVE ATE'S ESTIMATION

The S-learning algorithm is fine, but in practice, it has a problem. When you try to train a machine learning model to predict Y from variables X and Z, the training process implicitly uses the correlations among variables to create a prediction. Some of the behavior of X may be well predicted through variables Z. But in models like decision trees, which may select which variables to use, the model may not consider the value of X! This implies that the model f becomes insensitive to the value of X. So, when we evaluate $f(x, z_1^i, \ldots, z_p^i)$, we will see no differences if we change the value of X. And that's a problem because we will get an ATE of exactly 0: not because there is no effect from the treatment, but because of the numerical methods used in the process.

One way to address this is to take the subsample of cases where X takes value x instead of training a machine learning model with all the data. With that subsample, we can train a machine learning model. Of course, there is a caveat: because we have substantially reduced our dataset, we will have higher variance estimates. But usually it pays off, because the S-learner algorithm may produce very poor estimates. The T-learner algorithm can be summarized as follows:

1 Split the historical data $\{(y^i, z_1^i, \ldots, z_p^i)\}$ for $i = 1, \ldots, n$ into two subsets D_0 and D_1, the first corresponding to observations with $x = 0$ and the second analogously with $X = 1$. Then train two machine learning models f_0 and f_1 with each dataset. When Y is categorial, run a classifier; when Y is continuous, run a regressor. In both cases, the covariates should be all confounders $Z_1, \ldots, Z_p$.

2 For each observation $i = 1, \ldots, n$ (in the entire dataset), make two predictions using models $f_0(z_1^i, \ldots, z_p^i)$ and $f_1(z_1^i, \ldots, z_p^i)$.

3 Calculate the ATE (remember that this formula is also valid for the case where Y is binary):

$$\text{ATE} = E[Y|\text{do}(X = 1)] - E[Y|\text{do}(X = 0)] \approx \frac{1}{n} \sum_i \left[f_1\left(z_1^i, \ldots, z_p^i\right) - f_0\left(z_1^i, \ldots, z_p^i\right) \right]$$

Notice that the value of x has disappeared in the formulas. As explained earlier, we have a different function for each value of x: f_0 has been trained on the dataset $X = 0$, and f_1 has been trained on the dataset $X = 1$.

Exercise

We have explained that when training a machine learning model for applying the S-learner, the model may choose other variables over the treatment variable X, which becomes a problem because we will get an ATE of 0 (when it may not really be 0). Let's use a coded example to see how this can happen and how the T-learner solves this problem. To do so, we will create our own dataset. The data model is the following:

$$Z \sim N(0, 1)$$
$$X \sim Ber(p) \text{ where } p = p(Z) = logistic(\beta_z^x Z)$$
$$\text{and } logistic(s) = \frac{1}{1 + e^{-s}}$$
$$Y = \beta_z^y Z + \beta_x^y X + \varepsilon \text{ where } \varepsilon \sim N(0, 1)$$

Take a sample of size $n = 20$ generated with the previous description of the variables and parameters $\beta_z^x = \beta_z^y = 5$ and $\beta_x^y = 2$.

1   Calculate the difference in y between groups $x = 0$ and $x = 1$. Is it close to the value β_z^y (the effect of x into y)?

2   Apply the S-learner algorithm: train a decision tree (using the `rpart` library in R or `sklearn` in Python) with maximum depth 5, and calculate the ATE. Observe that the ATE is 0 (if it isn't, take a different sample; there is a small probability that it will not be 0, but it usually is). All predicted differences for each observation are also 0, which is the main problem of the S-learner.

3   With the same data, apply the T-learner algorithm and check that the ATE is not 0.

Notice that in this data, Z is a confounder because it affects not only the decision variable X but also the outcome variable Y. If you get lost in the mathematical formulas for generating the data, think about the following:

- The decision variable X follows a logistic regression model: the probability of X being equal to 1 depends on the factor Z. This means for each value of z, we need to calculate $p = p(z)$ with the earlier logistic function, and this probability p will tell us the probability that $x = 1$. Once this p is calculated, x will be a sample of a Bernoulli distribution with expectation p.
- The outcome y has three terms. The first is a linear dependency on z. The second is a linear dependency on x, which is the effect of x on y. The third is a noise term.

Now let's calculate the ATE based on the formulas of the data-generating process. When we set $x = 0$, the outcome y will behave like

$$y = \beta_z^y z + \varepsilon$$

But when $x = 1$, y will be

$$y = \beta_z^y z + \beta_x^y + \varepsilon$$

If we calculate the difference between setting $x = 0$ and $x = 1$ and measure the difference in effect on the outcome, we will have

$$\beta_z^y z + \beta_x^y + \varepsilon - \beta_z^y z + \varepsilon = \beta_x^y$$

So, in this model, the ATE (the difference between setting $x = 1$ ($do(X = 1)$) and $x = 0$ ($do(X = 0)$) and measuring the difference in the outcomes) will be precisely β_x^y. The problem is that if we use the S-learner, sometimes, depending on our data, the estimated ATE is exactly 0!

NOTE You can find a step-by-step coded solution on the book's website www.manning.com/books/causal-inference-for-data-science or in the GitHub repository at https://mng.bz/4pnQ.

4.2.5   *Cross–fitting: Avoiding overfitting*

There's an important caution when using machine learning in the adjustment formula: the risk of overfitting. *If we train a machine learning model on dataset D and then make predictions on the same dataset, we are prone to overfitting.* This means using the same dataset for both training and predicting is not advisable.

Overfitting in machine learning is different from what you may encounter in causal inference. In supervised learning, the goal is usually to pick a model that will perform best on a new, unseen set of data. However, the S- and T-learners make predictions on the same dataset they were trained on. This is why even if you perform cross-validation carefully to select the best model, making predictions on the training set can still lead to overfitting.

How overfitting works intuitively

If we want to predict Y from X, the goal of supervised learning is to estimate $E[Y|X]$, a quantity we don't observe. What we actually observe is the value of $Y|X$ for some X: that is, a dataset of $D = \{(x_i, y_i)\}$. We create the predictive model from these values, trying to fit the predictions $f(x_i)$ to y_i as much as possible. So, because the model we trained with D tries to mimic D for the x_i in the dataset, it will be biased toward predicting something near the observed value y_i rather than the value we want, which is $E[Y|x_i]$. We use cross-validation to prevent the model from mimicking the actual values too closely. It limits the complexity of the model (which means restricting the flexibility of the model we are using) and forces the model to focus more on $E[Y|x_i]$ instead of y_i. This is why training on a dataset D and predicting on the same dataset may produce biased results (overfitting), especially with more complex models.

Here's an alternative way to think about this. Whenever we have two variables Y and X, we can always describe the relationship between them in terms of the conditional expectation as $Y = E[Y|X] + \varepsilon$, where ε is an error term independent of X. This is straightforward because trivially, $Y = E[Y|X] + Y - E[Y|X]$. So, the term $\varepsilon = Y - E[Y|X]$ has zero mean conditioned on X: $E[\varepsilon|X] = E[Y|X] - E[Y|X] = 0$. In this expression, we cannot get any further information from X. That is, conditioned on X, ε is pure noise. Each time we observe a value x, we also observe a particular y, which usually is different from $E[Y|X] = f(x)$. In this approach, if the predictive model we create is closer to $y = E[Y|X] + \varepsilon$, rather than $E[Y|X]$, what we are fitting is ε, which is the noise.

Consider the example in the following figure, where the dashed line represents the underlying data-generation process (which we don't have access to), and we observe the dots that correspond to samples obtained from this process with some error. In supervised learning, we want to estimate the underlying process, but only using the data (points). Solid lines represent two different models. As we can see, the one closer to every point is also overfitting (its behavior far from the points is not good for making predictions). Instead, the curve that doesn't go through any point is better for making predictions because it is closer to the underlying data-generation process. The good model targets the conditional expectation (the expected value of the underlying process) rather than the points themselves.

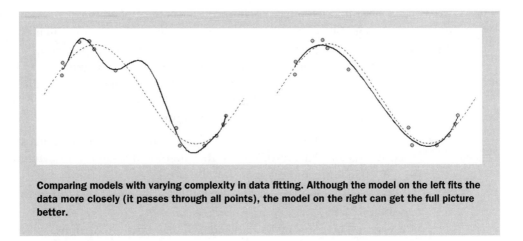

Comparing models with varying complexity in data fitting. Although the model on the left fits the data more closely (it passes through all points), the model on the right can get the full picture better.

The general approach to handling these situations, *cross-fitting*, splits the dataset to avoid overfitting. Let's start with the simplest case, a 50-50 split. We split our dataset in two: D_1, D_2. First we use D_1 to train machine learning models, and then we use D_2 to make predictions. Then we switch roles: train with D_2, predict on D_1. This process is shown in table 4.5.

Table 4.5   The difference between training and predicting on the same dataset with respect to applying cross-fitting

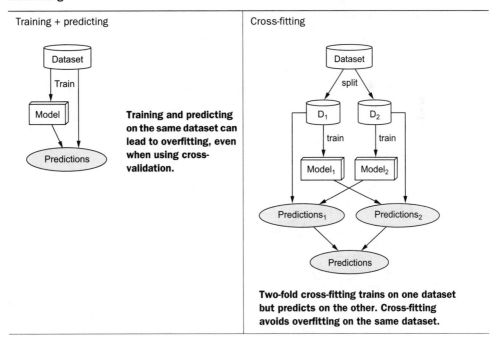

As we will see in future chapters, this approach can be applied in many situations, not only for the S- and T-learners. Moreover, just as we have k-fold cross-validation, we also have k-fold cross-fitting. That is, we can divide the dataset into k groups D_1, ..., D_k. For each dataset D_j, we train a machine learning model on the complementary of the dataset and then evaluate the predictions on D_j. Finally, we average all the predictions.

Let's see what two-fold cross-fitting would look like for the S-learner and T-learner algorithms. For simplicity, we will write it with continuous outcome Y:

1   Split the historical data $D = \{(x^i, y^i, z_1^i, \ldots, z_p^i)\}$ into two equal datasets D_1, D_2. To keep the dataset balanced, ensure that there is the same proportion of cases with $X = 0$ in both, and the same for $X = 1$.

2   Use the cases from D_1 to train a machine learning model f to predict Y from covariates X and Z_1, ..., Z_p.

3   For each observation in D_2 with index i, make two predictions, setting values $x = 1$ and $x = 0$, respectively.

4   Calculate the ATE for the data in D_2 using the model trained from D_1, f:

$$ate_2 \approx \frac{2}{n} \sum_{i \in D_2} f\left(1, z_1^i, \ldots, z_p^i\right) - f\left(0, z_1^i, \ldots, z_p^i\right)$$

5   Repeat steps 2–4, switching roles between D_1 and D_2 to obtain a new quantity ate_1.

6   Obtain $ATE = (ate_1 + ate_2)/2$

$$ATE = \frac{ate_1 + ate_2}{2}$$

Steps 1–4 are shown in figure 4.6. Step 5 should be done by switching roles between D_1 and D_2 in the figure.

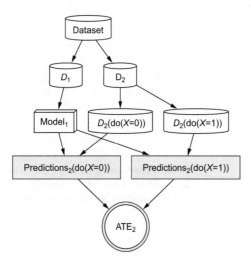

Figure 4.6   **Two-fold cross-fitting applied to the S-learner. We split the dataset into two and use one part to train the model. In the other part, we make two interventional predictions (do($X = 0$) and do($X = 1$)) and calculate the ATE. Finally, we switch the roles of the two datasets.**

As we have seen before, the S-learner may be inefficient. A better approach combines the T-learner with cross-fitting. The only difference in the cross-fitting algorithm for the T-learner is in step 2, where we use the subset of data with $X = x$ to train the model:

1 Split the historical data $D = \{(x^i, y^i, z_1^i, ..., z_p^i)\}$ into two equal datasets D_1, D_2. Make sure there is the same proportion of cases with $X = x$ in both to keep the dataset balanced.

2 Use the cases in D_1 to train two models $f_0(z_1^i, ..., z_p^i)$ and $f_1(z_1^i, ..., z_p^i)$ with covariates and $Z_1, ..., Z_p$.

3 For each observation in D_2 with index i, make two predictions, setting values $x = 1$ and $x = 0$, respectively.

4 Calculate the ATE for data in D_2 using the models trained from D_1, f_0, f_1:

$$ate_2 \approx \frac{2}{n} \sum_{i \in D_2} f_1\left(z_1^i, ..., z_p^i\right) - f_0\left(z_1^i, ..., z_p^i\right)$$

5 Repeat steps 2–4, switching roles between D_1 and D_2 to obtain a new quantity ate_1.

6 Obtain $ATE = (ate_1 + ate_2)/2$

Steps 1–4 are shown in figure 4.7. Step 5 should be done by switching roles between D_1 and D_2 in the figure.

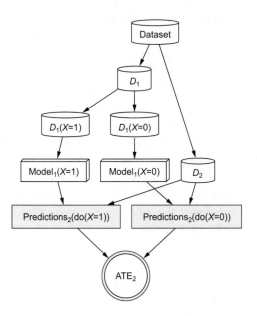

Figure 4.7 Two-fold cross-fitting applied to the T-learner. We split the dataset into two and use one part to train two models with $X = 0$ and $X = 1$, respectively. In the other part, we make two interventional predictions (do($X = 0$) and do($X = 1$)) using both previous models and calculate the ATE. Finally, we switch the roles of the two datasets.

Conclusion

To get good estimates of the adjustment formula, you should use the T-learner and cross-fitting to avoid overfitting from machine learning models.

4.3 Other applications of causal inference in machine learning

Until now, we've mainly talked about how causal inference relates to supervised learning. But the influence of causal inference is expanding into various areas of machine learning. In this section, we'll provide concise explanations of these connections. If you're eager to dive deeper, we've included some references. Keep in mind that they're not meant to cover every aspect, but they're a good starting point for further exploration.

4.3.1 Reinforcement learning

Reinforcement learning studies situations where one or more agents interact with an environment. Their actions lead to a reward, and we want to learn the optimal decisions these agents can make to maximize their reward. The agents are not required to know how the environment works, so part of their job is handling such unknowns. Typically, an optimal decision must balance the exploration of the environment (to find the best action) with exploitation (repeating an already known action to get the reward). A popular example is training computers to play games. You can have one computer play another for many games so that they end up learning optimal strategies.

The goals of causal inference and reinforcement learning are similar: making optimal decisions. However, there are big differences in when we can use each of them. In causal inference, we want to learn from past data. But in reinforcement learning, we can usually simulate the environment. Think about the example of two computers playing against each other. They can play the game as many times as needed, creating new data each time they play. Moreover, they can decide which actions agents take at each moment. So reinforcement learning has direct information about interventions, whereas causal inference does not (and must derive them from data). Causal inference can be applied in reinforcement learning problems where there is a mixture of intervened variables with others that cannot be intervened but merely observed.

Multiarmed bandits are a particular form of reinforcement learning closely related to A/B tests. Imagine that we run an A/B test to measure the efficacy of a new website, as in chapter 1. We decide that to have a big enough sample size, the experiment should last four weeks. However, after two weeks, there is strong evidence that alternative A performs better than B. Running an experiment is costly because it requires a particular setup for our website. But more importantly, when we assign participants to the worst option (in this case, B), we lose what we could potentially earn if they were assigned to the best option (in this case, A): that is, the opportunity cost. So, given evidence that A is better, is it a good idea to stop the experiment and conclude that A is better? No. During the four weeks, there will be fluctuations due to the random nature of the experiment. We can expect that A will be better in some periods than B; at other times, the opposite will be true. If we stop the experiment prematurely because A seems to do better, we are altering the results, introducing bias in favor of A.

But what if instead of stopping the experiment when A performs better, we just reduce the number of participants assigned to B from now on? That is precisely what multiarmed bandits do: they work like A/B tests that dynamically change the proportion assigned to each arm, allocating participants toward the better option without losing the opportunity to find the best option. During the experiment, they optimize a metric called *regret*, which is the opportunity cost of selecting the best option. As in reinforcement learning, we may have mixed settings with observational information in some situations where causal inference may help. Check out section 4.4 to find more literature about this topic.

4.3.2   *Fairness*

Imagine a bank that creates a credit score model that uses each customer's relevant characteristics (age, salary, etc.) to predict the probability of them repaying a loan in the agreed period of time. These predictions can be used to prioritize giving credit to customers who are more likely to pay back the money. In theory, nothing stops the model from using race to predict the chance of a customer repaying a loan. Empirically speaking, some races may have higher chances of returning the money than others, so including race in the model may increase its accuracy. However, deciding to make a loan based on someone's race is discrimination. Favoring or denying access to financing to specific groups can lead to serious social problems, so how you create a credit scoring model is not only a technical problem but also a social one.

Your first reaction may be that removing the "race" feature from the model will solve the problem. Not so. We can remove the customer's race but keep their address, which may be highly correlated with their race. So, removing the effect of race from a model requires understanding the relationships between the different variables included in the model.

Fairness is the area of machine learning devoted to understanding and correcting these problems. Here, causal inference may have a lot to say because understanding causal relationships between variables is its specialty. Check out section 4.4 for more reading on this topic.

4.3.3   *Spurious correlations*

Through supervised learning, machine learning has successfully achieved highly accurate predictions in many cases. However, some of these predictions are built on exploiting correlations among variables, and this can become a problem. Imagine a classifier that has to detect whether images show a dog or a fish. Suppose that in a particular historical dataset used to train the classifier, dogs usually appear lying on the grass, and fish are shown in the sea. Instead of learning the complex shapes, parts, and colors of both animals, the classifiers may learn that when the background is green, there is a high chance that the animal is a dog, but when the background is blue, the animal is probably a fish.

As we have explained, machine learning models work well as long as the past behaves like the future. This means that when we have a new image, the model will be accurate as long as the new images are similar to those from the training sample. The problem comes when an image shows a dog jumping through the air against a blue background: the model will detect the blue background and predict that the animal is a fish. The model is exploiting a *spurious correlation.* Causal inference can help us understand and develop methods to reduce these spurious correlations that may hurt our models. Check out section 4.4 to learn more.

4.3.4 *Natural language processing*

The collaboration between natural language processing (NLP) and causal inference is recent and in its early days. It seems intuitive that because humans give meaning to what we read, causality may have something to bring to the table. Section 4.4 lists more literature on this topic.

4.3.5 *Explainability*

Explainable AI (XAI) is, in simplistic terms, devoted to understanding what models predict and how and why they predict the way they do. Deep learning is especially (but not only) concerned with making accurate predictions and, when predictions fail, understanding why. There are also some examples of applications of causal inference in interpretability; see the references in section 4.4.

4.4 *Further reading*

The S- and T-learners are explained in "Metalearners for Estimating Heterogeneous Treatment Effects Using Machine Learning" by Künzel et al. Related techniques are explained in "Targeted Learning: Causal Inference for Observational and Experimental Data" by Mark J. van der Laan and Sherri Rose. Cross-fitting is introduced in "Double/Debiased Machine Learning for Treatment and Structural Parameters "by Chernozhukov et al., but be warned that it is a highly technical paper.

Following are some additional references for the previous sections:

- Reinforcement learning
  - Causal reinforcement learning tutorial by Elias Bareinboim at the International Conference on Machine Learning (ICML) 2020 (https://crl.causalai.net)
- Fairness
  - "Causal Fairness Analysis: A Causal Toolkit for Fair Machine Learning" by Drago Plečko and Elias Bareinboim (*Foundations and Trends in Machine Learning* vol. 17, no. 3, pp. 1–238, 2024): https://causalai.net/r90.pdf

– "Counterfactual Fairness" by Matt J. Kusner, Joshua R. Loftus, Chris Russell, and Ricardo Silva: https://arxiv.org/abs/1703.06856

– "Fairness and Machine Learning, Limitations and Opportunities" by Solon Barocas, Moritz Hardt, and Arvind Narayanan (2023): https://fairmlbook.org

- Spurious correlations
  – "On Calibration and Out-of-Domain Generalization" by Yoav Wald, Amir Feder, Daniel Greenfeld, and Uri Shalit: https://arxiv.org/pdf/2102.10395.pdf

  – "Invariant Risk Minimization" by Martin Arjovsky, Léon Bottou, Ishaan Gulrajani, and David Lopez-Paz: https://arxiv.org/pdf/1907.02893.pdf

  – "Why Should I Trust You?: Explaining the Predictions of Any Classifier" by Marco Tulio Ribeiro, Sameer Singh, and Carlos Guestrin: https://arxiv.org/pdf/1602.04938.pdf

  – "Causal Inference Using Invariant Prediction: Identification and Confidence Intervals" by Jonas Peters, Peter Bühlmann, and Nicolai Meinshausen: https://arxiv.org/pdf/1501.01332.pdf

- NLP
  – "Causal Inference in Natural Language Processing: Estimation, Prediction, Interpretation and Beyond" by Amir Feder, Katherine A. Keith, Emaad Manzoor, Reid Pryzant, Dhanya Sridhar, Zach Wood-Doughty, Jacob Eisenstein, Justin Grimmer, Roi Reichart, Margaret E. Roberts, Brandon M. Stewart, Victor Veitch, and Diyi Yang: https://arxiv.org/pdf/2109.00725.pdf

- Explainability

  – "Explaining the Behavior of Black-Box Prediction Algorithms with Causal Learning" by Numair Sani, Daniel Malinsky, and Ilya Shpitser: https://arxiv.org/pdf/2006.02482.pdf

  – "Toward Unifying Feature Attribution and Counterfactual Explanations: Different Means to the Same End" by Ramaravind Kommiya Mothilal, Divyat Mahajan, Chenhao Tan, and Amit Sharma: https://arxiv.org/pdf/2011.04917.pdf

4.5 Chapter quiz

As we conclude the chapter, it's important to ensure that you have a solid understanding of the key concepts. Here are the essential questions you should be able to answer clearly and concisely. If you can't, I suggest rereading the corresponding references:

1 Theoretically, which is the best predictor you can create in a regression problem?

    Answer in section "What does a supervised learning model aim for?"

2 What is the basic assumption in supervised learning?

    Answer in section 4.1.3

3   Imagine that you want to estimate the effect of a product's price on the probability of purchasing it. Name a scenario where training a supervised learning model is enough to obtain the causal effect.

Answer in section 4.1.4

4   Cross-validation is not a reliable metric for choosing the correct causal model. Why?

Answer in section "Why we cannot select models in causal inference based on their cross-validation error?"

5   Cross-validation is not enough to avoid over-fitting in causal inference estimates. Why?

Answer in section 4.2.5

Summary

- Supervised learning is all about prediction and works as long as the future behaves like the past. So, if you are going to make decisions that affect your environment based on machine learning models, consider first whether they are the right tool.
- Machine learning models provide causal estimates when you include all confounding variables.
- You should not choose your causal model based only on cross-validation.
- When you have many confounders, you can apply the adjustment formula using machine learning models:
  - A conditional probability appearing in a formula can be substituted in practice by a machine learning model.
  - Even when using cross-validation to choose your machine learning model, you still need to apply cross-fitting to avoid over-fitting.

Part 2

The adjustment formula in practice

Y ou may encounter challenges when attempting to apply the adjustment formula in real-life scenarios. One critical requirement for using this formula effectively is that the positivity assumption is met. This assumption mandates that every version of the treatment is applied across all subpopulations. In chapter 5, you will discover methods to identify when the positivity assumption does not hold and strategies to navigate this issue.

Until this point, our discussion has primarily focused on situations where the treatment or decision variable is binary. Chapter 6 introduces linear models to deal with the effect of continuous variables. You will also discover that linear models provide insights into how correlation and causation propagate through graphs. This understanding will be extremely useful in the following chapter.

Another challenge is figuring out which variables to include in the adjustment formula, especially if your graph is complex. Chapter 7 tackles this issue by explaining the back-door criterion, a graphical criterion to pick the right variables for adjustment.

You learned to use machine learning for the adjustment formula in chapter 4, and now chapter 8 introduces the double machine learning technique. This method is more efficient and flexible in estimating causal effects. You'll also see how to calculate confidence intervals: how sure you can be about your results. Plus, you'll learn to use the `DoubleML` library to estimate causal effects and their confidence levels.

Finding comparable cases with propensity scores

This chapter covers

- Using propensity scores to assess the positivity assumption
- Calculating the ATE using propensity-score techniques

Let's revisit the main point in causal inference: how to choose between two options when we can't use randomized controlled trials or A/B tests. Remember the kidney-stone example from chapter 2? We've used the adjustment formula to tackle problems like this. Now we have a modified version of this formula. Why do we need it? Because it's specifically made to determine whether the positivity assumption is true.

Remember from chapter 2 that the adjustment formula only works if the positivity assumption is true. Let's go over what this assumption means. Suppose you have two treatments, A and B. You give treatment A to both young and old people, but treatment B only to young people. If you want to figure out the effect of treatment B on everyone, both young and old, you hit a snag. You can't know how treatment B affects old people unless some of them also receive this treatment. To determine which treatment is better, you need to apply both treatments, A and B, to both age groups: older and younger.

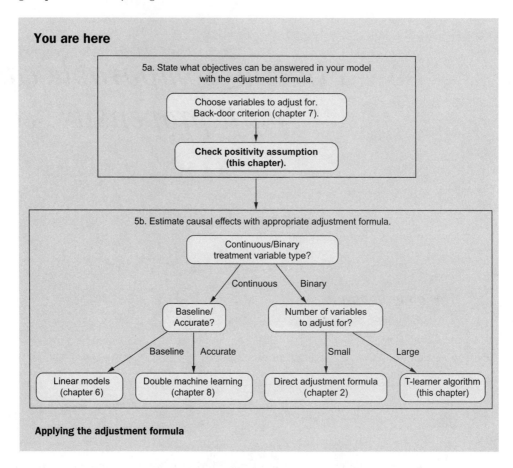

But you're not done. You probably also need to consider other important factors like gender and regular exercise. For instance, if older females who exercise often are receiving treatment A, some of them should also get treatment B. Without doing this, you won't get a clear picture of how treatment B works across the whole population. That's the essence of the positivity assumption: to evaluate the effects properly, both treatments, A and B, must be tested across all relevant subgroups within your patient population.

The positivity assumption can also be explained in a slightly different way. If you give treatment A to a specific group, such as older females who exercise often, you should also give treatment B to the same group. Similarly, if any group receives treatment B, some individuals from the same group should receive treatment A. Taking this idea to the individual level, it means that for every patient who receives one treatment, there should be a *match*: another patient with similar characteristics who receives the other treatment. Matching is straightforward when you only have one or two categories to consider. However, when dealing with many confounders, as we will see in the section 5.1.3, the matching process can get much more complicated.

The positivity assumption is equivalent to saying that for each patient, we can find another patient with similar characteristics who received the opposite treatment. In this chapter, we'll learn how to identify these matches using the *propensity score.* Formally, the *propensity score for a patient is the probability that any patient with the same characteristics will be given a specific treatment,* such as treatment A. This score ranges from 0 to 1.

If a patient's propensity score is 1, it means this patient, and all others like them, received treatment A, and none got treatment B. There's no matching patient in group B, so we can't tell how treatment B would affect this type of patient. Conversely, a propensity score of 0 indicates that the patient and all others with the same characteristics only received treatment B, with no matches in treatment group A.

Groups A and B are only *comparable* when their patients' propensity scores are strictly between 0 and 1—not exactly 0 or 1. This range ensures that for each patient with a score between 0 and 1, there is a match receiving the opposite treatment, thereby supporting the positivity assumption.

Propensity scores are not just for checking the positivity assumption; they can also be used in various ways in calculating the adjustment formula. In this chapter, we'll explore how both matching and propensity scores can be used to refine this formula.

Propensity scores are especially prominent in healthcare, where they're a popular tool for matching and evaluating adjustment calculations. This chapter is essential for those interested in healthcare data analysis. If you're familiar with healthcare literature, you'll notice that propensity scores are frequently mentioned. But their use extends beyond healthcare to other areas, such as recommender systems. Even if healthcare isn't your field, understanding how propensity scores function is beneficial.

Additionally, this chapter will help you better understand previous material. We'll revisit the adjustment formula—a concept we've already covered—but view it from a new angle: comparing treatment effects between similar patients. This perspective is not only insightful but also enhances your grasp of causal inference techniques.

> **When to use propensity scores**
> Propensity scores help you figure out if the positivity assumption is true, which then lets you know whether you can apply the adjustment formula. They are also useful for calculating average treatment effects (ATEs).

5.1 Developing your intuition about the propensity scores

Let's start with a straightforward example to demonstrate the practical use of propensity scores. This will lay the groundwork before we delve into more complex theories necessary to expand our understanding. First we need to reexamine how to calculate ATEs from a simpler, perhaps more intuitive, angle.

Consider the scenario shown in figure 5.1, where doctors, acting cautiously, opted not to administer a newer, more uncertain treatment to older individuals—a group at higher risk of complications. Let's assume age is the only factor considered when deciding the treatment allocation (making it the sole confounder). In this scenario, the treatment group includes only 20% (1/5) older individuals, and the control group (those not receiving the treatment) includes 75% (3/4) older individuals. Given that age likely influences recovery rates and clearly affects the distribution between the treated and control groups, age must be considered a significant confounder.

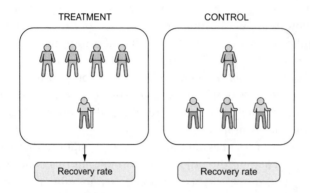

Figure 5.1   The age distribution in both groups is different. So, we cannot estimate the ATE with the difference in means between the two groups.

Keep in mind
Even though we will start analyzing simple examples with only one or two confounders, our goal is to learn how to deal with situations where we have a medium or large number of confounders.

5.1.1   *Finding matches for estimating causal effects*

If I told you that 80% of the treated group recovered well but only 50% of the control group recovered, given what you've learned in previous chapters, you would probably think (and you would be right) that this is not a fair comparison. The treatment group has a higher proportion of young people, who recover more easily, and the control group has a higher proportion of older people, who are usually more difficult to cure. The ratio of old versus young people is different in both groups.

Think first, read next
What if the comparison is at each age stratum, as in the following figure? For instance, if there is a 15% increase in recovery rate in young people but a 5% increase in recovery rate in older people in the treatment versus the control group, are these estimates unbiased?

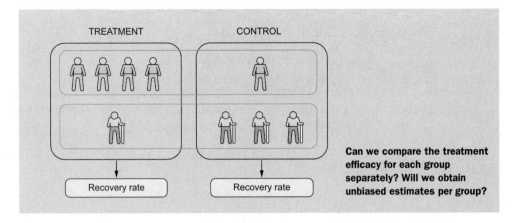

In this case, the estimation will be fair (unbiased). The intuition is as follows. Many factors affect a patient's chances of recovery, such as location, age, and so on. The number of factors can be huge. All of these factors, except age, have the same distribution in both groups (if there are 50% females in the treatment group, there is the same proportion in the control group). This means the two groups are very similar regarding all these variables (except age); the only difference is whether they were treated. The age variable is different because it was used to decide which treatment to give, so the proportion of, say, young people with respect to the total is different in both groups. However, when we select *only* young people, the proportion of young people is the same in both groups (actually, it is 100% because there are only young people!). Now all the variables that affect the outcome, including age, have the same proportion in both groups. All the characteristics are equal in both groups, the only difference being that one group was treated but the other wasn't. So, both groups are comparable, and we can estimate the causal effect of the treatment just by measuring the difference in outcomes between the groups.

We can arrive at the same conclusion following the logic from the section "Conditioning is part of the solution" in chapter 2. As shown in figure 5.2, we have only one confounder. When we select a particular stratum and condition on young people, the confounder is fixed (has no variation), so all the correlation between treatment and the outcome comes from their causal relationship.

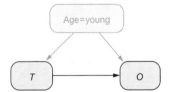

We can only compare the recovery rate of a treated patient with a nontreated patient if they both share the same characteristics (in this case, age). To calculate the ATE, we can follow the path called *matching*, where for each type of treated patient, we look at the same type in the nontreated group and make comparisons among them.

Figure 5.2   When we control for age, we fix age as a constant. Thus, in the group where Age = young, age no longer influences the outcomes. Therefore, age is no longer a confounder in this scenario. *T* stands for Treatment and *O* for Outcome.

Which variables should we match on?

Long story short: the set of all confounders. The confounders, by definition, can potentially affect the decision about which treatment to give, so we can expect to have a different distribution of each confounder in each treatment group. At the same time, we worry that this distribution is different because these variables affect the outcome, and that prevents us from comparing both groups directly (because we have an unfair comparison).

5.1.2   *But is there a match?*

The real problem arises when there is a subgroup with characteristics found in only one of the two groups, as in figure 5.3, where there are no young people in the treatment group. In this case, we cannot use matching because young treated patients have no counterpart in the control group. The characteristics of a specific subpopulation can be different in the treated and control groups (20% older in treatment versus 75% older in control), but there is a problem when a particular subpopulation appears in only one of the two groups. And that is precisely what the positivity assumption worries about! In figure 5.3, the proportion of young people in the control group is 0%. Equivalently, we can say that for young people, the probability of being in the control group is 0%, which can be mathematically expressed as

$$P(T = 0 | young) = 0\%$$

But this is nothing more than saying that the propensity score for young people (their probability of being treated) is $P(T = 1 | young) = 100\%$. So, as we can see, checking the positivity assumption is equivalent to checking for which patients have a propensity score of either 0 or 1.

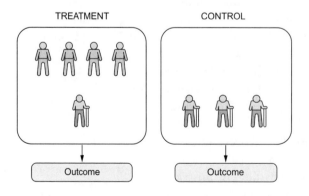

Figure 5.3   We can't compare the effectiveness of the treatment across different age groups because the control group doesn't include any young patients.

5.1.3   *Why matching can be hard*

In our age-related example, finding a match for each group is pretty easy. But in real life, finding a match can get much more complicated. Let's look at why this happens.

DEALING WITH CONTINUOUS VARIABLES

The positivity assumption cannot be proved; it is just supported by statistical arguments. This fact is easier to understand when we are working with continuous variables. Imagine that preoperation blood pressure (a continuous variable) is the only confounder, and we need to check whether the positivity assumption holds. Unlike the previous example, where we can make groups that have the exact same characteristics (young/old), with blood pressure, patients can have very similar yet not exact values. For instance, knowing that systolic blood pressure usually ranges from 90 mmHg to more than 120 mmHg, imagine that a patient in the treatment group has a reading of 100 mmHg and the closest patient in the control group has a reading of 101 mmHg. Are these two comparable? Can we match one with the other to calculate the effect of the treatment? Formally, as we introduced the positivity assumption, we should say it doesn't hold because, for patients with 100 mmHg, there is no match in the control group. On the other hand, going from 100 to 101 mmHg doesn't have a significant effect on the recovery rate of patients. If that is the case, we can safely match these two patients and regard them as having the same blood pressure.

One solution in practice to deal with continuous variables is to bin blood pressure in ranges ([less than 80), [80, 85), …,). That is what we actually did with age. Binning requires some work to decide the number of bins to create: if the bins are too large, we put very different cases in the same basket; but if they are too small, each bin contains few observations and thus has poor statistical performance.

MORE THAN ONE CONFOUNDER

A major problem arises when we have not one but many confounders (which is almost always the case). Imagine that both age (as a continuous variable) and preop blood pressure are confounders. We can still make bins: say, five bins for age (A_1, …, A_5) and five bins for blood pressure (BP_1, …, BP_5). Each patient will have a combination of the two, so in total we will have 5×5 = 25 bins (A_i, BP_j) for i, j = 1, …, 5. When we only considered blood pressure, if we used five bins, all the patients had to be distributed among those five bins. Now that we have two variables, the same number of patients must be distributed among 25 bins. Every time we consider a new variable binned into five categories, the number of bins multiplies by five, increasing exponentially. *So, as the number of confounding variables increases, the number of patients in each bin decreases,* potentially achieving a sample size that is too small in each bin and thus leading to poor statistical performance. If you are thinking about avoiding this problem by reducing the number of variables in the analysis, that is a very bad idea! The variables that need to be included in the analysis are the entire set of confounders, and we know from experience that not considering a relevant confounder can make our analysis flawed (remember Simpson's paradox).

Additionally, there's another problem to consider. Confounding factors may affect the outcome differently. For instance, in a given scenario, a 10 mmHg difference in blood pressure (ranging from 90 to 100 mmHg) may have a smaller effect on the outcome than a five-year age difference (between 80 and 85 years old). It's not just about the different scales of these variables (mmHg and years) but also about how they uniquely contribute to the outcome. So, if age affects the outcome more than blood pressure, age bins should be proportionally smaller than blood pressure bins: recall that in each bin, there shouldn't be differences in the outcome due to age, only differences due to treatment. That makes the two treatment groups comparable among patients in the same bin. Fortunately, there is a technique that solves all these problems cleanly and uses (as you may have guessed) propensity scores.

5.1.4 *How propensity scores can be used to calculate the ATE*

Recall that the propensity score is the probability of a type of patient being treated. For instance, in the example shown in figure 5.4, four out of five young people are treated, so the propensity score for young people is $PS(\text{young}) = 4/5 = 80\%$. Analogously, the propensity score for older people is $PS(\text{old}) = 1/4 = 25\%$.

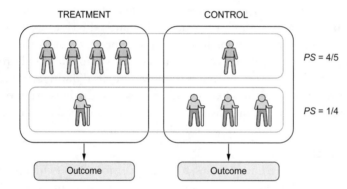

Figure 5.4 Example of calculating propensity scores. In a group of young patients, four out of five received treatment. Therefore, the probability of being treated in the young group, or the propensity score for this group, is 4/5. The same method applies to calculate the score for older patients.

Propensity scores offer a solution to the challenges we discussed earlier. In simpler terms, instead of hunting for patients with precisely similar attributes, you just need to compare patients with *similar propensity scores*. This comparison helps check the positivity assumption, find matches, or calculate the adjustment formula. It may seem odd initially, but look at figure 5.5 for a clearer picture. Consider a new group of patients: children. Some of them end up in the treatment group, but doctors are cautious about administering the new treatment to children.

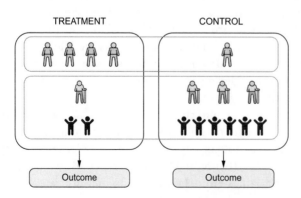

Figure 5.5 To calculate the ATE, we can put together two groups of patients if both groups share the same propensity score. For instance, older patients and children have the same probability of being treated: in other words, they have the same propensity scores.

If you remember, the original problem that prevented us from comparing treated versus nontreated was that the ratio of young/old was different in each treatment group. However, the ratio of children/old (2 to 1) is the same in both groups (treated and control), so they are comparable! And that is the idea of propensity scores: you can group patients with different characteristics as long as they have the same propensity score and deal with them as the same group.

For instance, we can measure the ATE first in the group of young people by calculating the difference in outcome between the two groups:

$$ATE_{young} = P(O = 1|young) - P(O = 0|young)$$

This is an unbiased estimation of the ATE because in this example, there is only one confounder, and the group of younger people in the treated group is comparable with the group of younger people in the control group. We can repeat this process, but instead of dealing with children and old people separately, we can consider them in the same group (because they are comparable) and calculate the following (children+old means the union of both groups):

$$ATE_{children+old} = P(O = 1|children+old) - P(O = 0|children+old)$$

We can put together children and old people because the ratio between two different categories of a confounder (older or children, for age) is the same in both the treatment and control groups: these categories have the same propensity score, so they are comparable. In other words, *among those with a particular propensity score, their characteristics appear in the same proportion in the treated and experimental groups.* Read this twice if you need to, because it will appear many times in this chapter.

5.2 *Basic notions of propensity scores*

In the previous section, we first encountered the new tool called a propensity score. Typically, in practice, propensity scores are used as shown in figure 5.6.

The first step in figure 5.6 is exploring the data and describing the basic characteristics of the population. This simple step helps us detect subpopulations that have been assigned to only one of the two groups (treatment or control) so they can be discarded. Then we calculate the propensity scores using machine learning techniques. Once the propensity scores are calculated, in step 3, we visually assess whether the positivity assumption holds (whether for each patient we can find a match in the other treatment group), which typically leads to one of the three possible outcomes:

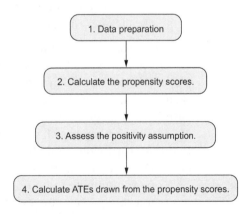

Figure 5.6 Four steps describing the typical process with propensity scores

- We can move on with the analysis because both groups are comparable.
- We cannot perform the analysis because the two groups are very different.
- The groups are not comparable, but we can use the analysis for a particular subset of our population.

If we conclude that we can move on with the analysis, we draw on the already-calculated propensity scores to calculate ATEs.

Before jumping into using propensity scores, we need to set some foundations and specify the situations we are working with and some problems we may face.

5.2.1 Which cases are we working with?

We will start by introducing the notation used in the rest of the chapter and describing the cases where we can use propensity scores. In particular, we want to consider situations that arise frequently in practice, where we have many confounders. The characteristics of the population described by those confounders are diverse, which may become a problem when assessing the positivity assumption. Throughout this chapter, we will assume that the data we want to analyze follows a directed acyclic graph (DAG), as in figure 5.7, with the following variables:

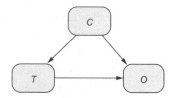

Figure 5.7 Main diagram for this section. *C* denotes a vector of confounders, *T* stands for treatment, and *O* stands for outcome.

- The treatment variable (T) has two possible outcomes: treated/nontreated or two different types of treatment. In this chapter, we will consider treated versus nontreated, which will be encoded as 1 and 0, respectively.
- The outcome variable (O) is the outcome we want to analyze, such as recovery from an illness. Unless stated otherwise, we will assume that O is also binary. However, the propensity-score techniques can also be used with continuous variables (we will explain how when required).
- A vector of confounders (C) comprises all confounding variables (typically age, sex, location, and so on).

We know from chapter 2 that whenever our problem is described by a graph such as the one in figure 5.7, ATEs can be calculated using the adjustment formula. For example, consider a surgical group at a hospital that's started using a promising new surgical technique. They observe that surgeries performed with this new technique seem to have better outcomes than those without it. To accurately assess how significant this effect is, the best approach would be to conduct a randomized controlled trial (RCT). In this RCT, patients would be randomly assigned to either receive the new technique or undergo surgery without it.

Moreover, suppose the surgical group is curious not only about the effectiveness of this new technique but also about the efficacy of other techniques they've been using. In this case, they would need to carry out a series of RCTs, conducting one experiment at a time for each technique to systematically evaluate each technique's effectiveness.

Performing RCTs can be expensive in terms of direct costs, such as money (because new treatments may be more costly) or time, and also opportunity costs. If a new treatment proves ineffective, the patients who received it during the trial may have been better off receiving standard care. Therefore, the surgical group needs to carefully prioritize which experiments to run, focusing on those with a higher likelihood of success.

To make these decisions more strategically, the group can use causal inference methods to estimate the causal effect of each treatment based on historical data. By calculating the ATE of each treatment, they can identify which ones show the most promise. Then they can start with RCTs for treatments that have a higher estimated ATE, thus optimizing their resources and increasing the likelihood of beneficial outcomes.

To calculate the ATE for a specific medical technique using observational data, it's crucial to account for confounders—variables that influence both the treatment decision and the outcome. Because the data isn't from a controlled experiment, there's a risk of bias due to these confounders.

The first step is to identify potential confounders. We can begin by consulting with the physicians involved in the treatment decisions and asking each physician what factors they considered when deciding whether to use this particular technique for a patient. Collectively, the factors mentioned by all physicians form a preliminary set of potential confounders.

Next, we evaluate this list to determine which factors are true confounders. For a variable to be considered a confounder, it must influence not only the decision to use the treatment but also the treatment outcome. If we are not certain that a particular variable affects the outcome, we can safely exclude it from our list. But if there's any doubt about whether a variable affects the outcome, it's generally safer to include it to avoid bias.

Common examples of confounders in this context include age, sex, the hospital where the treatment was administered, radiological findings, and the patient's history of previous illnesses or surgeries. By carefully selecting and adjusting for these confounders, we can more accurately estimate the ATE and thereby assess the true effectiveness of each medical technique.

Think first, read next

Imagine that physicians want to know the effect of undergoing surgery versus not having surgery. Generally speaking, what are the confounders?

Hint: Think about who is involved in deciding whether a patient undergoes surgery and which factors they take into account.

Even though calculating the effect of surgery may seem similar to calculating the effect of a particular treatment, there is a huge difference in terms of potential confounders. We can have a good idea of the confounders involved in choosing a treatment when the physicians make this decision and let us know their choice. Having surgery is a different story because the decision is generally agreed on between the physician and the patient! In this case, to list all possible confounders, in addition to asking the doctors, we should ask each patient what made them decide to undergo surgery. Patients can give rational reasons, but we should assume that there are also irrational reasons that are difficult to explain or measure (or put in a table with a numeric quantifier).

In our first example, where the doctors are the only ones to decide whether to use a new technique, we may still miss some confounders: maybe a doctor has subconscious biases or decided based on an intuition that can't be made explicit in a database. But the set of potentially missed confounders is still much smaller than the set for the decision to have surgery, which includes all the confounders from the patient's side.

For the rest of the chapter, we'll focus on calculating the ATE of a particular technique. Let's assume that we have all the potential confounders and are dealing with the data-generating process shown in figure 5.7.

5.2.2   *What are the propensity scores?*

The definition of the propensity score of a particular patient, given their characteristics, is their probability of being treated. Mathematically speaking, if $c = (c_1, ..., c_p)$ is a vector with all the values of each confounder, the propensity score (S) is defined as

$$S(c) = P(T = 1 | C = c)$$

The conditional probability $P(T = 1 | C = c)$ is a function of c: for each value of c, we calculate the probability of being treated for all those patients with attributes c, so the resulting value $P(T = 1 | C = c)$ is different for every c.

> ### Why can we compare groups based only on their propensity scores?
>
> The key idea that lets us calculate ATEs using the propensity scores is, as we saw in the previous section, the following: *the ratio between two different categories of a confounder (older people or children for age, in the previous example) is the same in both the treatment and control groups, because these categories have the same propensity score, which makes the two categories comparable.*
>
> In other words, if two different categories have the same propensity score, you can treat them as one group in the evaluation of the ATE.

The example from the previous section should help us understand. You can also find a mathematical proof in section C). This idea was formalized in 1983 by Paul R. Rosenbaum and Donald B. Rubin (see section 5.5) in the paper "The Central Role of the Propensity Score in Observational Studies for Causal Effects," and propensity scores have been popular ever since.

5.2.3   *The positivity assumption is ... an assumption*

The positivity assumption doesn't check something about the data itself. If that were the case, when we find lots of patients without an exact match in the opposite group (such as in section 5.1.3), we shouldn't calculate ATEs. However, we understand that even if we don't have the same exact value, we can use patients with similar values. The formal way to support this is the following. If the positivity assumption holds in the long run, when we get a very large sample size, we are sure that for each patient, we will be able to find a match in the opposite group. The probability distribution in the long run is the data-generation process, as described in chapter 2. The positivity assumption is formally stated on this distribution, saying that for all *c*,

$$0 < P_0(T = t|C = c) < 1$$

Because we only have access to the data, but not this limiting distribution, the positivity assumption is just an assumption, not something that can be formally verified from data. But as we have seen throughout this chapter, data can support such an assumption.

5.3   *Propensity scores in practice*

In this section, we will learn how to execute each of the steps we saw earlier, repeated for convenience in figure 5.8.

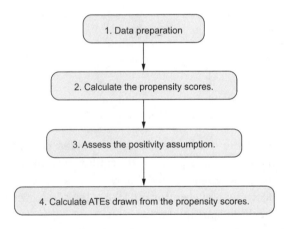

Figure 5.8   Four steps describing the typical process with propensity scores

5.3.1   *Data preparation*

We usually perform a preliminary exploratory analysis of the data to discard obvious differences between groups: for instance, if the control group only contains older patients and the treatment group contains both young and old, as in figure 5.3 earlier. In this situation, it is clear that we cannot proceed with the analysis. However, there is a convenient solution: just analyze older patients. Whatever results we obtain from an analysis with only older patients will only apply to older people and cannot be extrapolated to young people. This selection may alter the objective of the analysis, so if you continue such an analysis with a subset of patients, remember to inform everyone who should be kept in the loop.

It is recommended that we visually (or by statistical means) check each confounder to find clear evidence of subpopulations missing a match in the opposite group. We will select a viable subpopulation from each variable, and the subpopulation subject to further study should be the intersection of each subpopulation found on each confounder.

5.3.2 Calculating the propensity scores

In real-world scenarios, we commonly deal with several confounding factors. As explained in "More than one confounder," calculating propensity scores may be a problem. Luckily, as seen in chapter 4, we can use machine learning models to estimate conditional probabilities, particularly the propensity score $P(O = 1 | C = c)$. Because the outcome is binary (whether the patient is treated: $T = 1$), we can use any classifier. To calculate propensity scores, you should have data organized in the format shown in table 5.1: each row contains information from a different patient, and we can find whether they received the treatment (column T, taking a value of either 0 or 1) and their value for each confounder (the remaining p columns $C_1, ..., C_p$).

Use equations 5x - 8x for the C's in this table that have superscripts and subscripts

Table 5.1   Table describing whether each patient was treated (variable T) and their description in terms of confounders ($C_1, ..., C_p$)

T	C_1	...	C_p
t^1	c_1^1	...	c_p^1
...	...	...	...
t^n	c_1^n	...	c_p^n

Of the available models to predict the treatment variable from the confounders, a logistic regression model is frequently used, especially in healthcare applications. Saying that logistic regression is a machine learning model may be overkill, because statisticians used it before machine learning was even invented, but logistic regression can be regarded as a model in the machine learning toolbox.

To make accurate predictions, we typically try many alternative machine learning models to find which one works best for our particular dataset. In addition to logistic regression, popular models include random forests and boosting (and deep learning), and we may want to try them. You can use whatever predictive model you see fit; the question is, how do you pick the best one? The answer is to perform the usual cross-validation for supervised models and choose the one with higher predictive capability on the test set.

Machine learning classifiers can produce two types of outcomes: predicting the label itself (in this case, 0 or 1) or predicting the probability of the label. For the propensity scores, we are interested in the probability of the score being 1 (by definition). In this case, it is desirable to evaluate the models using the area under the curve (AUC) instead of accuracy. If this concept is new to you, check out Tom Fawcett's "An introduction to ROC analysis" at https://mng.bz/754m. As explained in section 7 of that paper, the

AUC of a classifier is equivalent to the probability that the classifier will rank a randomly chosen positive instance higher than a randomly chosen negative instance.

Besides the fact that propensity scores can be calculated using standard machine learning techniques, there are small details we need to consider. Let's take a look at them.

Is a higher AUC better?

Typically, in machine learning, the higher the accuracy or AUC of our model, the more useful the model is, because higher accuracy means our model is more capable of predicting what will happen.

> **Think first, read next**
> But when we calculate propensity scores, the lower the AUC is, the better. Why?

Think for a moment about the extreme situation where we hypothetically have an accuracy of 1. This means we can predict which patients will be treated and which will not, based on their characteristics in the set of confounders. If that is the case, the positivity assumption doesn't hold because for all c,

$$P(T = 1 | C = c) \text{ is either 1 or 0}$$

Let's consider the opposite situation where the model with the highest possible performance has an AUC of 0.5 (the lowest AUC a model can have in terms of performance). This means the model cannot find any relationship between confounders and the treatment assignment: that is, the variables T and C are independent. Thus, by the definition of independence,

$$P(T = 1 | C = c) = P(T = 1)$$

We can safely assume that at this point, our study includes some treated and untreated patients (otherwise, there is nothing to do from the causal perspective), written mathematically as $P(T = 1) > 0$. So, the positivity assumption is satisfied automatically.

Saying that the confounders C and the treatment T are independent corresponds to the situation where we have performed an RCT, which, from the causal inference perspective, is a desired situation. Does this mean that when training the machine learning model, we shouldn't aim for the highest AUC? Of course not. We should try to get the highest accuracy possible; and later, the lower the accuracy is, the closer we will be to an RCT, so the luckier we will be.

Don't include variables in a model just because they make the model more accurate

In machine learning, it's common to choose variables that boost a model's accuracy. But when it comes to causal inference, you should select variables based on domain knowledge, not just model accuracy. This is a complex topic, and we will talk about it more in chapter 7 when we introduce the backdoor criterion to explain which variables you should adjust for. For now, know that picking the wrong variables can seriously bias your ATE estimate or increase the variance of your results, and you may not even realize it.

BE CAREFUL: YOU CAN STILL OVERFIT USING CROSS-VALIDATION!

Yes, you heard it: even with train–test splitting (as typically done in machine learning), you can still overfit. If this sounds weird, it may be because you are used to training the machine learning model with one historical dataset (using the correct train–test splitting) but later using the model (in production, for instance) with new data the model hasn't seen. For instance, imagine that you want to create a model that can read car license plates, which can be used to automatically read license plates at the entrance and exit of a parking garage. You will train the model on a dataset containing images and car registration numbers, but when the model runs with images from the parking garage, you should expect that it will mostly read plates different from those in the historical dataset. In that sense, propensity scores are different because we have a historical database with patient information, and we want to calculate the propensity scores of these particular patients. Once we have a machine learning model, it will be used to make predictions (propensity scores) for this historical database.

We talked about this phenomenon in chapter 4, and one solution is to run a cross-fitting:

1 Split your data into (for simplicity of this explanation) two datasets D_1, D_2.
2 Train a machine model on each dataset (also executing the corresponding cross-validation on each one), and obtain two predictive models f_1, f_2.
3 Calculate propensity scores on each dataset using the corresponding opposite predictive function: that is, for patients with data in D_1, use the predictive model f_2; and for patients with data in D_2, use the predictive model trained with data in D_1.

This way, we will not predict on the same data used to train the model.

5.3.3   *Assess the positivity assumption*

One of the main advantages of propensity scores is that they provide a concise way to check whether the positivity assumption holds. Let's assume that each patient has a description $c = (c_1, \ldots, c_p)$ in terms of the set of confounders (for instance, if the only confounder is age, a patient may have the description $c = (\text{old})$). The positivity assumption says that for this particular type of patient, there are patients in both the treatment and control groups, which can be written mathematically as selecting (conditioning on) all those older patients; we can potentially find them in both groups:

$$0 < P(T = 1|\text{older}) = \frac{1}{4} < 1$$

The positivity assumption written in general mathematical notation says that for every c,

$$0 < P(T = 1|c) < 1$$

Thanks to the propensity scores, as we said earlier, there is no need to check each of the possible combinations of values of *c*. We can group patients with the same propensity score, as we did when we aggregated children and older people (because they had the same propensity score of 1/4). Grouping patients by the same propensity score, instead of the raw patient description, is more convenient because each propensity score groups more samples.

WHY WE CAN GROUP BY PROPENSITY SCORES: MATHEMATICAL REASONING

We have offered some intuitive explanations about why we can group patients by propensity score. However, we need actual math that supports this statement. Before going into the details of the mathematical reasoning, try to answer the following question.

> ### Think first, read next
> Given a patient with characteristics c and propensity score s = S(c), what is the relationship between $P(T = 1|c)$ and $P(T = 1|s)$?

The difficulty of this question is related to mathematical notation, because we already have the answer. They are the same!

$$P(T = 1|c) = P(T = 1|s)$$

The reason is as follows. Pick all those patients with characteristics *c*. Then calculate their propensity score *s=S(c)*. On the other hand, pick all the patients with the same propensity scores as our selected patient with *C = c*. This operation is the same as conditioning on *s*. To answer the "Think first, read next" question, we need to know what $P(T = 1|s)$ is, which is a bit like answering the popular Spanish phrase: "Which is the color of Santiago's white horse? (¿De qué color es el caballo blanco de Santiago?)". White, of course! If you can answer the riddle, you are prepared to answer the following one: what is the probability of being treated for those patients who have a probability of being treated of *s*? This sentence is the exact definition of the mathematical expression $P(T = 1|s)$, and the answer is *s*, of course! So, we have

$$s = P(T = 1|c) = P(T = 1|s)$$

This formula justifies the fact that we can put all the patients with the same propensity score in the same basket, because checking

$$0 < P(T = 1|c) < 1$$

for all vector characteristics *c* is the same as checking

$$0 < P(T = 1|s) < 1$$

for all values of *s*.

VISUAL ASSESSMENT

A great deal of literature provides tools to assess the positivity assumption. But one of the more basic ways is to visually inspect the distribution of propensity scores of both groups. Saying that for a propensity score s, we have $0 < P(T = 1 \mid s) < 1$ is equivalent to saying that for that particular s, there are samples of both groups. The idea is to make a plot where we show, for each value of s, the number of patients around this point. And for that, we use density plots. Let's look at some typical situations; the figures have been created with synthetic data to show the point of the analysis.

Look at figure 5.9. On the x axis, every vertical line represents the value of a patient's propensity score. Patients in the treatment group have a dashed line, and those in the control group have a solid line. You can see the density distribution of both groups; the groups are strictly separated. For a propensity score higher than approximately 0.55, there are no control patients, whereas for a propensity score lower than .5, there are no treatment patients. The *support*—by definition, the range of values of the distribution—of the treatment group is [0.55, 1], and the support for the control group is [0, 0.5]: *there is no overlap*. In this case, there is nothing to do. The

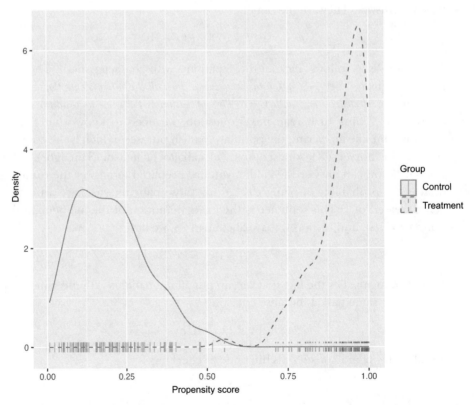

Figure 5.9   The distribution of propensity scores between the two groups shows no overlap, indicating that there are no matches between the groups. Consequently, we cannot calculate ATEs.

assignment is deterministic (you can tell with 100% accuracy who is in each group), which is the opposite of we want—a totally random assignment such as in RCTs. This is the worst-case scenario, and we should admit that we cannot proceed to calculate ATEs, because the positivity assumption doesn't hold at any propensity-score value.

We would ideally like to find the scenario shown in figure 5.10, where the support of both distributions is approximately the whole interval [0, 1]. There is *full overlap between supports*, and for every propensity score *s*, we can find patients in both groups with very similar propensity scores. In this case, we can safely proceed to calculate ATEs.

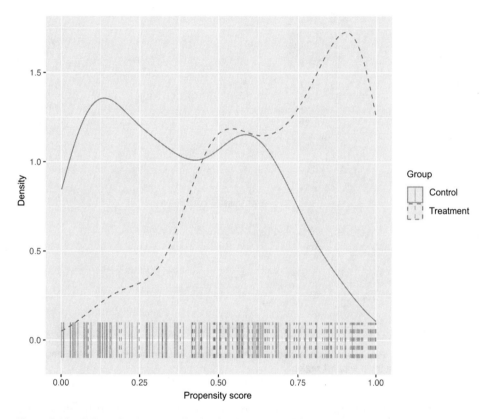

Figure 5.10 Full overlap between distributions' supports. This is the ideal scenario to calculate ATEs.

In practice, we may find ourselves in an in-between situation where *there is overlap on a subset of patients*, as in figure 5.11. In this case, there is overlap in approximately the interval [0.25, 0.75] (if we want to be more conservative, we should shrink this interval). For patients with a propensity score in this interval, we can find a match in the opposite group. The physician (or whoever chose the assignment) had doubts about which group these patients should be in. This contrasts with patients outside the overlapping region, who clearly are in only one group (they don't have a match in the opposite group). At this point, we have two options: stop the analysis by saying we cannot assume that the positivity assumption holds, or continue the analysis with only the subset of patients who have a match: that is, those whose propensity score lies in the interval [0.25, 0.75].

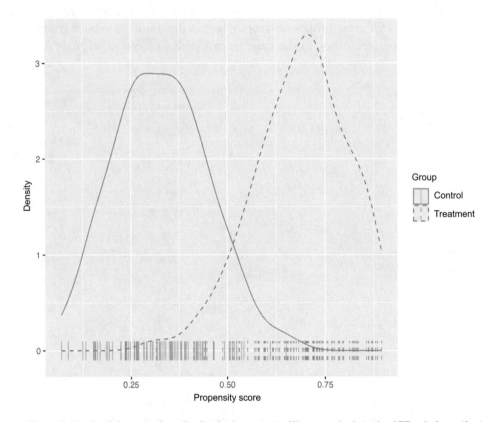

Figure 5.11 Partial overlap in a distribution's supports. We can calculate the ATE only for patients within the common support region.

The second solution is convenient because it lets us move on but at the expense of analyzing only a particular subpopulation. We must ask ourselves whether using only this subpopulation still fits the objective of the analysis, knowing that the results cannot be extrapolated to the rest of the patients who are dropped from the study. There is no general answer to this question, and it should be studied case by case. To make this decision, it helps to know this subpopulation better: Who are they? Does any characteristic define them well? You can try to combine basic descriptive statistics and better understanding by asking physicians how the decision process was made. Unfortunately, in general, do not expect to get a clear picture of who the patients are. If you decide to move on with the overlapping subpopulation, remember to keep all stakeholders informed.

The last example, in figure 5.12, is a particular case of the previous one. There is not full overlap, but the overlapping subpopulation is clearly defined: it's the treatment group. The support of the distribution of the treatment group is approximately the interval [0.6, 1], and the support of the distribution of the control group is approximately the interval [0.3, 1]. There is a match for every patient in the treatment group, so we can calculate the ATE on the treated group. This leads us to the notion of *average treatment effect on the treated* (ATT), which means to calculate the ATE only for the subpopulation of treated patients. Alternatively, we can define the *average treatment effect on the control* (ATC).

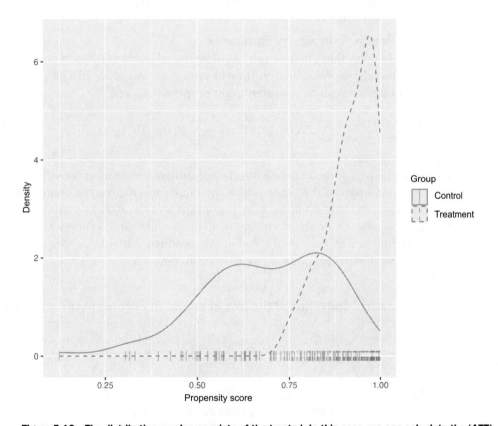

Figure 5.12 The distribution overlap consists of the treated. In this case, we can calculate the (ATT).

ATT and ATC

The ATT and ATC are defined independently of propensity scores and matching. We introduced them here because they arise naturally in this context, but they are variations of the ATE that are frequently calculated in healthcare analysis.

Of course, in this example, we can only calculate the ATT, not the ATC, because there is not a match for every patient in the control group.

5.3.4   *Calculating ATEs drawn from the propensity scores*

Now that we have calculated the propensity scores of all patients and have supported the positivity assumption, let's see how to reuse the already-calculated propensity score to calculate ATEs. We know that because we are working with the graph in figure 5.7, ATEs can be calculated using the adjustment formula introduced in chapter 2. So, we will start by showing how propensity scores can be used in the adjustment formula, and then we will learn two numerical implementations of it. Finally, we will introduce a different relationship between the adjustment formula and propensity scores called *inverse probability weighting.*

PROPENSITY SCORES IN THE ADJUSTMENT FORMULA

We have said many times that we can calculate the adjustment formula based on previously calculated propensity scores. It turns out, as we will prove in a second, that the adjustment formula can be rewritten using propensity scores:

$$\sum_c P(O = 1|t, c)P(c) = \sum_s P(O = 1|t, s)P(s)$$

The left-hand part of the expression is the adjustment formula explained in chapter 2. The right-hand part of the expression is the same formula, but the confounding vectors *c* are replaced by the values of the propensity score *as if the propensity scores acted as the sole confounder.* Once again, the adjustment formula using propensity scores is an unbiased estimator of the causal effect of the treatment variable, as long as we are not missing any relevant confounders, as assumed in figure 5.7.

Mathematical derivation of the role of propensity scores in the adjustment formula

This mathematical proof is not required to follow the rest of the book. However, if you are curious, I recommend giving it a try. The proof is short and accessible enough to be included in this book.

Before delving into the mathematical derivation, we need to acknowledge two facts:

- For every patient description *c* and its propensity score $s = s(c)$, we have that $P(c|t,s) = P(c|s)$. We already talked about this relationship in section 5.1.4, and you can find a proof in Appendix C The math behind propensity scores and population distributions. It says that if we group patients by the same propensity score, the distribution of each confounder (characteristics) is the same in the treatment and control groups.
- The following relationship holds: for every treatment *t*, and for every patient description *c* and its propensity score *s*, we have that $P(O = 1|t, c, s) = P(O = 1|t, c)$. This formula says that we can remove the *s* from the conditioning part. The reason is that conditioning on *c* is more restrictive

than conditioning on *s*. That is, selecting patients with characteristics *c* and their corresponding propensity score s = s(c) is redundant. It is enough to say that we condition on patients with characteristics *c*.

Now we can go step by step through the mathematical derivation. We start from the adjustment formula and apply the definition of conditional probability, slicing through the different values of s:

$$\sum_c P(O = 1|t, c)P(c) =$$

$$\sum_c \sum_s P(O = 1|t, c)P(c|s)P(s)$$

Now we apply the already-discussed relationship $P(O = 1|t,c) = P(O = 1|t, c, s)$, obtaining

$$\sum_c \sum_s P(O = 1|t, c)P(c|s)P(s) =$$

$$\sum_c \sum_s P(O = 1|t, c, s)P(c|s)P(s)$$

We switch the order of summation and apply the fact that $P(c|t,s) = P(c|s)$, so we get

$$\sum_c \sum_s P(O = 1|t, c, s)P(c|s)P(s) =$$

$$\sum_s \sum_c P(O = 1|t, c, s)P(c|t, s)P(s)$$

and summing over *c*, we can make *c* disappear from the formula, arriving at

$$\sum_s \sum_c P(O = 1|t, c, s)P(c|t, s)P(s) =$$

$$\sum_s P(O = 1|t, s)P(s)$$

In summary,

$$\sum_c P(O = 1|t, c)P(c) = \sum_s P(O = 1|t, s)P(s)$$

as we originally said.

Whenever the outcome variable O takes many values, we can follow the reasoning explained in chapter 2 and get the relationship

$$E[O|do(T = t)] = \sum_c E[O|T = t, C = c]P(C = c) =$$

$$\sum_s E[O|T = t, S = s]P(S = s)$$

COVARIATE ADJUSTMENT

The equality formula

$$\sum_c P(O = 1|t, c)P(c) = \sum_s P(O = 1|t, s)P(s)$$

tells us that we can apply the adjustment formula but use propensity scores instead of confounders. In practice, once we have calculated the propensity scores, we can add a new column to our database, as in table 5.2.

Table 5.2   Available data with propensity scores calculated

O	T	C_1	...	C_p	S
o_1	t^1	c_1^1	...	c_p^1	s_1
...	...	...	...	...	...
O_n	t^n	c_1^n	...	c_p^n	s_n

Actually, we only need columns *O*, *T*, and *S*, as in table 5.3, to apply the numerical methods described in chapter 4 as the T-learner, where the only confounder is the variable *S*. Recall that when using machine learning models, you can still overfit (as explained in subsection 5.3.4), so you should also use cross-fitting.

Table 5.3   Necessary data with propensity scores calculated to apply the adjustment formula

O	T	S
o_1	t^1	s_1
...	...	...
O_n	t^n	s_n

MATCHING

We will now see how matching, which was introduced at the beginning of this chapter, can be numerically implemented. There is a lot of literature and variations on matching. Here we will explain the most basic method because giving all the variations is outside the scope of this book. We will start with simple cases and end up seeing that matching is nothing but a particular case of the adjustment formula.

Imagine that we have the same number of treated patients (n_t) and untreated patients (n_c). Then for each treated patient, we can find a match in the control group. Recall that it is enough to compare patients using only their propensity scores rather than their full description variables. We can start with one patient in the treatment group, calculate their propensity score, and look for a control patient with the closest propensity score. We can repeat the process, never repeating already-matched patients, until we run out of patients. In this way, for each patient i, if we denote the patient in the control group by $m(i)$, we can guess what would have happened to this patient (or any with similar characteristics) if they were in the control group, calculating the *treatment effect* as the difference in their outcomes:

$$d_i = O_i - O_{m(i)}$$

Then we can calculate the ATE by averaging the differences among all the patients:

$$\text{ATE} \sim \sum_i d_i$$

You may say that in practice, we rarely have the same number of treated and untreated patients. You are right. We need a way to calculate the ATE when the sample size of the groups differs.

Actually, we can run the same algorithm even though the groups are different sizes. If we have fewer treated patients than untreated patients, $n_t < n_c$, then for each treated patient, we can always find an untreated patient without repeating already-chosen untreated patients. On the other hand, if there are more treated than control patients, $n_t > n_c$, we are obliged to repeat control patients; otherwise, some treated patients will have no match.

Notice that with this procedure we are calculating not the ATE but the ATT. To see this, think of the situation where there are fewer treated than control patients, $n_t < n_c$, because it is easier to understand. We are only estimating the difference between being treated and untreated for the treated patients. And that is precisely the definition of ATT! Notice that there are some patients in the control group for whom we haven't calculated the treatment effect.

> **Reminder of the definition of ATT**
> You may find it helpful to look at figure 5.12 and its explanation, and see how it fits with the matching algorithm we just described.

There is another problem with the matching algorithm introduced in this section. For each patient, we are only looking for a unique match. But due to luck or because the outcomes have a lot of variance, some matches are extreme or infrequent cases. To put it another way, given a treated patient, estimating the treatment effect relying on a sample size of 1 (so far, we are choosing only one patient from the control group) seems like a poor choice from a statistical point of view.

If you have some knowledge of machine learning, finding matches based on covariates may sound familiar. It is nothing but *k-nearest neighbors* (kNN)!

We will explain how to combine kNNs and the adjustment formula to calculate the ATE. Let's separate the dataset in table 5.3 into treated and control datasets called D_t (table 5.4) and D_c (table 5.5), respectively.

Table 5.4   Treatment data to be used with kNN, $D_{t \cdot n\_t}$ is the number of patients in the treatment group.

O	S
O_1	S_1
...	...
O_{n_t}	S_{n_t}

Table 5.5   Control data to be used with kNN, $D_{c \cdot n\_c}$ is the number of patients in the control group.

O	S
O_1	S_1
...	...
O_{n_c}	S_{n_c}

Using kNN, we can create predictive models of the outcome O for the datasets called p_t and p_c, respectively. Notice that the only feature is the propensity score of each patient, and the outcome is the variable O. The number of patients to match with is precisely k for the kNN algorithm. From the point of view of supervised learning, k is a hyperparameter that should be chosen using cross-validation. This way, we can address answer the problem of choosing the correct number of patients to match with!

Consider a treated patient i with propensity score s_i. The treatment effect can be calculated using the kNN trained on the control group to predict the expected outcome for a patient with propensity score s_i:

$$d_i = O_i - p_c(s_i)$$

The same can be done with the control group. For each control patient j, we use the kNN model trained in the treatment group to calculate the treatment effect:

$$d_j = p_t(s_j) - O_j$$

Now we can average the n treatment effects, obtaining

$$\text{ATE} \approx \frac{1}{n}\left[\sum_i O_i - p_c(s_i)\right] + \frac{1}{n}\left[\sum_j p_t(s_j) - O_j\right]$$

where i runs over treated patients and j over control patients.

Matching formula is just an approximation of the adjustment formula

The formula we have just seen

$$\text{ATE} \approx \frac{1}{n}\left[\sum_i O_i - p_c(s_i)\right] + \frac{1}{n}\left[\sum_j p_t(s_j) - O_j\right]$$

is just an approximation of the adjustment formula with the propensity scores:

$$\text{ATE} = \sum_s P(O=1|T=1,s)P(s) - P(O=1|T=0,s)P(s)$$

Let's sketch the idea of why this is so for the mathematically curious reader. Notice that in the first formula, the summation runs over patients, whereas in the second, the summation runs over different values of the propensity scores. Suppose l patients have the same value of $s = s_i$. Some of them, l_t, are in the treatment group, and others, l_c, are in the control group (with $l_t + l_c = l$). We need to see that for this particular s,

$$P(O=1|T=1,s)P(s) - P(O=1|T=0,s)P(s) =$$

$$\frac{1}{n}\left[\sum_{i,s_i=s} O_i - p_c(s_i)\right] + \frac{1}{n}\left[\sum_{j,s_j=s} p_t(s_j) - O_j\right]$$

If we have l patients with propensity score s, then $P(s) = l/n$. Substituting this information on the previous equation, and given that for these patients, $s_i = s_j = s$, we can simplify terms to obtain

$$l[P(O=1|T=1,s) - P(O=1|T=0,s)] =$$

$$\left[\sum_{i,s_i=s} O_i - p_c(s)\right] + \left[\sum_{j,s_j=s} p_t(s) - O_j\right]$$

Let's now focus on the term $P(O=1|T=1,s)$, because the term $P(O=1|T=1,s)$ is treated the same way. If we see that

$$lP(O=1|T=1,s) = \sum_{i,s_i=s} O_i + \sum_{j,s_j=s} p_t(s)$$

then we are done. On the one hand,

$$p_t(s) \approx P(O=1|T=1,s)$$

because $p_t(s)$ is a predictive model of outcome O. But for those patients i in the treatment group,

$$\frac{1}{l_t}\sum_{i,s_i=s} O_i \approx P(O=1|T=1,s)$$

(continued)

by definition, because $P(O = 1|T = 1,s)$ is just the average (expectation) of the outcome O over those treated patients with propensity score s. So,

$$\sum_{i,s_i=s} O_i + \sum_{j,s_j=s} p_t(s) = l_t\left[\frac{1}{l_t}\sum_{i,s_i=s} O_i\right] + l_c p_t(s) \approx$$

$$l_t P(O = 1|T = 1, s) + l_c P(O = 1|T = 1, s) =$$

$$l P(O = 1|T = 1, s)$$

INVERSE PROBABILITY WEIGHTING

An alternative formula relates the adjustment formula and propensity scores. Starting from the adjustment formula and multiplying and dividing by the same quantity $P(T = t|c)$,

$$\sum_c P(O = 1|t, c)P(c) = \sum_c \frac{P(O = 1|t, c)P(t|c)P(c)}{P(t|c)}$$

Noticing that $P(O = 1|t,c)P(t|c)P(c) = P(O = 1, t, c)$ is just the joint distribution, we obtain what is called the *inverse probability weighting* formula:

$$\sum_c P(O = 1|t, c)P(c) = \sum_c \frac{P(O = 1, t, c)}{P(t|c)}$$

In the case where we have two treatments $t = 0,1$, the empirical version (using data) of this formula is

$$\frac{1}{n}\sum_i \frac{o_i I(t_i = t)}{p(t|c_i)}$$

where $I(t_i = t)$ equals 1 for patients i with treatment t_i equal to t, and $p(t|c_i)$ must be calculated from data. Actually, the ATE

$$\text{ATE} = P(O = 1|do(T = 1)) - P(O = 1|do(T = 0))$$

can be calculated using the previous formula and substituting for $t = 1$ and $t = 0$

$$\text{ATE} \approx \frac{1}{n}\sum_i \frac{o_i I(t_i = 1)}{s(c_i)} - \frac{1}{n}\sum_i \frac{o_i I(t_i = 0)}{1 - s(c_i)}$$

where we use the fact that $p(t = 0|c) = 1 - p(t = 1|c) = 1 - s(c)$, where $s(c)$ is the propensity score that can be calculated from data.

It is good to know about inverse probability weighting because it may appear in the literature, but in general, using it is not recommended unless you have a good reason to do so. Propensity scores appear divided in the formula. For some patients, the propensity score may be very small, close to zero. From a numerical point of view, dividing by quantities close to zero is discouraged because small errors in estimation may translate into large errors in the resulting formula, and thus the variance of your estimate of the ATE may increase significantly.

5.4 *Calculating propensity score adjustment: An exercise*

Now we're going to give you a practical exercise with real data. We'll explain the goal and the steps involved. In the book's code repository (www.manning.com/books/ causal-inference-for-data-science or on GitHub at https://mng.bz/o0AN), which includes both R and Python, you'll find starting code called *exercise starter*, so you don't have to begin from scratch. There's also code for the solution. Note that this exercise is for learning purposes only; it shouldn't be used to draw any medical conclusions.

The exercise has several objectives, and the primary one is to calculate the ATE for a specific problem using propensity scores. In this exercise, you'll learn the following:

- How to calculate propensity scores using machine learning models
- The importance of cross-fitting to avoid overfitting your data
- How to compute ATEs using covariate adjustment (see section 5.3.4) and the T-learner (see chapter 4)

We will use the Right Heart Catheterization (RHC) dataset (https://hbiostat.org/ data/repo/rhc), which can be used to study the effect of performing an RHC—an invasive test that provides many measurements such as blood pressure and cardiac output—on the chances of survival of critically ill patients. You can find more information (and an exploratory analysis) at https://github.com/opencasestudies/ocs-right -heart-catheterization. The treatment variable is *swang1*, and it takes the value RHC when the test is performed. The outcome variable, *death*, indicates whether the patient survived. You can find rhc.csv file containing data from https://hbiostat.org/ data/ (courtesy of the Vanderbilt University Department of Biostatistics) and a list of the available variables at https://hbiostat.org/data/repo/crhc.

Before starting the exercise, you need to know the list of confounders. The book's code repository includes a file called confounders.yml with a list of variables to be considered confounders. In practice, this list of variables should have been thoroughly discussed with expert physicians. In this case, the variables in the confounders file have been selected for the sake of the exercise.

5.4.1 *Exercise steps*

1 Propensity scores first attempt. Train a model for the propensity score (PS) with the treatment variable *swang1*.

2 Overfitting. Use the trained model to make predictions (probabilities) on the same dataset and calculate its AUC. Verify that the AUC with respect to the predicted probabilities is greater than the AUC reported from the cross-validation.

3 Propensity scores with cross-fitting. Calculate the PS using two-fold cross-fitting: split the dataset into two equally sized datasets D_1 and D_2. Train a model for PS using D_1 and predict on D_2, and vice versa. Calculate the AUC with the new propensity score.

4 Visual inspection. Make the plot of the density of the PS by treatment group. Are the two groups comparable?

5 ATEs with T-learners and cross-fitting. Calculate ATEs using T-learner and cross-fitting to estimate the effect of *swang1* on *death*:

   – Split the dataset into two equally sized datasets D_1 and D_2.
   – Take D_1 and and train two models:
     ▪ With *swang1* = RHC, called $f_{1,R}$
     ▪ With *swang1* = non-RHC, called $f_{1,N}$

6 Repeat the process with D_2 and train two models.

7 Calculate on D_2 the estimated treatment effect vector of $f_{1,R}(x) - f_{1,N}(x)$, where x ranges for all observations in D_2.

8 Switch roles between D_1 and D_2 and calculate the ATE.

Train a model means to execute cross-validation (train–test split) over a subset of hyperparameters and choose the one with a higher AUC. The simplest method is to use grid search. You can find both R and Python functions that perform grid search (run the cross-validation over the set of hyperparameters), such as the `caret` and `tune` packages in R and `scikit-learn` in Python. Among the available machine learning models, we propose to use boosting, a fairly popular and effective model. You don't need to know how boosting works in detail for this exercise. It is just another predictive method that can be called from the previously mentioned packages.

The exercise starter files in the book's repository calculate propensity scores using logistic regression. It can be used as a baseline model to compare with the boosting model proposed in the exercise.

> **Solution**
> You will find a proposed step-by-step coded solution in the book's repository.

5.5   *Further reading*

Propensity scores were proposed by Paul R. Rosenbaum and Donald B. Rubin in the paper "The Central Role of the Propensity Score in Observational Studies for Causal Effects" (1983).

There is a large body of literature about propensity scores, especially in healthcare. Here we have only given an introduction to the subject. If you want to become a propensity score expert, you can expand your knowledge by reading specialized papers on the topic. We recommend the introductory paper "An Introduction to Propensity Score Methods for Reducing the Effects of Confounding in Observational Studies" by Peter C. Austin, and the references therein; or check out the book *Propensity Score Analysis* by Shenyang Guo and Mark W. Fraser (SAGE Publications, 2009).

5.6   *Chapter quiz*

As we conclude the chapter, it's important to ensure that you have a solid understanding of the key concepts. Here are the essential questions you should be able to answer clearly and concisely. If you can't, I suggest rereading the corresponding references:

1 Why is matching patients from different treatment groups based on their covariates more complex than it sounds in practice?
   Answer in section 5.1.3

2 Which variables should we consider when calculating the propensity scores?
   Answer in the section "Which variables should we match on?"

3 Why do we need to use machine learning models to estimate propensity scores?
   Answer in section 5.3.2

4 When training a machine learning model to estimate the propensity score, we aim for the highest accuracy. However, we hope for the worst accuracy. Why?
   Answer in the section "Is a higher AUC better?"

5 Imagine that you gather all patients with a similar propensity score into a group, regardless of their individual traits. Can you estimate the ATE for this group by comparing the average outcomes of those who were treated versus those who were not?
   Answer in section 5.1.4

6 The answer to the previous question is "yes." Why?
   Answer in section 5.1.4

7 What is the average treatment effect on the treated?
   Answer in the section "Visual assessment"

Summary

- Propensity scores are a flexible tool that lets us assess whether the positivity assumption holds. When the assumption is not held in our data, we can try to look for a subset of patients where it holds.
- Once we have calculated the propensity scores, we can reuse them to calculate ATEs.
- If we have many outcomes, propensity scores can be calculated and the positivity assumption assessed once and then reused on each outcome for calculating ATEs.

Direct and indirect effects with linear models

6

This chapter covers

- Calculating causal effects using linear regression when the treatment is a continuous variable
- Decomposing the effect of a variable into direct and indirect effects
- Propagating correlations through the graph

Up to now, we've focused on treatment variables that take just two values, typically 0 or 1. However, many real-world scenarios involve continuous treatment variables. For instance, consider a company trying to determine how flight pricing affects demand to find the optimal price that maximizes profits. For flights from Barcelona to Mallorca, the price may be set at discrete intervals (like 80€, 85€, or 90€), or it can vary continuously within a range (from 80€ to 90€).

When dealing with continuous variables, linear models are one of the simplest and most interpretable methods available. A *linear model* is used to describe the relationship between variables. Practically, to build a linear model from data, we perform a *linear regression*. This method calculates the coefficients of the linear model that best fit our data.

150

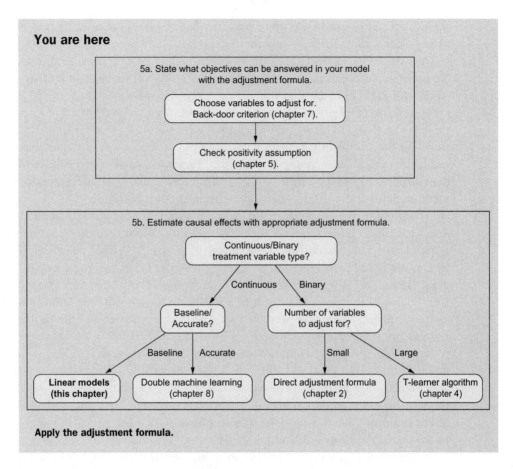

Although linear models are traditional, they remain widely used in many fields, including statistics, econometrics, and machine learning, demonstrating their enduring relevance and utility in both research and practical applications.

Let's use the example of airline seat price versus demand to see the relationship between causal effects and the coefficients of linear regression. For instance, the company wants to learn the relationship between price and demand from its historical data. So, the data scientists model such a relationship with a linear model in which demand, measured as the number of booked seats for each flight, is expressed in terms of the price of the flight and whether the flight takes place on a holiday. Here is the formula they use to express this relationship:

$$\text{seats} = \beta + \beta_1 \text{ price} + \beta_2 \text{ holidays} + \varepsilon$$

ε is the random term that represents all the rest of the factors related to *seats* but not related to the variables *price* and *holidays*. The coefficient β_1 measures the increase in the number of booked seats when *price* increases by one unit and the rest of the variables—in this case, *holidays*—remain unchanged.

At first, it may seem that β_1 measures the effect of *price* on *seats*. But be careful! Now that we know a little about causal inference, we can see that things may not be so straightforward. Imagine that the airline drops the price of flights during economic crises and increases prices when times are good. If so, we may find that whenever the price is low, demand is low, and when the price is high, demand is high. So, when we calculate the coefficient β_1 from data using linear regression, the coefficient will be positive because, historically speaking, a higher price is correlated with higher demand. But a positive coefficient β_1 contradicts basic economic theory because an increase in price should negatively affect the demand, decreasing it.

The problem that arises from this example is that the coefficients obtained from the dataset through linear regression do not reflect a causal relationship—only correlations. However, we need to know the causal relationship between price and demand so we can predict what will happen if we set a particular price. Finding correlations is not good enough because they only reflect what happened in the past in a particular context. So, we cannot trust the result of a linear regression until we know more details about the possible effects of other factors. And that is what we will learn in this chapter: *when we can interpret the regression coefficients as causal effects, and when we cannot.*

This chapter is divided into two sections. In simple terms, we'll tackle the same topic in each section but from two different angles: first from a programming perspective and then from a mathematical standpoint. We'll work with causal models involving three variables: treatment, outcome, and a third variable whose role changes in the different examples. We'll explore how the coefficients of a linear regression are affected by the causal model we use and the variables we choose to include in the regression.

In section 6.1, we will work with an example similar to the airline's situation. We will see in more detail how to estimate causal effects with linear models. The main take-home message of this section is that linear models are very useful for studying problems where the treatment variable is continuous, but depending on the variables we include in the regression, the result may change dramatically. So, we need a methodology that helps us determine which regressions run in each scenario. We will also find that a variable may affect an outcome through different paths: a flight being on a holiday increases demand because people have more free time (a *direct effect: holiday → ticket sales*), but at the same time, if the company decides to raise prices on holidays, the higher price will reduce sales (an *indirect effect: holiday → price → ticket sales*).

Up to now, we have worked with a few simplified examples of graphs. However, in your daily work, you will encounter many situations that lead to a wide variety of causal graphs. In chapter 7, we will see how to work with any type of graph. But before going into the general tools explained in the next chapter, we need to practice with linear models, because they are much easier to understand. So, in section 6.2, we will examine the math behind the application of linear models to causal models. In doing so, we will develop our intuition about how causality and correlations propagate through a graph and why each does so differently.

> ### When should linear models be used in causal inference?
> In the early stages of your analysis, it's a good idea to start with linear models. They are straightforward to understand and simple to use, and they provide initial insight into what your results may be. Additionally, you can use linear models to estimate causal effects whenever your decision or treatment variable is continuous.

6.1 *Estimating causal effects with linear models*

This section focuses on using linear models with causal models to get unbiased estimates. We'll begin with a coded example that introduces some of the challenges you may encounter when applying linear models in causal inference. This example will provide a basic understanding, which will be formally detailed in section 6.1.2.

6.1.1 *Simulating a pricing problem: A walkthrough*

Let's warm up with a practical example. Imagine a fictitious company that we will call Land2Hotel, which owns properties in many towns and has decided to build hotels on them. The properties are located in the center of a town, in its suburbs, or in the countryside. Once each hotel is built, the company sets a price according to the hotel's location. In this example, people want to be near the town, so hotels in the center tend to be more expensive than those in the suburbs, which, in turn, are more expensive than those in the countryside. Two years later, the strategy has been successful and the hotels have become very popular. Seeing the results, Land2Hotel wants to repeat the experience. Unlike the first time, now the company has a lot of data it can analyze. In particular, the company wonders what the effect is of price on the number of customers, and which location is optimal for a hotel. Imagine that we are the analysts in charge of answering these questions.

As explained in chapter 1, I suggest starting to learn a new technique by practicing with made-up data instead of real data. This way, when you reach a conclusion, you can easily check whether it's correct. This idea applies to our hotel-building analysis: we begin by studying a problem for which we already know the answer, using it to figure out the right regression method. Then we can use what we learned to apply linear regression to new situations where we don't know the answer.

We will first synthetically generate our own data from a ground-truth model representing the problem description. Then we will analyze the data with linear models and compare the results with the correct values of the ground-truth model. First we will outline the main steps for the do-it-yourselfers who want to try this on their own. Then we will walk through the process, applying it to our example.

Here are the steps:

1 Draw the graph. Think first about the relevant variables that appear in the description of the problem. These are the nodes. When a variable affects another, draw an arrow between them.

2 Generate the data. Given the variables Price (P), Distance (D), and Customers (C), simulate a sample size of $n = 1,000$ that follows these relationships:

- D takes three possible values: 0 (center of town), 0.5 (suburbs), and 1 (countryside), uniformly at random
- $P := 10 - 3D + \varepsilon_P$, with $\varepsilon_P \sim N(0, 0.5)$
- $C := 30 - 2P - 10D + \varepsilon_C$, with $\varepsilon_C \sim N(0, 2)$

3 Figure the effect of price. We want to know the effect of price on the number of customers. How would you do that using linear regression and the simulated data?

4 Figure the effect of distance. We want to know the effect of distance on the number of customers. How would you do that using linear regression and the simulated data?

Feel free to spend some time working on the problem with just the information provided in these four general steps. To check your solutions (or to skip right to my walk-through), here are the steps applied to our problem.

DRAW THE GRAPH

The description of the problem can be represented with the graph in figure 6.1. Because the price of each hotel is set based on the distance from the town, distance affects the price. To have an arrow in the other direction (Price → Distance), the situation would have to be different: something like the company first deciding on the price and then looking for a property it thought could match the expectations of that price.

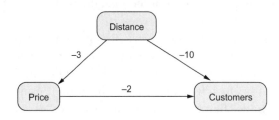

Figure 6.1   Graph illustrating the data-generation process for creating synthetic data, as described in the example. The arrows in the graph are labeled with their corresponding linear coefficients, all of which are negative, as this fits the context of the data modeled.

Notice that all the coefficients of the model (–3, –2, –10) are negative, but it makes sense:

- The further from the town, the lower the price
- The further from town, the fewer customers are willing to come
- The higher the price, the fewer the customers

GENERATE THE DATA

The following two listings (R and Python, respectively) generate the ground-truth data that will be analyzed with linear models with.

Listing 6.1 (R) Creating synthetic data for Land2Hotel

```
set.seed(1234)
n = 1000
D <- sample(c(0,0.5, 1), n, replace = TRUE)
P <- 10 - 3*D + rnorm(n, sd = 0.5)
C <- 30 - 2*P - 10*D + rnorm(n, sd = 2)
```

Listing 6.2 (Python) Creating synthetic data for Land2Hotel

```
from numpy.random import choice, normal
import random
import pandas as pd
random.seed(1234)
n = 1000
distance = choice([0, 0.5, 1], n)
price = 10 - 3*distance + normal(loc=0, scale=.5, size=n)
customers = 30 - 2*price - 10*distance + \
    normal(loc=0, scale=2, size=n)
df = pd.DataFrame({
    'price': price, 'distance': distance, 'customers': customers
})
```

EFFECT OF PRICE

The first thing that comes to mind may be to analyze the effect of price by running a regression of *C* and *P*. Let's see how this works by analyzing the data with a linear regression as shown in the next two listings.

Listing 6.3 (R) Regression `customers ~ price`

```
lm(customers ~ price)
```

Listing 6.4 (Python) Regression `customers ~ price`

```
import statsmodels.formula.api as smf
mod = smf.ols(formula='customers ~ price', data=df)
mod.fit().summary()
```

The results in table 6.1 show that the model that fits the data best is $C = 0.7902 + 0.8535P$. Hmm—this doesn't make sense! The model is saying that the higher the price, the greater the number of customers! But we know for a fact that the effect of price on the number of customers is –2 because we created the data that way.

Table 6.1 Results in R of the regression `customers ~ price`

Coefficient	Estimate	Std error
Intercept	0.7902	0.5164
Price	0.8535	0.0606

Can it be a problem with the linear regression? Does it do something fancy that over-complicates things? Figure 6.2 shows an increasing trend: when price increases, the number of customers increases, too.

Price vs. customers

Figure 6.2   Graph showing the relationship between price and number of customers, with a line representing the linear regression. This linear regression highlights an increasing trend in the data.

Think first, read next

Why don't the results from the regression give the expected result?

The problem is that the variable D is a confounder and messes things up. In figure 6.3, we can see that even though the price trend is positive, the trend is negative in each distance group. We have found ourselves, once again, in a Simpson's paradox.

Price vs. customers including distance

Figure 6.3   Graph showing price versus number of customers, segmented by distance groups. Although the overall global trend is positive, each group shows a negative trend. This phenomenon is known as Simpson's paradox.

When we had a binary treatment variable in the presence of confounders, we applied the adjustment formula. With linear regression, we will follow a different path (even though—spoiler alert—we will end up again with the adjustment formula). Instead of regressing C with respect to P, we will also include D.

Listing 6.5   (R) Regression `customers ~ price + distance`

```
lm(customers ~ price + distance)
```

> **Listing 6.6 (Python) Regression** `customers ~ price + distance`

```
mod = smf.ols(formula='customers ~ price + distance', data=df)
mod.fit().summary()
```

The coefficient obtained, including the distance is –1.992 (see table 6.2), which is almost the correct coefficient, –2.

Table 6.2 Results in R of the regression `customers ~ price + distance`

Coefficient	Estimate	Std error
Intercept	29.9413	1.3491
Price	–1.9915	0.1345
Distance	–9.9004	0.4355

Our conclusion is that to correctly estimate the effect of price on the number of customers, we need to include distance in the regression. We still don't know why distance has to be included or what it has to do with the adjustment formula, but the reasons are related to the fact that it is a confounder, and checking it empirically with data gives the expected result of the coefficient of the price (–2).

EFFECT OF DISTANCE

What about the effect of distance on the number of customers? You may think that the regression in the previous section in listing 6.6 or 6.5 already does the job. It shows us (in R) that the weight of the distance is –9.900, which is very close to the real –10. However, this is only part of the story. In the past, the location of the hotel also affected the decision of which price to set. When a hotel is further from town, fewer people are willing to come, which is a negative effect; but at the same time, prices are lower, which is appealing to customers, thus creating a positive effect. The first is a direct effect, and the second is an indirect effect.

At this point, we need to ask ourselves whether we are going to use the same pricing policy as in the past. If we are, the effect of distance on the number of customers is not only –10 but the sum of the direct and indirect effects: the total effect.

The questions now are these: What is the total effect in our model? How do we calculate it from the data? The equations will help us answer the first question. Because $P := 10 - 3D + \varepsilon_P$, we can substitute P in the second equation:

$$C := 30 - 2P - 10D + \varepsilon_C = 30 - 2(10 - 3D + \varepsilon_P) - 10D + \varepsilon_C =$$
$$10 + (6 - 10)D - 2\varepsilon_P + \varepsilon_C = 10 - 4D - 2\varepsilon_P + \varepsilon_C$$

When we change D, through the direct and indirect paths, C changes with a coefficient of –4. The total effect is –4, the direct effect is –10, and the indirect effect is $-2 \times (-3) = 6$. But where does this 6 appear in the regression we run earlier? It doesn't appear anywhere, so we probably need to run a different regression. The main point here is, which confounders are between the distance and the number of customers?

There are none! In chapter 2, we saw that when there are no confounders, we shouldn't apply the adjustment formula: we can measure the effects of one variable on the other with direct calculations (difference in means) without considering any other variable. So, let's try to run a simple regression of *D* into *C*.

Listing 6.7   (R) Linear model regressing customers respect with respect to distance

```
lm(customers ~ distance)
```

Listing 6.8   (Python) Linear model regressing customers with respect to distance

```
mod = smf.ols(formula='customers ~ distance', data=df)
mod.fit().summary()
```

We obtain a coefficient of –3.898 (table 6.3), which is close to –4, the correct coefficient.

Table 6.3   Results in R of the regression `customers ~ distance`

Coefficient	Estimate	Std error
Intercept	10.02	0.12
Price	–3.90	0.18

If, on the other hand, we want to use a different pricing policy from the one used in the past, we should calculate the effect distance will have in the future with the new strategy. For instance, if we are going to lower the price by 2.5 (instead of 3, as in the past), the expected total effect (with the estimated data) is as follows (using the rationale with the earlier equations):

$$P := 10 - 2.5D + \varepsilon_P C := 29.941 - 1.992P - 9.900D + \varepsilon_C =$$
$$-1.992(-2.5D) - 10D + \text{other factors} =$$
$$-5.02D + \text{other factors}$$

The total effect is –5.02. Notice that the new pricing policy is something we can decide on our own, whereas the effect of distance and price on the customers is something that reality decides.

We conclude that to estimate the effect of distance on the number of customers, we need to consider direct and indirect effects. And in this case, we can calculate their sum, called the total effect, using linear regression without including price as a regressor.

In causal inference, choosing a model based on its fitting error may be a mistake

This example highlights an important difference between causal inference and supervised learning: selecting the model with the lowest error can be misleading in causal inference. For instance, if you want to determine the total effect of distance on the number of customers, a regression model like $C \sim D + P$ may show a lower fitting error. However, the correct model to use would be $C \sim D$, even though it has a higher fitting error.

6.1.2 Direct and indirect effects

In the previous section, we informally introduced different ways a variable can affect another: the direct and indirect effects. Let's give formal definitions for them, plus the definition of total effect.

Decomposition of effects of a variable X into a variable Y

- *Total effect*—When we change the value of X, how does it change the value of Y?
- *Direct effect*—When we change the value of X, but the values of the rest of the system's variables excluding Y are fixed, how does the value of Y change? This corresponds to the direct arrow from X to Y.
- *Indirect effect*—When we change the value of X, how does it change the value of Y through all the paths excluding the direct path?

Direct and indirect effects can also be defined with nonlinear models. However, their definition is more involved and requires the knowledge of counterfactuals, a notion that is outside the scope of this book.

In linear models we always have

total effect = direct effect + indirect effect

But be aware that this is not the case with nonlinear models.

Change of notation

In the remainder of this chapter and in chapter 7, we are going to change the variable notation to X, Y, Z instead of T, C, O. The main reason is to get used to seeing the same graph from different perspectives. For example, depending on the analysis we want to do, a variable may play the role of the treatment, the mediator, or a confounder.

We began this approach in chapter 3 with the topic/pageviews example, as shown in the figure. For instance, if we're analyzing the effect of the topic on pageviews, the platform serves as a mediator. Conversely, if we want to determine which platform performs better, the platform is treated as the treatment variable.

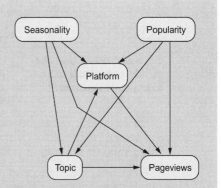

Graph illustrating the influence of Topic on Pageviews. This graph can help us understand how the topic affects the number of pageviews a page receives. Additionally, we may also explore how the platform affects pageviews.

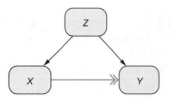

Figure 6.4   Causal path $X \to Y$ with a confounder. In causal diagrams, causality is transmitted through these paths. For example, a change in X leads to a change in Y because of the influence that X exerts on Y via the path between them.

In any DAG, causal effects (total, direct, or indirect) from a variable X to a variable Y only propagate through directed paths: those paths starting from X and ending on Y, $X \to Z_1 \to \dots \to X_k \to Y$, where Z_i are nodes in the graph. For instance, a path $X \leftarrow Z \to Y$, as found in the presence of confounders, is not a causal path. Remember that the direction of the arrows in a DAG—for instance, $X \to Y$—means if you alter the value of X, the value of Y can change, but altering the value of Y does not affect X. So, the path $X \leftarrow Z \to Y$ is not a causal path because altering X will not affect Z, and thus Y (through this path). In figure 6.4, the causal path is $X \to Y$.

DIRECT AND INDIRECT EFFECTS IN PRACTICE USING REGRESSION

Whenever we have a three-node DAG with variables X, Y, and Z and we want to find the causal effect from X to Y, as shown in table 6.4, the variable Z can take one of the following roles:

- *Confounder*—Z is a common cause of both X and Y.
- *Mediator*—X is a cause of Z, and Z is a cause of Y.
- *Collider*—X and Y are both causes of Z.

Table 6.4   In a three-node graph where X influences Y without any independence assumptions, there are only three possible roles for node Z.

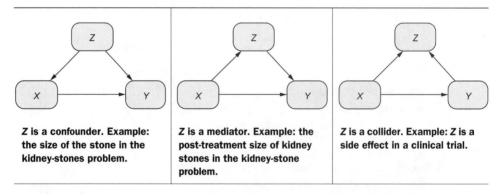

| Z is a confounder. Example: the size of the stone in the kidney-stones problem. | Z is a mediator. Example: the post-treatment size of kidney stones in the kidney-stone problem. | Z is a collider. Example: Z is a side effect in a clinical trial. |

Example of a collider

We've just introduced colliders for the first time in this book. Let's see an example. Imagine running an RCT where you want to test a new treatment to cure a specific illness. This new treatment is far from perfect, and even though it seems to cure more people than the previous treatment did, it may have side effects.

To describe this situation with a graph, in addition to Treatment and Recovery nodes, we need a Side Effects node. This node depends on the treatment each patient receives. We can also assume that experiencing side effects depends on whether the patient recovered from the illness. So, there is an arrow from Recovery to Side Effects. In this graph, Side Effects plays the role of a collider between Treatment and Recovery.

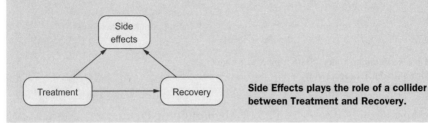

Side Effects plays the role of a collider between Treatment and Recovery.

The objective of this section is to learn how to decide which effect you are interested in (total, direct, or indirect) and which variables you need to include in your linear regression to obtain the expected effects. Now, let's formulate intuitively how to find direct and indirect effects in linear models in three different situations: with confounders, with mediators, and with colliders.

Test your knowledge

Before diving into the details for each case in table 6.4, ask yourself these questions:

- What are the causal paths between X and Y?
- What is the direct effect of X on Y? Should you include the variable Z in the linear regression to get such an effect?
- What is the total effect of X on Y? Should you include the variable Z in the linear regression to get such an effect?

You may need to experiment with the equations to find the answers.

NOTE Throughout the rest of the chapter, we have removed the intercepts in the linear equations because they don't affect the conclusions we are obtaining, and removing them simplifies the notation.

CONFOUNDER EFFECTS

Let's answer the questions posed in the previous "Test your knowledge" box, first when Z is a confounder, as in table 6.5:

1. Direct effect from X to Y: a (the direct arrow)
2. Total effect from X to Y: also a because when we alter the value of X, the only way it can affect Y is by the direct path.

Table 6.5   Confounder: causal path

DAG	In equations
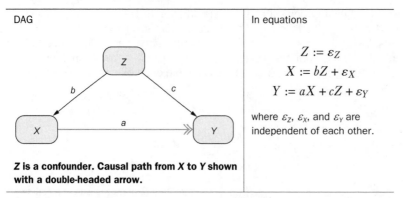 **Z is a confounder. Causal path from X to Y shown with a double-headed arrow.**	$$Z := \varepsilon_Z$$ $$X := bZ + \varepsilon_X$$ $$Y := aX + cZ + \varepsilon_Y$$ where ε_Z, ε_X, and ε_Y are independent of each other.

We know from chapters 2 and 5 that confounding factors can easily lead us to wrong estimates and that an adjustment is necessary. In the pricing example, confounding factors can also mess up our analysis if we are not careful, even when we are working with linear models. This shouldn't be a surprise because when deriving the adjustment formula, we made no assumptions about functional form (the particular equations that relate variables among themselves). So, the same adjustment formula should also work with linear models. That is the case, and we will see how in section 6.2.4.

In the pricing example, we saw that including the confounding variable in the regression (including distance, when looking for the causal effect of price on the number of customers) gave us the correct answer. Now we will see why this is the case.

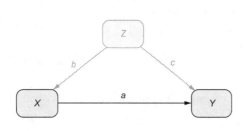

Figure 6.5   Confounding disappears when we condition on Z = 1.

For simplicity, imagine that the variable Z is binary and only takes the values 0, 1. We have already argued in chapters 2 and 5 that when we select a particular subpopulation of the confounder—say, the data for $Z = 1$—the confounding effect disappears. As reflected in figure 6.5, when we condition on $Z = 1$, the variable Z is fixed, so it no longer varies and doesn't affect X or Y.

This means if we regress Y to X, $Y \sim X$, using only the data $Z = 1$, we will obtain a regression coefficient of X, which we will call a_1, that estimates well (without bias) the real coefficient of X in the model: a. This is a good solution but not optimal because we have only used a smaller subset of data (with $Z = 1$). We can then run another regression $Y \sim X$ with the rest of the data, with $Z = 0$, and obtain another unbiased estimate a_0. Finally, having two unbiased estimates, it is natural to calculate the mean of both to get an unbiased estimate of the coefficient a.

But what happens when Z is not binary? We cannot run a regression for each value of Z, because if Z is continuous, in most cases each value of $Z = z$ will appear once in the dataset (for instance, if Z is the age of a client measured in minutes, you are unlikely to see two clients with the same age)!

Fortunately, there is no need to run many regressions, one for each value of Z. The way to go is to directly run a regression with X and Z, $Y \sim X + Z$ as we did in the pricing example, including the confounder distance: such a regression can handle continuous values of Z and correctly estimate the coefficient of X.

MEDIATOR EFFECTS

Now let's answer the "Think first, read next" questions when Z is a mediator, as in table 6.6:

1 Direct effect from X to Y: a
2 Total effect from X to Y: using the same logic as in the previous pricing example when calculating the effect of distance on the number of customers, we can substitute Z in Y by its dependency on X:

$$Y := aX + cZ + \varepsilon_Y = \varepsilon_X + c(bX + \varepsilon_Z) + \varepsilon_Y = (a + cb)X + c\varepsilon_Z + \varepsilon_Y$$

So the total effect is $a + cb$.

Table 6.6 Mediator: causal paths

DAG	In equations
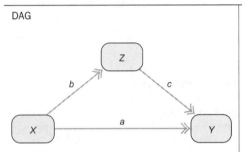 Mediator: causal paths shown with double-headed arrows comprise the direct path from **X** to **Y** and the path that goes through **Z**.	$$Z := bX + \varepsilon_Z$$ $$X := \varepsilon_X$$ $$Y := aX + cZ + \varepsilon_Y$$ where ε_Z, ε_X, and ε_Y are independent of each other.

To calculate the direct effect, we must include the mediator in the regression $Y \sim X + Z$. The direct effect is the coefficient of X in that regression. To understand why, the same argument that we used in the confounder case works here: if we are conditioning on Z, the value of Z is fixed, so we are removing its effect, and the only remaining causal effect comes from the direct arrow $X \to Y$.

On the other hand, if we want to capture all the influence that X exerts on Y, we should run the regression $Y \sim X$. One way to see this is that because there are no confounders between X and Y, a difference in means without adjusting for confounders will work.

COLLIDER EFFECTS

The third and last case we can construct with three variables is shown in table 6.7, where the arrows of X and Y point toward Z. In this case, we say that Z is a *collider*:

1 Direct effect from X to Y: a
2 Total effect from X to Y: a

In this case, there are no confounding factors between X and Y, so no adjustment is necessary. Moreover, Y only depends on X and not Z. So, running a regression $Y \sim X$ estimates both the direct and total effects.

Table 6.7   Collider: only the direct path is a causal path.

DAG	In equations
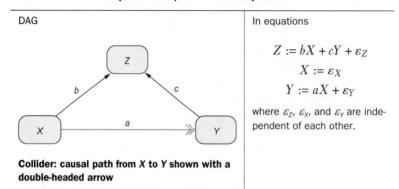 Collider: causal path from *X* to *Y* shown with a double-headed arrow	$$Z := bX + cY + \varepsilon_Z$$ $$X := \varepsilon_X$$ $$Y := aX + \varepsilon_Y$$ where ε_Z, ε_X, and ε_Y are independent of each other.

SUMMARY OF THE TYPES OF EFFECTS AND WHICH LINEAR REGRESSIONS TO USE IN EACH CASE

Table 6.8 summarizes the three scenarios so you can check the differences between them. In each case, the regression coefficient corresponding to the X variable gives you the estimate.

Table 6.8   Effects between X and Y, and how to estimate them

Case	Direct effect	Estimation direct effect	Total effect	Estimation total effect
Confounder	a	$Y \sim X + Z$	a	$Y \sim X + Z$
Mediator	a	$Y \sim X + Z$	$a + bc$	$Y \sim X$
Collider	a	$Y \sim X$	a	$Y \sim X$

So far we have talked about the case where we have three variables X, Y, and Z. What happens when we have many confounders: when Z is a vector? The rationale for the three cases (confounder, mediator, and collider) when Z is a vector is the same, so table 6.8 is still useful.

Conclusion

Notice that all three cases are different. So, for each causal problem you face, before jumping into analyzing the data, ask yourself the following:

- Which case are you working on? Check the model you created for your problem, and see which situation fits your case best.
- Which effect are you interested in? It should be aligned with the objective of the analysis.
- Which is the correct regression to apply? Check out table 6.8.

6.2   Understanding causal dynamics through linear models

So far, we have worked with a simplified set of graphs in this book. We have mostly seen confounders, colliders, and mediators, which can be either variables or vectors of variables. But in your daily work, you will face a wide variety of graphs that do not fit the examples we have shown: confounding variables for which there is no data, variables that may be a confounder in some paths and a collider in other paths, different levels of confounding, and so on. And in each case, you will need to know whether you can estimate the causal effects you want and how to do so.

Chapter 7 explains how to deal with complex graphs. It is a very important chapter, but it is not easy to understand. So, before diving deep into causal graph theory, this section provides a transition. Section 6.2.1 uses visualization as a metaphor, which will help you understand the next chapter.

You may find this section fairly technical or theoretical. If you grasp the ideas, you will have half the job done for chapter 7. However, if the math is too much for you, or you begin to lose interest, don't push it; you can always skip it and come back if you need it. I encourage you to at least give it a try!

6.2.1   The analogy of a gas flowing through pipes

There is a helpful analogy for understanding causation in graphs. Imagine correlation as a gas flowing through a pipe network, representing our graph. The key points are as follows:

- Each pipe has a direction, but the gas (correlation) can flow in any direction.
- Preferred paths, or causal paths, start at node X, end at node Y, and follow the direction →.
- Our goal is to measure how much gas flows through these causal paths: if we pump gas into X, how much reaches Y using only causal paths? Because we only measure correlations, we open and close noncausal paths and measure the resulting gas flow.
- We can control paths by conditioning on (or fixing) variables in those paths.

For instance, in figure 6.6, the causal path is $X \to Y$. The correlation can flow through the path $X \to Y$ but also the path $X \leftarrow Z \to Y$ (remember the crazy examples from the Spurious Correlations website where two causally unrelated quantities are shown to be highly correlated because they h*ave a common factor: the confounder). When we condition on Z, we are closing the path* $X \leftarrow Z \to Y$, so the remaining correlation takes the causal path. The challenge is how to play this opening–closing paths game when we have complex graphs (which will be seen in the next chapter).

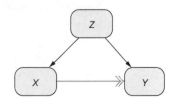

Figure 6.6   Causal path in the confounder case

6.2.2   *How correlation flows through a graph*

The task for this section is to mathematically calculate the correlation of the three cases we have worked with (confounders, mediators, and colliders) and see how conditioning affects the correlation. This calculation will lead us to what is known as *path analysis,* which was discovered by Sewall Wright in 1921 and explains how to calculate correlations from the effects of each path.

For the confounder, mediator, and collider cases, we want to answer the following:

1 What is the correlation between X and Y? Calculate the regression coefficient of X in the regression $Y \sim X$.

2 Calculate the regression coefficient of X in the regression $Y \sim X + Z$.

3 How are the previous quantities related to the direct and total effects?

You can follow this section as a walkthrough exercise that you try on your own, and later you can check your results with the ones shown here. You can also read it as a step-by-step example if you prefer. If you find the math hard to swallow, don't push yourself too hard. You can always revisit it. We're going to work on some correlations next; just check that they make sense to you. The intuition is the same as in the previous sections.

We will need some basic statistical equations. They are shown next; be sure you know them!

Reminder of basic equations about variance, covariance, and correlation

If X, Y, and Z are random variables and a and b are constants:

- Relationship between variance and covariance: $var(X) = cov(X, X))$
- Behavior of constants in the variance formula: $var(aX) = a^2\,var(X)$
- Covariance of a linear combination: $cov(aX + bY, Z) = a\,cov(X, Z) + b\,cov(Y, Z)$
- Variance of the sum of two independent variables X, Y: $var(X + Y) = var(X) + var(Y)$

Definition of correlation: $cor(X, Y) = \dfrac{cov(X, Y)}{var(X)^{\frac{1}{2}} var(Y)^{\frac{1}{2}}}$

Reminder of basic equations coefficients in linear regression

When doing a linear regression of Y into X, we assume that the expectation of Y given X has a linear form $E[Y|X] = a + bX$. The formula for the regression coefficient b that we obtain running a linear regression from data that we will write as $Y \sim X$ is

$$b = \frac{cov(X, Y)}{var(X)}$$

When doing a linear regression of Y into X and Z, we assume that the expectation of Y given X has a linear form $E[Y|X] = a + bX + cZ$. The formula for the regression coefficient b that we obtain running a linear regression from data that we will write as $Y \sim X + Z$ in this case is a little more involved:

$$b = \frac{\mathrm{cov}(Y, X) - \mathrm{cov}(X, Z)\mathrm{cov}(Z, Y)}{1 - \mathrm{cov}(X, Z)^2}$$

Throughout this exercise, we will assume that variables X, Y, and Z are standardized (sometimes called normalized) because the equations become much easier to handle:

- $E[X] = E[Y] = E[Z] = 0$
- $\mathrm{var}(X) = \mathrm{var}(Y) = \mathrm{var}(Z) = 1$

You can always standardize a variable X if you transform it into $\frac{X - E[X]}{\mathrm{var}(X)}$.

Note that because the variables are standardized, the correlation between any two of them is the covariance. For instance,

$$\mathrm{cor}(X, Y) = \frac{\mathrm{cov}(X, Y)}{\mathrm{var}(X)^{\frac{1}{2}}\mathrm{var}(Y)^{\frac{1}{2}}} = \mathrm{cov}(X, Y)$$

because $\mathrm{var}(X) = \mathrm{var}(Y) = 1$. At the same time, the covariance coincides with the regression coefficient of X in the regression $Y \sim X$, because $\frac{\mathrm{cov}(X, Y)}{\mathrm{var}(X)} = \mathrm{cov}(X, Y)$. So, for this exercise, the correlation and the covariance are the same quantity.

CONFOUNDER CORRELATION

Let's analyze the confounder's diagram shown in table 6.9.

Table 6.9 Confounder case

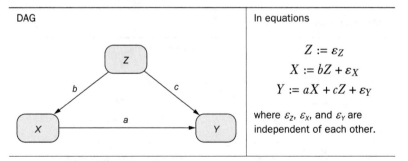

DAG	In equations
	$Z := \varepsilon_Z$ $X := bZ + \varepsilon_X$ $Y := aX + cZ + \varepsilon_Y$ where ε_Z, ε_X, and ε_Y are independent of each other.

1 Calculate the regression coefficient of X in the regression $Y \sim X$. Let's first calculate

$$\mathrm{cov}(X, Z) = \mathrm{cov}(bZ + \varepsilon_X, Z) = b\,\mathrm{cov}(Z, Z) = b\,\mathrm{var}(Z) = b$$

Then

$$\text{cov}(X, Y) = \text{cov}(X, aX + cZ + \varepsilon_Y) = a + cb$$

2 Calculate the regression coefficient of X in the regression $Y \sim X + Z$. Let's first calculate

$$\text{cov}(Z, Y) = \text{cov}(Z, aX + cZ + \varepsilon_Y) = \text{cov}(Z, aX) + \text{cov}(Z, cZ) = ba + c$$

We need to calculate the long formula:

$$\frac{\text{cov}(Y, X) - \text{cov}(X, Z)\text{cov}(Z, Y)}{1 - \text{cov}(X, Z)^2} = \frac{a + cb - b(ba + c)}{1 - b^2} = a$$

3 We see that the correlation is $a + c\,b$, which involves all the paths from X to Y. That's why the analogy is gas propagating through all the paths, as in figure 6.7. On the other hand, when we condition on Z, the resulting coefficient is a, the direct effect.

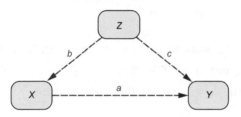

Figure 6.7   Confounder case. Correlation propagation goes through every arrow.

MEDIATOR CORRELATION

Let's analyze the mediator's diagram shown in table 6.10.

Table 6.10   Mediator case

DAG	In equations
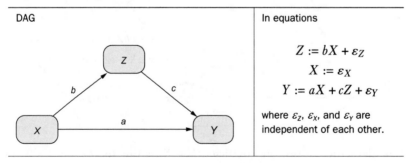	$Z := bX + \varepsilon_Z$ $X := \varepsilon_X$ $Y := aX + cZ + \varepsilon_Y$ where ε_Z, ε_X, and ε_Y are independent of each other.

1 Calculate the regression coefficient of X in the regression $Y \sim X$. Using the expression of

$$Y := aX + cZ + \varepsilon_Y = aX + c(bX + \varepsilon_Z) + \varepsilon_Y = (a + cb)X + c\varepsilon_Z + \varepsilon_Y$$

we have that

$$\text{cov}(X, Y) = \text{cov}(X, (a + cb)X + c\varepsilon_Z + \varepsilon_Y) = a + cb$$

2 Calculate the regression coefficient of X in the regression $Y \sim X + Z$. We need to calculate

$$\text{cov}(Z, X) = b\,\text{cov}(X, X) = b$$
$$\text{cov}(Z, Y) = \text{cov}(Z, aX + cZ + \varepsilon_Y) = \text{cov}(Z, aX) + \text{cov}(Z, cZ) = ba + c$$

Now we can apply the long formula:

$$\frac{\text{cov}(Y, X) - \text{cov}(X, Z)\text{cov}(Z, Y)}{1 - \text{cov}(X, Z)^2} = \frac{a + cb - b(ba + c)}{1 - b^2} = a$$

3 In this case, the correlation and the total effect coincide; see figure 6.8. But when we control for the variable Z, we cut the correlation that goes through the indirect path, obtaining only the correlation that goes through the direct path.

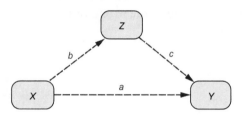

Figure 6.8   Mediator case. As in the confounder case, correlation propagates through every arrow.

COLLIDER CORRELATION

Let's analyze the colliders's diagram shown in table 6.11.

Table 6.11   Collider case

DAG	In equations
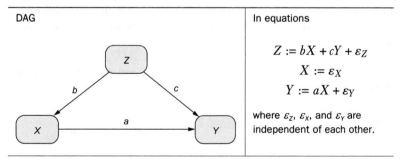	$Z := bX + cY + \varepsilon_Z$ $X := \varepsilon_X$ $Y := aX + \varepsilon_Y$ where ε_Z, ε_X, and ε_Y are independent of each other.

1 Calculate the regression coefficient of X in the regression $Y \sim X$. We have that

$$\text{cov}(X, Y) = \text{cov}(X, aX + \varepsilon_Y) = a$$

2 Calculate the regression coefficient of X in the regression $Y \sim X + Z$. We need to calculate

$$\frac{\text{cov}(X,Y)}{\text{var}(X)} = \text{cov}(X,Y) = a$$

3 Which coefficient of X do we get when we regress Y into X and also Z? We need to first calculate

$$\text{cov}(Z,X) = b \, \text{cov}(bXcY\varepsilon_Z, X) = b + c \, \text{cov}(Y,X) = b + ca$$
$$\text{cov}(Z,Y) = \text{cov}(bX + cY + \varepsilon_Z, Y) = b \, \text{cov}(X,Y) + c \, \text{cov}(Y,Y) = ba + c$$

Now we can apply the long formula:

$$\frac{\text{cov}(Y,X) - \text{cov}(X,Z)\text{cov}(Z,Y)}{1 - \text{cov}(X,Z)^2} = \frac{a - (b+ca)(ba+c)}{1 - (b+ca)^2}$$

which gives an expression that cannot be simplified as in the other cases.

4 We see that correlation cannot flow through a collider, as in figure 6.9. Moreover, if we estimate the direct or total effects, including the variable Z in the regression, it will include bias, giving us the wrong result.

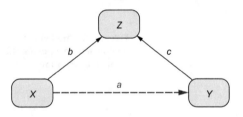

Figure 6.9   **Collider case. Correlation only propagates through the causal path.**

CORRELATION AND CAUSATION COMPARISON

Putting together the three cases, table 6.12 illustrates the differences between causal paths (double-headed arrows) and paths through which correlation propagates (dashed lines). These are the sources of conflict when we try to estimate causation from correlation!

Table 6.12   Differences between causal paths (dashed lines) and correlation propagation (double-headed arrows)

Case	Causal paths	Correlation propagation
Confounder	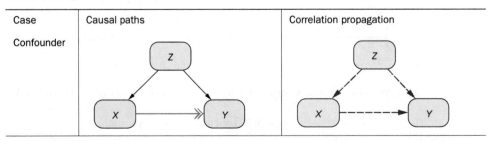	

Table 6.12   Differences between causal paths (dashed lines) and correlation propagation (double-headed arrows) *(continued)*

Mediator	
Collider	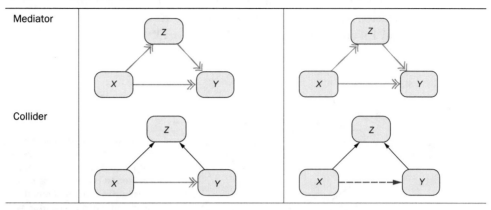

6.2.3   *Calculating causation and correlation from the arrows' coefficients*

Now that we have experience calculating total effects and correlations, we can find a pattern that lets us work them out without having to do the algebraic calculations. At the end of the day, we calculated these quantities based on the coefficients on the graph's arrows.

CORRELATIONS

Let's attempt to generalize how correlations are calculated using the cases in the sections "Confounder correlation," "Mediator correlation," and "Collider correlation" where all the variables are normalized. We have seen that correlation propagates through causal paths but also through paths containing a confounder. The only paths correlation can't go through are those containing colliders. The correlation that flows in each path is the multiplication of its coefficients (keep in mind the indirect paths in the sections "Confounder correlation" and "Mediator correlation"). So, to calculate correlation, we need to multiply the coefficients on each path that propagates correlation and then add them up.

In 1921, Wright demonstrated that our initial approach is a valid method. He showed that to find the correlation between two variables based on the linear coefficients in a graph's arrows, we just need to follow these steps when all variables are normalized (the non-normalized case is a bit more complex):

1 Consider all the paths from X to Y, except those that at some point contain a collider. The paths should contain consecutive arrows of the type $\rightarrow\rightarrow$, $\leftarrow\leftarrow$, or $\leftarrow\rightarrow$, but no part of the path should be like this: $\rightarrow\leftarrow$.

2 For each of the selected paths, multiply all the coefficients of the path. For instance, in the path in figure 6.10, the propagated correlation between X and Y is the product $a\,b\,c$.

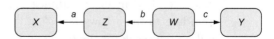

Figure 6.10   A path between X and Y with a confounder. The correlation between X and Y can be calculated by multiplying the coefficients (when variables are normalized): *a b c.*

3 Then the correlation is the sum of all the obtained products through all the selected paths. For example, in figure 6.11, there are only two (of the three) selected paths: $X \leftarrow Z \leftarrow W \rightarrow Y$ and $X \rightarrow E \rightarrow Y$. And the correlation between X and Y if all variables are normalized is $cor(X, Y) = abc + de$.

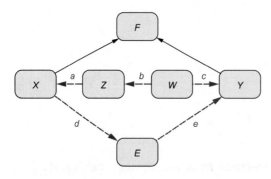

Figure 6.11   **A graph with three paths from X to Y: a path with a mediator, a path with a confounder, and another with a collider. In this case, the correlation only propagates through the path with a confounder and a mediator, which is abc + de (if variables are normalized).**

CAUSAL EFFECTS

Is there a similar procedure for calculating not correlation but total effects? Yes, there is. Moreover, it works whenever variables are standardized. The example shown in table 6.13 is probably the best one to give us a clue about how it is done.

Table 6.13   **DAG and linear models of a mediator scenario**

DAG	In equations
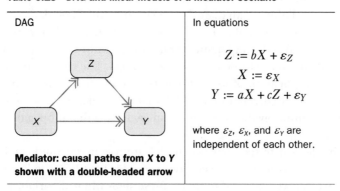 Mediator: causal paths from X to Y shown with a double-headed arrow	$$Z := bX + \varepsilon_Z$$ $$X := \varepsilon_X$$ $$Y := aX + cZ + \varepsilon_Y$$ where ε_Z, ε_X, and ε_Y are independent of each other.

Recall that to calculate the total effect, we substituted the definition of Z into Y

$$Y := aX + cZ + \varepsilon_Y = aX + c(bX + \varepsilon_Z) + \varepsilon_Y = (a + cb)X + c\varepsilon_Z + \varepsilon_Y$$

which resulted in the multiplication of the coefficients of the indirect path, corresponding to the arrows $X \rightarrow Z$ and $Z \rightarrow Y$. The total effect can then be obtained by adding the result for the direct and indirect paths. This process is correct whether we have paths with 2 arrows, as in this example, or paths with 1,000 arrows. The process is still the same. So, to calculate the total effects based on the values of the arrows, we will do the following:

1 Consider all the causal paths from X to Y, which include paths $X \to \dots \to Y$, where all the arrows are of the type $\to\to$.

2 For each of the causal paths, multiply all the coefficients of the path.

3 Sum all the products obtained in the previous step for each causal path.

6.2.4 *Linear models and the "do" operator*

So far, we have seen how to estimate causal effects in linear models. But how do these relate to the techniques we have learned in other chapters? The regression techniques used in this chapter are a particular variation of the adjustment formula and the do operator.

> ### Controlling for covariates
>
> In linear regression jargon, instead of saying that we adjust for some variable Z, we say that we *control for* variable Z. That means we are including Z as a covariate in a linear regression between variables X and Y so that the resulting coefficient of X can be interpreted causally.

Let's see this relationship between linear regression and the "do" operator. Consider the DAG in table 6.14, which shows a combination of a confounder, a direct effect, a mediator, and a collider.

Table 6.14 DAG and linear models combining a mediator, collider, and confounder.

DAG	In equations
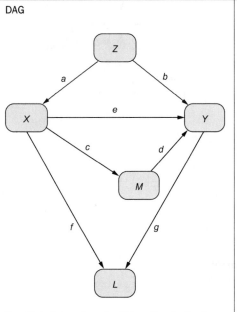 Combining a confounder (**Z**), a direct effect, a mediator (**M**), and a collider (**L**)	$$Z := \varepsilon_Z$$ $$X := aZ + \varepsilon_X$$ $$M := cX + \varepsilon_M$$ $$Y := bZ + eX + dM + \varepsilon_Y$$ where ε_Z, ε_X, ε_M, and ε_Y are independent of each other.

Recall that when we have a treatment variable with two options A and B, the effect of the treatment on an outcome variable Y—the average treatment effect (ATE)—is $ATE = E[Y|do(X = A)] - E[Y|do(X = B)]$. The ATE is our first objective in causal inference. How can we apply this notion to our current graph with linear models?

The first difference is that now, the X, the variable that does the role of the treatment, is continuous and can take not only two options but any real number. So, comparing two by two would take a lot of work! Because that is not practical, we will take another approach. Given a particular value of the variable $X = x_0$, we will calculate the effect of increasing X by one unit. That is,

$$\text{ATE}(x_0) = E[Y|do(X = x_0)] - E[Y|do(X = x_0 + 1)]$$

As you may have realized, this ATE varies for every x_0. Fortunately, as we will see in a minute, the *ATE for linear models is constant (independent of x_0)*. This gives us a global ATE, which is much more convenient.

Table 6.15 shows the effect of the "do" operator: removing all incoming arrows to X (actually, there is just only one). We know from the developments in this chapter that the direct effect is e and the total effect is $e + cd$.

Table 6.15 **DAG and linear models after an intervention on node x_0.**

DAG	In equations
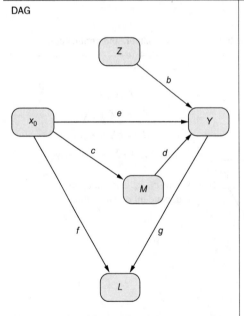	$$Z := \varepsilon_Z$$ $$X := x_0$$ $$M := cX + \varepsilon_M$$ $$Y := bZ + eX + dM + \varepsilon_Y$$ where ε_Z, ε_X, ε_M, and ε_Y are independent of each other.

The effect of an intervention do($X = x_0$) on the DAG in table 6.14. You can see that the arrow from Z to x_0 has been removed, and the value of X is set to x_0.

Now, using the equations that describe the DAG in table 6.15, using the linearity of the expectation E, we can calculate (taking into account that the error terms ε have zero expectation)

$$
\begin{aligned}
E[Y|\mathrm{do}(X = x_0)] &= E[bZ + eX + dM|\mathrm{do}(X = x_0)] \\
&= E[bZ + eX + d(cx_0)|\mathrm{do}(X = x_0)] \\
&= bE[Z|\mathrm{do}(X = x_0)] + ex_0 + dcx_0 \\
&= bE[Z|\mathrm{do}(X = x_0)] + (e + dc)x_0
\end{aligned}
$$

Repeating the process with $x_0 + 1$ (which is practically the same), we can calculate the difference

$$
\mathrm{ATE} \ = E[Y|\mathrm{do}(X = x_0)] - E[Y|\mathrm{do}(X = x_0 + 1)] = e + dc
$$

Well, well, well, it turns out that the ATE is precisely the total effec introduced in this chapter! As you can see, it does not depend on the value of x_0 that we selected.

But what if, instead of estimating causal effects with the techniques developed in this chapter, we wanted to use the adjustment formula from chapter 2? To make a long story short, we would arrive at the same result. For the curious, the following mathematical derivation shows why. Remember that the adjustment formula for the case when the outcome takes many values is

$$
E[Y|\mathrm{do}(X = x_0)] \approx \frac{1}{n}\sum_i E[Y|X = x_0, Z = z_i]
$$

To evaluate it, we proceed in two steps:

1 Estimate the terms $E[Y|X = x,\ Z = z_i]$. Although in chapter 4 we did this using machine learning techniques such as the S- and T-learners, when dealing with linear models, we estimate $E[Y|X = x,\ Z = z_i]$ by running a linear regression from our own data.

2 Average through the different values of z_i.

In the first step, if we run a regression with our data, the result is a pair of coefficients $\widehat{\beta}_1, \widehat{\beta}_2$ that describe the relationship:

$$
Y = \widehat{\beta}_1 X + \widehat{\beta}_2 Z
$$

If we compare this expression with the real relationships between the variables

$$
\begin{aligned}
Y := bZ + eX + dM + \varepsilon_Y &= bZ + eX + d(cX + \varepsilon_M) + \varepsilon_Y = \\
(e + cd)X &+ bZ + d\varepsilon_M + \varepsilon_Y
\end{aligned}
$$

and match the coefficients of variables X and Z, we see that the coefficient $\widehat{\beta}_1$ estimates the value of $e + cd$, whereas the coefficient $\widehat{\beta}_2$ estimates the value of b.

Now we proceed with the second part. We need to calculate the following with the regression obtained in the previous step:

$$E[Y|\mathrm{do}(X = x_0)] \approx \frac{1}{n} \sum_i E[Y|X = x_0, Z = z_i] =$$

$$\frac{1}{n} \sum_i (\widehat{\beta_1}x_0 + \widehat{\beta_2}z_i) = \widehat{\beta_1}x_0 + \widehat{\beta_2}\frac{1}{n} \sum_i z_i$$

Finally,

$$E[Y|\mathrm{do}(X = x_0)] - E[Y|\mathrm{do}(X = x_0 + 1)] \approx$$
$$\widehat{\beta_1}x_0 - \widehat{\beta_1}(x_0 + 1) = \widehat{\beta_1} \approx e + cd$$

arriving at the same estimated value, the total effect, that can be obtained with the linear regression $Y \sim X + Z$.

6.3 *Chapter quiz*

As we conclude the chapter, it's important to ensure that you have a solid understanding of the key concepts. Here are the essential questions you should be able to answer clearly and concisely. If you can't, I suggest rereading the corresponding references:

1 What are total, direct, and indirect effects?
   Answer in section 6.1.2

2 What are total effects, the sum of direct and indirect effects?
   Answer in section 6.1.2

3 Consider a graph with three nodes: X, Y, and a confounder Z. What do we need to control for to calculate the direct effect?
   Answer in the section "Summary of the types of effects and which linear regressions to use in each case"

4 Consider a graph with three nodes: X, Y, and a mediator Z. What do we need to control for to calculate the direct effect?
   Answer in the section "Summary of the types of effects and which linear regressions to use in each case"

5 Consider a graph with three nodes: X, Y, and a confounder Z. What do we need to control for to calculate the direct effect?
   Answer in the section "Summary of the types of effects and which linear regressions to use in each case"

6 What is the relationship between the "do" operator and controlling for variables in a linear model?
   Answer in section 6.2.4

7 What does Wright's method say?
   Answer in section 6.2.2

Summary

- Linear models are an intuitive tool in causal inference. It is recommended that they be used as a preliminary analysis.
- Linear models cannot always be interpreted causally. To do that, you need to answer these questions:
  - Which case are you working on? Are there confounders, mediators, colliders, and so on?
  - Which effect are you interested in: direct, indirect, or total? They should be aligned with the objective of the analysis.
  - What is the correct regression to apply? (See table 6.4.) In other words, which variables should you control for?
- Causal paths from X to Y are those paths starting from X and arriving at Y and always having the same direction $X \to \ldots \to Y$. They represent the different ways X can affect Y causally.
- To decide which variables you need to adjust for, you can use the metaphor of gas through pipes to imagine how correlations propagate and which paths you need to close.

Dealing with
complex graphs

7

This chapter covers

- A mathematical definition of a causal model
- Deriving conditional independencies between variables with d-separation
- Using the back-door criterion to decide which variables to put in the adjustment formula

We now know that one way to remove the effect of confounders is by using the adjustment formula. In real life, we work with complex DAGs, and we will have doubts about which variables to adjust for. Therefore, in this chapter, we answer the following question: given a particular DAG (simple or complex), a treatment, and outcome variables, which variables should we adjust for to estimate the average treatment effect (ATE)?

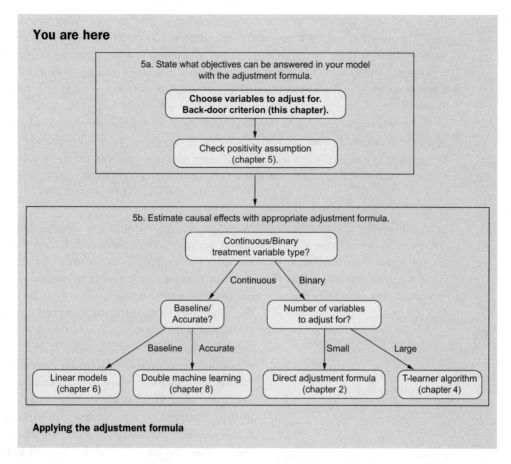

You are here

Applying the adjustment formula

You may wonder why we didn't have trouble choosing the right confounders in the previous chapters. We were working essentially with just one type of graph: the DAG in figure 7.1, where all confounders are known, observed, and without causal relations among them. So, to estimate the causal effect between X and Y, we need to adjust for confounders $Z_1, \ldots, Z_k$. However, you will frequently find unobserved confounders with complex interactions in practice.

For instance, imagine that we work in a company that wants to find the optimal price for a pair of shoes. The company wants to specify several prices and learn the expected number of sales for each one. This way, it can calculate the price that maximizes profits. So, we want to estimate the causal effect of the price on sales. Historically, the company has tried different prices, but no A/B tests were performed.

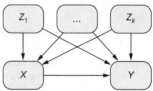

Figure 7.1 We want to estimate a causal effect between X and Y. In this graph, all confounders are known, so there is no problem with unobserved confounders.

This is the same problem we encountered earlier in the book when we wanted to estimate the causal effect of a medical treatment on the outcome of that treatment on patients' health. Here, price substitutes for treatment and the number of sales are the equivalent of the outcome. If you recall, the first step in estimating the causal effect of a factor on an outcome is to identify the confounders that are playing a role in our problem.

So, we go to the pricing department and ask how they set the prices, what policies or guidelines they follow, and what specific information they consider when setting the price. They tell us that they base the price of a pair of shoes on the available stock at the moment: if there are only a few units left, they increase the price, and if there are many left, they reduce the price. They also tell us that they have never run out of stock of any shoe.

Even though the number of shoes in stock affects the price, the variable Stock is not a confounder. Remember, a confounder must affect both X and Y. In this case, it affects X, the price of the shoes, but it does not affect Y, the number of shoes sold. However, that doesn't mean there are no confounders. For example, the country's economic situation affects items sold, determining the remaining stock. In addition,

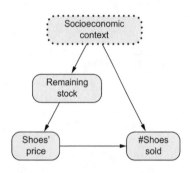

Figure 7.2 Socioeconomic context is the only confounder, but it is unobserved. The remaining stock is observed and can be used to adjust for it.

the remaining stock is the only basis for the current price. But at the same time, the country's economic situation determines future sales. So, the country's economic situation is a confounder. Similarly, other factors, such as the company's competition and new laws, are also confounders. Therefore, we can group all these concepts in a socioeconomic context. Because some of these factors are unobserved, the socioeconomic context is represented as an unobserved confounder in figure 7.2.

To summarize the problem, we know we need to adjust for confounders, but we don't have information about them. Is all hope lost, or do we still have a chance of finding out the effect of price on sales?

One of the things we will learn in this chapter is how to know whether we can overcome the lack of information about confounders. We will also learn to identify DAGs whose causal effects can be estimated from data and detect DAGs for which estimating causal effects from data is impossible.

Another example of a complex graph is shown in figure 7.3; it's adapted from the 2008 paper by Shrier and Platt (see section 7.7). Imagine that we want to know how warm-up exercises may prevent injuries. Shrier and Platt described the whole process and all the variables they considered relevant to this problem.

The relationship between Warm-up Exercises (the treatment variable) and Injury (the outcome) in figure 7.3 goes through many different paths. As a result, the DAG is much more complex than the graphs we have seen in previous chapters.

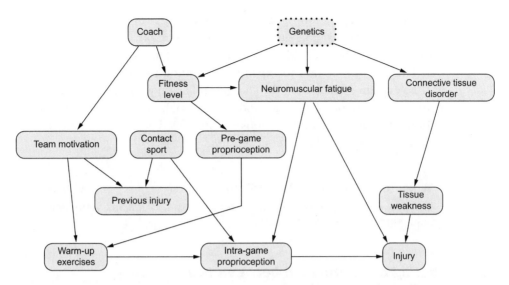

Figure 7.3 Graph describing the complex relationship between warm-up exercises and being injured in sports. As you can see, DAGs can become complex to analyze. (If you aren't familiar with the term, *proprioception* is the sense of self-movement, force, and body position.)

The plan for this chapter is the following, as shown in figure 7.4. The objective is to be able to determine which variables we should adjust for. What do we need to achieve this? Let's open the curtain and see what we need at each stage. The most popular tool for selecting variables to adjust for is the *back-door criterion* (3 in figure 7.4). With the back-door criterion, we can analyze the DAG and remove spurious correlations by conditioning on particular graph nodes. The back-door criterion is an application of

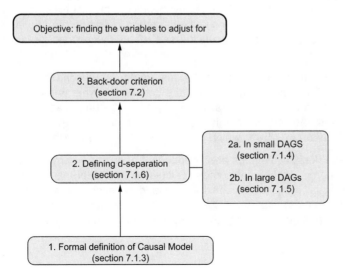

Figure 7.4 Chapter roadmap. We will start from point 1.

the notion of d-separation (2 in figure 7.4), which gives a graphical criterion for how to make two variables independent by conditioning on a third one. To understand d-separation, we will start with elementary three-node graph examples (2a in figure 7.4). Then we will see how to expand d-separation to any type of graph (2b in figure 7.4). To explain d-separation, the chapter will begin with a formal (mathematical, 1 in figure 7.4) definition of a causal model (that's right: we haven't yet provided a formal definition!). The remaining sections will help us digest the content and understand the applications of the back-door criterion.

> **When to use the back-door criterion**
>
> The back-door criterion helps you determine which variables you should choose to adjust in the adjustment formula.

7.1   *Altering the correlation between two variables conditioning on a third one*

In section 6.2.1 in chapter 6, we looked at how correlation is like a gas flowing through a network. We are also interested in measuring how much gas can go through a particular set of pipes called *causal paths*. To do that, we can open or close paths by conditioning on specific variables so the gas only flows through the causal paths.

> **A refresher on probability independence**
>
> The notions of conditioning and independence appear a lot in this chapter. If you don't feel comfortable with conditioning, I recommend you revisit section 1.6.2 in chapter 1. And this sidebar will remind you about probability independence.
>
> Imagine tossing a perfectly balanced coin twice. The probability of getting two heads in a row is 25%. There's a 50% chance of getting heads on the first toss. Then, given heads on the first toss, there's a 50% chance of getting heads on the second toss. Thus, 50% × 50% = 25%. The first result doesn't affect the second because the events are independent.
>
> Now, imagine a different game. If the first toss is heads, the second toss is forced to be heads. If the first toss is tails, we toss the coin again. What is the probability of getting two heads in a row? There is a 50% chance of getting heads on the first toss. In these cases, the second toss is automatically heads. So, the probability of getting two heads in a row is 50%, which differs from the previous example.
>
> Mathematically speaking, two events are independent of one another when the probability of both happening at the same time is calculated by multiplying each probability separately. That is, if D_1 and D_2 are the first and second tosses, respectively, $P(D_1 = \text{heads}, D_2 = \text{heads}) = 50\% \times 50\% = P(D_1 = \text{heads}) \times P(D_2 = \text{heads})$. In general, given two events A and B, we say that they are independent whenever $P(A, B) = P(A) \times P(B)$.

Independence can be combined with conditioning. For example, we say that two events A and B are independent conditioned on C if, conditioning on C (we focus ourselves in those cases where C happens), A and B become independent, which is mathematically written as

$$A \perp B | C$$

This idea that the correlation between two variables can be removed by conditioning on a third one is called *conditional independence*. Let's see some examples.

7.1.1 Arrival time example of conditional independence

Jane and Joe work in the same company. They tend to arrive late at work, and usually, when one is late, the other is, too. Surprisingly, they don't know each other or have common colleagues, friends, or family. The only thing they have in common is that they live outside of town and commute by train every day. Their arrivals are correlated because trains break down frequently and are affected by the same train incidents.

If X and Y are the variables that tell whether Jane and Joe arrive late, respectively, X and Y are highly correlated. However, if on a particular day, the train service, denoted by the variable $Z = 1$, works well, whether Jane arrives late tells you nothing about whether Joe will also arrive late. So, given $Z = 1$, X and Y are independent.

Notice that the situation would be different if, let's say, Jane and Joe met halfway to work and came together. Given that the train service worked well when Jane arrived late, it would be highly probable that Joe also arrived late. Thus, X and Y would not be independent given $Z = 1$.

7.1.2 Mathematical example of conditional independence

Let's now look at another example of conditional independence with a more mathematical flavor. Take a number Z from 1 to 10 uniformly at random. Now take two more numbers at random, X_1, X_2 which are a small perturbation of Z: $X_1 = Z + \delta_1$ and $X_2 = Z + \delta_2$, where δ_1, δ_2 are independently drawn from a random variable that takes values -1, 1 with probabilities 0.5, 0.5, respectively. See figure 7.5 for a representation of this process.

Figure 7.5 Example of conditional independence. First we choose the value of Z at random. Then we choose X_1 and X_2 at random, but close to the value of Z. If we know the value of X_1, we know that X_2 must be close. But if we also know the exact position of Z, the position of X_1 does not provide any useful information.

In general, variables X_1 and X_2 tend to be close to Z, which is also between them. So, if I tell you that $X_1 = 3$, it means Z is either 2 or 4. Thus X_2 can only be 1, 3, or 5. Variables X_1 and X_2 are not independent: if you know the value of one, you have some hints about the whereabouts of the other. But the story changes completely if I tell you that $Z = 2$. Knowing the value of X_1 doesn't help you know more about the variable X_2 because the only information you need is that $Z = 2$. That is, X_1 and X_2 are not independent, but conditionally on Z, they are.

THE ROLE OF GRAPHS IN CONDITIONAL INDEPENDENCE

The notion of conditional independence is probabilistic or statistical. It is defined in terms of probabilities or frequencies. But because we also work with graphs, you may wonder if there is a way to find conditional independencies of variables from their graph structure. As we will see in this chapter, the answer is yes.

Let's go back to our first example with the DAG in figure 7.6: there is no direct causal relationship between Jane and Joe. Nonetheless, they are related to bad train service. The only path connecting X and Y is through Z. And we have deduced that X and Y are independent given Z without seeing any dataset about the process. What we suspect is true is that we can determine some conditional independencies only with the graph and no further data. We will see in this section that when a variable Z d-separates (a notion properly defined later) two variables X and Y in the graph (a graphical notion), the variables X and Y are independent conditioning on Z (a statistical notion).

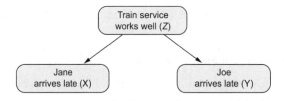

Figure 7.6   Train service affects whether Jane and Joe arrive late. Their lateness is connected. But if we know the train is running smoothly, one being late doesn't necessarily mean the other will be late, too.

Curves ahead

From a theoretical point of view, the following sections are probably the most challenging ones in this book. But they cover key ingredients for working with graphs. If this chapter is too much for you right now, please skip it. You can come back to it once you start working with causal inference and need to use d-separation and the backdoor criterion. And don't forget: you can pose questions on Manning's forum for this book at https://livebook .manning.com/forum?product=ruizdevilla&page=1.

We will start this section by understanding conditional independence on simple graphs containing only three variables. Then, in section 7.1.6, we will formally define d-separation with any number of variables and how it relates to conditional independence and give some examples. In section 7.2, we will see how d-separation helps us decide which variables should be included in the adjustment formula.

7.1.3 Breaking a causal model into independent modules

We know from experience that when we want to analyze a phenomenon—say, how the price of a product affects sales—we need to include in our analysis only those variables relevant to our problem, such as seasonality, what the competition does, etc. It may seem obvious, but we don't need to consider how the entire world works. It is sufficient to focus on these relevant variables. Causal systems can be decomposed into smaller subsystems and analyzed separately.

So far, we have dealt with causal models from an intuitive point of view. But in this section, we will see a formal definition of a causal model. Then we will see how the idea of independent systems working together arises naturally from such a definition. Finally, we will end the section by analyzing the most elementary modules in a graph: chains, confounders, and colliders.

Let's begin by defining a causal model. Imagine working with the problem represented by figure 7.7. In causal inference, when we draw a graph like this one, we implicitly say that we have three variables Z, X, and Y that are causally related. To know the value of X, we need to know the value of Z; and to know the value of Y, we need to know the values of X and Z. These variables are the lead characters of our work, and they are called *endogenous*. We also assume that these variables aren't isolated in the void but may be affected by

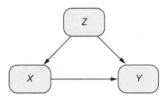

Figure 7.7   Typical three-node DAG with confounding. Z is a confounder for X and Y.

other factors we are not explicitly aware of. For each variable, we group all these unknown and unobserved factors in variables U:

- Z is affected by some variables U_Z.
- X is affected by some variables U_X.
- Y is affected by some variables U_Y.

These unobserved (not stored because we don't have them or because we have concluded that we don't need them) variables are called *exogenous* and represent the boundary between our variables of interest, the endogenous variables, and the rest of the world.

One way to put all this information together mathematically is by saying that there are three different functions f_X, f_Z, and f_Y that describe the relationship of each one of the variables with those they depend on, called their *parents*:

$$Z := f_Z(U_Z)$$
$$X := f_X(Z, U_X)$$
$$Y := f_Y(X, Z, U_Y)$$

In chapter 6, we assumed that such relationships were linear:

$$X = f_X(Z, U_X) = a + bZ + U_X$$

In chapter 4, we modeled them, separating the exogenous from the endogenous part

$$X = f_X(Z, U_X) = f_X(Z) + U_X = E[Z|X] + U_X$$

with flexible machine learning models that don't assume linearity. Still, in practice, we will never know exactly which these functions are, except on rare occasions, because they represent the laws of nature that we try to discover but don't have direct access to. Fortunately, not knowing them is not a blocker to our analysis because, as we have seen in previous chapters, we can calculate ATEs anyway.

> **NOTE**   Saying that $X := f_X(Z, U_X)$ without saying anything else about the function f_X is a very general statement. In particular, the case when X doesn't depend on Z can be written the same way, taking $f_X(Z, U_X) = U_X$. You may remember from "The meaning of an arrow" in chapter 3 that when we draw an arrow, we are saying there may be a causal relationship. However, the existence of an arrow also includes the case where there is no causal relationship between variables. The fundamental assumption comes when we don't draw an arrow between variables. The same thing happens with functions: when we write $X := f_X(Z, U_X)$, we are saying there is a possible causal relationship between Z (and U_X) and X. It shouldn't be a surprise because, as we have said, drawing an arrow between variables implicitly says that a function describes their behavior. Also remember that we use the symbol := to highlight the fact that the relationship between variables is an assignment relationship: the value of Z (possibly) changes the value of X, but the value of X never changes the value of Z.

What can the DAG tell us about the probability distribution of its variables? To make a long story short, the DAG helps us to calculate the probability of observing any particular combination of values $X = x$, $Z = z$, $Y = y$ out of probabilities of other parts of the graph as if it were a Lego toy. Let's see how.

When we gather data for variables X, Z, and Y, such as in table 7.1, we have information about the joint distribution of the three variables $P(X, Z, Y)$. That is, we have information about the frequency with which the variables take values $X = x$, $Z = z$, $Y = y$ simultaneously. Applying the definition of conditional probability (iteratively, if necessary), we can always factorize the joint probability in conditional probabilities

$$P(X, Z, Y) = P(Y|Z, X)P(X, Z) = P(Y|Z, X)P(X|Z)P(Z)$$

Table 7.1   Data table of variables Z, X, Y with sample size *n*

X	Z	Y
x_1	z_1	y_1
...	...	...
x_n	z_n	y_n

This decomposition works whenever we have three variables (independently of the DAG they belong to). When, in addition to the data, we use a causal model such as figure 7.8 (a pure confounder structure) to describe the data, we add more information about how $P(X, Z, Y)$ can be calculated. The equations describing this case are

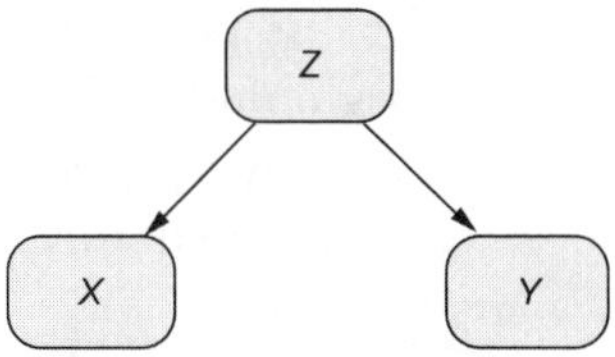

Figure 7.8   Pure confounder structure. Z is a confounder for X and Y.

$$Z := f_Z(U_Z)$$
$$X := f_X(Z, U_X)$$
$$Y := f_Y(Z, U_Y)$$

The main difference from figure 7.7 is that as the equation $Y := f_Y(Z, U_Y)$ shows, Y no longer depends on X. We can calculate the probability of Y given X and Z only considering the value of Z: $P(Y|X, Z) = P(Y|Z)$. This is because the variable $Y|X = x, Z = z$ is the resulting variable from selecting only those cases where $X = x$ and $Z = z$. Thus, using the functional relationship between Y and Z, we can express

$$Y|[X = x, Z = z] := f_Y(z, U_Y)$$

where we have only substituted Z for the particular value z in the function $f_Y(Z, U_Y)$. Such a small change may seem subtle to you. But we are saying that instead of considering Z a variable that may change, we are fixing its value to the particular z. More importantly, $X = x$ plays no role in $f_Y(z, U_Y)$! So we can certainly conclude that $Y|X, Z$ can be expressed as $Y|Z = z$, which implies that $P(Y|X, Z) = P(Y|Z)$.

Thus we can factorize the joint probability distribution of the model in figure 7.8 as

$$P(X, Z, Y) = P(Y|Z, X)P(X|Z)P(Z) = P(Y|Z)P(X|Z)P(Z)$$

More generally, if we denote the *parents* of W (those variables it directly depends on) by $\mathrm{pa}(W)$, then

$$P(X, Z, Y) = P(Y|\mathrm{pa}(Y))P(X|\mathrm{pa}(X))P(Z|\mathrm{pa}(Z))$$

Because Z has no parents, $\mathrm{pa}(Z)$ is the empty set. Such decomposition is not specific to the graph in figure 7.8 but works with any general graph. If variable Y depends directly on variables $Z_1, ..., Z_l$ (Y has incoming arrows from those variables) and not other $X_1, ..., X_m$ (there are no direct arrows from any of those into Y), $Y := f_Y(Z_1, ..., Z_l, U_Y)$ and, moreover,

$$P(Y|Z_1, \ldots, Z_l, X_1, \ldots, X_m) = P(Y|Z_1, \ldots, Z_l)$$

and by definition

$$P(Y|Z_1, \ldots, Z_l, X_1, \ldots, X_m) = P(Y|pa(Y))$$

This is precisely the formal way to express the modular notion introduced at the beginning of the section: *we can calculate the joint probability of our system based only on the relationships of each variable with its parents.* Now we are in a position to give the abstract definition of what a causal model is.

Structural causal models

A *structural causal model* (SCM) is a collection of variables U, V and set of functions F, where

- The set of variables U are called exogenous and represent the variables that affect our model in reality, but we don't have information about them. Variables U are independent of one another.
- The set of variables V, called endogenous, are the ones we work with.
- The set F of functions describes the relationship between variables. We can always tell how the value of a variable depends on its parents and its associated exogenous variable $x := f_x(\text{pa}(x), U_x)$, with f being a function of the set F.

Because each variable x depends only on its parents $\text{pa}(x)$, we can factorize the joint probability

$$P(V) = \Pi_x P(X|pa(X))$$

A DAG is a (visual) representation of a causal model: whenever we draw a DAG, we assume we are defining a causal model, as explained here.

Data is not enough (once more)

We have seen that every DAG we can consider induces a factorization of its joint probability distribution. Does this work the other way around? The answer is no. The fact that we can factorize the probability distribution of some variables doesn't determine the direction of the arrows in the graph.

Consider the case of only two variables, X and Y. We can always factorize $P(X, Y) = P(Y|X) P(X) = P(X|Y) P(Y)$. This means there is no possible way (unless you make extra assumptions) to decide only from a dataset with variables X and Y which causes the other: in other words, whether $X \rightarrow Y$ or $Y \rightarrow X$.

In summary, from the causal point of view, it is different having $X \rightarrow Y$ than $Y \rightarrow X$. The former means you can change Y by changing X, whereas the latter does not. But from the probability point of view, there is no way to know which case we are in; we just have data from the joint distribution $P(X, Y)$. So we see once more that *we cannot infer a causal relationship based only on data.*

7.1.4   *The bricks of DAGs: Factorizing probability distributions*

As we have already stated, we are interested in analyzing how correlation flows through different graph paths. Understanding how the minimal modules that shape a graph determine how their probability distributions factorize will be very helpful. Given any three nodes in a path, we can find only one of the following three situations:

- Paths of type $\rightarrow\rightarrow$ or $\leftarrow\leftarrow$, which we will call *chains*
- Paths of type $\leftarrow\rightarrow$, which we will call *forks*
- Paths of type $\rightarrow\leftarrow$, which we will call *colliders*

CHAINS

Picture a rainy day where the street is soaked. When you get home, your wet shoes can make the floor dirty. Use the following variables:

- X denotes whether it rains.
- Y denotes whether the street is wet.
- Z denotes whether your shoes make the floor dirty.

This process can be described by the DAG and structural causal model in table 7.2.

Table 7.2   Chain DAG

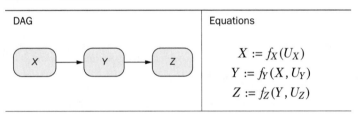

DAG	Equations
$X \longrightarrow Y \longrightarrow Z$	$X := f_X(U_X)$ $Y := f_Y(X, U_Y)$ $Z := f_Z(Y, U_Z)$

In this case, to know the distribution of Z, we only need to know the value of Y, so

$$P(Z|Y, X) = P(Z|Y)$$

This equation says that to determine whether your shoes will dirty the floor (Z), you just need to know whether the street is wet (Y). Once you have that information, the details about the weather (X) are irrelevant.

Thus, the joint distribution is

$$P(X, Y, Z) = P(Z|Y, X)P(Y, X) = P(Z|Y)P(Y|X)P(X)$$

This implies that Z is conditionally independent of X given Y:

$$Z \perp X|Y \tag{7.1}$$

Because

$$P(Z, X|Y) = \frac{P(X, Y, Z)}{P(Y)} = P(Z|Y)P(Y|X)\frac{P(X)}{P(Y)} = P(Z|Y)P(X|Y)$$

In causal inference jargon, we say that if we condition on Y, Y blocks X and Z.

Let's test the condition in equation (7.1) with code by simulating and analyzing synthetic data. The data-generation process is the following:

$$X := B(0.5)$$
$$Y := X \times B(0.3) + (1 - X) \times B(0.7)$$
$$Z := Y \times B(0.1) + (1 - Y) \times B(0.9)$$

where $B(p)$ is drawn from Bernoulli distribution with expectation p. This process is a chain because Y is determined solely by X, and Z is determined solely by Y. The process is simulated in the following two listings. Notice how $cor(X, Z) = 0.32$ is not zero.

Listing 7.1   (R) Creating a synthetic dataset with the structure of a chain

```
set.seed(1234)
n <- 10000
x <- rbinom(n, 1, 0.5)
y <- x * rbinom(n, 1, 0.3) + (1-x)*rbinom(n, 1, 0.7)
z <- y * rbinom(n, 1, 0.1) + (1-y)*rbinom(n, 1, 0.9)
cor(x, z)
```

Listing 7.2   (Python) Creating a synthetic dataset with the structure of a chain

```
from numpy.random import seed, binomial
from numpy import corrcoef
seed(1234)
n = 10000
x = binomial(1, 0.5, n)
y = x * binomial(1, 0.3, n) + (1 - x) * binomial(1, 0.7, n)
z = y * binomial(1, 0.1, n) + (1 - y) * binomial(1, 0.9, n)
corrcoef(x, z)[0][1]
```

However, when conditioning on $y = 1$ or $y = 0$, the correlation becomes close to zero: $cor(X, Z \mid = Y = 1) = 0.007$ and $cor(X, Z \mid = Y = 0) = 0.015$ (R results), as seen in the next two listings, which provides evidence of the relationship in equation 7.1.

Listing 7.3   (R) Conditional correlations of *X* and *Z* given *Y*

```
print(cor(x[y == 1], z[y == 1]))
print(cor(x[y == 0], z[y == 0]))
```

Listing 7.4   (Python) Conditional correlations of *X* and *Z* given *Y*

```
print(corrcoef(x[y == 1], z[y == 1])[0][1])
print(corrcoef(x[y == 0], z[y == 0])[0][1])
```

FORKS

Consider the process shown in table 7.3. In this case, X and Y may not be independent in general (think about all the examples of spurious correlations), but given the value of Z, they are: given $Z = z$, the value of X does not depend on Y, because $X := f_X(z, U_X)$ (and analogously for Y). This implies that

$$P(X|Z, Y) = P(X|Z)$$

Table 7.3   Pure fork DAG

DAG	Equations
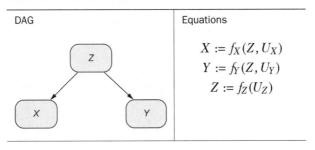	$X := f_X(Z, U_X)$ $Y := f_Y(Z, U_Y)$ $Z := f_Z(U_Z)$

So,

$$P(X, Y|Z) = \frac{P(X, Y, Z)}{P(Z)} = \frac{P(X|Z, Y)P(Z, Y)}{P(Z)} = P(X|Z)P(Y|Z)$$

and thus X and Y are conditionally independent given Z:

$$X \perp Y|Z \tag{7.2}$$

In causal inference jargon, we say that if we condition on Z, Z blocks X and Y.

You may wonder why we call this structure a fork rather than a confounder. The reason is that, as we will see later, not all forks are confounders. For example, in figure 7.9, Z is a fork but not a confounder between X and Y, because Z is not a cause of either of them.

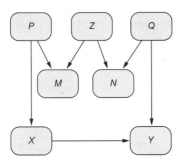

Figure 7.9   Example of a fork that is not a confounder. Z is a fork, but because it doesn't directly influence M and N, it is not a confounder. This structure is known as an *M-structure* in the causal inference literature (because it resembles the letter M).

Let's test the condition in equation 7.2 with code by simulating and analyzing synthetic data. The data-generation process is the following:

$$Z := B(0.5)$$
$$Y := Z \times B(0.3) + (1 - Z) \times B(0.7)$$
$$X := Z \times B(0.3) + (1 - Z) \times B(0.7)$$

This process is a fork because Y and X are determined solely by Z. The process is simulated in the following two listings. Notice how $cor(X, Y) = 0.17$ is not zero.

Listing 7.5   (R) Creating a synthetic dataset with the structure of a fork

```
z <- rbinom(n, 1, 0.5)
y <- z * rbinom(n, 1, 0.3) + (1-z)*rbinom(n, 1, 0.7)
x <- z * rbinom(n, 1, 0.3) + (1-z)*rbinom(n, 1, 0.7)
cor(y, x)
```

Listing 7.6   (Python) Creating a synthetic dataset with the structure of a fork

```
z = binomial(1, 0.5, n)
y = z * binomial(1, 0.3, n) + (1-z)*binomial(1, 0.7, n)
x = z * binomial(1, 0.3, n) + (1-z)*binomial(1, 0.7, n)
corrcoef(y, x)[0][1]
```

However, when conditioning on $z = 1$ or $z = 0$, the correlation becomes close to zero: $cor(X, Y | Z = 1) = 0.013$ and $cor(X, Y | Z = 0) = 0.015$ (R results), as seen in the next two listings, which provides evidence of the relationship in equation 7.2.

Listing 7.7   (R) Conditional correlations of X and Z given Y

```
print(cor(x[z == 1], y[z == 1]))
print(cor(x[z == 0], y[z == 0]))
```

Listing 7.8   (Python) Conditional correlations of X and Z given Y

```
print(corrcoef(x[z == 1], y[z == 1])[0][1])
print(corrcoef(x[z == 0], y[z == 0])[0][1])
```

COLLIDERS

The collider's case is a little different from the previous ones (see table 7.4). X and Y are already independent. What happens when we block on Z? Let's first talk about Berkson's paradox.

Table 7.4   Collider DAG. Z is a collider for X and Y.

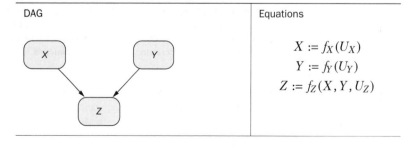

DAG	Equations
	$X := f_X(U_X)$
	$Y := f_Y(U_Y)$
	$Z := f_Z(X, Y, U_Z)$

Imagine that you work at a university and want to study the relationship between the two scores necessary for students to be accepted to the university: the SAT and GPA. To make it simple, students with an average of the two scores greater than a certain threshold will be accepted. The accepted students are above the left-hand diagonal line in figure 7.10. However, students with much higher qualifications—those above the right-hand diagonal line—will probably go to more popular universities. Thus, students who enter your university are those between the two lines. If you were a teacher who wanted to understand your students' profiles and only had access to your university's data, you would conclude that GPA and SAT are negatively correlated. But in reality, if you had complete information for all students, you would see that they are positively correlated. This effect is called *Berkson's paradox*. We can model this scenario with the DAG in figure 7.11. Conditioning on a particular subset of data—in this case, those accepted to your university—can change the direction of the correlation of two variables.

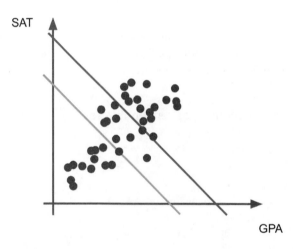

Figure 7.10   Example of Berkson's paradox: There's a positive correlation between SAT scores and GPA overall. However, if we only look at students accepted to our university, between the diagonal lines, this correlation turns negative.

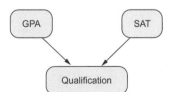

Figure 7.11   Student university acceptance DAG, based on GPA and SAT results. Qualification is a collider. Conditioning on a collider can change the correlation between the collider's parents.

A very similar example is the following. Suppose you throw two dice, X and Y, and calculate their sum. The results of the two dice are independent: if you know that X resulted in a 2, it tells you absolutely nothing about the result of Y. But if you stick to cases where the sum of both dice is $Z = 5$, as in table 7.5, knowing that the value of

$X = 2$ tells you that the value of Y can only be $Y = 3$. In fact, X and Y become negatively correlated! This is because Z is a collider, as shown in figure 7.12.

Table 7.5   Collider DAG

X	4	3	2	1
Y	1	2	3	4
Z	5	5	5	5

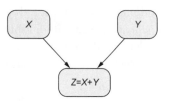

Figure 7.12   Sum of two dice DAG. Conditioning on Z creates new correlations between X and Y that were not there before conditioning.

So, if Z is a collider of X and Y, Z already blocks them. That's right: not conditioning on Z leaves them independent. That's why in causal inference jargon, we say that Z blocks them. If we condition on Z, we are potentially opening new correlation paths, so we can no longer ensure that X and Y are independent.

Which distributions does conditional independence refer to?

In the first graph, X and Y are not independent *in general*, but conditioning on Z, X and Y are independent. What does this mean?

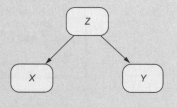

Pure confounder

When we say that conditioning on Z, X and Y are independent, we mean that for all probability distributions compatible with the DAG, X and Y are independent. But when we say that X and Y are not independent *in general*, it doesn't mean X and Y are never independent! Rather, there are *some* distributions compatible with the graph in which X and Y are not independent. But there may be others in which they are!

For example, the second DAG is a particular case of the previous one. Remember that arrows also model cases in which there are no causal relationships. In this case, conditioning on Z, X and Y are independent. But it turns out that X and Y were independent from the beginning.

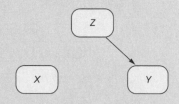

A real situation we may not be aware of: there is no effect from Z to X, so in reality, Z is not a confounder.

Analogously, conditioning on a collider *does not always* open a new correlation path between variables. In some cases it will, but in others it will not. Being cautious, we need to assume that conditioning on a collider will open a new correlation path.

Let's see how conditioning on a collider can make two variables correlated when originally they are not. The data-generation process is the following:

$$X := B(0.5)$$

$$Y := B(0.5)$$

$$Z := (1 - X_Y) \times B(0.2) + X_Y \times B(0.8)$$

This process is a collider because Y and X determine Z. The process is simulated in the following two listings. Notice how $\text{cor}(X, Y) = 0.002$ is approximately zero.

> **Listing 7.9   (R) Creating a synthetic dataset with the structure of a collider**

```
x <- rbinom(n, 1, 0.5)
y <- rbinom(n, 1, 0.5)
z <- (1-x*y) * rbinom(n, 1, 0.2) + x*y*rbinom(n, 1, 0.8)
cor(y, x)
```

> **Listing 7.10   (Python) Creating a synthetic dataset with the structure of a collider**

```
x = binomial(1, 0.5, n)
y = binomial(1, 0.5, n)
z = (1 - x * y) * binomial(1, 0.2, n) + x * y * binomial(1, 0.8, n)
corrcoef(y, x)[0][1]
```

However, when conditioning on $z = 1$ or $z = 0$, the correlation is nonzero: $\text{cor}(X, Y \mid Z = 1) = 0.33$ and $\text{cor}(X, Y \mid Z = 0) = -0.30$ (R results), as seen in the next two listings.

> **Listing 7.11   (R) Conditional correlations of X and Z given Y**

```
print(cor(x[z == 1], y[z == 1]))
print(cor(x[z == 0], y[z == 0]))
```

> **Listing 7.12   (Python) Conditional correlations of X and Z given Y**

```
print(corrcoef(x[z == 1], y[z == 1])[0][1])
print(corrcoef(x[z == 0], y[z == 0])[0][1])
```

7.1.5   *What's the d-separation about?*

In section 6.2.1 in chapter 6, we talked about an analogy where the correlation is a gas that flows through a pipe network, and we are interested in measuring how much flow goes through a particular set of paths—the causal paths. To do that, we try to open and close some paths so that all the correlation flows only through the causal paths. In our causal model, we can close and open paths analogously by conditioning on certain variables. For example, we saw in the previous section that conditioning on intermediate variables cuts the correlation for chains and forks. Meanwhile, if we condition on a collider, we may open new correlation paths.

> ## Causal paths refresher
>
> Recall that the causal paths between variables X and Y are those paths that represent an effect from X to Y. In a graph, they are those paths starting from X where all the arrows have the same direction $X \rightarrow \ldots \rightarrow Y$, meeting no fork or collider.

In this section, our goal is to eliminate all the correlations between a pair of variables by conditioning on in-between variables. To achieve this, we need to block all the paths that link them. Conditioning on a variable may close a path while opening another simultaneously. This means we must be thoughtful about which variables to condition on. Let's apply what we've learned so far and work through an exercise to develop your intuition.

For this example, we will reuse the graph from chapter 6 shown in figure 7.13. Clearly, X and Y are not independent in general for many reasons. The first is that there is a causal path $X \rightarrow E \rightarrow Y$. Another is that there is a confounder W in the path $X \leftarrow Z \leftarrow W \rightarrow Y$. If we want to make X and Y independent by conditioning on some variables, which variables should they be?

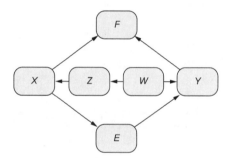

Figure 7.13   A graph with three paths from X to Y: a causal path, a path with a confounder, and another with a collider

There are three paths from X to Y:

- $X \rightarrow E \rightarrow Y$
- $X \leftarrow Z \leftarrow W \rightarrow Y$
- $X \rightarrow F \leftarrow Y$

To block the first one, because it is a chain, we should condition on E. We have two options for blocking the second path. We either condition on the collider W or condition on the "chain" part of the path. That is, conditioning on Z, we block the part $X \leftarrow Z \leftarrow W$, and consequently, the entire path gets blocked. Notice that the third one is already blocked because it contains a collider.

Notice that to block a whole path, you only need it to be blocked at one particular variable. Using the analogy of the gas flowing through a pipe, if you cut off the flow at any section of the pipe, the gas stops moving through the entire pipe.

Test your knowledge

We'll work with the DAG about sports and injuries shown in the figure. I highly recommend practicing path blocking with the exercises provided. Remember, the same variable may act differently in separate paths; it can be a fork in one path and a collider in another (see exercise 7.4 for details).

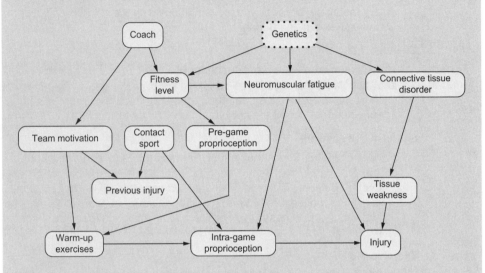

Graph describing the relationship between warm-up exercises and being injured in sports

Exercise 7.1

1   Are Genetics and Coach independent?
2   If you condition on Fitness Level, are Genetics and Coach independent?
3   If you condition on Neuromuscular Fatigue, are Genetics and Coach independent?
4   If you condition on Previous Injury, are Genetics and Coach independent?
5   If you condition on Intra-game Proprioception and Previous Injury, are Genetics and Coach independent?

Exercise 7.1 answers

1   Yes, because any path linking them has a collider in the middle.
2   In general, no. Fitness Level is a collider with respect Genetics and Coach, so you can introduce correlations between them both.
3   In general, no. If you choose some participants with a particular level of Neuromuscular Fatigue, those participants will have a specific type of Fitness Level. So, conditioning on Neuromuscular Fatigue alters the distribution of Fitness Level, which, being a collider, may introduce correlations between Coach and Genetics.

(continued)

4   Yes, they are. Even though Previous Injury is a collider, there are two colliders in the path Coach → Team Motivation → Previous Injury ← Contact Sport → Intra-game Proprioception ← Neuromuscular Fatigue ← Genetics. So although conditioning on Previous Injury may open correlations between Team Motivation and Contact Sport, it is cut off by the collider Intra-game Proprioception.

5   In general, no, because you are conditioning on the only two colliders on a path linking Genetic and Coach.

Exercise 7.2

1   Are Warm-up and Coach independent?

2   Which variables should you condition on to make them independent? To do that, you must first check all the paths that link them. Then, condition on the variables that cut all the correlation off between them.

Exercise 7.2 answers

1   Not in general. Coach may affect Warm-up through Team Motivation.

2   The only paths that do not contain a collider, thus the only open paths, are Coach → Team Motivation → Warm-up and Coach → Fitness Level → Pregame Proprioception → Warm-up. Conditioning at the same time on Team Motivation and Fitness Level, or Team Motivation and Pregame Proprioception, will do the job.

Exercise 7.3

1   Why are Previous Injury and Intra-game Proprioception not generally independent?

2   If you condition on Team Motivation, which other variables should you condition on to make Previous Injury and Intra-game Proprioception independent?

3   Are there other combinations of variables such that conditioning on them, Previous Injury and Intra-game Proprioception are independent?

Exercise 7.3 answers

1   Because they have confounders Team Motivation and Contact Sports.

2   Team Motivation closes one path, but you still need to close the path Previous Injury ← Contact Sport → Intra-game Proprioception, so you need to condition on Contact Sport.

3   Yes. You always need to condition on Contact Sport, but you can close the other path in other ways. If you don't condition on Team Motivation, you must condition on Warm-up. Otherwise, the path Previous Injury ← Team Motivation → Warm-up → Intra-game Proprioception is open. But if you condition on Warm-up, you open the path Previous Injury ← Team Motivation → Warm-up ← Pregame Proprioception ← Fitness Level → Neuromuscular Fatigue → Intra-game Proprioception. So, if in addition you condition on Neuromuscular Fatigue, you close this path and at the same time close the other path left open Previous Injury ← Team Motivation ← Coach → Fitness Level → Neuromuscular Fatigue → Intra-game Proprioception.

Exercise 7.4

In the following figure, which single variable should you condition on so that X and Y are independent?

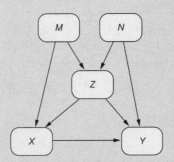

DAG for exercise 4. This is the M-structure introduced before but with additional arrows beginning at Z. Z is a collider and a confounder at the same time, depending on the path taken to relate X and Y.

Exercise 7.4 answer

In this case, it is impossible to make X and Y independent conditioning on a single variable. Because you have a confounder, $X \leftarrow Z \rightarrow Y$, you need to condition on Z. But then, because Z is a collider for the path, $M \rightarrow Z \leftarrow N$, conditioning on Z opens this path.

7.1.6 Defining d-separation

Imagine a complex graph with many nodes and many paths. Pick two nodes, which we will call X and Y. These two have a bunch of paths relating to one another. Some paths start with incoming arrows to X, such as $X \leftarrow ...$, and others leave X, such as $X \rightarrow ....$ We are only interested in those paths that finally end up at Y $(... \rightarrow Y)$ because these are the ones that play a role in the effect of X into Y. So, we can forget about paths like $X \leftarrow ... \leftarrow Y$. Any path you can think of ending at Y will fall into one of the three following categories:

- The path starts from X and keeps the same direction until it arrives at Y: $X \rightarrow ... \rightarrow ... \rightarrow Y$. These are the causal paths between X and Y. This means changing the value of X will affect Y through these paths. If we want to, we can close the path, conditioning on any intermediate node.

- The path starts from X, but at some point there is a reversed arrow at a variable Z, which becomes a collider: $X \rightarrow ... \rightarrow Z \leftarrow ....$ There is no correlation flowing through this path. But if we condition on this collider, we may open the path.

- The path starts pointing at X: $X \leftarrow ....$ If the path ends at Y, it must have a fork Z at some point: $X \leftarrow ... \leftarrow Z \rightarrow ... \rightarrow Y$. There may be a spurious correlation flowing through this path, and when estimating the causal effect, we will be interested in blocking it.

The previous categorization prepares the way for the definition of d-separation. The intuitive idea is that a set of variables Z d-separates or blocks X from Y if, conditioning on the variables in Z, we cut off all the correlation between X and Y.

Descendants

A *descendant* of a node X is any node for which there is a causal path starting from X and ending in Z, $X \rightarrow \dots \rightarrow Z$. Descendants can never be confounders. For example, in the DAG $X \rightarrow M \rightarrow Z_1 \leftarrow C \rightarrow Z_2 \leftarrow Y$, both M and Z_1 are descendants, but Z_2 is not.

Definition of d-separation

Given two nodes X and Y and a path p linking them, a set of nodes $M = \{Z_1, \dots, Z_p\}$ d-separates X from Y if one of the following is true:

- There is some Z is in the middle of a chain: $\dots \rightarrow Z \rightarrow \dots$.
- Some Z is a fork: $\dots \leftarrow Z \rightarrow \dots$.
- None of the variables Z is a collider nor a descendant of a collider.

A set of variables M block X from Y if it blocks all the paths from X to Y.

DEFINITION NOTE 1

Notice that the definition rules out descendants of colliders to block a path. Why? Descendants of a collider Z_1 are those nodes, call them Z_2, for which a causal path starts on Z_1 and ends on Z_2.

For example, imagine the case in figure 7.14, where Z_1 and Z_2 are highly correlated. Even worse, imagine the extreme case where Z_2 is an exact copy of Z_1. Conditioning on Z_2 is the same as conditioning on Z_1, thus potentially opening the path between M and N. If Z_1 and Z_2 are not the same but are strongly correlated, conditioning on Z_2 will give us information about the values Z_1 takes and at the same will potentially open a path between M and N.

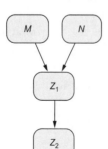

Figure 7.14 Conditioning on a descendant (Z_2) of a collider (Z_1) can open new correlations (between M and N).

DEFINITION NOTE 2

The "or" in the definition tells us that if one of the conditions is not met, the path can still be blocked if another condition is. For instance, in figure 7.15, we have many ways of blocking X from Y.

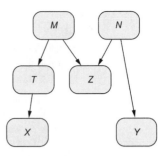

We can condition on

- M or N, or $\{M, N\}$ at the same time, because they are confounders
- T, because it is in a chain
- Combinations of the previous: $\{T, M\}, \{T, N\}, \{T, M, N\}$

Figure 7.15 There are many valid ways to block the correlation between X and Y.

We cannot condition on Z alone because we open a new path. But we can still condition on Z as long as we condition on another variable that closes the path. For example, we can condition on

- $\{Z, M\}, \{Z, N\}, \{Z, M, N\}$
- $\{Z, T\}$
- $\{Z, T, M\}, \{Z, T, N\}, \{Z, T, M, N\}$

Any subset of $\{T, M, Z, N\}$ will do the job, except taking only Z. As long as we condition on at least one of the variables $\{T, M, N\}$, we will block X from Y.

D-separation (d stands for directional) is a vital notion relating the graph's structure with the variables' probability distribution. As the following theorem says, whenever variables are d-separated, they also are conditionally independent.

Theorem

If a DAG G describes a process (probability distribution), and a set of variables Z d-separates two variables X and Y in G, the variables X and Y are independent if we condition on the variables Z.

7.2 *Back-door criterion*

In the last section, we saw how we can cut off all correlation between two variables X and Y by blocking all the related paths. But actually, this is not what we are looking for when we want to calculate causal effects. If we cut all the correlation from treatment and outcome variables, and they become independent, there is nothing left to calculate! We want to calculate the correlation between two variables, but only the correlation that goes through causal paths. We don't want to estimate the correlation that flows through confounders because this correlation does not reflect the effect of X into Y, but other common causes between X and Y that affect them both at the same time.

Strategy

Generally speaking, our strategy to estimate causal correlation in any graph will be the following:

- Keep all the causal paths without blocking.
- Block all the paths that contain confounders.
- In the process, avoid opening any new paths by conditioning on colliders.

The three types of paths are shown (with only one node for each one) here.

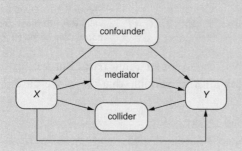

Simplified types of paths between X and Y. Any path between X and Y is either a direct path or contains one of the three elements: a confounder, a mediator, or a collider. If the graph gets complex, we can have paths with more than one of these elements.

Consider the example from the beginning of the chapter about pricing shoes in figure 7.16. Which variables should we condition on to block the correlation from colliders but still keep the causal paths?

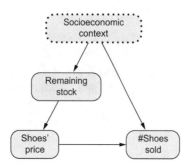

Figure 7.16 Socioeconomic context is the only confounder, but it is unobserved. We need to find an alternative to adjust for. Otherwise, we cannot estimate the causal effect between shoe prices and the number of shoes sold.

If we condition on Remaining Stock, we block all the confounders represented by Socioeconomic Context, and at the same time, we keep the causal path Shoe Price → # Shoes Sold open. But on the other hand, we cannot condition on Socioeconomic Context because we don't have these variables!

Let's look at another example. Consider the simplified version (made up for the sake of the exercise) of the sports DAG at the beginning of the chapter, shown in figure 7.17.

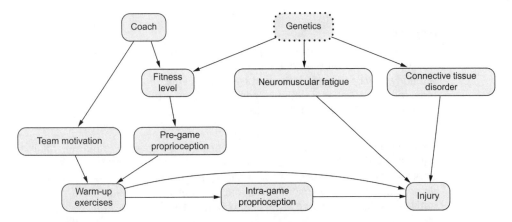

Figure 7.17   Graph describing the relationship between warm-up exercises and being injured in sports

Test your knowledge
Exercise 7.5

Which variables should we condition on to block all paths with confounders while keeping causal paths open between Warm-up Exercises and Injury?

1 List all possible paths (directed and undirected) starting at Warm-up Exercises and ending at Injury (without loops).
2 Among them, identify all the causal paths
3 Pick the combinations of variables (there is more than one!) that block all paths with confounders and keep the causal paths open.

Exercise 7.5 answer

Let's go step by step:

1 We have these paths (variables are shortened for convenience):
   - Warm-up → Injury
   - Warm-up → Intra-game → Injury
   - Warm-up ← Team ← Coach → Fitness ← Genetics → Connective → Injury
   - Warm-up ← Team ← Coach → Fitness ← Genetics → Fatigue → Injury
   - Warm-up ← Pregame ← Fitness ← Genetics → Connective → Injury
   - Warm-up ← Pregame ← Fitness ← Genetics → Fatigue → Injury
2 The only causal paths are Warm-up → Injury and Warm-up → Intra-game → Injury. So we have to avoid conditioning on Intra-game because, in that case, we would be closing this causal path.
3 We need to close the remaining noncausal paths:
   - Warm-up ← Team ← Coach → Fitness ← Genetics → Connective → Injury
   - Warm-up ← Team ← Coach → Fitness ← Genetics → Fatigue → Injury
   - Warm-up ← Pregame ← Fitness ← Genetics → Connective → Injury
   - Warm-up ← Pregame ← Fitness ← Genetics → Fatigue → Injury

(continued)

Notice that any noncausal path must go first through the Coach or Pregame node. So, we can block all the noncausal paths just conditioning on Coach and Pregame. Similarly, any noncausal path must go through Fatigue or Connective, so we can also block all the noncausal paths by conditioning on Fatigue and Connective. There are other options, though. For instance, the paths that go through Coach are the same as those of Motivation. Thus, an alternative would be Motivation and Pregame.

A similar argument can be made with Fitness. If we condition on it, we will block the path that goes through Pregame. But Fitness is a collider, and it opens the path Coach → Fitness ← Genetics. So, as long as we block those, too, we will be fine. To do so, we just need to condition on Coach or Motivation. In summary, two other alternatives are Motivation and Fitness and Coach and Fitness.

There are many more combinations of nodes blocking all noncausal paths. Those we have found are the minimal ones. Any other combination is obtained by adding more nodes to the solutions we have already seen. For instance, the set Team, Pregame, Fitness also blocks all noncausal paths.

So far, we have focused on sets of variables to adjust for. We have seen that many admissible sets can be considered. But are some sets better than others? If we apply the adjustment formula to any of them, we will get unbiased estimates of the causal effect. Thus, from the bias perspective, all of them are equally suitable. However, some are statistically more efficient (with a lower variance) than others. Even though finding statistically efficient adjustment sets is a complex topic, we will introduce it later.

Analyzing the results of the previous exercise, we can see that a path that contains a confounder Z for a treatment variable X and outcome Y takes one of the two following forms:

$X \leftarrow \ldots \leftarrow Z \rightarrow \ldots \rightarrow Y$ (no colliders in the path)

$X \rightarrow \ldots \rightarrow C \leftarrow \ldots \leftarrow Z \rightarrow \ldots \rightarrow Y$ or $X \leftarrow \ldots \leftarrow Z \rightarrow \ldots \rightarrow C \leftarrow \ldots \rightarrow Y$, where C is a collider (it has some collider).

We don't have to worry about the second case because even though the path has a confounder Z, it also has a collider, so the path is already closed.

A path with an incoming arrow into X, $X \leftarrow \ldots$, is called *back-door path*. If a back-door path links X and Y, it must have a fork at some point. *So, these are the paths responsible for creating spurious correlations between variables X and Y*, and these are the paths that we need to worry about. We can now finally state the back-door criterion.

Back-door criterion

Given a treatment variable X and an outcome variable Y, if a set of variables Z satisfies the following

- Z blocks every back-door path
- Z does not contain any descendant of X

we say that Z satisfies the back-door criterion.

Note that we have excluded descendants of X because if we conditioned on them, we would be blocking causal paths, such as Intra-game in the previous example.

Informally speaking, the back-door criterion between X and Y tells us which variables we need to condition on to cut all the spurious correlations without unintentionally removing any effect of X to Y. Another way of expressing the back-door criterion, which is close to the explanation we have offered so far, is the following. Given a DAG G, consider the DAG $G_{X\rightarrow}$ as the same DAG, but with the arrows leaving X removed (you can see an example in table 7.6). You can see that the only paths left connecting X and Y are precisely the back-door paths. So, if a set Z d-separates X from Y in the graph without descendants of X, $G_{X\rightarrow}$, and Z doesn't include any descendant of X, Z satisfies the back-door criterion.

Table 7.6   Example of original G and $G_{X\rightarrow}$ with leaving arrows removed

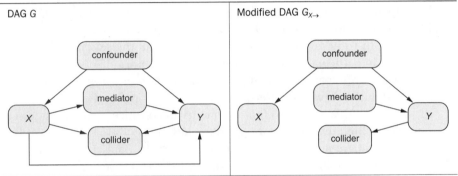

7.2.1   *The importance of the back-door criterion*

The back-door criterion tells us if a set of variables can be used in the adjustment formula (which we learned in chapter 2) to calculate ATEs.

> **Theorem**
> Suppose a set of variables Z satisfies the back-door criterion for the treatment X and outcome Y. In that case, the effect of intervening $X = x$ can be calculated by applying the adjustment formula with variables Z:
>
> $$E[Y|\text{do}(X = x)] = \sum_z E[Y|X = x, z]P(z)$$

TIP   In previous chapters, we have seen many variations of the adjustment formula: using machine learning in chapter 4, running propensity scores in chapter 5, and using linear models in chapter 6. Regardless of your chosen algorithm, you still must find which variables to adjust. The back-door criterion helps you to do it. But remember, the choice of the statistical method in no case substitutes the work of determining which variables you must adjust for.

For instance, in the second example of this chapter (figure 7.3), if we wanted to calculate the causal effect from X (Warm-up) to Y (Injury), we could apply the adjustment formula with any of the following sets as adjustment sets:

- Coach, Fitness Level
- Coach, Pregame Proprioception
- Connective Tissue Disorder, Neuromuscular Fatigue
- Fitness Level, Genetics
- Fitness Level, Team Motivation
- Neuromuscular Fatigue, Tissue Weakness
- Pregame Proprioception, Team Motivation

At this point, you may ask, how did we determine that these are the sets? One way is to follow the procedure in exercise 7.5 (listing all paths, making sure you close all the back doors, etc.). Fortunately, there is software that tells you which adjustment sets satisfy the back-door criterion. One example is the website Dagitty (www.dagitty.net/dags.html#): you draw a graph, and it computes all the sets satisfying the back-door criterion. In particular, in Dagitty, you can find an example of a warm-up injury.

And now you may be thinking, "Wait: if a computer can tell me which sets of variables I should use, why are we spending so much time and effort on understanding the back door?" Well, not so fast! Let me try to convince you that understanding the rationale behind the back-door criterion is advantageous for you.

You may have noticed that we haven't analyzed a dataset in this chapter. The discussion has been about DAGs. And with just the DAG, we can conclude whether we can estimate the causal effect (with the adjustment formula)—all before seeing any data. Not only can we know whether we can apply the adjustment formula, but we can also tell which variables we need to estimate causal effects. This is a huge advantage of this method!

My point is that the back-door criterion can help you plan the variables you will need for your analysis before gathering any data. For example, imagine a situation where you want to estimate some causal effects, but the data has not been collected yet. You can sit down with your colleagues, draw a DAG of the process you will analyze, and tell in advance which variables you will need to collect.

Imagine now that after analyzing the DAG, you conclude that there are no adjusting sets, so you cannot proceed with the adjustment formula. If you understand the back-door criterion, you can still consider alternative adjusting sets not considered before. This is something a computer cannot do (at least for now) because the computer cannot understand the context of the problem or derive the potential causal relations.

Let's look at a hypothetical story about searching for variables that close the back-door paths. Imagine that we want to understand the effect of price on sales for a pair of shoes. As we saw initially, the price may depend on many factors, such as the competition's prices, marketing campaigns, the country's economic situation, and so on. We may not have the historical values of this information, so we regard all of these as unobserved variables that we call Socioeconomic Context. This situation is represented on the left in table 7.7, and we cannot estimate the causal effect because there are confounders that we can't adjust for.

To understand the process better, we ask the pricing department how prices are set. They tell us that prices are decided in the middle of the week, depending on the remaining stock. They increase the price if they think they will run out of stock before the end of the week. So, the Remaining Stock variable is the only information required to set shoe prices. That is good news! Now we are in the situation shown in the center in table 7.7: the variable Remaining Stock closes all the back-door paths, so, adjusting for it, we can calculate the causal effect we are searching for.

Unfortunately, we were too optimistic. After talking with the IT department, we realize that they don't store the variable Remaining Stock in any database. We are in trouble again because we haven't closed the back-door path yet. Thinking a bit more, we conclude that Remaining Stock only depends on the weekly new shoe purchase orders and the number of shoes sold last week. Both of them may depend on Socioeconomic Context. If we have these two variables, as shown on the right in table 7.7, we don't even need to calculate Remaining Stock. We can adjust for them by closing the back-door path again. But if we only have one or none, we cannot estimate the causal effect.

Table 7.7   Different stages in searching for back-door closing variables

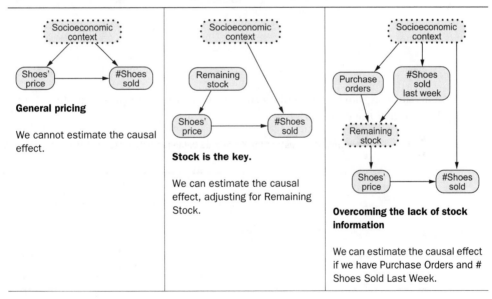

7.3   Good and bad controls

The back-door criterion helps us know which variables to adjust for in various situations. Let's now see some examples from the paper "A Crash Course in Good and Bad Controls" (2022) by Carlos Cinelli, Andrew Forney, and Judea Pearl. If you are curious about anything else, check out the paper!

Examples of good and bad controls simulated and analyzed

Simulating good and bad controls is an excellent exercise to convince yourself of the results we are explaining. I was going to write the code for the simulations, but it turns out the people from the Dive into Causal Machine Learning group (https://d2cml-ai.github.io/d2cml.ai/) already did that in R (https://mng.bz/V2mr) and Python (https://mng.bz/x6Aq).

7.3.1 Good controls

In any of the examples in table 7.8, conditioning on *Z*, we block the only back-door path, so *Z* is an adjustment set for the back-door criterion.

Table 7.8   Good controls 1: adjusting for Z gives us unbiased estimates for the causal effect between X and Y.

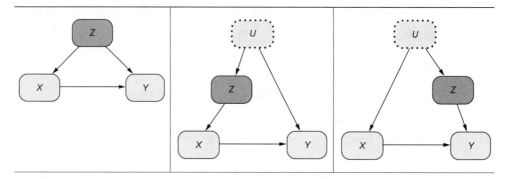

The same argument and conclusion apply to the examples in table 7.9, in which we have added the extra variable *M*.

Table 7.9   Good controls 2: adjusting for Z gives us unbiased estimates for the causal effect between X and Y.

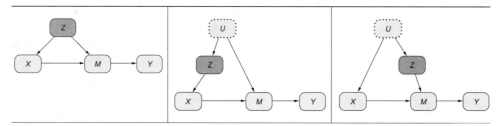

7.3.2 Neutral controls

The examples in table 7.10 are called *neutral* because we get unbiased estimates regardless of whether we adjust for them. The reason is that formally, *Z* is an adjustment set for the back-door criterion: *Z* is not a descendant, and if we condition on *Z*, we block all back-door paths. So, in the case on the left, it closes the only back-door path. And on the right, it also closes all back-door paths because there are none. So, we can use *Z* for the adjustment formula.

Table 7.10   Neutral controls: there is no difference adjusting for Z in terms of bias.

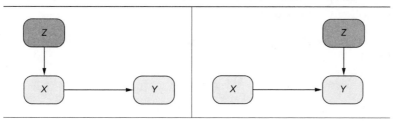

At the same time, conditioning on *Z*, we are blocking a path already blocked by default because there is no connection from *X* to *Y* going through *Z* (*Z* is not a con-founder). So if we don't adjust for *Z*, we still get unbiased estimates.

7.3.3   Bad controls

The two DAGs in table 7.11 are bad controls. They don't satisfy the back-door crite-rion because they are descendants of *X*. Both of them may induce the effect known as *selection bias*. In the first one (the argument for the second one works the same way), if we condition on *Z*, we change the distribution on *Y*. So, if we analyze the effect of *X* into *Y*, conditioning on *Z*, the result may have bias. For example, let *X* be the treat-ment with some drug for a particular illness, *Y* the number of days it takes each patient to recover from the disease, and *Z* the number of days it takes the patient to return to work. If we condition on those patients who went back to work soon and analyze the effect of the treatment for those patients, we will conclude that the drug works better than it does if we consider the whole population.

Table 7.11   Bad controls 1: adjusting for Z will provide, in general, biased estimates for the causal effect between X and Y.

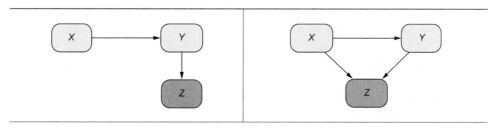

Biostatisticians and econometricians have known for a while that if we want to analyze the effect of a variable *X* into another *Y*, we may need to adjust for some variables. They also knew that not all variables are valid for adjustment. As we have seen, variables depending on the treatment variable *X* (called *post-treatment*) may induce selection bias or reduce the estimated causal effect from *X* to *Y*. So they knew these were not good for adjusting. Before the back-door theory was developed, there were many discussions about which variables we should adjust for. One hypothesis was that variables before the treatment (called *pre-treatment*) are always valid for adjustment. Pretreatment variables either affect *X* or not, but if they do, they never depend on *X* because they occur earlier in time. But are all pretreatment variables valid for the adjustment formula? The answer is no, as we will see in the examples shown in table 7.12.

Table 7.12 Bad controls 22: adjusting for *Z* generally provides biased estimates for the causal effect between *X* and *Y*.

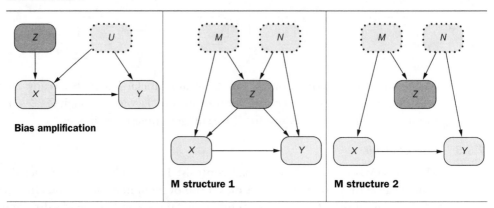

In the first DAG in table 7.12, we fail to adjust for the true confounders because they are unobserved. So the question is whether we should adjust for *Z*. Mistaking *Z* for a confounder can easily happen because it affects the treatment variable. But adjusting for *Z* doesn't solve the real problem: confounding due to *U*. It turns out that adjusting for *Z* harms our estimations when models are linear. It would take some time to explain why; if you want to understand this effect in more detail, see the references at the end of the chapter.

The second DAG is known as the M structure. Variables *M* and *N* are unobserved, and the pretreatment variable *Z* is both a collider and a confounder. Because *Z* is the only confounder, we must condition on *Z*, but if we do, we open the path $X \leftarrow M \rightarrow Z \leftarrow N \rightarrow Y$. There is no way to estimate the causal effect in this case.

There is no confounding in the third DAG of in table 7.12. The back-door path is closed because it contains *Z*, a collider. So, adjusting for *Z* can potentially introduce bias.

7.4   *Revisiting previous chapters*

Now that we have learned more about the variables we need to use for the adjustment formula, we can revisit some of the ideas that appeared in previous chapters from this new point of view.

7.4.1   *Efficient controls*

We have seen many times in this chapter that to calculate a specific causal effect from *X* to *Y*, we can apply the adjustment formula with different combinations of variables.

The question is, which is the best? If we have many candidates for unbiased estimators, the best is the one with less variance (so it requires the least data to obtain a good estimate). Knowing a priori the best set of adjustment variables is still an active area of research. In this book, we will not see a definitive solution to this problem, just some hints. See the further reading at the end of the chapter for further references.

To get an idea of the kind of reasoning used to select good adjustment sets, we will use the examples of neutral controls from earlier in the case of linear models. These simple examples will help give you the idea. In both cases in table 7.13, we get unbiased estimates independently of adjusting for the variable Z. The question is, is it better to adjust for Z?

Table 7.13   These controls are neutral in terms of bias, but not variance. The outcome predictor generally decreases the variance of your estimations, whereas the treatment predictor may increase them.

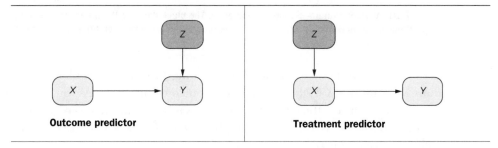

Let's start with the linear model on the left in table 7.13. The model can be written as

$$Y := a + bX + cZ + \varepsilon_Y$$

If we run a regression $Y \sim X + Z$, the remaining error term is ε_Y. On the other hand, when we run a regression $Y \sim X$, the remaining error is the combined term $cZ + \varepsilon_Y$, which has variance $\text{Var}(cZ + \varepsilon_Y) = c^2\text{Var}(Z) + \text{Var}(\varepsilon_Y) > \text{Var}(\varepsilon_Y)$, which is strictly greater than $\text{Var}(\varepsilon_Y)$. So, the estimator of the first regression has a lower variance and is thus preferable to the second.

Let's see the intuition. The variable Y has some background noise (the remaining error term). We want to estimate the causal effect of X that is hidden amid all this noise. So, reducing the background noise will make it easier to estimate the causal effect from X. And one way to reduce the noise is to add other predictive variables of Y, in this case, Z.

Another way to visualize this idea is the graph shown in chapter 1, repeated for clarity in figure 7.18. On the left, we show a sample of some variable y. On the right, the same data is split by two different values of x (horizontal axis), giving conditional distributions for different xs. The variance of the figure on the left is greater than the variance of each of the groups on the right.

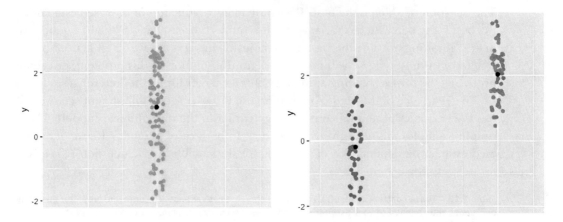

Figure 7.18 Variance versus conditional variance. The black dots are the means for each group. On the left is the unconditional expectation, and on the right is each group's conditional expectation.

Let's create a synthetic example. The following two listings simulate the two regressions $Y \sim X$ and $Y \sim X + Z$ for the case of an outcome predictor. As you can see in tables 7.14 and 7.15, the coefficient of the variable X is similar in the two regressions, but the standard deviation is three times higher (0.3167 versus 0.09373) when we don't include Z as a predictor.

Listing 7.13   (R) Adding a predictor to improve estimation of coefficient x

```
set.seed(1234)
n <- 100
z <- rnorm(n, sd=.5)
x <- rnorm(n, sd=.5)
y <- 3*x + 3*z + rnorm(n, sd=.5)
summary(lm(y ~ x))
summary(lm(y ~ x + z))
```

Listing 7.14   (Python) Adding a predictor to improve estimation of coefficient x

```
from numpy.random import normal, seed
import statsmodels.formula.api as smf
import pandas as pd
seed(1234)
n = 100
z = normal(loc=0, scale=.5, size=n)
x = normal(loc=0, scale=.5, size=n)
y = 3*x + 3*z + normal(loc=0, scale=.5, size=n)
df = pd.DataFrame({'x': x, 'y': y, 'z': z})
smf.ols(formula='y ~ x', data=df).fit().summary()
smf.ols(formula='y ~ x + z', data=df).fit().summary()
```

Table 7.14 Model results (R) regressing Y ~ X

Variable	Estimation	Standard deviation
Intercept	−0.1581	0.1628
x	3.0122	0.3167
z	-	-

Table 7.15 Model results (R) regressing Y ~ X + Z

Variable	Estimation	Standard deviation
Intercept	0.08179	0.04874
x	3.08832	0.09373
z	3.08051	0.09633

Efficiency in A/B tests

The figure on the left in table 7.13 describes a frequent situation in A/B tests or RCTs. Even though the treatment variable is selected randomly, we may still have predictive variables of the outcome. For instance, in an RCT where we give a treatment to cure a particular illness, the patient's recovery will depend on their age, gender, where they live, and so on. So, all of them are predictors of the outcome. They are not confounders because they have not been used to decide the treatment.

We know now that adjusting for these variables does not introduce bias in our estimations. However, they may benefit our estimates because they may reduce the variance.

In practice, whether to adjust for them depends on the sample size and the number of predictive variables we have. For example, suppose we have only 10 patients and 20 predictive variables. In that case, we have more variables than observations, and from the statistical point of view, it is not a good idea to include them in a linear regression. But if we have enough data, including them will reduce the variance. If you want to learn more about covariate adjustment in RCT, I suggest looking at specialized literature on this topic.

We will see now that in the treatment predictor case on the right in table 7.13, it is better not to control for Z. The variable Y only depends directly on X, so we can write

$$Y := a + bX + \varepsilon_Y$$

However, we can also think that it also depends on Z, but with a coefficient of zero:

$$Y := a + bX + 0 \times Z + \varepsilon_Y$$

The discussion of the difference in remaining error terms between regressing $Y \sim X$ or $Y \sim X + Z$ doesn't help much in this case because they both have the same error term ε_Y. The argument here is different. The covariates X and Z can be highly correlated. If it helps, you can imagine the artificial extreme case where X is a mere copy of Z, $X := Z$. Then we have a case of multicollinearity: the variables X and Z highly correlated, so the regression has a hard time knowing how much effect comes from X and how much comes from Z. Mathematically speaking, this effect is translated into higher *standard error* (the standard deviation of the coefficient) when including the variables Z into the regression. In the extreme case $X := Z$, because both are exactly equal, there is an infinite set of solutions for the regression problem. Thus the model is incapable of giving a unique set of regression coefficients.

Listings 7.15 and 7.16 show an experiment for the two regressions. Notice that the noise term in the definition of X has a standard deviation of 0.1. The smaller the standard deviation, the larger the correlation between Z and X is. Results (in R; in Python should be similar) are shown in tables 7.16 and 7.17. The situation is reversed from the outcome predictor case. When we regress only for X, the standard deviation is 0.08915, and when we also control for Z, the standard deviation is 0.41669 (more than four times larger).

Listing 7.15   (R) Adding a treatment that worsens the estimation of coefficient *x*

```
z <- rnorm(n, sd=.5)
x <- z + rnorm(n, sd=.1)
y <- 3*x + rnorm(n, sd=.5)
summary(lm(y ~ x))
summary(lm(y ~ x + z))
```

Listing 7.16   (Python) Adding a treatment that worsens the estimation of coefficient *x*

```
z = normal(loc=0, scale=.5, size=n)
x = z + normal(loc=0, scale=.1, size=n)
y = 3*x + normal(loc=0, scale=.5, size=n)
df = pd.DataFrame({'x': x, 'y': y, 'z': z})
smf.ols(formula='y ~ x', data=df).fit().summary()
smf.ols(formula='y ~ x + z', data=df).fit().summary()
```

Table 7.16   Model results (R) regressing $Y \sim X$

Variable	Estimation	Standard deviation
Intercept	−0.06823	0.04665
x	3.03378	0.08915
z	-	-

Table 7.17 Model results (R) regressing Y ~ X + Z

Variable	Estimation	Standard deviation
Intercept	−0.06981	0.04608
x	2.27345	0.41669
z	0.77902	0.41730

7.4.2 Propensity score

In chapter 5, we saw that in a situation like that shown in figure 7.19, instead of adjusting for all the variables $Z_1, ..., Z_k$, we can adjust using only a variable called the propensity score that is calculated as $PS(Z_1, ..., Z_k) = E[X|Z_1, ..., Z_k]$ (remember that PS is a function that depends on the Z variables). Because the propensity score adjustment is a variation of the adjustment formula, now we know that we can apply it as long as the set $Z_1, ..., Z_k$ satisfies the back-door criterion.

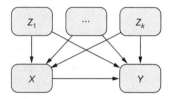

Figure 7.19 Multiple observed confounders

We will see now that the propensity score can be interpreted as a variable closing all back-door paths. That explains why it is enough to adjust for the propensity score. If we want to include the propensity score as a new variable in the DAG, we need to describe its relationship with any other variable. We draw an arrow from each Z into PS because the propensity score depends on $Z_1, ..., Z_k$ to be calculated. Then we must relate the PS to the treatment X. Recall that the definition of propensity scores for a particular patient is its probability of being treated. So, we can draw an arrow from the PS to the treatment variable X. In addition, we saw that given a value of the propensity score, the distribution of each of the Z covariates is the same for the treated and not treated groups. That is, given a value of PS, the variables X and $Z_1, ..., Z_k$ are independent. This is equivalent to say that the PS d-separates X from $Z_1, ..., Z_k$.

Thus, we can represent the propensity scores as in figure 7.20, as if it summarized all the necessary information from the Z variables into one, and conditioning on this PS blocks all back-door paths.

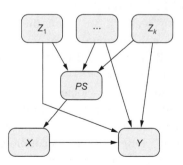

Figure 7.20 The effect of confounders on the treatment is channeled through the propensity score PS variable.

7.4.3 Again: Don't include variables in your model just because they make the model more accurate

In chapter 5, we mentioned that when creating a propensity-score model, we shouldn't choose variables just to maximize accuracy. Now we have the concepts needed to better understand this idea. The goal of the propensity score is twofold: to check the positivity assumption for the variables we are adjusting for, and to apply the adjustment formula. Therefore, the variables used to calculate the propensity score should be chosen based on the back-door criterion. If we pick the wrong variables, we can get very biased estimates of the ATE.

But there's more to the story. In section 7.4, we saw that variables that predict the treatment well but don't affect the outcome can increase the variance of our ATEs. So, if we select the variables for our propensity score aiming to maximize accuracy, we may end up using a variable that makes the propensity score very accurate but increases the uncertainty of the ATE.

7.4.4 Should you adjust for income?

In chapter 5, we proposed an exercise for computing a propensity score adjustment. We wanted to evaluate whether performing a right heart catheterization (RHC) test affected patient survival. To know in detail which variables we should adjust for, we should talk to an expert on the matter. For the sake of the exercise, we take for granted that all the variables provided in the dataset are confounders (except the treatment and the outcome, of course).

Because most of us are not cardiologists, we will focus on a more familiar variable. Should we adjust for the variable Income? We will not provide a definitive answer because it depends on the specifics of how the data was obtained. But we will get an idea of how to analyze different potential scenarios.

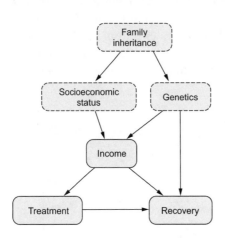

Figure 7.21 Even though Family Inheritance is a confounder, we can remove its effect conditioning on Income.

The level of income depends on many factors including genetics (natural skills for the job) and socioeconomic status, both inherited from the patient's family. In addition, income may affect the treatment because some insurance plans cover the treatment and others don't. Suppose that figure 7.21 is a reliable representation of the process. Then, if we close the only back door by conditioning on income, we get an unbiased estimate of the effect of the treatment on recovery.

However, if socioeconomic status affected the treatment in other ways, the problem would be more complicated. For instance, inherited socioeconomic status may determine where the patient lives. That also affects which hospital the patient went to for treatment. If that is the case, as in figure 7.22, we must adjust for Income and Home Location. These two variables close all the back-door paths. Missing one of them may potentially incur bias.

7.4.5 Linear models

As we have said, the back door is useful for knowing which variables we should adjust for. How can the back door be applied in linear models? It turns out the intuition developed in this chapter also applies to linear models: to find the total effect, we need to adjust for a set closing all back-door paths. And to find the direct effect, we need to adjust for a set closing all back-door paths and all paths containing mediators. Let's see this in detail.

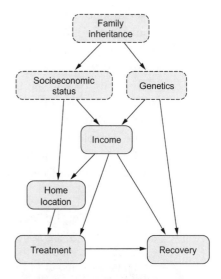

Figure 7.22 **Income plays a collider role, so conditioning only on Income can open new correlation paths. We also need to condition on Home Location.**

In the DAG in table 7.18 (explained in chapter 6), we find confounders, mediators, and colliders. We know that if we run the regression $Y \sim X$, the resulting coefficient of X will not be the causal effect of X to Y because there is a confounder that may add bias to our estimation. The direct effect is e (see the equations describing the system), and the total effect is $e + cd$. The total effect is related to the "do" operator as follows:

$$E[Y|\mathrm{do}(X = x)] - E[Y|\mathrm{do}(X = x + 1)] = e + cd$$

Table 7.18 **Combining confounders, direct effect, mediators, and colliders**

DAG	In equations
	$Z := \varepsilon_Z$ $X := aZ + \varepsilon_X$ $M := cX + \varepsilon_M$ $Y := bZ + eX + dM + \varepsilon_Y$ where ε_Z, ε_X, ε_M, and ε_Y are independent of each other.

How can we obtain the total and direct effects from the data? Which linear regressions should we run? Which variables should we control for? Notice that in linear models, we "control for" variables when we include them as covariates in the regression, aiming to find the correct coefficient in the model. This is slightly different than "adjusting for" variables, which means including them in the adjustment formula, aiming to estimate the causal effect of an intervention.

In the DAG in table 7.18, if we want to measure the total effect, we need to control for the variable Z. This is because Z blocks all back-door paths. However, we must control for Z and the mediator M to estimate the direct effect. This rationale works in general, as the two following theorems state.

> **Theorem: Total effect**
>
> Given a DAG G, if a set of variables Z blocks all back-door paths and doesn't contain any descendant of X, the resulting coefficient of X in the regression $Y \sim X + Z$ is an unbiased estimator of the total effect of X into Y.

The result for the estimation of the direct effect is similar. In this case, we also need to block the mediators. How can we express this? We cannot say that Z should block all the descendants of X because colliders can also be descendants of X, and we don't want to control for them. The difference is that colliders can be descendants from Y, whereas mediators are not. So, to calculate the direct effect, we need to control all paths starting from X and ending in Y, regardless of whether they contain descendants of X, except the direct path. We also must avoid including colliders, and thus descendants of Y (potential colliders). Formally speaking, we can state this idea as follows.

> **Theorem: Direct effect**
>
> Given a DAG G, consider $G_{X \to Y}$, the same DAG with the arrow $X \to Y$ removed (the precise one we want to estimate). If a set of variables Z
>
> 1 D-separates X from Y in this new DAG $G_{X \to Y}$
> 2 Doesn't contain descendants of Y (to avoid colliders)
>
> then the resulting coefficient of X in the regression $Y \sim X + Z$ is an unbiased estimator of the direct effect of X into Y.

7.5   An advanced tool for identifying causal effects: The do-calculus

The adjustment formula is not the only way to find the causal effect of a variable X into another variable Y, but it is probably the most popular. There are situations where we cannot use the adjustment formula, but we can use other formulas to find the value of the intervention $E[Y \mid do(X = x)]$.

A theoretical tool, much less used in practice, is called *do-calculus*. It tells us whether, in a particular problem with a graph G, there is another way to estimate the causal effect and which formula to apply. The objective of this section is not to go deep into do-calculus but just to mention it and show what it looks like, in case you ever see it in the literature or need it. I recommend reading Andrew Heiss's post at www.andrewheiss .com/blog/2021/09/07/do-calculus-backdoors to understand it better.

We need first to introduce some notation. Given a DAG G, $G^{X \leftarrow}$ is the DAG where we keep all the incoming arrows to X and remove all the leaving edges from X. Similarly, $G_{X \rightarrow}$ is the graph with all the arrows leaving X while removing all the incoming ones to X.

The do-calculus consists of a set of three rules. It turns out (some theorems ensure it) that any possible formula to find a causal effect in a graph can be found using these rules. Even reading and understanding them requires an effort—again, the objective is not to understand them but just to know what they look like:

- Rule 1 (insertion/deletion of observations):

  if X, W d-separate Y, Z in the graph $G_{X \rightarrow}$

  $P(y|do(X{=}x), z, w) = P(y|do(X{=}x), w)$

- Rule 2 (action/observation exchange):

  if X, W d-separate Y, Z in the graph $G^{Z \leftarrow}_{X \rightarrow}$

  $P(y|do(X{=}x, Z{=}z), w) = P(y|do(X{=}x), z, w)$

- Rule 3 (insertion/deletion of actions):

  if X, W d-separate Y, Z in the graph $G_{X \rightarrow, Z(W) \rightarrow}$

  $P(y|do(X{=}x, Z{=}z), w) = P(y|do(X{=}x), w)$

where $Z(W)$ is the set of nodes in Z that are not ancestors of any node in W in the graph $G_{X \rightarrow}$ (if you finished this sentence, congratulations on your perseverance!).

7.6 Further reading

A key reference for this chapter is the paper "A Crash Course in Good and Bad Controls" by Carlos Cinelli, Andrew Froney, and Judea Pearl (https://mng.bz/Aa7E, revised 2022). It provides examples of when to control for covariates and when not to, along with additional references.

Figure 7.3 is from the 2008 paper "Reducing Bias through Directed Acyclic Graphs" by Shrier and Platt (https://mng.bz/ZVvj).

If you want to go deeper into finding efficient controls, as explained in section 7.4, I suggest you read the paper "Graphical Criteria for Efficient Total Effect Estimation via Adjustment in Causal Linear Models" (2019) by Leonard Henckel, Emilija Perkovi?, and Marloes H. Maathuis. They give graphical conditions for choosing good adjustment sets for the case of linear models. In addition, "Efficient Adjustment Sets for Population Average Treatment Effect Estimation in Nonparametric Causal Graphical Models" (2019) by Andrea Rotnitzky and Ezequiel Smucler sgeneralize the previous results to any kind of model, not necessarily linear ones.

7.7   *Chapter quiz*

As we conclude the chapter, it's important to ensure that you have a solid understanding of the key concepts. Here are the essential questions you should be able to answer clearly and concisely. If you can't, I suggest rereading the corresponding references:

1. Consider a chain $X \rightarrow Y \rightarrow Z$. If we condition on Y, do X and Z become independent?
   Answer in section 7.1.4
2. Consider a fork $X \leftarrow Y \rightarrow Z$. If we condition on Y, do X and Z become independent?
   Answer in section 7.1.4
3. Consider a collider $X \rightarrow Y \leftarrow Z$. If we condition on Y, do X and Z become independent?
   Answer in section 7.1.4
4. What is the definition of d-separation?
   Answer in section 7.1.6
5. How are d-separation and independence related?
   Answer in section 7.1.6
6. What is the back-door criterion? Informally speaking, what does it say?
   Answer in the section "Back-door criterion"
7. Why do we need the back-door criterion?
   Answer in section 7.2
8. In general, does adjusting for the treatment increase the variance of estimations?
   Answer in section 7.6
9. Can the back-door criterion be used to estimate total effects in linear models?
   Answer in section 7.4.5

Summary

- The main takeaway is that data is generally insufficient to build a DAG. We also need domain knowledge.
- Conditioning on variables in a DAG can open and close correlation paths. D-separation is a graphical criterion that can be applied on the particular DAG that lets us know which variables to condition on to make two variables independent.
- D-separation is the main ingredient for the back-door criterion: to estimate a causal effect between two variables X and Y, we need to close all the paths containing a confounder, carefully opening new paths when we condition on colliders.
- The back-door criterion helps us know which variables we should adjust for when applying the adjustment formula. Such selection should be made independently of which variation of the adjustment formula we use: linear models, propensity scores, using machine learning, etc.
- Learning and understanding the back-door criterion lets us plan in advance which variables we need to carry out our causal analysis.

Advanced tools with the DoubleML library

8

This chapter covers

- Estimating the effect of a continuous decision variable with double machine learning
- Learning to calculate confidence intervals for the ATE
- Combining two estimators to get a better one with doubly robust techniques

In the previous chapters, we covered the basic theory and practice of removing the effect of confounders using the adjustment formula. In this chapter, we will go one step further and explore three separate techniques that will improve the accuracy and reliability of our causal estimates. These techniques, double machine learning, confidence intervals, and doubly robust techniques, are used when precision is paramount. For instance, people working in healthcare or finance may apply these approaches.

Even though learning these techniques takes a while, using them is straightforward with open source libraries. Fortunately, the methods discussed in this chapter have already been implemented in the DoubleML library (https://docs.doubleml .org), available for both R and Python. After delving into the theoretical foundations, we will explore how to effectively employ these methods using this library.

> **NOTE** You don't need to read this chapter to be able to follow the rest of the book. If these topics are not a priority or are too technical, you can skip this chapter and return later when you need to learn about these tools.

Let's start with a brief definition of three techniques. Then we'll spend the rest of the chapter on the details.

First is *double machine learning* (DML). It is generally recommended to begin your analysis using linear models due to their simplicity of implementation and interpretation. Linear models serve as a valuable starting point as they establish a baseline model that helps identify potential data problems and provides a benchmark for evaluating the performance of more advanced models.

However, as you delve deeper into your analysis, you may encounter situations where linear models are insufficient for capturing complex relationships in the data. Nonlinearities, for example, require more flexible modeling techniques. In such cases, machine learning models come into play.

In chapter 4, we explored the S-learner and T-learner approaches, which combine machine learning with the adjustment formula to handle nonlinearities. Now we will introduce a new approach called double machine learning. This technique has the following advantages over the previous methods we have seen:

- DML works with continuous and binary treatment variables.
- DML uses machine learning to model causal relationships, increasing the accuracy of your causal estimations.
- DML is data efficient. That is, it requires less data than other methods to obtain the same level of precision.
- DML can estimate heterogeneous treatment effects. In other words, it can be used to estimate causal effects on different subpopulations: for example, estimating the difference in the effect of price between loyal and infrequent clients.

In this chapter, we will look at the primary algorithm used when implementing DML and see how to apply the process with the DoubleML package.

The second technique is using *confidence intervals*. Estimating causal effects helps us make better-informed decisions. That is, if the ATE (as the difference in effect between a new treatment and an old one) is positive, we will conclude that the new treatment works better and use it from now on. However, basing our decisions only on the ATE is not a good idea. It is a recommended practice to always provide confidence intervals with causal estimates.

Generally speaking, we use our data to estimate the ATE. But the resulting ATE would be different if we had a different dataset. So, in addition to any result we obtain,

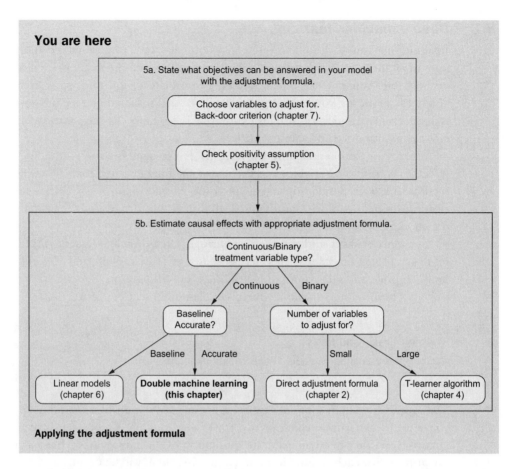

You are here

5a. State what objectives can be answered in your model with the adjustment formula.

Choose variables to adjust for. Back-door criterion (chapter 7).

Check positivity assumption (chapter 5).

5b. Estimate causal effects with appropriate adjustment formula.

Continuous/Binary treatment variable type?

Continuous   Binary

Baseline/ Accurate?   Number of variables to adjust for?

Baseline   Accurate   Small   Large

Linear models (chapter 6)   **Double machine learning (this chapter)**   Direct adjustment formula (chapter 2)   T-learner algorithm (chapter 4)

Applying the adjustment formula

we must also communicate how much this result can change if our data changes. And that is precisely what confidence intervals provide. We will explain the two major approaches for calculating confidence intervals: using a statistical formula whenever available or using resampling techniques that rely on computer simulations.

The third technique is the use of *double robust estimators*. In our daily work, once we have obtained a first causal estimate, usually there is little or no margin for further improvement. But for some applications, such as healthcare, accuracy is critical. In these cases, one option is to use doubly robust (DR) techniques. These are tools that let us combine two available estimations of a causal parameter to obtain a more accurate new one.

When to use double machine learning techniques

In general, it's better to use the adjustment formula with double machine learning techniques rather than the S- and T- algorithms, as they are more data-efficient and flexible.

8.1   *Double machine learning*

Imagine that you work in a travel agency, and you want to understand the effect on sales of an increase in the price of a flight ticket. Because the ticket price is a continuous variable, you can use linear models to estimate causal effects, as explained in chapter 6. However, you know from experience that seasonality is a confounder. That is, it affects price and sales. You also know that seasonality can have intricate nonlinear effects on both price and sales.

We can use double machine learning (DML) to combine the estimation of causal effects in continuous variables and the use of machine learning tools. We will start this section with a simplified approach called the *partially linear model* (PLM), where the relationship between price and sales is still linear, but the rest of the relationships in our model can be nonlinear.

In a more realistic and complex scenario, it is reasonable to assume that the effect of ticket prices on sales varies across seasons. This implies that the relationship between price and sales is not only nonlinear but also season-specific. We will have to wait a bit to solve this situation, which is explained in section 8.1.4.

> **Think first, read next**
>
> Could we use linear models in the pricing example?

The answer is yes. On some occasions, a linear model is all you need. For instance, if you want to determine which of two travel destinations is more sensitive to a price change, you don't need an accurate estimation of the causal effect. Just calculating a linear trend for each destination and comparing them will be enough.

> **Basic assumptions**
>
> Throughout this chapter, we will assume that we have the situation shown in the figure. Variable D is the treatment or decision variable, O is the outcome, and C is a set of confounders for which we need to adjust. Recall that the back-door criterion from chapter 7 can assist in deciding which variables we need to choose. If you are uncomfortable with this abstract representation, pick a problem with this structure and bear it in mind throughout the chapter—for instance, a pricing problem for an airline company:
>
>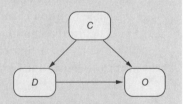
>
> Graph used throughout this chapter. C denotes the vector of confounders, D stands for decision, and O is the outcome.
>
> - D is the ticket price, which is usually a continuous variable.
> - O is the number of ticket sales.
> - C are contextual variables, such as seasonality and annual inflation rate.

Informally speaking, the idea of DML is the following. In the situation in the figure shown in "Basic assumptions," try to predict as well as possible treatment D using as inputs confounders C. Calculate the residuals—the actual values of D minus their predictions—representing information that depends on factors other than C and thus cannot be predicted from C. These residuals will be used later. Then create a second model predicting the outcome O from confounders C. Again, calculate its residuals. Once you have removed the influence of C from D and O, the remaining residuals are enough to estimate the causal effect. You can run a linear regression between the two sets of residuals, and the resulting coefficient is the causal effect you are looking for. The precise algorithm for the DML is shown in figure 8.1.

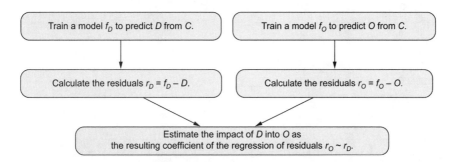

Figure 8.1   Steps to run the DML algorithm. The main goal of this algorithm is to first get rid of the influence of confounder C on both the decision and outcome variables. This is done using two predictive models. What remains after their predictions, called residuals, is used to estimate the causal effect from D to O.

We will explain a simplified version of the DML technique with linear models. Once we get the idea, we will develop a more elaborate solution with machine learning models. Finally, we will discuss using DML to calculate heterogeneous treatment effects.

8.1.1   FWL theorem: The predecessor of DML

DML draws on a well-known theorem in linear models discovered by Frisch, Waugh, and Lovell (called the FWL theorem for short). Consider the situation where all the relations in figure 8.2 are linear. We know from chapter 6 that to estimate the effect of D into O, we need to control for the vector C. So, we should run the linear regression $O \sim D + C$, and the resulting coefficient of D in the linear model is the effect of variable D.

It turns out that there is another way to calculate the same coefficient. *Intuitively, if we remove the effect that confounder C exerts on D and also on O, we may remove the overall effect of the confounder on the system—and with the remaining values, we can estimate without bias the effect of D into O.* More precisely, given a dataset like the one in table 8.1, we can run the following steps, shown in figure 8.2:

1　Run a regression $D \sim C$ to estimate the effect of the confounders on D. Use the resulting model to predict $\widehat{d_i}$ for each row in the dataset. Calculate the residuals (the real value of the treatment minus the prediction) $r_i^d = d_i - \widehat{d_i}$. We have subtracted the effect of the confounders from the treatment.

2　Repeat the process using the outcome O instead of the treatment. Run a regression $O \sim C$, and use the resulting model to predict $\widehat{o_i}$ for each row in the dataset. Calculate the residuals $r_i^0 = o_i - \widehat{o_i}$.

3　With the remaining residuals r_i^d, r_i^o, run a regression $R^O \sim R^D$. The resulting coefficient is the effect of D into O.

Table 8.1　Available data with propensity scores calculated

O	D	C^1	...	C^p
o_1	d_1	c_1^1	...	c_1^p
...	...	...	...	...
O_n	d_n	s_n^1	...	c_n^p

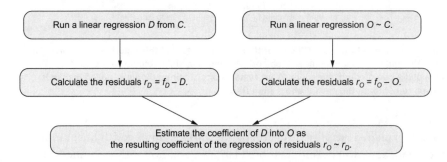

Figure 8.2　DML strategy applied to linear regressions to calculate the coefficient from D to O

Sounds like fun, but how can this possibly work? For simplicity, we will assume that C is only one variable (instead of a vector) and that the models don't have intercepts (this can be achieved by standardizing the variables). Then the equations describing the graph are

$$D = aC + \varepsilon_D$$
$$O = \beta D + cC + \varepsilon_O$$

where ε_D, ε_O are independent from one another. The coefficient we are interested in is the term β, the effect of the treatment on the outcome.

The first step of the procedure asks to run a linear model $D \sim C$, used for making predictions $\hat{D}$ (for each observation). If we have enough data, predictions $\hat{D}$ will be close to the true value D. So, the residual $R^d = D - \hat{D}$ will be close to the actual error term ε_D.

The second step asks for a regression $O \sim C$ of the outcome only with confounders C. As we did in previous chapters, to understand what this regression will estimate, we need to fully express the relationship of O with respect to C, substituting the value of D in the equation:

$$O = \beta D + cC + \varepsilon_O = \beta(aC + \varepsilon_D) + cC + \varepsilon_O = (a\beta + c)C + \beta\varepsilon_D + \varepsilon_O$$

When we run the regression $O \sim C$, the error term is not ε_O (as it would be if regressing with respect to C and D) but rather the noise term $\beta \varepsilon_D + \varepsilon_O$ from the resulting equation. So if we run a regression $O \sim C$ and later use this model to predict the value of O with respect to C, obtaining the predictions $\hat{O}$, the residuals $R^O = O - \hat{O}$ will be close to error term $\beta \varepsilon_D + \varepsilon \sim O$.

Thus, running a regression of the residuals $R^O \sim R^D$ will be like running a regression of the outcome residual $\beta \varepsilon_D + \varepsilon \sim O$ with respect to the treatment residual ε_D: the resulting coefficient of the regression will be approximately β, which is the correct answer.

Think first, read next

It seems that the effect of the treatment on the outcome in the graph in "Basic assumptions" can be calculated two different ways:

- Using a linear model that controls for confounders
- Creating two linear models to predict the treatment and outcome, respectively, and then calculating a regression with the residuals of the two previous models

Which algorithm do you think works better?

The answer is surprising: the two give the *exact same result* (numerically speaking). This result is known as the Frisch, Waugh, and Lovell theorem. Let's see an example with code using simulated data.

Listing 8.1 (R) Creating synthetic data

```
set.seed(1234)
n <- 100
treatment_effect <- 5
confounder <- runif(n)
treatment <- -3*confounder + rnorm(n)
outcome <- -2*confounder + treatment_effect*treatment + rnorm(n)
df <- data.frame(confounder, treatment, outcome)
```

Listing 8.2 (Python) Creating synthetic data

```
from numpy.random import seed, normal, uniform
import pandas as pd
```

```
import statsmodels.api as sm
seed(1234)
n = 100
treatment_effect = 5
confounder = uniform(size=n)
treatment = -3*confounder + normal(size=n)
outcome = -2*confounder + treatment_effect*treatment + \
    normal(size=n)
df = pd.DataFrame({
    'confounder': confounder,
    'treatment': treatment,
    'outcome': outcome
})
```

Then we can run the linear regression $O \sim D + C$ as shown next, with the results (in R) shown in table 8.2. The coefficient we are interested in is the effect of the treatment on the outcome: in this case, 4.9473069, which is very close to the true treatment effect, 5.

Listing 8.3 (R) Linear estimation controlling for confounders

```
coefficients(lm(outcome ~ confounder + treatment ))
```

Listing 8.4 (Python) Linear estimation controlling for confounders

```
model = sm.OLS(outcome, df[['treatment', 'confounder']]).fit()
model.params
```

Table 8.2 Resulting coefficients from regressing $O \sim T + D$ (in R)

Coefficients	Estimate
(Intercept)	0.1147036
confounder	-2.0984803
treatment	4.9473069

Now we can run the FWL strategy. The results are shown in table 8.3: we get the same number (4.947307) as before with the regression $O \sim D + C$ (there may be slight differences, but they are due to rounding errors).

Listing 8.5 (R) Linear estimation with the FWL strategy

```
res_y <- outcome - predict(lm(outcome~confounder, df), df)
res_d <- treatment - predict(lm(treatment~confounder, df), df)
coefficients(lm(res_y ~ res_d))
```

Listing 8.6 (Python) Linear estimation with the FWL strategy

```
model_treatment = sm.OLS(treatment, confounder).fit()
residuals_treatment = treatment - model_treatment.predict(confounder)
```

```
model_outcome = sm.OLS(outcome, confounder).fit()
residuals_outcome = outcome - model_outcome.predict(confounder)
sm.OLS(residuals_outcome, residuals_treatment).fit().params
```

Table 8.3 Resulting coefficients from regressing *O* ~ *T* + *D* (in R)

Coefficients	Estimate
(Intercept)	-2.486900e-15
treatment	4.947307

8.1.2 *Nonlinear models with DML*

We have seen with the FWL theorem an alternative way to estimate the effect of a variable in a linear model. But does the same algorithm work with nonlinear models fitted with machine learning models? The answer is yes; let's see why.

THE PARTIALLY LINEAR MODEL

DML is a general technique that has many variations. For the sake of simplicity, we will work with the PLM. We will assume that the outcome can be written as

$$O = \beta D + g(C) + U$$

Here we are saying that the relationship between D and O is linear, but unlike in linear models, the relationship between the set of confounders C and the outcome O can have any kind of relationship, potentially nonlinear, through a function g. This combination of linear dependence from D but nonlinear for C is why this model is called *partially linear. Notice that a linear relationship in the treatment variable means the effect is constant for all values of the treatment.* For instance, consider the example of estimating the effect of a particular product's price (D) on its sales (O). If we increase the price by \$1, the effect on sales (β) remains the same whether the initial price is \$10 or \$20.

The term U represents the exogenous unobserved variables affecting O. We will make the technical assumption that given a particular value of D and C, the expectation of the term U is zero, and $E[U|D, C] = 0$. If this assumption sounds weird or unnatural, I suggest you look at chapter 4, which explains in more detail.

We will also assume that the relationship between confounders and the decision variable can be potentially nonlinear and is expressed through a function m

$$D = m(C) + V$$

where V are the exogenous unobserved variables affecting D. Similarly to the previous case with U, we will assume that $E[V|C] = 0$.

We don't know the functions g and m, and we must estimate them using machine learning models. Nor do we know the parameter β, which is decision variable D's effect on outcome O. This is the objective of our analysis.

WHY DOES THE FWL STRATEGY WORK IN THIS CASE?

Let's understand why the algorithm described in figure 8.3 (the same as the introduction, repeated for convenience), which follows the linear version of figure 8.2, works to estimate causal effects. But first, let's answer where the "ML" in DML comes from.

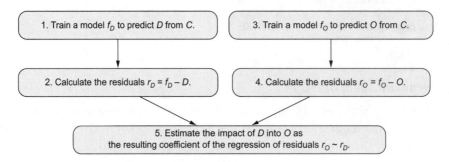

Figure 8.3 Steps to execute the DML algorithm

The function m is the conditional expectation $E[D|C]$.

$$E[D|C] = E[m(C)|C] + E[V|C] = m(C)$$

because $E[V|C] = 0$; and given a value of C, the value of $m(C)$ does not vary, and thus its expectation is correspondingly $m(C)$. Recall that in chapter 4, we learned that conditional expectations can be approximated using machine learning models. That means in step 1 in figure 8.3, we are approximating the function $m(C)$ by training a machine learning model f_D that predicts D from C.

We can think then that function g is the expectation of O conditioned on C. But this is not the case! Outcome O depends on C through C but also through D, which also depends on C. So,

$$E[O|C] = \beta E[D|C] + E[g(C)|C] = \beta\, m(C) + g(C)$$

So in step 3 in figure 8.3, we are approximating the value of $\beta\, m(C) + g(C)$.

If f_D is a good predictor of D (thus approximating $f_D \approx m(C)$ well) and f_O is a good predictor of O (thus approximating $f_O \approx \beta m(C) + g(C)$ well), then because we have the relationships

$$D = m(C) + V \approx m(C) + V$$

and

$$O = \beta D + g(C) + U \approx \beta\, m(C) + g(C) + U$$

the residuals will be good approximations of the values

$$r_D = f_D(C) - D \approx V$$
$$r_O = f_O(C) - O \approx \beta(D - m(C)) + U = \beta V + U$$

So, when we run the linear regression $r_O \sim r_D$, we are approximating the linear regression $\beta V + U \sim V$, and the expected coefficient is precisely our objective β.

DML works with binary and continuous decision variables

When I first read about DML in the original paper by Chernozhukov et al. (check out section 8.4), it felt weird that it also worked with binary decision variables D. I'm used to seeing error terms that are continuous variables. But the specification of D

$$D = m(C) + V$$

does not work if the error term V is continuous. The reason is that D takes only two values (0 or 1). For a given C, the term $m(C) = E[D|C]$ is a constant, so $V = D - m(C)$ can take only two different values at most. Then I realized that it was not a problem. Nowhere did the paper assume that V would be continuous. Consequently, the DML specification also works when D is binary.

EFFICIENCY OF THE DML ESTIMATOR

When it comes to estimation, a frequent concern is determining sufficient data to draw reliable conclusions. In particular, DML exhibits data efficiency, meaning it can yield a reliable estimate of the causal effect using a smaller dataset than other methods, such as the T-learner mentioned in chapter 4. But how do we come to this conclusion? In this section, we will delve into the reasoning behind this concept.

Hypothetically speaking, you may be inclined to assess the required sample size for the DML through experimentation. To do so, you can follow these steps:

1 Generate multiple datasets with different characteristics.
2 Apply DML to each dataset using varying sample sizes.
3 Measure the disparity between the estimated and actual causal effects.

By analyzing the results of these experiments, you can determine the necessary sample size to achieve a specific level of accuracy in your estimations. However, it's important to note that these results would only describe how quickly DML works in the specific datasets you tested. It wouldn't guarantee similar performance on other datasets you might encounter in the future.

To ensure the performance of DML with any dataset, experimentation alone may not be sufficient. It is essential to rely on advanced statistical and mathematical proofs. Fortunately, the paper that introduced DML provides such proof, demonstrating that under reasonable conditions, DML converges rapidly to the expected causal effect. This result offers a solid foundation for relying on DML beyond specific experimental scenarios.

What does "fast convergence" mean? The statement "DML converges fast" can be expressed more formally as the DML estimator being *root*-n *consistent*. In the rest of this subsection, we will see different convergence rates, define what *n*-root convergence means, and explain why it is faster than other types of convergence.

Let's start with convergence rates. The succession $1, 1/2, 1/3, \ldots$ can be expressed as $1/n$ where n is a natural number. As n increases, the term $1/n$ decreases, so the sequence tends to zero. Another succession tending to zero is $1, 1/\sqrt{2}, 1/\sqrt{3}, \ldots$ which can be written as $1/\sqrt{n}$. As you can see in figure 8.4, the sequence $1/n$ approaches zero faster than $1/\sqrt{n}$.

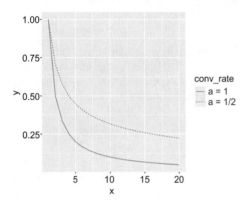

Figure 8.4 **Convergence rate for sequences $1/n$ and $1/\sqrt{n}$. We can see that $1/n$ converges faster to 0 than $1/\sqrt{n}$. The convergence rate of an algorithm tells us how fast this algorithm converges to its objective. In statistics and machine learning, the faster an estimate converges, the less data we need.**

In general, any succession $1/n^a$ where $a > 0$ tends to zero as n tends to infinity. And the higher a is, the faster the sequence approaches zero.

A root-n consistent estimator approaches the expected value at rate $1/\sqrt{n}$. In other words, if T_n is the estimator obtained from a sample of size n, the variance of T_n is of the order of $1/\sqrt{n}$.

In the original paper on DML, Chernozhukov et al. prove that the DML estimator is root-n consistent under some reasonable assumptions. The proof is highly technical and requires advanced math knowledge. You can find a more formal statement in the sidebar "Formal theorem on the convergence of DML for the partially linear model."

Why do we consider n-root convergence to be fast? To assess its speed, we need a point of comparison. Let's consider one of the simplest estimators: the sample mean. In statistics, the central limit theorem (CLT) is a fundamental result stating that the sample mean approaches its expected value at a rate of $1/\sqrt{n}$. Additionally, the sample mean is *efficient*, meaning this rate cannot be surpassed by other unbiased estimators. Therefore, because the sample mean, a straightforward estimator, exhibits n-root convergence and cannot be improved on, achieving n-root convergence for the DML method is a highly favorable outcome!

In comparison, the S-learner and T-learner are not root-n consistent. They converge much more slowly. Understanding why is not easy, but if you want to check the details, I suggest you read the section "4.1 Plug-in bias and how to remove it" from the paper by Hines et al. (see section 8.4).

Central limit theorem

The CLT states that if we take the mean of a sample for a large sample size, the outcome will behave like a normal distribution. Formally speaking, assume that we have a sample $X_1, \ldots, X_n$, where all variables have the same distribution with expectation $E[X_i] = \mu$ and variance $V[X_i] = \sigma^2$, they are independent of one another, and n is large enough. Then the sample mean for a large enough n is

$$\frac{1}{n} \sum_i X_i \sim N\left(\mu, \frac{\sigma^2}{n}\right)$$

In particular, the standard deviation of the sample mean is $\sigma/\sqrt{n}$. So, the sample mean converges to μ at a rate of $1/\sqrt{n}$.

Finally, let's give the formal result showing that the DML estimator (for simplicity, only in the case of the PLM) is n-root consistent.

Formal theorem on the convergence of DML for the PLM

If the data has been generated using the PLM

$$D = m(C) + V$$
$$O = \beta D + g(C) + U$$

and we use the DML partially linear estimator to obtain an estimation $\hat{\beta}$, then as the sample size n increases, the resulting estimation $\hat{\beta}$ behaves as a normal distribution

$$\hat{\beta} \sim N\left(\beta, \frac{\sigma^2}{n}\right)$$

where $\sigma^2 = E[U^2 V^2]/E[V]^2$. In particular, because the standard deviation is $\sigma/\sqrt{n}$, the DML estimator for the PLM is n-root consistent and efficient.

Check section 8.4 for further references where you can find the proof of this theorem.

8.1.3 *DML in practice*

DML and some of its variations are implemented in R and Python in the DoubleML library (https://docs.doubleml.org) following the original paper on DML. The DoubleML package works with the popular Python and R packages scikit learn (https://scikit-learn.org/stable/) and mlr3 (https://mlr3.mlr-org.com/), respectively.

We will not explain the library here because the website has good tutorials and examples that show how to use it. You can start with the Workflow page (https://docs.doubleml.org/stable/workflow/workflow.html), which explains the general steps to follow to calculate the causal effect of one variable on another. The documentation contains many algorithms; the one explained in this chapter is called *partially linear regression* (PLR) in the documentation. Even though the name only references regression, this method works with regression and classification problems.

The class responsible for estimating the causal effect is `DoubleMLPLR` (both in R and Python). It has two arguments:

- `ml_m`: a machine model to predict the treatment from confounders (step 1 in 8.3)
- `ml_l`: a machine model to predict the outcome from confounders (step 3 in 8.3)

For a more realistic example, look at the 401(k) introductory tutorial. 401(k) plans are pension accounts sponsored by employers. The tutorial studies the causal effect of enrolling in a 401(k) plan on net financial assets (*net_tfa*). Net financial assets is a financial measure computed as the sum of IRA balances, 401(k) balances, checking accounts, saving bonds, other interest-earning accounts, other interest-earning assets, stocks, and mutual funds, less nonmortgage debts. The tutorial uses the PLR model in Python (https://docs.doubleml.org/stable/examples/py_double_ml_pension.html) and in R (https://docs.doubleml.org/stable/examples/R_double_ml_pension.html) combined with different machine learning models to estimate the causal effect of 401(k) plans.

READING THE DOUBLEML DOCUMENTATION

If you explore the DoubleML documentation, you'll notice that it introduces several concepts and terminologies that may differ from what you're accustomed to (depending, of course, on your previous exposure to data science). This subsection provides an overview of the process described in the documentation and translates the terminology into the concepts discussed in this book. We won't delve into the intricate technical details, as they can get complex. The goal is to ensure that you can navigate the documentation without feeling overwhelmed by these technicalities, enabling you to effortlessly use this exceptional package.

So far, we have only talked about the PLM. However, the DoubleML library provides tools to estimate many types of causal effects under a wide range of DAGs. Besides the PLM, you can also find the interactive regression model (IRM), instrumental variables (IVs), and differences in differences (DiDs). The IRM will be explained in section 8.3, and IVs and DiDs will be explained in later chapters.

DML is just a particular case of a more general technique called *orthogonalization*. Orthogonalization is a method that takes existing estimators, enhances them with machine learning techniques, and transforms them into root-*n* consistent estimators.

The orthogonalization method presents the causal effect as the solution to an equation. This equation is formulated in relation to a *score* function. If you're familiar with machine learning, you can consider this score function similar to a loss function. There is a specific score function for each combination of DAG and causal parameters. Throughout the documentation, you'll come across these score functions frequently. Don't be intimidated by them! You don't need to understand them well to use DoubleML properly.

You'll also come across the term *nuisance* often. It refers to secondary functions necessary to estimate the primary causal parameter of interest. For instance, the propensity score is a function required to apply the adjustment formula, but it's not inherently of interest. In this case, the propensity score is considered a nuisance function.

Finally, keep in mind that this library tries to handle three types of biases at the same time:

- Confounding bias addressed by the DML algorithm
- Overfitting bias, addressed by cross-validation
- Bias due to predicting over the same dataset, addressed by cross-fitting

AVOIDING OVER-FITTING WITH CROSS-FITTING

DML is sensitive to over-fitting. The reason can be intuited in figure 8.3. When we apply DML, we use a dataset to train a machine learning model; later, we need to make predictions on the same dataset. As explained in chapter 4, this procedure can lead to over-fitting. The solution to this problem is to perform cross-fitting (introduced in the paper by Chernozhukov et al.; see section 8.4), as also explained in chapter 4 (look at chapter 4 again if you don't remember).

Cross-fitting algorithm applied on DML

The steps to apply a two-fold cross-fitting to DML, as shown in the figure, are the following:

1 Split the dataset into two equally sized datasets D_1, D_2.
2 Train two machine learning models in D_1.
3 Use those machine learning models to make predictions in D_2, and calculate the linear regression coefficient.
4 Switch the roles of D_1 and D_2. The resulting coefficient is the average of the two linear regressions.

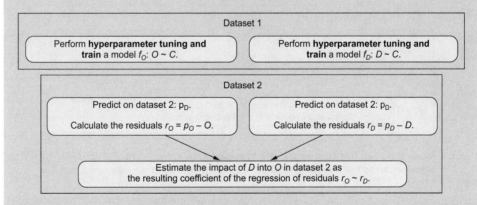

Two-fold cross-fitting applied to the DML algorithm. Once the process is finished, you must switch roles between datasets 1 and 2. This process can be generalized to *k*-fold cross-fitting by breaking the data into *k* datasets instead of two.

Cross-fitting is encouraged by the DML package (check the documentation at https://docs.doubleml.org/stable/guide/resampling.html). Fortunately, *k*-cross fitting can be easily performed by DML: pass the argument `n_folds = k` (i.e., `n_folds = 5` performs five-cross fitting) to the `DoubleMLPLR` class.

HYPERPARAMETER TUNING

Before fitting a machine learning model to our data, we need to specify a particular set of parameters called *hyperparameters* (for instance, the *k* in kNN, the regularization parameter in linear regression, and so on). Unfortunately, a poor choice of hyperparameters can lead to bad model performance. In practice, finding a good set of parameters is done with *hyperparameter tuning*:

1 Take some candidate sets of hyperparameters.
2 Run a cross-validation on each of them.
3 Choose the set with the lowest error.

How do we incorporate hyperparameter tuning in the cross-fitted DML algorithm (shown in the "Cross-fitting algorithm applied on DML" sidebar)? The answer is to replace both appearances of "Train a model" in the algorithm with "Run a hyperparameter tuning and then train a model."

For instance, when we perform a cross-fit, we split the data into two groups—call them *A* and *B*. We use *A* to train a model and make predictions on *B*. In this case, we run a hyperparameter tuning on *A*, train a model on *A* with the chosen set of hyperparameters, and make predictions on *B*, as shown in figure 8.5.

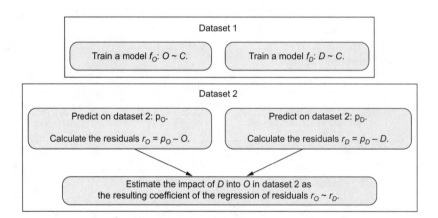

Figure 8.5   Two-fold cross-fitting with hyperparameter tuning applied to the DML algorithm. Once the process is finished, we switch roles between datasets 1 and 2.

Hyperparameter tuning is implemented in the `DoubleMLPLR` class from the DoubleML package. First we create a list with the candidate sets of hyperparameters and pass it to the `tune` function. You can find the syntax for R and Python in the package documentation at https://docs.doubleml.org/stable/guide/learners.html.

Unfortunately, the process described in figure 8.5 can be time-consuming. That is, if k_1 is the number of splits for cross-fitting, k_2 is the number of folds in cross-validation, and N_C is the number of hyperparameter candidate sets we want to try, we will need to train $k_1 \times k_2 \times N_C$ models for each one of the predictive models ($O \sim C$ and $D \sim C$).

In practice, some degree of bias is tolerated to reduce computational time. For example, DoubleML provides an alternative that consists of the following steps:

1   Perform the hyperparameter fine-tuning with the whole dataset.
2   Run the DML algorithm with cross-fitting again in the whole dataset, using the optimal hyperparameters obtained by the previous step.

This process is represented in figure 8.6. This way, we only need to train $k_1 + k_2 \times N \sim C$ models.

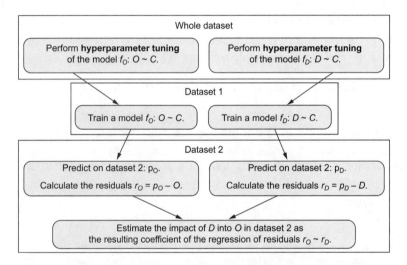

Figure 8.6   Faster but potentially biased fine-tuning strategy, where we first perform hyperparameter tuning and later perform the DML algorithm. As usual, the roles of datasets 1 and 2 have to be switched after running this algorithm.

You can decide which strategy to use for the DoubleML package via the `tune_on_folds` argument of the `tune` function:

- `tune_on_folds = True` chooses the unbiased but more computationally intensive task in figure 8.6.
- `tune_on_folds = False` (the default option) chooses the second strategy in figure 8.6, decreasing computational time at the expense of potentially incurring some bias.

You can also pass the `n_folds_tune` argument to the `tune` function to specify the number of folds to perform in the cross-validation (typically 5 or 10).

8.1.4   *Heterogeneous treatment effects*

Let's revisit the pricing example we discussed earlier. Imagine that you're employed at a travel agency and want to assess the influence of a price increase on flight ticket sales. Based on your experience, you know that seasonality plays a role in determining prices. Additionally, you suspect that the effect of a price increase may vary across different seasons. For instance, a $5 increase in a $50 ticket during holidays would likely have a lesser effect than the same $5 increase outside of holiday periods. In this case, where the causal effect is not constant, we say there are *heterogeneous treatment effects.*

The PLM introduced previously is not enough for this problem. If you remember, the PLM assumes that the relationship between variables is the following:

$$\text{sales} = \beta \, \text{price} + g(\text{season}) + V$$

In particular, a price increase always affects β units in sales.

In our case, we are interested in measuring the ATE for different seasons. An ATE stratified by a variable different from the treatment is called the *conditional average treatment effect* (CATE). In interventional notation, if D, O denote the treatment and outcome variable, and X is the variable we want to stratify for,

$$\text{CATE}(x) = E[O|\text{do}(D = 1), X = x] - E[O|\text{do}(D = 0), X = x]$$

Heterogeneous effects in linear models are called interactions

Imagine that we model the price, season, and sales relationship with linear models and heterogeneous treatment effects. Let P, S, L denote the price, season, and sales variables, respectively.

The linear model

$$L = a + bP + cS + U$$

where a, b, and c are the coefficients and U is the noise would be inappropriate to reflect heterogeneous effects. The reason is that a price increase will always affect a units of sales. The alternative is to use a model with *interactions*—that is, variables that multiply themselves:

$$L = a + bP + cS + dP \times S + U$$

For simplicity, imagine that the season variable only takes two values (autumn, winter = 0 / spring, summer = 1). Then by evaluating the model under the two scenarios, we can see how the model responds. That is, when $S = 0$, we will have

$$L = a + bP + U$$

From this equation, we can see that the intercept is a and the slope is β. Meanwhile, when $S=1$,

$$L = a + bP + c + dP + U = a + c + (b + d)P + U$$

That is, the intercept changes from a to $a + c$ and the slope from β to $b + d$.

This way, we can model different slopes in different seasons.

Similar scenarios can arise with regard to different user groups. For example, you may suspect that the causal effect of price varies among different types of customers. If you have personal data about your clientele, you may be interested in measuring the price effect between older and younger individuals or between people residing in different locations.

However, it's important to note that this formulation assumes that the variable X is distinct from the treatment variable. Suppose that D, X, Z, and O are the treatment, stratification, confounders, and outcome. In particular, X can be part of the confounders. Most current libraries implementing the CATE make the following assumption:

$$O = g(X)D + h(W) + U$$

That is, the effect of the treatment variable D on O is linear. However, the crucial point is that despite this linearity, it affects each stratum of X in a nonlinear manner. In other words, the effect of the treatment can vary significantly across different levels or categories of X.

For more details, check the documentation of the DoubleML package at https://docs.doubleml.org/stable/examples/py_double_ml_cate.html or the example at https://docs.doubleml.org/stable/guide/heterogeneity.html. It is worth mentioning that the CATE version of DoubleML makes an additional assumption. The method works well when X has few components (1, 2, 3, ...), because it uses a classic technique called *splines*, which works well with a small number of covariates.

8.2 Confidence intervals

Imagine that you obtain a positive estimate of the ATE using your initial data, but you subsequently calculate a negative ATE when analyzing a new sample. The conclusion can be puzzling and may raise concerns about the reliability of the results.

In practice, we often have access to only a single dataset, which limits our ability to observe multiple estimates of the ATE. However, it is important to recognize that if we had multiple datasets, we would likely obtain different results due to sampling variability. This situation is shown in figure 8.7: we obtain a different result for each dataset.

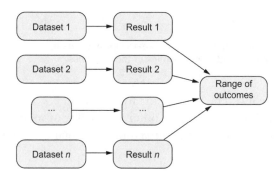

Figure 8.7 **If we repeat the process of obtaining and analyzing data, we get different results. We need confidence intervals to assess how much these different results may change.**

Confidence intervals estimate the possible range of values our results would have if we obtained many samples of the same process. Generally speaking, there are two ways to obtain confidence intervals:

- Rely on simulations and computational power using resampling methods.
- Use an analytical formula derived ad hoc for each different problem whenever this formula is available or possible to obtain.

In this section, we will learn about both. (We will not delve into the details of confidence intervals because basic information can be found in any introductory statistics textbook.) We will also see how to calculate them using the DoubleML library.

8.2.1 *Simulating new datasets with bootstrapping*

In practical scenarios, we often have only one dataset at hand. We can overcome this limitation by generating simulated datasets using a computer. One of the simplest ways to create similar datasets is through resampling methods.

Imagine your dataset, where columns represent variables and rows represent observations. Let's assume your sample size is denoted as n. To generate a new dataset, you can randomly select n rows from the original dataset. It's important to allow rows to repeat in the process: otherwise, you will end up with the original dataset in a different order without significant changes.

To obtain a confidence interval of level a (usually $a = 0.05$), calculate the causal effect using each dataset separately. You can use whatever method you wish. Then calculate the $a/2$ and $1 - a/2$ (typically 0.025 and 0.975) percentiles of the outcomes. This process is shown in figure 8.8.

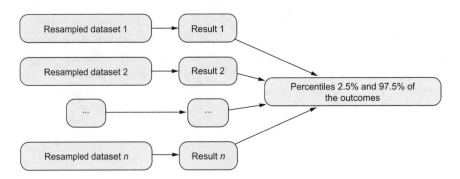

Figure 8.8 A 95% confidence interval with bootstrapping. We create new datasets by resampling our original ones, and then we calculate the quantiles of the outcomes.

This method is adaptable because it can be applied to any causal inference estimator. However, it can be computationally demanding. In other words, if your method takes t minutes to execute, and you bootstrap your dataset m times, the total computational time will be $m \times t$.

The time required to estimate the causal effect can vary significantly depending on the complexity of your analysis. For instance, if you're running a linear model with a small number of variables, the estimation process may be nearly instantaneous. On the other hand, more computationally intensive methods like DML (where cross-validation for hyperparameter tuning and cross-fitting are necessary) can be more time-consuming.

It's important to consider the trade-off between computational time and the accuracy of your causal effect estimates. Although some methods require more time to execute, they may provide more robust and reliable results. Ultimately, choosing the appropriate method depends on the specific requirements of your analysis and the available computational resources.

Exercise 8.1

Calculate confidence intervals of the ATE estimation for the kidney stone data from chapter 2. Follow these steps:

1. Repeat 2,000 times.
2. Resample the original dataset.
3. Estimate and store the ATE.
4. Calculate percentiles 2.5% and 97.5% of the stored results.

You can find the solution at the book's website (www.manning.com/books/causal -inference-for-data-science) or in the GitHub repository (https://mng.bz/1ang).

BOOTSTRAPPING IN DOUBLEML

In the DoubleML package, you can easily get confidence intervals for individual estimates. However, when you want to assess the causal effects of multiple treatment variables at once, there's an advanced option. In this case, you can obtain confidence intervals through bootstrapping (see the documentation at https://mng.bz/PNMP). But this method uses a computationally more efficient variation of bootstrapping, different from the resampling method explained earlier. This advanced option goes beyond our discussion, but I wanted to mention it for completeness.

8.2.2 Analytical formulas for confidence intervals

Sometimes confidence intervals can be calculated using a statistical formula, which is faster than bootstrapping. However, it's important to note that not all problems have readily available analytical formulas to calculate confidence intervals.

To use an analytical formula, we need to understand the distribution of the estimator when the sample size increases. Take the sample average as an example. We know by the CLT (included again here for convenience) that when the sample size tends to infinity, the sample average tends to behave like a normal distribution no matter what original distribution the sample has.

Central limit theorem

The CLT states that for a large sample size, the mean of a sample will behave like a normal distribution. Formally speaking, assume that we have a sample $X_1, \ldots, X_n$, where all variables have the same distribution with expectation $E[X_i] = \mu$ and variance $V[X_i] = \sigma^2$, they are independent of one another, and n is large enough. Then the sample mean for a large enough n is

$$\frac{1}{n}\sum_i X_i \sim N\left(\mu, \frac{\sigma^2}{n}\right) \tag{8.1}$$

In particular, the standard deviation of the sample mean is $\sigma/\sqrt{n}$.

Suppose you have a sample $x_1, \ldots, x_n$, where each observation has been obtained independently from the others. If $\hat{\mu}$ and $\hat{\sigma}$ are the sample average and standard deviation, a confidence interval of level a can be obtained as

$$\left(\hat{\mu} - \frac{z_a \hat{\sigma}}{\sqrt{n}}, \ \hat{\mu} + \frac{z_a \hat{\sigma}}{\sqrt{n}}\right)$$

where z_a is the value where a standard normal distribution accumulates $1 - a/2$ of the probability.

CONFIDENCE INTERVALS IN LINEAR MODELS

In chapter 6, we learned that linear models can be used to calculate causal effects. When dealing with confounding variables, we only need to include the variables that meet the back-door criterion from chapter 7 in our regression analysis. To determine the confidence intervals, we can use traditional statistical tools for linear regression.

For instance, popular tools like the `lm` or `glm` functions in R and the `statmodels` library in Python offer built-in functionality to compute confidence intervals. These functions generate output including the desired confidence intervals and other relevant statistical information.

CONFIDENCE INTERVALS IN DOUBLEML

In DoubleML, confidence intervals of individual estimations can be obtained analytically. Fortunately, the original DML paper provides asymptotic approximations of the distribution of the resulting estimators. We saw an example of such approximations in section 8.1.2, "Efficiency of the DML estimator," repeated here for convenience.

Formal theorem on the convergence of DML for the partially linear model

If the data has been generated using the PLM

$$D = m(C) + V$$
$$O = \beta D + g(C) + U$$

and we use the DML partially linear estimator to obtain an estimation $\hat{\beta}$, then as the sample size n increases, the resulting estimation $\hat{\beta}$ behaves like a normal distribution

$$\hat{\beta} \sim N\left(\beta, \frac{\sigma^2}{n}\right)$$

where $\sigma^2 = E[U^2 V^2]/E[V]^2$

Quantities β and σ^2 can be approximated from data and used to create confidence intervals in the same way as in equation 8.1 in the "Central limit theorem" sidebar. Therefore, this process is calculated automatically by DoubleML using the `fit` method. Confidence intervals can also be accessed by the `summary` function. See the example at https://docs.doubleml.org/stable/guide/se_confint.html for more details.

8.3   *Doubly robust estimators*

In certain situations, it is crucial to estimate causal effects accurately. Therefore, we need tools that offer improved estimates, even if they require more effort. Specifically, this book introduces a set of estimators that can be further enhanced using doubly robust techniques. Doubly robust (DR) tools allow us to combine two causal estimators to create a new one, ensuring that if either of the two estimators is unbiased, the resulting estimator will also be unbiased. So, a DR estimator provides a safety net if we do something wrong with a model.

DR techniques can become intricate. Therefore, this section will focus exclusively on explaining the augmented inverse probability weighting (AIPW) method. (This method and the notion of DR estimators were introduced in the 1994 paper "Estimation of regression coefficients when some regressors are not always observed" by James M. Robins, Andrea Rotnitzky, and Lue Ping Zhao.) AIPW combines the machine learning–based approaches discussed in chapter 4 with the propensity score–based methods explained in chapter 5, using the IPW formula based on propensity scores.

Imagine that T denotes a binary treatment variable, Y is the outcome variable, and C is all the confounders between T and Y. Also assume that there are no unobserved confounders. To estimate the causal effect between T and Y, we can use the adjustment formula. In that case, we will have a dataset like the one in table 8.4.

Table 8.4   Available data with propensity scores calculated

Y	T	C_1	...	C_p
y_1	t^1	c_1^1	...	c_p^1
...	...	...	...	...
y_n	t^n	c_1^n	...	c_p^n

In addition, suppose that we use two different variations of the adjustment formula to estimate

$$\text{ATE} = P(Y = 1 | \text{do}(T = 1)) - P(Y = 1 | \text{do}(T = 0))$$

- We apply the T-learner from chapter 4 and, through the process, obtain the functions $f_0(c), f_1(c)$, where c is the values of the confounders that approximate $f_0(c) \approx E[Y|c, T = 0]$ and $f_1(c) \approx E[Y|c, T = 1]$. The ATE with the T-learner is

$$\widehat{\text{ATE}}_t = \frac{1}{n} \sum_i f_1(c_i) - f_0(c_i)$$

- We apply IPW and, through the process, estimate the propensity scores $s(c)$, where s is the approximation to the probability of being treated $s(c) \approx P(T = 1|c)$. The ATE with IPW is

$$\widehat{\text{ATE}}_{ipw} = \frac{1}{n} \sum_i \frac{y_i t_i}{s(c_i)} - \frac{y_i(1 - t_i)}{1 - s(c_i)}$$

The AIPW estimator combines the two previous estimators to create a new one with this formula:

$$\widehat{\text{ATE}}_{aipw} =$$

$$\frac{1}{n} \left[\sum_i f_1(c_i) - f_0(c_i) \right] + \frac{1}{n} \left[\sum_i \frac{(y_i - f_1(c_i))t_i}{s(c_i)} - \frac{(y_i - f_0(c_i))(1 - t_i)}{1 - s(c_i)} \right]$$

Using the AIPW estimator whenever possible is highly recommended. It offers several advantages:

- It is doubly robust (for more details, see the proof in appendix D).
- It is n-root consistent, which means it converges rapidly. This implies that you can achieve accurate results with a smaller sample size than other methods.
- It is efficient. That is, it converges quickly to the ATE and minimizes the asymptotic variance among ATE estimators as the sample size tends to infinity. For further exploration, refer to the tutorial "Semiparametric doubly robust targeted double machine learning: a review" by Edward H. Kennedy.

8.3.1   AIPW in practice

You can use the AIPW in the DoubleML package under the name *interactive regression model* (IRM). The IRM and its relationship with AIPW are explained in the original DML paper. The model description and code examples in R and Python can be found at https://mng.bz/JNnv.

> **Exercise 8.2**
>
> Consider the right-heart catheterization (RHC) dataset from the exercise in chapter 5. Calculate the ATE and its confidence interval of the treatment variable *swang1* on the variable *death* using the DoubleML library. Use hyperparameter tuning as explained at https://mng.bz/w5mQ, with the option `tune_on_folds=True`.
>
> You can find the solution at the book's website (www.manning.com/books/causal -inference-for-data-science) or in the GitHub repository (https://mng.bz/1ang).

8.4   *Further reading*

Double machine learning (DML) was introduced in the original paper "Double/ debiased machine learning for treatment and causal parameters" by Victor Chernozhukov et al. (https://arxiv.org/pdf/1608.00060.pdf). Because this paper is highly technical, if you are interested in further details, I recommend starting from the simplified versions:

- "DoubleML—an object-oriented implementation of double machine learning in R" by Philipp Bach, Victor Chernozhukov, Malte S. Kurz, and Martin Spindler (https://arxiv.org/pdf/2103.09603.pdf). The simplest version of the formal theorem on the convergence of DML for the partially linear model is shown in Theorem 1 in this paper. The version of this theorem in the original DML paper is much more involved.
- "Double/debiased/Neyman machine learning of treatment effects" by Victor Chernozhukov et al. (https://arxiv.org/pdf/1701.08687.pdf)

To learn more about influence functions, you can read the paper "Demystifying statistical learning based on efficient influence functions" by Oliver Hines, Oliver Dukes, Karla Diaz-Ordaz, and Stijn Vansteelandt (https://mng.bz/q0z2).

8.5   *Chapter quiz*

As we conclude the chapter, it's important to ensure that you have a solid understanding of the key concepts. Here are the essential questions you should be able to answer clearly and concisely. If you can't, I suggest rereading the corresponding references:

1   What are the benefits of DML?
    Answer in the chapter introduction
2   Does DML require cross-fitting?
    Answer in section 8.1.3, "Avoiding over-fitting with cross-fitting"
3   Does the partially linear model deal with nonlinearities in the treatment variable?
    Answer in section 8.1.2, "The partially linear model"
4   From the statistical perspective, is it better to perform hyperparameter tuning before cross-fitting or after data splitting on each cross-fitting fold?
    Answer in section 8.1.3, "Hyperparameter tuning"

5 Is the DML for the PLM statistically efficient?
    Answer in the sidebar titled "Formal theorem on the convergence of DML for the partially linear model" in section 8.2.2
6 What are the benefits of the AIPW over the original IPW estimator?
    Answer in section 8.3

Summary

- You can improve the reliability of your analysis and reduce the required sample size of your dataset by using any of the three techniques we have seen. They are all implemented in R and Python in the `DoubleML` package:

- When the treatment variable is continuous, it is recommended to use double machine learning (DML). In particular, DML is root-n consistent and efficient, which means it converges quickly to the expected causal effect. It is also efficient, meaning it asymptotically achieves the lowest possible variance. More specifically, it converges faster than the S- and T-learners from chapter 4.

- It is always recommended to incorporate confidence intervals in your estimations. These intervals provide a measure of uncertainty around your estimated causal effect. You can obtain confidence intervals through resampling methods or, if available, using analytic formulas provided by the chosen estimation method.

- When working with a binary treatment variable, using the doubly robust augmented inverse probability weighting (AIPW) estimator is recommended. This estimator is efficient as it is root-n consistent and asymptotically achieves the lowest possible variance.

    - For these methods to work well, we assume that you have measured all the confounders or have carefully selected the variables to adjust for using tools like the back-door criterion.

Part 3

Other strategies beyond the adjustment formula

Parts 1 and 2 of this book focus on understanding and applying the adjustment formula. But this formula requires you to know a lot about confounders. Sometimes, figuring out all the confounders can be challenging. When that happens, you may need to use different strategies.

A simple yet effective trick is the instrumental variables method. This approach, as explained in chapter 9, derives causal estimations by taking advantage of the presence of an independent source of variation.

Chapter 10 introduces the potential outcomes framework, another way to think about cause and effect. This approach is important because many methods are based on it, especially those we discuss in chapter 11. In this chapter, you'll learn about techniques for time series data. These techniques don't require you to know all the confounders because they work on stronger assumptions. Specifically, you'll learn about synthetic controls, regression discontinuity design, and differences in differences.

Instrumental variables

This chapter covers

- Learning different ways to estimate causal effects with instrumental variables
- Identifying situations where you can apply instrumental variables
- Learning how to apply instrumental variables with different Python and R packages

Using *instrumental variables* (IVs) is a technique to estimate causal effects that differ from the adjustment formula. It is applicable only in specific scenarios, particularly when your DAG follows the structure in figure 9.1. Some parts of this DAG are already familiar, such as the typical three-node confounder structure with the decision or treatment variable D, the outcome Y, and the set of confounders C, which we assume is unobserved. Additionally, you may have noticed an extra variable Z, called the *instrument*, a crucial requirement for applying the IV method.

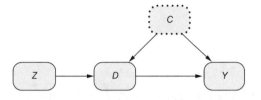

Figure 9.1   Basic instrumental variables diagram. Confounders are unobserved. Variable *Z* plays the role of an instrument. This structure lets you overcome the lack of information about confounders in estimating the effect of *D* into *Y*.

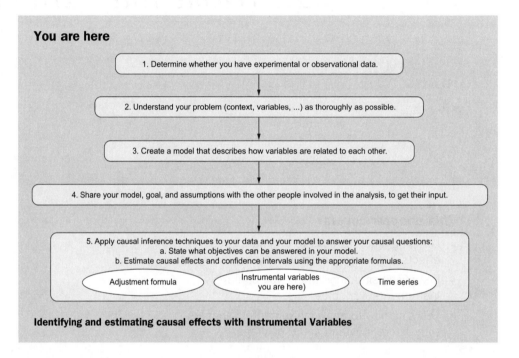

Identifying and estimating causal effects with Instrumental Variables

We've spent almost two-thirds of the book discussing the adjustment formula. Unfortunately, we cannot apply the adjustment formula in figure 9.1 to estimate the causal effect between X and Y because the set of confounders is unobserved. Indeed, the Achilles heel of the adjustment formula is that our lack of knowledge about confounders can lead us to incorrect conclusions. Here's where IVs come into play. The IV technique uses the fact that the instrument is unaffected by any other variable to bypass the influence of confounders.

The IV method finds application in various scenarios. For instance, it can be used in noncompliant RCTs in clinical trials, where patients have the option to take the assigned drug. Similar situations arise in A/B tests measuring customer engagement with an optional new feature. IVs are widely employed in econometrics and are emerging as a valuable tool in genomics, using genetic information for making causal inferences about the connection between a risk factor and an outcome.

In section 9.1, we will clarify and define the assumptions for applying the IV method. Then, in section 9.2, we describe the IV estimator with different assumptions.

Finally, we will see how to apply the IV estimator and interpret the results using R and Python libraries.

> **When to use instrumental variables**
>
> You can use IVs as an alternative to the adjustment formula for calculating ATEs. IVs are particularly useful when your understanding or data about confounders is limited and you have an independent source of randomness (an instrument) available.

The next chapter will revisit IVs using the potential outcomes framework. Although it may be more logical to explain potential outcomes first, I chose to introduce IVs earlier. This is because IVs can be understood using only graphs. From a teaching perspective, this chapter aligns better with the book's graphical approach.

9.1 Understanding IVs through an example

Let's look at an example where an A/B test alone cannot estimate the causal effect we are looking for. However, the data from the A/B test can be analyzed differently using IVs to obtain the causal effect we are interested in. This situation may arise from time to time. That is why IVs are important, especially in digital companies that perform A/B tests regularly.

Consider this scenario: you work at an e-commerce company, and management is keen on integrating a chatbot into the website. However, before investing in a full-fledged chatbot, they opt for a trial run with a basic version. This prudent step will allow them to assess its effectiveness.

To gauge how users interact with the chatbot, an A/B test is conducted. The primary objective of this test is to address a fundamental question: does chatbot usage increase user engagement? Engagement will be measured by the rate of user actions, such as making purchases or signing up for services.

> **Think first, read next**
>
> How would you design an A/B test to answer the question "Does chatbot usage increase user engagement?"

The first idea that crosses your mind is probably to create two groups: the experimental group exposed to the chatbot and the control group with no chatbot. Then run the experiment, and finally calculate which group engages more.

The problem with this approach is that it doesn't tell us if using the chatbot increases engagement. It only tells us if providing a chatbot on the website increases engagement. Although these may appear similar, they are not the same. Let's explore why. Imagine an extreme situation where only 5% of customers with access to the chatbot end up using it. However, those who do find it extremely valuable.

In such a scenario, the A/B test results would tell us that there is not much of a difference in engagement between having and not having the chatbot. This is because 95% of the customers in the experimental group don't use it, resulting in average engagement similar to the control group. However, it's essential to note that chatbot usage increases engagement among those who have tried it because they loved it.

At this point, it is clear that two different business questions emerge:

1 What is the effect of providing a chatbot to customers?
2 How does chatbot usage increase engagement?

To determine which matters more for the business, we need to see how the answers affect our decisions. At first glance, we are mostly interested in question 1, because if customers do not use the chatbot, it may mean investing resources in its development and maintenance may not be worth it.

But question 2 can still be useful. If we find out the chatbot is helpful for those who use it, we can get creative and find ways to encourage more customers to use it, such as making it easier to access or creating videos and tutorials.

But which tools do we need to answer each question? Question 1 can be answered by analyzing the results of the A/B test that we designed earlier. Unfortunately, as we will see in a minute, we can't create an A/B test that effectively addresses question 2: we need to use IVs. Before moving too quickly, let's take a moment to explore how we might try to design an A/B test for question 2 (and fail in the process).

> **Think first, read next**
> In an A/B test designed to estimate the effect of chatbot usage on engagement, which variable would serve as the treatment?

The A/B test needs to work. The treatment variable is chatbot usage. So, we need to form two groups. The control group will not have access to the chatbot, so their usage is zero. The experimental group, on the other hand, will actively use the chatbot. It's important for the A/B test to work properly so participants in the experimental group use the chatbot as intended. If they don't, they're essentially behaving like the control group, and that messes up the A/B test design.

Let me emphasize this: we want both groups to strictly follow our instructions, regardless of their personal preferences. It is crucial in an A/B test that *participants don't get to choose their group*. If they do, the treatment isn't randomized anymore, and we risk introducing factors like participants' characteristics that can confound the relationship between the treatment and the outcome.

Thus, an A/B test to estimate the effect of chatbot usage on engagement has two problems. First, the result from the A/B test would not be representative of how people would behave naturally if we provided the chatbot for everyone. The reason is that some participants in the experimental group have to artificially use the chatbot, even though they would not use it outside the experiment. This is a structural problem of the experiment because it does not provide an unbiased answer to our question.

The second challenge is that to be sure participants follow instructions, we either need volunteers or have to compensate them. Either way, by letting customers decide whether to participate, we introduce *selection bias* into the experiment; participants are a specific subset of customers, often motivated by being fans of the website or the prospect of earning money. So they are not representative of the overall clientele.

In this chapter, you will learn how question 2 can be answered in two steps:

1 Perform the A/B test to answer question 1, randomizing who has access to the chatbot and who doesn't.

2 Use the data from the A/B test to apply the IV method to answer question 2.

9.1.1 The example's DAG

Let's draw the graph and discuss why question 2 cannot be answered using the adjustment formula. The data generation process is shown in figure 9.2. Each customer will have different characteristics and be in a different situation. Such a context will be described by a set of variables called *Customer Context*. The variable *Randomization* determines the two groups in experiment 1 in which each customer will be: those exposed to the chatbot and those without access to it. Whether the customer decides to choose the chatbot is described by the variable *Chatbot Usage*. And finally, the outcome is the *Engagement* variable.

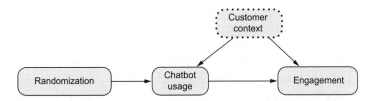

Figure 9.2 Instrumental variables diagram. The variable *Randomization* plays the role of an instrument, and the set of confounders *Customer Context* is unobserved.

Customer context is a confounder between chatbot usage and engagement. Because each customer's situation determines whether they use the chatbot and whether they engage in the platform, we cannot expect to have customer context variables in detail. We would need to understand all the factors influencing customers' decisions to use the chatbot and engage the platform, and that is not achievable. So, *Customer Context* is an unobserved confounder.

The presence of confounders prevents us from directly estimating the causal effect of chatbot usage. In this chapter, we will see how to use the *Randomization* variable with IVs to estimate the causal effect of *Chatbot Usage* on *Engagement*.

9.1.2 IV assumptions

Figure 9.2 in the previous example can be written with generic variables as in figure 9.3, in which Z is the instrument, D is the decision variable, Y is the outcome, and C is the set of unobserved examples. Before applying the IV method, explained shortly, you need to be sure that your graph satisfies the following assumptions:

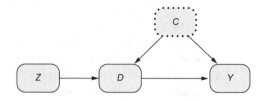

Figure 9.3 When we create this graph, we assume there are no other relationships between the variables. As we've discussed in previous chapters, the key assumptions in a DAG are about the arrows that are not shown rather than the ones that are.

- *Relevance*—Z should have an effect on variable D. Such an assumption is represented by an arrow $Z \rightarrow D$. As we will see later, the stronger the effect Z has on D, the better our estimates will be.
- *Exogeneity*—Z cannot be influenced by any confounders C, represented by the lack of arrows between C and Z in the graph.
- *Exclusion*—All the effect that Z exerts on the outcome Y has to be through D. We emphasize this by not having a direct arrow from Z to Y in the graph.

Is it bad if any of these assumptions are not true? Yes: things can go south very easily and can be as misleading as the conclusions in Simpson's paradox. For example, in an A/B test comparing two different webpage background colors to see which one users prefer, we should not assume that the randomization has any effect on the chatbot. In other words, we cannot assume that the relevance assumption holds.

Let's see an example where the exogeneity assumption (the instrument is not affected by the confounders) is not met. Consider a different scenario: Instead of conducting an A/B test, you decide to inform your customers about the new chatbot functionality through an email. The marketing platform provides information about whether customers open the email, and you plan to use this "opened the email (yes/no)" variable as an instrument in your analysis. That is not a good idea because the exogeneity assumption will not hold! As shown in figure 9.4, the act of opening the email is determined by the type of user receiving it. At the same time, the type of user is a confounder between using the chatbot and customer engagement. So, there is an arrow between a confounder and the instrument.

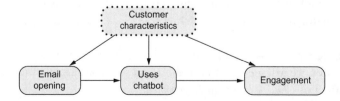

Figure 9.4 The exogeneity assumption fails because customer characteristics affect whether an email is opened. This is represented by an arrow from the set of unobserved confounders to the hypothetical instrument.

Finally, let's see an example where the exclusion restriction does not hold. Imagine a company conducting an A/B test to measure the effect on engagement of a package that includes various elements: access to a new chatbot, links to posts on a topic of interest, a curated list of YouTube videos, and more. Let's consider the randomization variable—whether you receive the full package—as the instrument Z. This case does not meet the exclusion restriction. Engagement may increase not only due to the new chatbot. Thus, Z affects the outcome Y through different paths. As shown in figure 9.5, there would be an arrow from Z to Y that wouldn't go through D.

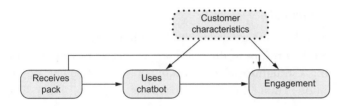

Figure 9.5 **The exclusion restriction does not hold because the instrument,** *Receives Pack,* **affects the outcome through two different paths.**

It's important to be cautious about the exclusion restriction, as it is often overlooked. Some instruments may appear suitable at first glance, but they can affect the outcome in various ways, as explained in the paper by Jonathan Mellon et al. (check section 9.4).

9.1.3 IVs in RCTs

Sometimes, in healthcare clinical trials, a variant of RCTs is performed where patients in the experimental group can decide whether to take the treatment. These RCTs are referred to as *noncompliant.* The problem with noncompliant RCTs is that you cannot estimate the effectiveness of the treatment with the difference in means $E[Y|D=1] - E[Y|D=0]$. This is because the decision to consume the treatment is now influenced by the patient's characteristics, making those characteristics confounding variables.

Noncompliant RCTs can be described with IV dynamics, such as in figure 9.3. The instrument is the group randomization, and the decision variable D is whether they took the treatment. As we will see, IV estimation can provide unbiased estimates of the effectiveness of the treatment.

In healthcare literature, besides using IVs, there is a specific nomenclature for the measured effects in the graph:

- *Intention to treat (ITT)* measures the causal effect of the randomization on the outcome and is defined mathematically as $E[Y|Z=1] - E[Y|Z=0]$.
- *Per protocol* is the difference in means, mathematically expressed as $E[Y|D=1] - E[Y|D=0]$. Due to the presence of confounders, per-protocol estimation is a potentially biased estimation of the causal effect of taking the treatment on the outcome.

9.2 *Estimating the causal effect with IVs*

Let's now move into explaining how the IV method provides unbiased estimates of the causal effect from D to Y in the general IV diagram in figure 9.3. Remember that we can't adjust for confounders between D and Y because they are unobserved. Fortunately, the IV method provides a mathematical formula to estimate this causal effect.

Unfortunately, as explained in section 9.2.4, there is no generic formula that works for any graph with the structure of 9.3. To apply the IV method, we need to make additional assumptions.

9.2.1 *Applying IVs with linear models*

In causal inference, when learning a new method, it's helpful to try applying it with the assumption that all relationships in the graph are linear. Linear models are easier to understand, providing a straightforward intuition about how the method works.

So, our first assumption is that all relationships in the graph are linear. The corresponding DAG with its linear coefficients is shown in figure 9.6. Thus, we can write the equations that relate the variables as

$$D := w_D + aZ + c_D C + \varepsilon_D$$
$$Y := w_Y + bD + c_Y C + \varepsilon_Y$$

where the terms ε_D and ε_Y are random variables, one independent of the other with zero expectation.

> **Think first, read next**
> In this model, which quantity reflects the effect of D in Y?

Let's answer this question. As explained in chapter 6, the question can be rephrased as follows: if we can intervene in the system and arbitrarily increase the value of D in one unit, what will be the change in Y? For simplicity, let's assume we want to calculate the effect on Y of changing $D = 0$ to $D = 1$. Mathematically speaking, we are wondering what the difference is between $E[Y|\mathrm{do}(D = 1)]$ (intervening in the system and setting the value $D = 1$) and $E[Y|\mathrm{do}(D = 0)]$ (intervening in the system and setting the value $D = 0$). Let's run the calculations:

$$E[Y|\mathrm{do}(D = 1)] = E[w_Y + bD + c_Y C + \varepsilon_Y|\mathrm{do}(D = 1)] = w_Y + b + E[c_Y C]$$
$$E[Y|\mathrm{do}(D = 0)] = E[w_Y + bD + c_Y C + \varepsilon_Y|\mathrm{do}(D = 0)] = w_Y + E[c_Y C]$$

So, the effect of D on Y is the coefficient

$$E[Y|\mathrm{do}(D = 1)] - E[Y|\mathrm{do}(D = 0)] = b$$

The goal of the IV method is to offer an unbiased mathematical formula for estimating the coefficient b. This method should solely rely on data and the assumption of linearity in the model. It shouldn't demand additional information about the coefficients.

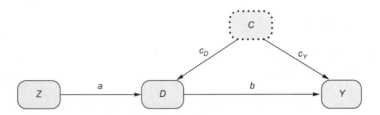

Figure 9.6 Instrumental variables diagram with linear models, with instrument Z. Each letter in an arrow represents the coefficient in the corresponding linear model.

We know that due to the presence of confounders, the causal effect of D into Y cannot be directly estimated from data unless we apply the adjustment formula. In chapter 6, we learned that in linear models, applying the adjustment formula is equivalent to controlling for confounders by including them in the regression analysis. However, in this case, we assume that the confounders are unobserved present in the dataset. Hence, we must explore alternative methods to estimate their effects and incorporate them into our analysis.

Fortunately, the IV approach provides a strategy to overcome this difficulty. The strategy operates as follows. First, it's important to note that there are no confounding variables between the instrument Z and both the treatment D and the outcome Y. This means we can obtain the effect of Z on D by conducting a linear regression of D on Z, $D \sim Z$, and extracting the coefficient associated with Z. Similarly, we can obtain the effect of Z on Y by conducting a regression of Y on Z, $Y \sim Z$. Consequently, we can estimate the causal effect of D on Y by calculating the ratio between these two estimates.

Now, let's delve into the details of this methodology. To understand how the IV strategy estimates the causal effect between D and Z, we need to know how the previous regressions relate to the coefficients in our model.

Remember, our model is described by the following equations:

$$D := w_D + aZ + c_D C + \varepsilon_D$$
$$Y := w_Y + bD + c_Y C + \varepsilon_Y$$

- To estimate the causal effect of D on Y, our goal is to obtain the coefficient b from data. Indeed, when we intervene in the system and change the value of D in one unit, the value of Y changes in b units. We know that if we run the regression $Y \sim D$, the coefficient associated with D is a biased estimator of b due to confounding. So, this regression is not an option.

- The effect of Z into D is given by its corresponding coefficient from the first equation a. Because there are no confounders between Z and D, the regression $D \sim Z$ estimates a without bias.
- All the effect of Z into Y is mediated by D. That is, when we intervene in Z and change its value, Z affects D and D affects Y. So, to find the total effect of Z into Y, we need to express Y in terms of Z by substituting the value of D, $D := w_D + aZ + c_D C + \varepsilon_D$, as follows:

$$Y := w_Y + bD + c_Y C + \varepsilon_Y = w_Y + b(w_D + aZ + c_D C + \varepsilon_D) + c_Y C + \varepsilon_Y =$$
$$w_Y + bw_D + abZ + bc_D C + b\varepsilon_D + c_Y C + \varepsilon_Y$$

This last expression shows us that in our model, when we change a unit of Z, Y changes in $a \times b$ units. Because there are no confounders between Z and Y, the regression $Y \sim Z$ estimates $a \times b$ without bias. The results are summarized in table 9.1.

Table 9.1   Expected coefficients obtained from data using linear regression

Regression	Expectation of the resulting coefficient
$D \sim Z$	a
$Y \sim Z$	$a \times b$

Now, here comes the trick. Dividing the coefficients associated with Z in the regressions $Y \sim Z$ and $D \sim Z$, we obtain $a \times b / a = b$, an unbiased estimate of b.

Mathematical IV formula for estimating causal effects

Let's now write a simple formula for the strategy just explained. First, we need to write the formulas for the slope of the linear regressions, and then divide one over the other.

For any two random variables M and R, the associated coefficient of the linear regression $M \sim R$ is given by the formula $\text{cov}(M, R)/\text{var}(R)$. Let's apply it to our case:

- The resulting coefficient from the regression $D \sim Z$ is $\text{cov}(D, Z)/\text{var}(Z)$
- The resulting coefficient from the regression $Y \sim Z$ is $\text{cov}(Y, Z)/\text{var}(Z)$
- The estimator of the causal effect from D to Y is obtained by dividing the previous quantities (notice that the term var(z) cancels), leading to

$$\hat{b} = \frac{\text{cov}(Y, Z)}{\text{cov}(D, Z)} \tag{9.1}$$

9.2.2   *Applying IVs for partially linear models*

Unfortunately, the linear assumption does not apply in our chatbot example. The treatment variable D is binary, so it cannot be expressed linearly as $D := w_D + aZ + c_D C + \varepsilon_D$! We need to develop the IV estimator for a different setting.

Now that we have found the IV estimator for causal effects in equation 9.1, let's see a more relaxed specification of the IV model that lets us deal with binary variables. Consider the following partially linear IV assumptions.

Variable Y can be expressed as

$$Y := w_Y + bD + h(C) + \varepsilon_Y$$

where the function $h(C)$ can be potentially nonlinear and the term ε_Y is independent from Z and D.

How does this differ from the linear assumptions from the previous section in our chatbot example? Unlike in the linear case, these new assumptions let the relationship between confounders C (*Customer Characteristics*) and Y (*Engagement*) have complex nonlinear interactions.

As in section 9.2.1, the effect of the variable D into Y is b (to find it, you can follow the same steps as in section 9.2.1). Notice that there are no further assumptions regarding Z and D or the linearity between them. Nonetheless, we are denoting this model as partially linear because we are assuming that we can decompose the effect of variables C and D on Y additively as $bD + h(C)$. The corresponding DAG is shown in figure 9.7.

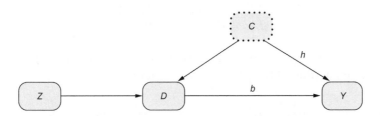

Figure 9.7   Instrumental variables diagram with binary treatment and with instrument Z

With these assumptions, the IV estimator leads us to the same formula as before:

$$\hat{b} = \frac{\text{cov}(Y, Z)}{\text{cov}(D, Z)}$$

That is, using the linear property of the covariance (seen in chapter 7), we see that

$$\text{cov}(Y, Z) = \text{cov}(w_Y + b\,D + h(C) + \varepsilon_Y, Z) = b\,\text{cov}(D, Z)$$

due to the fact that $\text{cov}(w_Y, Z) = 0$ (because w_Y is constant), $\text{cov}(h(C), Z) = \text{cov}(\varepsilon_Y, Z) = 0$ (because Z is independent from both terms). So,

$$\frac{\text{cov}(Y, Z)}{\text{cov}(D, Z)} = b$$

In conclusion, for our chatbot example, we can apply the same IV formula as the one with linear models.

9.2.3   *An alternative formula for the IV method*

Instead of the IV formula given in this chapter, you may find the following alternative formula in other resources:

$$\hat{b} = \frac{E[Y|Z = 1] - E[Y|Z = 0]}{E[D|Z = 1] - E[D|Z = 0]} \tag{9.2}$$

The two formulas give the *exact same result*, so feel free to use the one you find more preferable. The reason relies on the fact that for any variable Q and binary variable R, the covariance and difference of conditional expectations are related (see appendix E for the details) as

$$\mathrm{cov}(Q, R) = (E[Q|R = 1] - E[Q|R = 0])P(R = 1)P(R = 0)$$

Thus,

$$\hat{b} = \frac{\mathrm{cov}(Y, Z)}{\mathrm{cov}(D, Z)} = \frac{(E[Y|Z = 1] - E[Y|Z = 0])P(Z = 1)P(Z = 0)}{(E[D|Z = 1] - E[D|Z = 0])P(Z = 1)P(Z = 0)} = $$
$$\frac{E[Y|Z = 1] - E[Y|Z = 0]}{E[D|Z = 1] - E[D|Z = 0]}$$

Equation 9.2 has a nice interpretation. Because there is no confounding between Z and D, we can estimate the ATE as the observed difference between when $Z = 1$ and $Z = 0$:

$$\mathrm{ATE}(Z \rightarrow D) = E[D|Z = 1] - E[D|Z = 1]$$

Analogously, for the same reason, we can estimate the causal effect of Z on Y as

$$\mathrm{ATE}(Z \rightarrow Y) = E[Y|Z = 1] - E[Y|Z = 1]$$

So, the causal estimate of $D \rightarrow Y$ is

$$\mathrm{ATE}(D \rightarrow Y) = \frac{\mathrm{ATE}(Z \rightarrow Y)}{\mathrm{ATE}(Z \rightarrow D)}$$

Let's interpret this formula to our chatbot example. Variable Z is the exposure to the chatbot, and D is chatbot usage. The effect of Z to D can be interpreted as the level of appeal that the chatbot holds over its users.

Let's see how the term $\mathrm{ATE}(Z \rightarrow D) = E[D|Z = 1] - E[D|Z = 0]$ numerically affects the previous formula. If the chatbot has not been exposed, $Z = 0$, there is no usage $D = 0$, so $P(D = 1|Z = 0) = E[D|Z = 0] = 0$. On the other hand, among those who have access to the chatbot $Z = 1$, a proportion $P(D = 1|Z = 1) = E[D|Z = 1]$ will use it. Of course, it may happen that no one uses it, $E[D|Z = 1] = 0$. In these cases, the relevance assumption doesn't hold. Let's consider those cases where some customers use the chatbot, $E[D|Z = 1] > 0$. Then $E[D|Z = 1] - E[D|Z = 0] = E[D|Z = 1] > 0$. Moreover, because variable the variable D is either 0 or 1, the proportion of usage is a number between 0 and 1,

$$0 < P(D = 1|Z = 1) = E[D|Z = 1] = E[D|Z = 1] - E[D|Z = 0] \Leftarrow 1$$

In conclusion, our quantity of interest $\text{ATE}(D \rightarrow Y)$ is obtained by the total effect the randomization has on the outcome $\text{ATE}(Z \rightarrow Y)$ divided by a number between 0 and 1. When we divide by a number between 0 and 1, we are basically making the numerator larger. For instance, if half of the people who see the chatbot end up using it, $P(D = 1|Z = 1) = 0.5$, this means $\text{ATE}(D \rightarrow Y) = \text{ATE}(Z \rightarrow Y)/0.5 = \text{ATE}(Z \rightarrow Y) \times 2$.

So, the effect of the chatbot on engagement $\text{ATE}(D \rightarrow Y)$ can be interpreted as the effect of exposing the chatbot $\text{ATE}(Z \rightarrow Y)$ rescaled by the proportion of customers that use the chatbot $P(D = 1|Z = 1)$.

9.2.4 *The lack of a general formula for the general IV graph*

But what about other IV settings, without making any assumptions about the relationship of the variables? Is it possible to obtain an analogue of the adjustment formula for the IV problem? The answer is no; there is no general formula capable of finding the causal effect using an instrumental variable, as was shown by Balke and Pearl in 1993 (see section 9.4). So, any variation you may find in the literature needs to make further assumptions on top of the causal graph in figure 9.4 to be able to estimate the causal effect.

9.3 *Instrumental variables in practice*

Let's see how the IV method works by applying it to a synthetic dataset. The equations for generating the data are the following:

- $Z := B(0.5)$: The instrument is a binary variable following a binomial distribution.
- $C := B(0.3)$: There is only one unobserved confounder with a binomial distribution.
- $D := U(0,1) \leq 0.7Z + 0.4C$: The treatment is also a binary variable that takes the value of 1 when a sample from a $(0, 1)$ uniform distribution is smaller than the combination $0.7Z + 0.4C$ and takes the value of 0 otherwise.
- $Y := 30 - 2 \times D + 10 \times C + \varepsilon_Y$ where ε_Y follows a centered normal distribution with standard deviation 2.

Notice that the effect of the treatment on the outcome, what we want to estimate, is -2.

First we load the packages and create the synthetic dataset.

Listing 9.1   (R) Naive estimation

```r
library(AER)
library(ggplot2)
library(DoubleML)
library(mlr3learners)
set.seed(1234)
n <- 1000
instrument_effect <- 0.7
treatment_effect <- -2
confounder <- rbinom(n, 1, 0.3)
instrument <- rbinom(n, 1, 0.5)
treatment <- as.numeric(runif(n) <= instrument_effect *
  instrument + 0.4 * confounder)
outcome <- 30 + treatment_effect*treatment + 10 * confounder +
  rnorm(n, sd=2)
df <- data.frame(instrument, treatment, outcome)
```

Listing 9.2   (Python) Naive estimation

```python
from numpy.random import seed, normal, binomial, uniform
from numpy import cov
import statsmodels.formula.api as smf
from pandas import DataFrame
from seaborn import kdeplot
import doubleml as dml
from sklearn.linear_model import LinearRegression, LogisticRegression
seed(1234)
n = 1000
instrument_impact = 0.7
treatment_effect = -2
confounder = binomial(1, 0.3, n)
instrument = binomial(1, 0.5, n)
treatment = (uniform(0, 1, n) <= instrument_impact*instrument + \
  0.4*confounder).astype(int)
outcome = 30 + treatment_effect*treatment + 10 * confounder + \
  normal(0, 2, n)
df = DataFrame({
  'instrument': instrument,
  'treatment': treatment,
  'outcome': outcome
})
```

In listings 9.3 and 9.4, we provide naive estimations of the causal effect solely using the treatment and outcome variables. We will go first with linear regression and with the difference in means later.

The resulting (in R) coefficient of the linear regression is 1.0005, which gives the same result as naive the difference of means, 1.0004. This number is far from the expected –2.

Listing 9.3   (R) Naive estimations

```r
print(summary(lm(outcome~treatment, data=df)))
outcome_1 <- mean(df[df$treatment==1, 'outcome'])
```

```
outcome_0 <- mean(df[df$treatment==0, 'outcome'])
print(outcome_1 - outcome_0)
```

Listing 9.4   (Python) Naive estimations

```
outcome_1 = df[df.treatment==1].outcome.mean()
outcome_0 = df[df.treatment==0].outcome.mean()
print(outcome_1 - outcome_0)
smf.ols(formula='outcome ~ treatment', data=df).fit().summary()
```

Now we can apply the IV formula with covariances (but the alternative equation (9.2) is valid as well). The result is –1.8898, much closer to –2 than the previous biased estimation.

Listing 9.5   (R) IV estimation

```
print(cov(outcome, instrument)/cov(treatment, instrument))
```

Listing 9.6   (Python) IV estimation

```
print(cov(outcome, instrument)/cov(treatment, instrument))
```

In R, we can use the AER package as in listing 9.7. Notice that the package uses the bar | to specify which variable is the instrument and differentiate it from other covariables. The obtained result is the same, –1.8898. But in addition, the AER package gives us the standard deviation of our estimation, in this case, 0.1492.

Listing 9.7   (R) IV estimation with AER package

```
model <- ivreg(outcome~treatment|instrument, data=df)
summary(model)
```

What about Python? Some Python packages estimate instrumental variables. But they use an alternative technique, which is explained in the following section.

9.3.1   *Two-stage least squares (2SLS) algorithm*

There is an alternative way to get the same result in the estimation of IVs, called the *two-stage algorithm*. So, why do we need to learn it? First, because it is commonly used and not overly complex, it is worth the effort to learn it now. Second, it is easier to adjust the 2SLS estimator for more general cases where many instruments are used. However, using many instruments is beyond the scope of this book.

The two-stage algorithm shares a similar approach with double machine learning. The steps are essentially the same. First we estimate a model. Second, we estimate the causal model using the residuals (the difference between the real variable and its predictions). Specifically, the process of the two-stage algorithm unfolds as follows:

1 Predict treatment from instrument. Create a model to predict the treatment from the instrument and calculate the prediction. By predicting the treatment, we effectively isolate the variation in the treatment explained by the instrument.

2 Regress outcome on predicted treatment. With the predicted treatment from stage 1, you then regress the outcome variable of interest against this predicted treatment. The resulting coefficient is the effect we are searching for.

Let's apply the two-stage algorithm step by step to our already generated synthetic dataset from the previous section. The first step is creating a predictive model of the treatment with respect to the instrument.

Listing 9.8   (R) Creating a two-stage model

```
model_1 <- lm(treatment~instrument, data=df)
```

Listing 9.9   (Python) Creating a two-stage model

```
model = smf.ols(formula='treatment ~ instrument', data=df).fit()
```

Once we have the model, we apply step 2, regressing the outcome with respect to treatment prediction.

Listing 9.10   (R) Regressing with respect to the prediction

```
treatment_prediction <- predict(model_1, data=df)
lm(outcome~treatment_prediction)
```

Listing 9.11   (Python) Regressing with respect to the prediction

```
df['treatment_prediction'] = model.predict(df)
smf.\
  ols(formula='outcome ~ treatment_prediction', data=df).\
  fit().summary()
```

Alternatively, you can get the two-stage estimation in Python using the `linearmodels` package, as shown next. The result (in Python) is –1.95, with a standard deviation of 0.49.

Listing 9.12   (Python) Using the `linearmodels` package

```
from linearmodels.iv.model import IV2SLS
IV2SLS.\
  from_formula('outcome ~ 1 + [treatment ~ instrument]',df).\
  fit()
```

You may (or may not) have realized that in the two-stage algorithm, we have trained a (linear) model on our data and made predictions on the same data. So, what about cross-fitting? We should do cross-fitting, right? The answer is yes, but in practice, linear models with only one regressor rarely overfit unless you really have a very small sample size. So, there is no need to apply cross-fitting in this case.

9.3.2 Weak instruments

Using instrumental variables can be a handy approach, but there's a catch you should be aware of. The reliability of our estimates heavily depends on the effect the instrument has on the treatment variable. In other words, the instrument must be relevant and have some effect on the treatment variable to ensure accurate results.

In our chatbot example, picture the scenario where the chatbot is positioned in a small, nearly hidden, hard-to-find widget. Consequently, only a few participants in the experimental group will end up using it. As a result, the covariance between the instrument Z (indicating the group assignment) and the decision variable D (whether the participant uses it) is very small, approximately $cov(Z, D) \approx 0$, because variable D is mostly composed of zeroes.

Another explanation for the effect of group assignment on chatbot usage can be a lack of customer interest in the current chatbot setup. Consequently, customers may not use it. In this scenario, the company may make the chatbot more user-friendly to enhance its appeal and encourage usage.

When the effect of the instrument is low, even if the relevance assumption technically holds, we may face numerical and statistical challenges. More precisely, low relevance translates to a high variance in our estimation. In such cases, when an instrument has low relevance, we refer to it as a *weak instrument.*

To understand this better, let's explore it through the IV formula and then with some simulations. Recall that the IV formula is

$$\hat{b} = \frac{cov(Y, Z)}{cov(D, Z)} = \frac{E[Y|Z = 1] - E[Y|Z = 0]}{E[D|Z = 1] - E[D|Z = 0]} \tag{9.3}$$

Notice that we are dividing by $E[D|Z = 1] - E[D|Z = 0]$ (or by the closely related quantity $cov(D, Z)$), which is the causal effect of the instrument on the treatment. If Z has a low effect on D, $E[D|Z = 1] - E[D|Z = 0] \approx 0$. Here's where the problem arises: dividing by a value close to zero results in a larger value, which can magnify any inaccuracies in the numerator. So, if the covariance is small, even a small error in the estimation of the numerator can lead to a much larger error in the overall IV estimate, increasing its variance.

Let's see how bad the effect of weak instruments on the IV estimator can be by running some simulations. From the synthetic dataset above, we will create two scenarios. In the first one, the effect of the instrument on the treatment is 0.3, and in the second, we will consider a lower effect of 0.1. In each case, we will repeat the following steps 1,000 times:

1 Generate the dataset.
2 Estimate the causal effect with equation 9.3.

Then we will plot the distribution of the estimates of each scenario. We expect that estimates for the 0.1 case will be much worse than those with the higher effect of 0.3.

In the following listings, we create the generation and estimation functions we just explained.

Listing 9.13   (R) Helper functions

```r
generate_data <- function(instrument_effect, n){
  confounder <- rbinom(n, 1, 0.3)
  instrument <- rbinom(n, 1, 0.5)
  treatment <- as.numeric(
    runif(n) <= instrument_effect*instrument + 0.4*confounder
  )
  outcome <- 30 + treatment_effect*treatment + 10 * confounder +
    rnorm(n, sd=2)
  data.frame(instrument, treatment, outcome)
}
estimate_impact <- function(df){
  cov(df$outcome, df$instrument)/cov(df$treatment, df$instrument)
}
```

Listing 9.14   (Python) Helper functions

```python
def generate_data(instrument_impact, n):
  confounder = binomial(1, 0.3, n)
  instrument = binomial(1, 0.5, n)
  treatment = (uniform(0, 1, n) <=
  instrument_impact*instrument + 0.4*confounder).astype(int)
  outcome = 30 + instrument_impact*treatment +
  10 * confounder + normal(0, 2, n)
  return(DataFrame({
    'instrument': instrument,
    'treatment': treatment,
    'outcome': outcome
  }))
def estimate_impact(df):
  num = cov(df.instrument, df.outcome)[0][1]
  denom = cov(df.instrument, df.treatment)[0][1]
  return num/denom
```

Now we set the effect of the instrument on the treatment to *0.3*. And then we simulate the generation and estimation steps 1,000 times.

Listing 9.15   (R) Simulating the IV method with a nonweak instrument

```r
sim_n <- 1000
instrument_effect_1 <- 0.3
estimates <- c()
for(i in 1:sim_n){
  df <- generate_data(instrument_effect_1, n)
  estimates <- c(estimates, estimate_impact(df))
}
results <- data.frame(
  estimates=estimates,
```

```
    instrument_effect=instrument_effect_1
)
```

Listing 9.16   (Python) Simulating the IV method with a nonweak instrument

```
sim_n = 1000
instrument_impact_1 = 0.3
estimates_1 = []
for i in range(sim_n):
  df = generate_data(instrument_impact_1, n)
  estimates_1.append(estimate_impact(df))
```

Next we repeat the same process with the effect of the instrument on the treatment being 0.1.

Listing 9.17   (R) Simulating the IV method with a weak instrument

```
instrument_effect_2 <- 0.1
estimates <- c()
for(i in 1:sim_n){
  df <- generate_data(instrument_effect_2, n)
  estimates <- c(estimates, estimate_impact(df))
}
```

Listing 9.18   (Python) Simulating the IV method with a weak instrument

```
instrument_impact_2 = 0.1
estimates_2 = []
for i in range(sim_n):
  df = generate_data(instrument_impact_2, n)
  estimates_2.append(estimate_impact(df))
```

Finally, we plot the results in figure 9.8. You can see that dividing by nearly zero is no joke. Remember that the effect we are estimating is –2. You can see in the plot that with the lower instrument–treatment impact, sometimes we obtain results below –15!

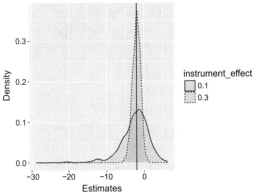

Figure 9.8   A lower effect of the instrument on the treatment variable leads to a higher variance in the estimation.

Meanwhile, the distribution of the estimates for the instrument–treatment effect (0.3) is much narrower. In conclusion, avoid using weak instruments. If you do really need them and don't have an alternative, I suggest you look for specialized references on the subject to deal with weak instruments.

9.3.3   IVs with DoubleML

You can also perform IV estimation using the DoubleML package (https://mng.bz/5Onz), which allows for a more general specification of causal relationships. This package accommodates the following features:

- That the instrument may depend on a set of observed confounding variables
- Nonlinear relationships with machine learning models

Let's delve further into these new specifications. Consider the scenario where variables Z and D are binary, and our DAG looks like figure 9.9. This graph has two sets of confounders: C (unobserved) and X (observed).

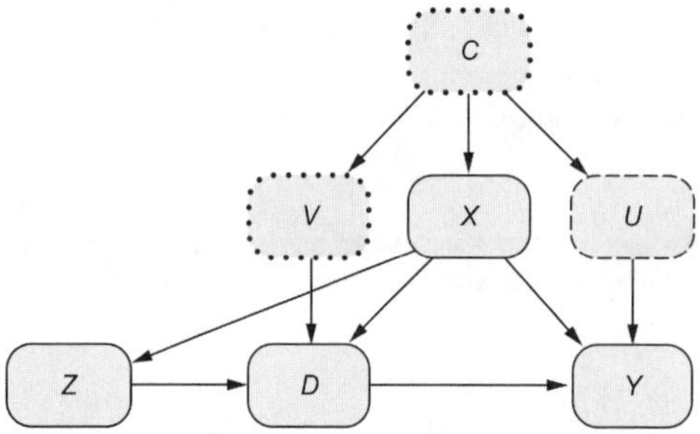

Consider our chatbot example. Suppose we have information about our customers' ages (collected during sign-up). We can assume that age is a confounder as it may influence the decision to use the chatbot (with younger individuals more inclined to adopt new technology) and the level of engagement. Although the original IV setting doesn't demand knowledge of any confounders, if we do have additional information, we can include it in the model and, consequently, reduce the variance in our estimations.

Fortunately, the DoubleML package offers the interactive IV model (IIVM)

Figure 9.9   An instrumental variables approach implemented in the DoubleML package. It focuses on the fact that we only consider confounders X that we can observe and that influence the instrument Z. This permits using a conditional instrumental variables technique tailored to account for the confounders we know and can measure.

approach. To apply this method, we need an additional assumption: the contributions of the observed and unobserved confounding can be separated additively. In other words, we will assume that the relationships between variables can be described by the following equations:

$$Y = l_0(D, X) + U$$
$$D = r_0(Z, X) + V \tag{9.4}$$
$$Z = m_0(X) + \varepsilon$$

For instance, variable Y can be split into two parts: $l_0(D, X)$ is a potentially nonlinear function that describes the effect of D and the observed confounding X on Y, and the term U channels the effect from the unobserved confounding C into Y. The equation $D = r_0(Z, X) + V$ follows the same logic.

NOTE The DAG in figure 9.9 represents a specific scenario where we apply the IIVM approach. But there are more. In more complex DAGs, if we want to apply the IIVM approach, we need to find a set of variables X that satisfy the back-door criterion (see chapter 7) with respect to Z and the other variables D and Y.

DoubleML Interactive IV model assumptions

In summary, we assume that

- Variables Z and D are binary.
- Variables X satisfy the back-door criterion for Z with respect to variables D and Y.
- The observed and unobserved confounding can be separated additively.

We will employ the identical dataset structure simulated in the preceding sections. There are no observed confounders in this scenario, enabling us to use the previously introduced IV formulas. Nevertheless, using this same dataset serves as a validation to ensure the method's effectiveness. For those seeking a more intricate dataset, the DoubleML IV documentation provides an option to explore at https://mng.bz/6Yvy.

In the following listings, we generate the dataset using the `generate_data` function from previous sections. Notice that we add a new variable x that takes a value of 1, which represents an observed confounder. Because the package requires an observed confounder, we are providing an artificial one that doesn't have any effect.

Listing 9.19 (R) Generating data

```
df <- generate_data(instrument_effect = 0.5, n)
df['x'] <- 1
obj_dml_data = DoubleMLData$new(
  df, y_col="outcome", d_col = "treatment", z_cols= "instrument"
)
```

Listing 9.20 (Python) Generating data

```
df = generate_data(0.5, 1000)
df['x'] = 1
obj_dml_data = dml.DoubleMLData(
  df, y_col='outcome', d_cols='treatment',
  z_cols='instrument'
)
```

In listings 9.21 and 9.22, we specify first the types of machine learning models we want to pass to the `DoubleMLIIVM` class. Then we call the `fit` method to estimate the causal effect. Finally, we print the results obtained from equation 9.1. Notice that in this case, because we are working with a simple example, both methods agree.

The `DoubleMLIIVM` class requires three machine learning models: `ml_m`, `ml_r`, and `ml_g`. These correspond to the equations

$$Y = g_0(Z, X) + U$$
$$D = r_0(Z, X) + V$$
$$Z = m_0(X) + \varepsilon$$

In case you wonder, these equations are slightly different but still valid for our graph in figure 9.10, than the ones set in equation 9.4. Instead of expressing Y depending on D and X through the function l_0, because D depends on Z, we express Y depending on X and Z through a new function g_0. That is why the following code requires a machine learning model called g.

Listing 9.21   (R) IV estimation using DoubleML

```
ml_g = lrn("regr.lm")
ml_m = lrn("classif.log_reg")
ml_r = ml_m$clone()
iv_2 = DoubleMLIIVM$new(obj_dml_data, ml_g, ml_m, ml_r)
iv_2$fit()
print(iv_2)
print(
  cov(df$outcome, df$instrument)/
  cov(df$treatment, df$instrument)
)
```

NOTE In the R code, if you call function `lrn("classif.log_reg")` twice, once for `ml_1` and another with `ml_r`, you will get an incorrect result. You need to use the `clone` method as in the preceding code.

Listing 9.22   (Python) IV estimation using DoubleML

```
ml_g = LinearRegression()
ml_m = LogisticRegression(penalty=None)
ml_r = LogisticRegression(penalty=None)
dml_iivm_obj = dml.DoubleMLIIVM(obj_dml_data, ml_g, ml_m, ml_r)
print(dml_iivm_obj.fit().summary)
print(estimate_impact(df))
```

The resulting estimation of the causal effect is -1.8907, with a standard deviation of 0.1955.

9.4   References

- "Rain, rain, go away: 195 potential exclusion-restriction violations for studies using weather as an instrumental variable" by Jonathan Mellon (2023; https://mng.bz/o0MM).

- "Nonparametric bounds on causal effects from partial compliance data" by Alexander Balke and Judea Pearl. UCLA Cognitive Systems Laboratory, Technical Report R-199 (https://mng.bz/n0yK).

9.5 Chapter quiz

As we conclude the chapter, it's important to ensure that you have a solid understanding of the key concepts. Here are the essential questions you should be able to answer clearly and concisely. If you can't, I suggest rereading the corresponding references:

1 Which variable plays the role of the instrument in a Noncompliant RCT?
   Answer in section 9.1.5
2 In a noncompliant RCT, which of the two effects can potentially be biased: ITT or per-protocol?
   Answer in section 9.1.3
3 Which are the three assumptions in an IV estimation model?
   Answer in section 9.1
4 Can we obtain an unbiased estimator for the causal effect in an IV directed acyclic graph if we refrain from assuming anything about the functional relationships between variables?
   Answer in section 9.2.4
5 What is a weak instrument?
   Answer in section 9.3.2

Summary

- When there is an independent source of variation, we can consider applying IV instead of the adjustment formula.
- The advantage of IVs is that we can overcome our lack of knowledge of confounders.
- To apply IVs, you need to make structural and functional assumptions:
- The structural assumptions are relevance, exogeneity, and exclusion restriction.
- The functional assumptions are related to the explicit formula that describes causal relationships between variables. We have seen the linear and partially linear models.
- When your decision variable is binary, you should use partial linear assumptions instead of linear ones.
- Two equivalent IV formulas are used in the literature.
- The two-stage algorithm provides the same results as the direct application of the IV formulas.
- Beware of weak instruments; they can inflate the variance of your estimations.

Potential outcomes framework

10

This chapter covers

- Explaining potential outcomes and their assumptions
- Understanding the relationship between potential outcomes and DAGs
- Using potential outcomes in the adjustment formula and instrumental variables

There are two main frameworks in causal inference: one based on graphs (DAGs) and another called *potential outcomes* (POs), also known as the Rubin causal model. These two frameworks are valid and consistent, allowing you to choose the one that suits your situation. We've spent parts 1 and 2 of the book on DAGs, and now, in part 3, we will get a taste of POs.

You may be wondering, why bother learning a new framework now? There are three reasons:

- A significant amount of literature is written using the PO framework, especially in econometrics, biostatistics, and epidemiology. So, if you come across it, understanding POs is essential.

- The PO notation operates at an individual level, making it more convenient for managing individual effects. Moreover, it is well-suited for dealing with counterfactuals, as expressing them in "do" notation can be cumbersome.

- Looking at the same concepts from a different perspective will help you assimilate the content covered so far.

We will begin the chapter by introducing PO notation and explaining how to define the average treatment effect (ATE) using this new notation. Additionally, we will outline the fundamental assumptions required for the proper use of POs.

Moving on, we will delve into the relationship between DAGs and POs. We will establish their equivalence through the first law of causal inference. Additionally, we'll offer a concise introduction to counterfactuals, addressing questions like this one: in a specific scenario, what would have occurred if different actions were taken? Counterfactuals are useful for finding the root cause of particular problems, estimating dosage effects in drug trials, and assessing the fairness of machine learning models. They are advanced, so we'll offer just a brief introduction. The final fourth sections will focus on the PO version of the adjustment formula and instrumental variables.

> **Why learn the potential outcomes framework?**
> It's important to learn the PO framework because a lot of literature uses this approach. Additionally, some prefer it over DAGs. The pros and cons of each method are a subject of debate. I suggest learning both to be well-rounded.

10.1   *What is a potential outcome?*

Let's start by learning the fundamental notation of POs. Consider a scenario where you wish to evaluate the effectiveness of a new treatment through an experiment. This experiment may not necessarily be a randomized controlled trial (RCT); you have the flexibility to randomly assign treatments based on certain criteria of your choosing or even delegate the assignment to others with an undisclosed policy.

We will describe the PO framework through this example, but of course, you can adapt the framework to other situations as long as you specify the roles of the treatment, outcome, and patients (see section 10.1.4 to be sure you can apply the framework). Although we will use index i to identify patients, in other scenarios, instead of patients, we use the term *units* and the corresponding subscript u.

10.1.1 *Individual outcomes*

Let's go through each step of the assignment and measurement process. To understand things clearly, we'll keep it simple. Here's what can happen to patient i: they either get the treatment or they don't. And once we're done with the experiment, they will either recover or they won't. So far, it doesn't seem complicated.

The important thing to remember is that the patient's response to the treatment *is already there before we decide on the treatment.* Let's explain this in mathematical terms. In PO notation, if a patient i is not treated, $t = 0$, we represent their response (whether they recover) with $Y_0(i)$. Analogously, if they are treated, $t = 1$, we use $Y_1(i)$ to denote their response. In general, for a given treatment t, the value Y_t is the PO corresponding to that treatment. The values $Y_0(i)$, $Y_1(i)$ are called *potential outcomes,* meaning they represent all the possible outcomes patient i can have based on whether they get treated. It's like saying, "What can happen if they get the treatment?" and "What can happen if they don't?" We're keeping track of both possibilities.

Let me really emphasize the meaning of POs. The responses a patient can have, $Y_0(i)$ and $Y_1(i)$, are not something we can directly see or know. They remain hidden from us. Here's where it gets interesting: at some point, we'll decide whether to treat the patient. If we do treat the patient, we'll get to observe $Y_1(i)$. But the tricky part is that we won't know the alternative outcome $Y_0(i)$! It stays unobserved to us.

So, after the assignment, we'll only be aware of one of the two POs, leaving us in the dark about the other. The response we observed is called the *factual* outcome because we see it in reality. But the one we can't observe is called the *counterfactual* (contrary-to-fact) outcome, as it's like imagining what would have happened in the alternative scenario where the patient wasn't treated. It's a bit like peeking into parallel universes but only seeing one side of the story.

On top of the POs, we can measure two more quantities: $T(i)$ is the final treatment patient i received, and $Y(i)$ is the measured response from patient i. You may notice that the notation is similar between the outcome $Y(i)$ and the POs $Y_0(i)$, $Y_0(i)$. But the difference in meaning is enormous! $Y(i)$ is something we can directly observe, whereas $Y_0(i)$ and $Y_1(i)$ are partially observed, meaning we only know one part of the story for each patient.

Table 10.1 gives a hypothetical example showcasing the main variables that play a role in this experiment:

- Drummer $(i = 1)$ has $Y_1(i) = Y_0(i) = 0$, which means they have no chance to recover independently of the treatment they received. So, even though they received the treatment, $T(i) = 1$, doctors observed that the patient wasn't cured, $Y(i) = 0$.
- Burton $(i = 2)$ is a strange case because they would naturally heal on their own, $Y_0(i) = 1$. But if they were given the treatment, they would have a negative reaction and not recover, $Y_0(i) = 0$. Unfortunately, the patient received the treatment, $T(i) = 1$ and didn't recover, $Y(i) = 0$.
- Holden $(i = 3)$ is what we would expect: they will recover if they receive the treatment, $Y_1(i) = 1$, but not otherwise, $Y_0(i) = 0$. Fortunately, they receive the treatment, $T(i) = 1$, and are cured, $Y(i) = 1$.
- Avasarala $(i = 4)$ is very healthy and will recover with or without treatment, $Y_1(i) = Y_0(i) = 1$. They didn't receive treatment, $T(i) = 0$, but it doesn't matter because they were cured anyway, $Y(i) = 1$.

Table 10.1 Hypothetical example of POs with assignment ($T(i)$) and observed recovery ($R(i)$)

Name	i	$Y_0(i)$	$Y_1(i)$	$T(i)$	$Y(i)$
Drummer	1	0	0	1	0
Burton	2	1	0	1	0
Holden	3	0	1	1	1
Avasarala	4	1	1	0	1

One of the main difficulties of the PO framework is always knowing which quantities are observable and which are not. To help identify each variable, table 10.2 provides a clear breakdown of each step in the experiment, focusing on the example of a treated patient. Here's what you'll find:

- *Before assignment*—At this stage, we have two unobserved POs that determine what would happen if the patient were treated ($Y_1(i)$) versus not treated ($Y_0(i)$).
- *Treatment assigned*—The patient receives treatment based on a specific policy, which can be random or nonrandom, determining the value of the variable T, shaded as $T(i) = 1$, to indicate that the patient was indeed treated.
- *Factual outcome*—Finally we observe the actual outcome. This is represented by the variable $Y(i)$, shaded as $Y(i) = Y_1(i)$, which tells us the real result of the patient's treatment.

Table 10.2 Stages in a causal process for the patient i (what changes in each step is shaded)

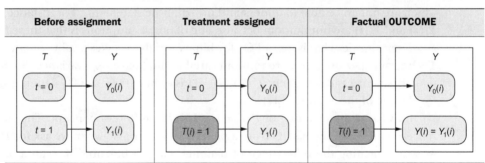

To make it easier to grasp, let's categorize all these variables in table 10.3.

Table 10.3 POs are (in principle) unobserved; we only have data about measured variables.

Potential outcomes (in principle unobserved)	Measured variables (observed)
• $Y_0(i)$: the outcome of patient i if they *were not* given the treatment • $Y_1(i)$: the outcome of patient i if they *were given* the treatment	• $Y(i)$ observed outcome of patient i • $T(i)$ treatment given to patient i

The relationship between observed and partially observed variables is expressed by the following equation, known as the *consistency* equation:

$$Y(i) = Y_0(i)(1 - T(i)) + Y_1(i)T(i) \tag{10.1}$$

When $T(i) = 0$, the measured outcome $Y(i) = Y_0(i)$, and when the patient is treated, $T(i) = 1$, $Y(i) = Y_1(i)$. The consistency equation is used later in the derivation of the adjustment and instrumental variable (IV) estimation formulas.

10.1.2 *Population outcomes*

In the same way that we have individual variables, such as those presented in table 10.3, we can have population values Y_0, Y_1, Y, T. How do we interpret them? Each of these quantities is a random sampling of the total population. In other words, if we have n patients, the value of T is sampling any of the individual $T(i)$ at random with probability $1/n$. The same reasoning applies to the other variables.

This means we can define the expectations of any of the variables Y_0, Y_1, Y, T as the average over individuals. For instance,

$$E[T] = \frac{1}{n} \sum_i T(i)$$

The expectation of the treatment is the mean over patients. In the same way, we can define other statistics, such as the variance.

It is important to always know which of the previous quantities are random and which are not, to be able to understand probabilistic statements. For instance, the POs $Y_1(i)$ and $Y_0(i)$ are not random because one of our assumptions is that these functions are deterministic. That is, each PO (for binary variables) takes a value of either 1 or 0. Technically speaking, they are random variables that have zero variance. So, for a particular patient i and treatment t, $P(Y_t(i) = 1)$ is either 100% or 0%, depending on the fixed value of the quantity $Y_t(i)$.

But what is the meaning of $P(Y_1 = 1)$? This is a different concept. The variable Y_1 represents a sampling of s PO from a patient at random. So when we ask for $P(Y_1 = 1)$, we are estimating the percentage of patients who will be cured if treated or, equivalently, whose PO satisfies $Y_t = 1$. That is, the *term probability* refers to the percentage of patients satisfying some criteria (in this case, $Y_1 = 1$). Notice that the quantity $P(Y_1 = 1)$ is not directly observable because the PO is a priori not observed!

In the same way, $P(T = 1)$ represents the percentage of people who are actually treated, and this quantity is straightforward to calculate. Similarly, the quantity $Y = 1$ is the proportion of patients who recovered, again a quantity that's easy to calculate.

10.1.3 *Causal effects*

When working with POs in causal inference, we come across different measures of treatment effects. However, it's important to note that because the POs $Y_1(i)$ (the outcome if individual i received the treatment) and $Y_0(i)$ (the outcome if individual i did not receive the treatment) are not observed simultaneously for the same individual, these measures cannot be directly calculated. Instead, they are theoretical constructs that we aim to estimate using specialized methods:

- *Individual treatment effect (ITE)*—$Y_1(i) - Y_0(i)$ is the difference in outcomes for patient i between being treated and not being treated. We will rarely be able to measure this quantity. There are some exceptions, however, such as crossover trials, where patients are initially assigned to one group and later switch to the alternative group. This allows us to observe both POs for each patient. But crossover trials come with their fair share of limitations and are only suitable for specific situations, such as patients with chronic conditions.

- *Average treatment effect (ATE)*—ITEs are hard to estimate, but ATEs can be calculated more often. The ATE, a concept we're already familiar with, is defined as its name says,

$$\text{ATE} = E[Y_1 - Y_0] = \frac{1}{n} \sum_i Y_1(i) - Y_0(i)$$

where n is the total number of patients.

- *Average treatment effect on the treated (ATET)*—The ATET was introduced in chapter 5 regarding the propensity score matching. As its name says, the ATET is the ATE, but calculated only on those who were treated:

$$\text{ATET} = E[Y_1 - Y_0 | T = 1] = \frac{1}{n_1} \sum_{i:T(i)=1} Y_1(i) - Y_0(i)$$

where n_1 is the total number of treated patients. You may have noticed that the only difference between the ATE and the ATET in the previous formulas is the index i: in the ATE, it runs over all patients, whereas in the ATET, it runs only over those who are treated (i such that $T(i) = 1$).

If we run an RCT, ATE = ATET. Because we are randomizing the treatment, the experimental group shares the same population characteristics as the control group. However, in general, the ATET and ATE may not be equal.

10.1.4 PO assumptions

To work with POs, we need them to be well defined. So, we will have a set of implicit assumptions from now on. If any of these assumptions are not likely to hold, you will need to look for specialized literature:

- *Deterministic POs*—We assume that given a patient i and a treatment t, the PO $Y_t(i)$ takes only one value. In other words, if we treat patient i, they will either recover or not: $Y_1(i)$ is either 1 or 0.

- *Well-defined interventions*—Only one type of treatment is considered, and the PO does not depend on how or why the treatment is given. This assumption would not hold if, for instance, we considered that different doctors applied different types of techniques or the treatment comprised different types of drugs.

- *Stable unit treatment value assumption (SUTVA)*—The PO of a unit doesn't depend on how other units are treated. In other words, there's no *interference* between units or patients. This assumption may sound simple, but in practice, it doesn't always hold true.

  Let's take an example to understand better. Imagine you run an e-commerce store selling bikes, and you want to figure out the best price for two bike models with similar features but from different brands; let's call them A and B. To do this, you randomly set the prices for each bike and brand.

  These two models are in competition with each other. If you lower the price of model A, it may reduce the chances of a customer buying the alternative model B. So, the treatment (price) of one item (A or B) ends up influencing the purchase of the other brand.

  In a way, we can say that the treatment of one bike affects the POs of the other bike's purchase. This situation violates the assumption of no interference between units or patients. Therefore, in this case, we would need to explore specialized literature that addresses this problem.

As we'll discover in the upcoming section, these assumptions work differently in DAGs; they don't require deterministic POs. Moreover, well-defined interventions and SUTVA assumptions are implicit in the construction of the graph.

10.2 How do POs relate to DAGs?

Are POs and DAGs completely different theories? Will we have to start learning an entirely new causal inference theory from scratch? Good news! They are not entirely different, and you don't need to start from square one. POs and DAGs talk about the same concepts; they just use different names for them.

10.2.1 The first law of causal inference

Let's see how we can translate POs into DAGs using what Judea Pearl calls the *first law of causal inference*. Recall the meaning of $Y_1(i)$: the outcome of patient i if we decided to give them the treatment. Now, imagine that we have a DAG G. This DAG can take whatever form we want. The variable Y in the DAG represents the outcome we are interested in, and the variable T denotes the treatment. We will have data for all n patients: $T(1), ..., T(n)$ and $Y(1), ..., Y(n)$. Furthermore, we assume that the same graph G is valid for each of them.

In DAG notation, giving patient i the treatment, regardless of context, means intervening in the graph with the "do" operator. So, we can see that the PO is the same as intervening in the graph $Y_1(i) = Y(i)|\mathrm{do}(T(i) = 1)$, where $Y(i)|\mathrm{do}(T(i) = 1)$ denotes the outcome of patient i once we have intervened in the graph.

> ### First law of causal inference
> The PO of patient *i* is nothing more than the result of intervening in the graph *G* with the "do" operator. In general, for a patient *i* and a treatment value *t* = 0, 1,
>
> $$Y_t(i) = Y(i)|\text{do}(T(i) = t)$$
>
> Essentially, the result of a "do" and the PO are the same.

The first law also tells us the relationship between causal estimates. Because expectations are averages over patients, we have that the effect of an intervention can be written with any of the two equivalent expressions: $E[Y_t] = E[Y|\text{do}(T = t)]$. Furthermore, the ATE can be written as

$$\text{ATE} = E[Y_1] - E[Y_0] = E[Y|\text{do}(T = 1)] - E[Y|\text{do}(T = 0)]$$

The relationship between POs and DAGs goes much further. A theorem proved by Judea Pearl (in his book *Causality*) says that *if a conclusion is valid in one framework, it is automatically valid in the other framework*. Informally speaking, the two frameworks are equivalent.

The point is that even though they are equivalent, each framework has strengths and weaknesses. So, the best option is to learn both and use the one that works better for your case!

10.2.2 *Expressing PO assumptions with DAGs*

We've established the equivalence of the PO and DAG frameworks. So, how do the assumptions from one framework translate to the other? The well-defined intervention and SUTVA assumptions from section 10.1.4 are embedded in the construction of the graph. Let's delve into this in more detail.

WELL-DEFINED INTERVENTIONS

The PO framework requires a unique definition of the treatment, whereas DAGs can handle multiple versions of the treatment, helping to clarify its scope. Let's look at an example. Suppose we want to measure the effect of undergoing surgery, and each surgeon has a different technique that may affect recovery differently. We can represent this scenario in a graph, as shown in figure 10.1.

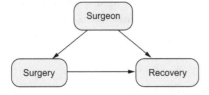

Figure 10.1   If different surgeons have varying effects on recovery and use different methods, we can't assume that the effect of the surgery type is the same for all because it changes from surgeon to surgeon.

If we assume that all surgeons have a similar effect on the surgery's outcome, we are interested in estimating the effect of a generic intervention, $P(Recovery = 1|do(Surgery = 1))$. However, if we want to evaluate each surgeon's effect individually, we are interested in the conditional intervention, $P(Recovery = 1|do(Surgery = 1), Surgeon)$. In the context of the PO framework, this means we either define the treatment as "undergoing surgery" or consider the surgeon's relevance, leading us to define multiple treatments, one for each surgeon.

SUTVA

In graphical approaches to causal inference, the SUTVA is not assumed. This is because the problem of interference pertains more to how we interpret interventions using the "do" operator than it is a limitation of the graph itself. Let's consider an example to illustrate this.

Consider the example in section 10.1.4, in which we randomize prices over two bikes A and B with similar characteristics. Let's assume that customers inspect both prices and then make their purchase based on this information, as shown in figure 10.2. For simplicity, let's assume customers can purchase zero, one, or two bikes. It may be more realistic to assume that each customer can buy only up to one bike, but this would make the model more complex.

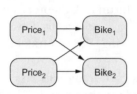

Figure 10.2 Price effect on competing products. There is interference between prices, so we cannot assume SUTVA.

The problem with using the tools we've discussed so far in this scenario is that they estimate the effect of $Price_1$ on $Bike_1$ assuming the prices of other items are randomized. However, the real question may be about estimating the effect in a different setting where other product prices are not randomized. Let's dive deeper into this.

At first glance, there seem to be no confounders, suggesting it should be easy to estimate the causal effect. But what exactly are we trying to measure? Perhaps we're interested in the probability $P(Bike_1 = Yes|do(Price_1 = p))$, meaning how likely it is that a customer buys the bike if we set its price to a specific price p.

Remember, the "do" operator's interpretation involves fixing the value of $Price_1$ while allowing the rest of the system to function normally. In this case, though, $Price_2$ is being randomized. So, we're essentially measuring the effect of $Price_1$ on $Bike_1$ under the condition of randomizing $Price_2$. This may not be the question we're actually interested in answering.

Estimating causal effects in this situation requires more sophisticated techniques that are beyond the scope of this book. However, once again, we can use graphs to explicitly state our assumptions and acknowledge the limitations of our current tools, indicating the need for more advanced techniques.

10.2.3 *Counterfactuals*

The word *counterfactual* is common in causal inference, but it can have different meanings in the PO and DAG frameworks. In the PO framework, counterfactuals appear from day one. They refer to a PO that we haven't actually observed. It's like asking, "What would have happened if we had given a different treatment to a patient?" We can't directly observe this outcome, but we can make educated guesses based on the data we have.

COUNTERFACTUALS ON DAGS

On the other hand, in the DAG framework, counterfactuals are an advanced concept. We explain them here to see the difference with respect to counterfactuals in the PO framework.

Counterfactuals in DAGs address a more general question: *for a specific situation, what would happen if we made a different choice or took a different action?* For instance, the ATET is a counterfactual quantity: what would happen to those who were treated if they were not treated? We are asking for a situation (no treatment) that contradicts what has actually happened (those who are treated).

Counterfactual example (advanced)

You may be wondering about the difference between the counterfactual definition we've just discussed and the definition of a PO, such as $Y_i(1)$. What would be the outcome for patient i if they received treatment?

The difference is subtle in wording but can be complex mathematically. I'll provide an example of a counterfactual using Pearl's approach. Counterfactuals can be tricky, so if it seems confusing, don't worry—it's something you can always revisit later.

Let's look at the following figure in the context of the kidney stone problem that we covered in chapter 2 when discussing z-specific effects. Here, treatment T influences the size of the stone after treatment, S, and both factors jointly influence the outcome, O. Here, S is a mediator.

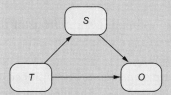

The size of the stone acts as a mediator. To figure out what would happen to patients with large stones after treatment if they were treated differently, we need to use a more advanced method known as counterfactuals. S stands for Size, T for Treatment, and O for Outcome.

Let's think about this scenario: suppose we want to study patients whose stone size increased after their treatment. We're curious what would happen if all these patients were treated with treatment A.

At first glance, this may seem contradictory. Some of these patients, if given treatment A, might not end up with large stones! Which should we consider first: the selection of the patients or the treatment they receive?

This is exactly why we use the concept of counterfactuals. It involves two steps:

- Select the group of patients. Mathematically, this means we condition on S = Large.

> **(continued)**
>
> - Apply a specific intervention to this group. In mathematical terms, we use $do(T = A)$.
>
> This is easier said than done! Applying these concepts mathematically is complex and goes beyond the scope of this book.
>
> A crucial aspect of Judea Pearl's definition of counterfactuals includes the phrase "for a specific situation." This refers to the possibility of first conditioning on a particular group or scenario before implementing any intervention. Thus, this notion of counterfactual is much more general than the one provided by the definition of POs.

In the DAG framework, counterfactuals are the third rung of what Judea Pearl calls the "Ladder of Causation." Here's what each rung focuses on:

- 1st rung: association. At this level, we focus on observing and exploring data. Tasks involve statistical tools for uncertainty assessment, exploratory data analysis, and predictive models. It helps us answer questions like, "Do people who take aspirin cure their headaches?" even if the recovery may not be attributed to the aspirin.
- 2nd rung: intervention. This level deals with questions related to changing the dynamics of the system. It allows us to estimate the effect of decisions, such as, "How many people will cure their headache if we give them aspirin?"
- 3rd rung: counterfactuals. Here, we encounter questions that inquire about what would have happened under different actions or choices. For instance, "Would my headache have disappeared without the aspirin?" Counterfactuals enable us to assess *actual causality*: that is, retrospectively analyzing the causes of an event.

Sometimes the intervention rung is devoted to estimating the "effects of the causes" (the effect of a decision), whereas counterfactuals are devoted to understanding the "causes of effects" (why did something happen?).

Counterfactuals in the DAG framework are considered an advanced topic that goes beyond the scope of this book. If you wish to explore this subject in depth, I recommend reading specialized literature, such as the book *Causality* book by Judea Pearl.

10.3   *Adjustment formula with potential outcomes*

The adjustment formula is the same for the PO and DAG frameworks. But here's the thing: the formula is helpful only when we can actually use it. In the DAG framework, we have the back-door criterion, which tells us when we need to use the adjustment formula. But this criterion relies on graphs. Because the PO framework doesn't use graphs, we need another way to figure out when the adjustment formula applies.

Back-door criterion reminder

The back-door criterion between *X* and *Y* tells us that if a set of variables *Z* satisfies the conditions

- Cuts all back-door paths of *X* (paths with incoming arrows on *X*)
- Does not cut causal paths departing from *X*

then we can adjust for *Z* in the adjustment formula to obtain an unbiased estimator of the ATE.

In this section, we will learn about the ignorability assumption for the PO framework, which tells us when we can apply the adjustment formula. The *ignorability* assumption states that we can adjust for covariates *X* as long as the POs are independent of the treatment, given the covariates *X*:

$$Y_1, Y_0 \perp T | X$$

Ignorability terminology

The assumption of ignorability varies in name and form across different books and sources. In some cases, you may encounter terms like *strong ignorability* or *exchangeability*. Additionally, the concept of ignorability may include a positivity assumption in certain contexts, whereas in others it may not.

If you find this expression difficult to digest, don't worry; we will go step by step. Let's start with a simple case: imagine that we run an RCT. Because the assignment is done at random, if the sample size is large enough, we expect to have the same proportion of any characteristics in both groups. For instance, there should be approximately the same proportion in both groups of patients of a specific age, specific socioeconomic class, specific sex, etc.

If we pick any age, let's call it *a*, we'll find that the probability of having that age in the group of treated patients $(T = 1)$ is the same as in the group of nontreated patients $(T = 0)$. This is shown in the math as $P(Age = a | T = 1) = P(Age = a | T = 0)$.

To put it simply, this mathematical expression tells us that the proportion of patients of a specific age doesn't change based on whether they are treated. That is, the variable *Age* and the variable *T* are independent of each other, according to the definition of probabilistic independence.

It's important to grasp that the PO $Y_1(i)$ is like any other characteristic of an individual, such as age or sex—it's determined before we even decide on the actual treatment. So, in an RCT, we expect to have the same proportion of patients with $Y_1(i) = 1$ in both groups:

$$P(Y_1(i) = 1 | T = 1) = P(Y_1(i) = 1 | T = 0)$$

which means $Y_1(i)$ and *T* are independent.

So, in an RCT, we will have

$$Y_1, Y_0 \perp T$$

Note that this statement may seem similar to suggesting that Y and T are independent, but that's not the case (usually!). In reality, we anticipate that treatment T does affect outcome Y, so they cannot be independent of each other. Although the notation appears similar, the meaning is significantly different.

What happens when we are not running an RCT, and there are confounders X? Imagine that you gave the treatment based on the age of the patient. Young patients were more prone to be treated. On the one hand, we can assume that age is correlated with patients' recovery capability if being treated. In other words, age is correlated with each of the POs Y_1, Y_0. On the other hand, in this experiment, age is correlated with the treatment. Thus, the treatment is no longer independent of the POs. However, if we choose a particular age group (we condition on age), age (a fixed variable) is independent of the treatment, and for this particular group, the treatment and the POs are independent.

This reasoning leads us to the ignorability assumption—given confounders X, the treatment and the POs are independent:

$$Y_1, Y_0 \perp T|X$$

Basically, the ignorability assumption ensures that there are no relevant confounders whose effect is not channeled by X.

The thing is, if the ignorability assumption holds, the ATE can be calculated with the adjustment formula

$$\text{ATE} = E_X[E[Y|T = 1, X]] - E_X[E[Y|T = 0, X]]$$

where E_X denotes the expectation with respect to variables X. At first sight, this formula may seem new because it is written using expectations. But it is the same as the adjustment formula in chapter 2. Check it out: for a binary outcome Y and categorical covariates X, we have

$$\text{ATE} = E_X[E[Y|T = 1, X]] - E_X[E[Y|T = 0, X]] =$$

$$\frac{1}{n}\left(\sum_x P(Y = 1|T = 1, X = x) - P(Y = 1|T = 0, X = x)\right)$$

Derivation of the adjustment formula from ignorability

This explanation is only for readers who are curious about the mathematical details of the adjustment formula under ignorability. If ignorability holds, because POs are independent of the treatment, given X, we have

$$E[Y_1|X] = E[Y_1|T = 1, X]$$

By equation 10.1, the outcome observed for the treated is precisely the PO, so

$$E[Y_1|T = 1, X] = E[Y|T = 1, X]$$

This means we can transform an expression depending on an unobserved quantity to an observed one: for a treatment $t = 0,1$,

$$E[Y_t|X] = E[Y|T = t, X]$$

Now we can apply the law of the total expectation to find

$$\text{ATE} = E_X[Y_1 - Y_0] = E_X[E[Y_1 - Y_0|X]] = E_X[E[Y_1|X]] - E_X[[Y_0|X]]$$

Finally, we can put together the previous equations into the adjustment formula:

$$\text{ATE} = E_X[E[Y|T = 1, X]] - E_X[E[Y|T = 0, X]]$$

Having established that we can adjust for a set of variables X whenever ignorability holds with respect to them, the next question arises: when does ignorability hold? Although some expert analysts can discern this in many cases, for most people it's challenging. This difficulty becomes a significant limitation of the PO framework: assessing the ignorability assumption is no easy task for the average person.

Relationship between the back door and ignorability

Fortunately, the back-door criterion is enough to determine ignorability. If we find a set of variables X that satisfies that back door with respect to two variables T and Y, we automatically confirm the ignorability assumption. In other words, the POs are independent of the treatment, given the covariates X.

10.4 IVs with potential outcomes

As the PO and DAG frameworks are equivalent, the estimation process we learned in the previous chapter using IVs remains valid. To get more practice with the PO notation, let's explore another variant of IVs.

In chapter 9, we learned that there is no general formula to estimate the causal effect from D to Y in figure 10.3. To estimate such a causal effect, we need to make further assumptions. In particular, we covered two variations. First, we assumed that all relationships in the graph were linear. Second, we assumed that the treatment was binary and that its effect on the outcome was partially linear.

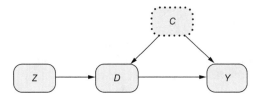

Figure 10.3 General DAG for IVs

We will concentrate on a variation that fits perfectly with the chatbot example. In this scenario, we conducted an A/B test in which customers were randomly assigned to either the experimental group, where they interacted with the chatbot, or the control group, where they had no access to the chatbot.

The role of each variable in figure 10.3 is as follows:

- D is the treatment or decision variable that represents whether a customer has used the chatbot.
- Z represents the group to which the customer has been assigned (with value 0 or 1).
- Y is the engagement of the customer in the platform.

In this example, a distinct characteristic allows us to estimate the causal effect on Y: customers in the control group have no access to the chatbot. Mathematically, this means the probability of using the chatbot among those in the control group is zero: $P(D = 1 | Z = 0) = 0$. As a result, we can drop the assumption of partial linearity that was required in the previous chapter, which is explained in the following result.

Imperfect compliance IVs

Variables Z and D are binary, and $P(D = 1 | Z = 0) = 0$. In this case, we can estimate the ATE on the treated with the following unbiased formula:

$$\text{ATET} = \frac{E[Y|Z = 1] - E[Y|Z = 0]}{E[D|Z = 1]}$$

The mathematically inclined reader can find the proof in appendix F. I highly recommend taking a look at it to gain practice with POs.

You may notice that this formula is identical to the one we saw in chapter 9, which also includes the fact that $E[D = 1 | Z = 0] = 0$. So why all the fuss about different IV variations if we keep getting the same result?

This is a valid question, and the answer lies in the interpretation of the results. Depending on the assumption we make, the same result may represent a different quantity or meaning. In this particular case, we are saying that we can only estimate the causal effect on those who are treated (those who used the chatbot). So, we don't know how those customers who didn't use the chatbot will react once they try it. This seems legitimate. If we don't have information about those who didn't use it, we cannot make guesses about how they will engage the chatbot.

But why didn't we have this problem in chapter 9? Because there, we assumed *homogeneous treatment effects*. For instance, when we assume the partially linear relationship $Y := w_Y + bD + h(C) + \varepsilon_Y$ (see the partially linear IV assumptions in section 9.2.2 in chapter 9), we are intrinsically saying that the effect of using the chatbot is the quantity b, no matter who uses it.

In this chapter, we are assuming *heterogeneity*: the effect of using the chatbot may be different for different customers. If we assume homogeneity, the effect on the treated population will be the same as that of the whole population, and the ATE and ATET will agree (ATE = ATET).

10.5 Chapter quiz

As we conclude the chapter, it's important to ensure that you have a solid understanding of the key concepts. Here are the essential questions you should be able to answer clearly and concisely. If you can't, I suggest rereading the corresponding references:

1 What are the three assumptions of the potential outcomes framework?
  Answer in section 10.1.4

2 Are the PO and DAG frameworks equivalent?
  Answer in section 10.2.1

3 What is the relationship between ignorability and the back-door criterion?
  Answer in the sidebar "Relationship between the back door and ignorability" in section 10.3

Summary

- Potential outcomes and DAGs are two equivalent frameworks. POs are more commonly used in the econometrics and biostatistics communities, and they are particularly helpful for handling counterfactuals and individual effects. On the other hand, DAGs offer graphical criteria, such as the back-door criterion, and allow us to be more explicit about the model's assumptions.
- The fundamental assumptions of a PO model are that POs are deterministic, interventions need to be well defined, and SUTVA must hold.
- In the PO literature, applying the adjustment formula typically requires the adjustment set to satisfy the ignorability assumption. This assumption is automatically met if the set satisfies the back-door criterion.
- There are several variations of instrumental variables that share the same formula. The crucial aspect is understanding the assumptions made to determine how we will interpret the results.
- Pearl's ladder of causation categorizes causal questions into three distinct rungs: association, intervention, and counterfactuals.

11

The effect of a time-related event

This chapter covers

- Synthetic controls, regression discontinuity designs and differences in differences
- Understanding the assumptions and limitations of these three methods
- Using these methods to estimate causal effects

In chapter 1, we used an example of evaluating the effect of a newly designed website. We learned that the best way to make such an evaluation was using A/B tests. However, as we already know, it is not always possible to perform A/B tests. Therefore, in this final chapter, we revisit how to assess the decision effect by comparing the situation before and after without relying on A/B tests. That is, we focus on understanding the effect of time-related events.

In this chapter, we'll explore three techniques for estimating the effect of a decision. Each technique works for a different situation. We'll stick to the following example as our guide; as we explore each technique, we'll modify the example accordingly to understand when the technique works, what assumptions it has, and how to use it to estimate the ATE.

Imagine that you work in a movie streaming service and you are about to launch the new movie *VII: The Force Awakens* (VII for short) from the *Star Wars* saga. You are interested in knowing if the launch will increase the views of the older *Star Wars* movie *III: Revenge of the Sith* (III for short). Understanding how the release of one movie affects the viewership of others can help the company decide which new movies are worth releasing.

Ideally, you would like to run an A/B test to measure the effect of the new movie on others from the service catalog. The experimental group would have access to the new film (VII), but the control group wouldn't. However, such an experiment is very impractical because, for reasons of popularity, you cannot release the movie only for an exclusive group of customers.

So, how can you estimate the ATE with nonexperimental time-related data? First, let's see what the data looks like. Figure 11.1 shows the Google Trends results for web searches for III in December 2015. The metric reported by Google Trends is called *interest* and represents the number of searches rescaled so that the maximum value equals 100. Keep in mind that the new movie VII was released on December 18.

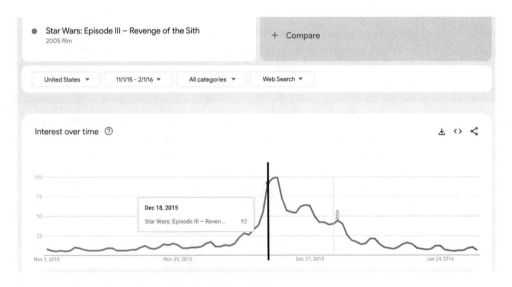

Figure 11.1 The release of a new *Star Wars* movie may increase the interest (metric reported by Google Trends) of previous *Star Wars* movies. Source: Google Trends.

NOTE We are using the Google Trends search as an illustrative example here. However, the primary focus of this section is on estimating how the release of a new movie affects the viewership of older films. This is a different metric than the web searches displayed in Google Trends.

Because there is a clear bump in the trend of the old movie, the data seems to support the hypothesis that the release of VII increased the views of III. But correlation is not causation, so this bump may not necessarily be caused by the new movie. As we know from chapter 1, relying on the differences in views before and after the release to estimate the effect can be very biased. The context before and after may not be comparable due to the existence of *simultaneous factors* (factors that happen at the same time) with the movie release that may affect movie viewership: possible simultaneous marketing campaigns and seasonality, and so on. The presence of simultaneous factors prevents us from estimating causal effects. However, we may frequently find ourselves in situations where it is reasonable to assume that there are no simultaneous factors, or at least their effect is limited. In these occasions, by delving deeper into the movie release process and incorporating sensible additional assumptions, we can enhance the reliability of our effect estimation.

We will explore three distinct approaches to estimate the effect of the movie release. Each method is tailored for a different situation, thus making a different set of assumptions. By learning the following three methods, you will have a stronger foundation on which to estimate causal effects:

- *Regression discontinuity design (RDD)*—The context before and after the release of VII may be very different and thus not comparable. But if we zoom in right around the release date, the differences get smaller. RDDs provide causal estimates under the presumption that data close to the release date can treated as if it were obtained from an A/B test.

- *Synthetic controls (SCs)*—Let's consider another popular movie franchise: *The Lord of the Rings* (*LoTR*). Both *LoTR* and *Star Wars* may exhibit similar patterns, especially in the case of movies released a long time ago. They share common factors that influence them, such as seasonality, a similar target audience, and similar competition. However, an event like the release of a new *Star Wars* movie can potentially affect older *Star Wars* films but not affect *LoTR*. Given the high correlation between *Star Wars* and *LoTR*, we can develop a predictive model to answer this hypothetical question: what would have happened to the viewership of the old *Star Wars* movies if the new one had never been released?

  The fascinating aspect of this approach, known as *synthetic controls*, is that we aren't limited to predicting changes based on other movie views alone. We can create the model with other related quantities, such as the number of movie tickets sold in different countries. As long as the model predicts well, we are fine!

- *Differences in differences (DiD)*—Just because we didn't start with a control group doesn't mean we can't find one later. Take the *LoTR* series, for example. It has a pretty similar pattern of views, but it's not influenced by (let's pretend) the new *Star Wars* movie. On the other hand, we may be interested in finding the effect of the new release not only on a particular *Star Wars* movie but on all previously released movies. DiD helps us figure out how much effect the new movie had on previous movies by comparing it to other movies with a similar trend.

This chapter is divided into three main sections, one for each method: RDD, SCs, and DiD. Each section follows the same structure, making it easier to understand the differences among them:

- *Introduction*—This section describes the technique and the basic intuition behind its assumptions.
- *Data simulation*—Before delving into theory, we'll create a synthetic dataset suited for the method.
- *Terminology*—Here we'll cover the names given to each variable in the method.
- *Assumptions*—This part explains what the method relies on and the situations where it can be applied.
- *Effect estimation*—Each method estimates a causal quantity, sometimes different than ATE, which we've seen before. Here we will see what each method actually estimates.
- *In practice*—In this section, we'll explore basic algorithms for each method and learn how to use programming libraries that implement them.

Just as in previous chapters, we'll test the algorithms using made-up data. The challenge with real data is that you can't be sure if your analysis results are accurate. But when you create the data yourself, you know the exact process used, allowing you to calculate the true ATE. This way, you can evaluate the effectiveness of your method by comparing its results with the true ATE. Trying methods on synthetic data builds confidence in the approach. Once you're confident, you can then apply the method to real-world datasets.

When to use time-related methods

You should use these techniques whenever you want to estimate the effect of a specific event in time. Generally, follow these guidelines:

- Use RDDs if there are no major sudden changes from factors other than the main event.
- Use SCs as long as you can correlate your time series with other time series.
- Apply DiD to estimate an event's effect on a group of elements.

11.1   Which types of data will we use?

Before moving on, we need to clarify the types of data that we will use throughout this chapter. There are three types of time-related data:

- *Cross-sectional data* involves many measurements taken at a single point in time. For example, it can be the number of views each *Star Wars* film received on the day of its release.
- *Time series data* focuses on tracking a single subject or element over a period of time. For instance, you may track the number of views the first *Star Wars* movie received over many days.

- *Panel data* combines both of the other two approaches. It involves tracking multiple elements over time. For instance, you can measure the daily views of all previously released *Star Wars* movies over a three-month period.

In the upcoming sections, we'll take a closer look at each of these methods step by step. The versions we're presenting here are the simplest forms of each technique. RDD and SCs will target time series data, and DiD, analyzing many *Star Wars* films at the same time, deals with panel data.

> **NOTE** There are variations of each method that don't involve time. For instance, we could use these techniques to assess the effect of a new environmental policy by comparing neighboring districts in a city that implement the policy differently. The good news is that once you understand how these techniques work with time-related events, applying them to other types of problems becomes straightforward. There's a wealth of literature available on these topics, and they're constantly advancing. If you need more tailored adaptations for your specific scenario, I suggest delving into specialized literature.

Throughout this section, keep in mind that our goal is to assess the influence of VII's release on III. The event of interest, which we will call the *main event*, is the launch of VII. The main event plays the role of the treatment. Such an event happens at time T. In our example, T is the time of release: 18 December 2015. To understand each of the methods well, we will work with a synthetic dataset that will be adapted to the necessities of each section.

11.2   *Regression discontinuity design*

Assume that the data related to the number of views of III looks like figure 11.2 (the code for generating the data is shown in section 11.2.1). The naïve way to try to figure out how much the new movie release affects viewership is to compare the number of people who watched the movie before and after it came out. But this method can be flawed if other things were happening at the same time that also influenced how many people watched the movie.

But don't worry, all hope is not lost. If these other factors that happened at the same time didn't cause sudden and drastic changes in viewership and instead had a gradual effect, we can still estimate the causal effects using RDD.

To understand how RDD works, you need to be familiar with the following idea: *if the effect of other factors is gradual, then the closer we are to the date of the event, the less effect those factors will have on the outcome.* In other words, something like seasonality may not have a big effect on daily movie viewership, but it can be a significant factor when explaining differences between two measurements that are six months apart. So, RDD exploits the idea that in the limit of approaching the time of the event, factors should be regarded as having the same influence before and after the event. Again, this is true as far as the effect of other simultaneous factors.

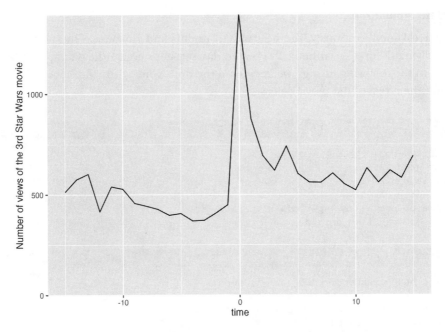

Figure 11.2 Data simulating the number of views of III. There is a spike in views, followed by a decreasing trend. We can check whether our algorithms are working correctly by testing them on simulated data.

Why can we estimate the causal effect of RDD even when there are simultaneous factors?

Informally speaking, when the effects of other factors happen gradually, you can picture the situation like this:

- Close to the event date T, there is a period of time $[t - s, T + s]$, where s is a small time interval, that can be regarded as if there were no simultaneous factors.
- In this time period $[t - s, T + s]$, because there are no simultaneous factors and the only potential effect is due to the main event, the data we are working with can be regarded as if it were obtained from an A/B test.

This way of thinking about RDD is just an approximation that can help you understand better how RDD is used in practice. Technically speaking, the assumption that we can treat data near the time of the event as random is called *local randomization*.

The reasoning behind RDD goes like this: because we assume that factors other than the main event don't cause sudden and dramatic changes in the outcome, if we do notice a substantial spike in the data at the timepoint T, we can attribute it to the main event. In other words, if there's a big jump in the data, we can interpret it as the effect of the main event.

11.2.1 Data simulation

As explained previously, the best way to understand how these methods work is by applying them to a synthetically created dataset. Let's create the data for this section.

In the following listings, we decide on the time window (the `periods_n` parameter) and the effect of the movie release.

Listing 11.1   (R) Synthetic data setup

```r
library(ggplot2)
set.seed(1234)
periods_n <- 15
impact <- 1000
time_points <- seq(-periods_n, periods_n)
n <- length(time_points)
```

Listing 11.2   (Python) Synthetic data setup

```python
from numpy.random import normal, seed
from numpy import abs, cos, mean, pi, arange
import statsmodels.formula.api as smf
import pandas as pd
from rdrobust import rdrobust
seed(1234)
periods_n = 15
impact = 1000
time_points = arange(-periods_n, periods_n + 1)
n = len(time_points)
```

Next we create the dataset. To do so, we need to generate the two potential outcomes (what would happen if the release happened and if it did not). We add a seasonality trend shown in figure 11.3 to make the example more realistic. To re-create a novelty effect, we simulate the maximum effect at time 0, decreasing over time.

Listing 11.3   (R) Data generation

```r
seasonality <- -cos(time_points/(2*pi))
D <- as.numeric(time_points >= 0)
Y_0 <- 500 + 100*seasonality + rnorm(n, sd=50)
Y_1 <- Y_0 + impact * D / (abs(time_points) + 1)
Y <- D*Y_1 + (1-D)*Y_0
```

Listing 11.4   (Python) Data generation

```python
seasonality = -cos(time_points / (2 * pi))
D = (time_points >= 0).astype(int)
Y_0 = 500 + 100 * seasonality + normal(size=n, scale=50)
Y_1 = Y_0 + impact * D / (abs(time_points) + 1)
Y = D * Y_1 + (1 - D) * Y_0
```

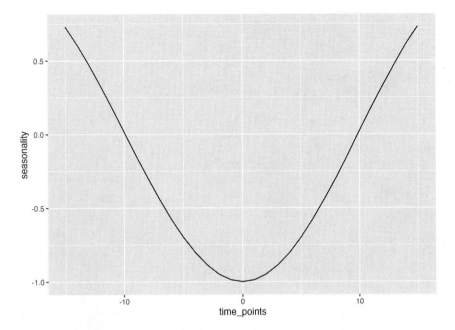

Figure 11.3 Simulated seasonality trend. We add this trend to our simulated data to make it more realistic.

11.2.2 RDD terminology

Before delving into the method itself, we need to introduce some terminology. In the basic RDD setting, we have three variables:

- t denotes the time variable, and the main event happens at $t = T$.
- $D(t)$ is the decision binary variable for each timepoint. In our example, $D(t)$ denotes whether the movie has been released. So, it is 0 before the event and 1 after the event,

$$D(t) = 0 \text{ for } t < T, \text{ and } D(t) = 1 \text{ for } t > T$$

- $Y(t)$ is the outcome time series variable. In our example, it's III movie views in the United States.

If we use the potential outcomes framework, we have more variables! $Y_0(t)$ is the outcome time series if the decision at time t is made, and $Y_1(t)$ is the outcome at the same timepoint if the decision is done. Remember that the variables $Y_0(t)$ and $Y_1(t)$ are partially observed (only if the corresponding decision has been actually made). Because we generated the dataset ourselves, we're aware of the possible outcomes, and we've illustrated them in figure 11.4. However, in real-life scenarios, we typically won't have access to both potential outcomes at the same time; we'll only have access to one of them, which is represented by the variable $Y(t)$.

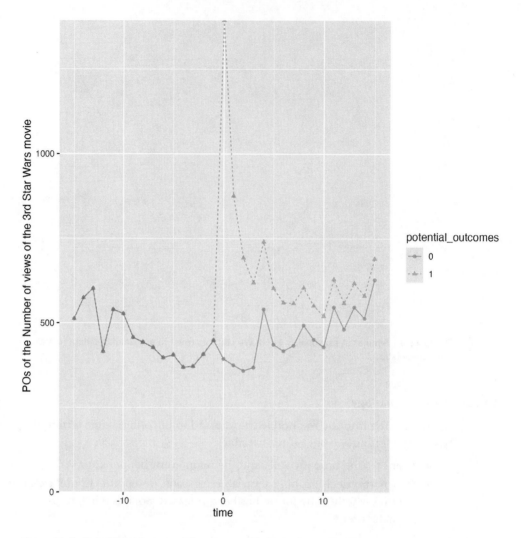

Figure 11.4   Potential outcomes of the process. We know them only because we generated the data synthetically. In real data scenarios, we can observe only one of the two outcomes.

Notice that in the pretreatment period (before time 0), the two potential outcomes overlap. This is because before the time of the event, the event itself has no effect on the outcome. We can write the fundamental relationship between the observed outcome $Y(t)$ and the potential outcomes:

$$Y(t) = Y_0(t)(1 - D(t)) + Y_1(t)D(t)$$

That is, if the decision is factually made, $D(t) = 1$, the observed outcome is $Y(t) = Y_1(t)$. But if the decision is not finally made, $D(t) = 1$, the observed outcome is

$Y(t) = Y_0(t)$. Because the decision is factually made after the event time T, the observed outcome for times after T, $t > T$, is $Y_1(t)$. Analogously, for times $t < T$, the observed outcome is the potential outcome $Y_0(t)$. So, in mathematical expressions, we have $E[Y(t)|t < T] = E[Y_0(t)|t < T]$ and $E[Y(t)|t > T] = E[Y_1(t)|t > T]$.

In this book, we will only consider the *sharp* design case: that is, when the main event is fixed at some time T. The alternative is called *fuzzy* design, in which the time of the event is random for x > 0.

11.2.3 Assumptions

To use the RDD method, we need to assume only one thing: the potential outcomes $Y_0(t)$ and $Y_1(t)$ need to change smoothly as time progresses. Technically speaking, the potential outcomes $Y_0(t)$, $Y_1(t)$ need to be continuous functions with respect to the time variable. In simple terms, this means right around event time T, the values of $Y_0(t)$ before and after the event should be pretty similar (the same goes for $Y_1(t)$). For instance, if we're looking at movie views around $T = 18$ December 2015, and there is no new movie release on that date, the number of views before and after T should be roughly the same.

When does this assumption not work? Well, when something besides the main event happening at the exact same time T that produces a drastic change (a discontinuity) in $Y_0(t)$ and $Y_1(t)$. For example, image that there's a big scandal related to the *Star Wars* saga, and it becomes public on the same date, 18 December 2015. If people decide to stop watching those movies, the number of views will suddenly drop right after date T. This creates a sudden change in the pattern of views over time, such as a jump in the data. Thus, the behavior of $Y_0(t)$ and $Y_1(t)$ will not be continuous around T.

Mathematically speaking, the *continuity assumption* at T is written in the following way:

$$\lim_{s \to 0} E[Y_0(T - s)] = \lim_{s \to 0} E[Y_0(T + s)]$$

and

$$\lim_{s \to 0} E[Y_1(T - s)] = \lim_{s \to 0} E[Y_1(T + s)]$$

with $s > 0$. This expression tells us that the expected value of $Y_0(t)$ and $Y_1(t)$ is the same whether you approach T from moments just before T, $\lim_{s \to 0} E[Y_0(T - s)]$, or from moments just after T, $\lim_{s \to 0} E[Y_0(T + s)]$.

RDD assumptions

To apply the RDD method at time T, we only require the continuity at T of the potential outcome assumption:

$$\lim_{s \to 0} E[Y_0(T - s)] = \lim_{s \to 0} E[Y_0(T + s)]$$

(continued)

and

$$\lim_{s \to 0} E[Y_1(T - s)] = \lim_{s \to 0} E[Y_1(T + s)]$$

11.2.4 Effect estimation

In addition to relying on our intuition for estimating causal effects, a formal proof provides stronger and more reliable support for our conclusions. In our example, the effect of the event at time T is the difference in the old movie views between what would have happened if there were no new release and if the new movie was released. In mathematical terms, the ATE

$$\text{ATE} = E[Y_1(T) - Y_0(T)]$$

defines the change of the outcome at time T due to the new release. The question is, how do we calculate the ATE from the data?

Recall that we can observe only one of the two potential outcomes $Y_0(t)$, $Y_1(t)$. In particular, at time T, we will only observe $Y_1(T)$. So, we need to find a way to estimate the unobserved potential outcome $Y_0(T)$. Fortunately, the continuity assumption tells us that the value of $Y_0(T)$ can be approximated by observed data $Y(t) = Y_0(T)$ before the main event time, $t < T$. That is, for $s > 0$,

$$E[Y_0(T)] = \lim_{s \to 0} E[Y_0(T - s)] = \lim_{s \to 0} E[Y(T - s)]$$

On the other hand, even though we can get the value of $Y_1(T)$ from data, it is just one observation. So, statistically speaking, the sample size is very low. It is more interesting to use data from after the main event to approximate the value $Y_1(T)$. That is,

$$E[Y_1(T)] = \lim_{s \to 0} E[Y_1(T + s)] = \lim_{s \to 0} E[Y(T + s)]$$

These two equations tell us that the unobserved ATE $E[Y_1(T) - Y_0(T)]$ defined by potential outcomes can be approximated by observed data $Y(t)$ near the main event time T:

$$\text{ATE} = E[Y_1(T) - Y_0(T)] = \lim_{s \to 0} E[Y(T + s)] - \lim_{s \to 0} E[Y(T - s)] \qquad \textbf{(11.1)}$$

11.2.5 RDD in practice

We'll explore three different algorithms. The first two are like a warmup. In real-world situations, we'll use the third one, but the first two will help us grasp the concept and see where RDD has its strengths and weaknesses.

An important part of these algorithms is deciding how long a time span to examine. These algorithms need data from a specific time range, denoted $[T - w, T + w]$, where w is a positive amount of time. Because we assume that things change gradually over time, we want to focus on the values of $Y(t)$ close to T. This means choosing a small time interval w. However, selecting a very small time window has its downsides. It gives us less data to work with, which can make our estimations less accurate due to higher variability.

So, there's a balance to strike when picking w: a smaller w reduces bias but increases variability, whereas a larger w does the opposite, increasing bias and decreasing variability. The challenge is that we don't know the exact bias in our estimations because it comes from factors we can't observe! Unfortunately, we can't objectively assess the influence of these factors without data from them.

Therefore, the choice of the time period should be based on your knowledge of the subject. One simple approach is to choose the longest time period possible for which you're confident other simultaneous factors don't change significantly.

DIFFERENCE OF MEANS

The first approach is calculating the difference between the mean of the outcome before and after the time of the event

$$\text{ATE} = \frac{1}{n_w^+} \sum_{T \le t \le T+w} Y(t) - \frac{1}{n_w^-} \sum_{T-w \le t < T} Y(t)$$

where n_w^- is the number of observations that fall in the interval $[T-w, T]$, and analogously n_w^+ for the interval $[T, T+w]$.

But as explained at the beginning of the chapter, this is precisely what we should not do! Well, kind of. The key point is that we are deciding on the time interval w.

In the following listings, we try various time intervals, ranging from 10 to 2 timepoints around the main event time. For each interval, we compute the effect by finding the difference between the means.

Listing 11.5   (R) Difference of means method with varying time window

```
results <- c()
time_windows <- 10:2
for(time_window in time_windows){
  ind <- abs(time_points) < time_window
  results <- c(
    results,
    mean(Y[ind & D == 1]) - mean(Y[ind & D == 0])
  )
}
data.frame(time_windows, results)
```

Listing 11.6   (Python) Difference of means method with varying time window

```
results = []
time_windows = arange(10, 1, -1)
for time_window in time_windows:
```

```
ind = abs(time_points) < time_window
results.append(mean(Y[ind & D == 1]) - mean(Y[ind & D == 0]))
pd.DataFrame({"time_window": time_windows, "estimate": results})
```

We show the results in figure 11.5. In the plot, you can distinguish the actual effect (top line) and the estimated effect (bottom line). This means for smaller time intervals, our estimation becomes more precise. It's important to note that this pattern may not apply universally; this happens because of the nature of our data, in which the effect decreases over time.

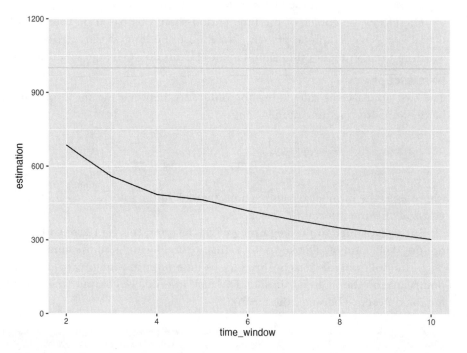

Figure 11.5   Effect estimation for different time windows. The *x* axis is the different time windows we have used. The *y* axis is the estimated effect of the algorithm. The horizontal top line depicts the real effect.

Limitations of the difference in means approach

This method has two problems:

- It can be greatly influenced by the choice of *w*.
- It doesn't capture any possible trend in the time period $[t - w, T + w]$.

LINEAR MODELS

We can use linear regression to capture trends in the analyzed time period. The objective is to fit the behavior of the pre and post regimes with a linear model, as shown in figure 11.6. As explained shortly, even though in the figure there seem to be two linear models, they are different parts of the same linear model.

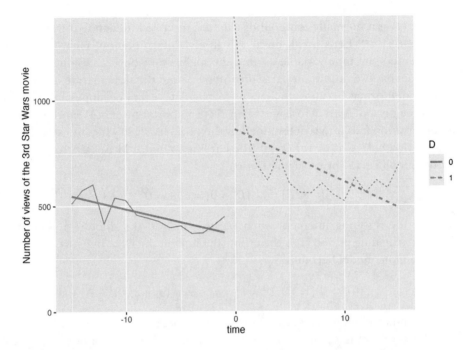

Figure 11.6 We can use linear models to estimate the effect in a RDD. The first step is to fit a linear model to the data, with different intercepts and slopes on each of the time regimes.

Let's see how to find such a linear model. Imagine that your dataset looks like table 11.1.

Table 11.1 Available data for a linear model RDD

i	t^i	D^i	Y^i
1	t^1	D^1	Y^1
...	...	...	...
n	t^n	D^n	Y^n

The index i indicates the observation number. The variable t^i denotes the time the information was measured. The decision D^i is a binary variable determining whether the observation is previous or following the main event time T: it takes the value 1 when $t^i > T$ and 0 when $t^i < T$. Finally, Y^i denotes the outcome of observation i. Notice that the total number of observations n depends on the time period $[t - w, T + w]$ we chose previously.

The linear model we are going to use is the following:

$$Y^i = a_0 + a_1 D^i + a_2(t^i - T) + a_3(t^i - T)D^i + \varepsilon^i(t)$$

where $\varepsilon^i(t)$ is a normally centered distributed variable independent from other $\varepsilon^j(s)$ and $E[\varepsilon^i(t)] = 0$. Let's break down this model interpretation. First, the expression $t^i - T$ centers the time variable around the main event time T. Second, every line in the model has two important parts: the intercept and the slope. We've chosen this specific model format because it allows us to calculate a unique slope and intercept for each time period, both before and after T. It's important to note that the time period an observation falls into is determined by the variable D^i. So when we're looking at the time period before T, we set $D^i = 0$ (the left line in figure 11.6). As a result, the linear model simplifies to (by replacing $D^i = 0$)

$$Y^i|[t^i < T] = Y^i|[D^i = 0] = a_0 + a_2(t^i - T) + \varepsilon^i$$

That is, the resulting intercept when $D^i = 0$ is a_0, and the slope is a_2. On the other hand, for the time period after the event (the line on the right in figure 11.6), we have $D^i = 1$. So, the model becomes

$$Y^i|[t^i > T] = Y^i|[D^i = 1] = a_0 + a_1 + (a_2 + a_3)(t^i - T) + \varepsilon^i$$

That is, the resulting intercept when $D^i = 1$ is $a_0 + a_1$, and the slope is $a_2 + a_3$.

The coefficients a_0, a_1, a_2, and a_3 are determined from data by running a linear regression. This means the difference in intercepts between the pre- and post-T period is a_1, and the difference in slopes is a_3, as shown in table 11.2.

Table 11.2   Resulting coefficients in a linear regression applying RDD

	Period	D^i	Intercept	Slope
	$t < T$	$D^i = 0$	a_0	a_2
	$t > T$	$D^i = 1$	$a_0 + a_1$	$a_2 + a_3$
Interpretation of the difference		Different time period	A jump in data of a_1	A change in slope of a_3

Let's calculate the ATE with equation (11.1). On the one hand, for instances before T, we should use the formula

$$Y|[t < T] = a_0 + a_2(t - T) + \varepsilon$$

(we have removed subscript i to represent the process in general, not for a particular observation i). So,

$$E[Y|t < T] = a_0 + a_2(t - T)$$

and (with $s > 0$)

$$\lim_{s \to 0} E[Y | t = T - s] = a_0$$

To calculate the limit, we have just substituted $t = T$. On the other hand, for $t > T$, we need to use the corresponding formula

$$Y | [t > T] = a_0 + a_1 + (a_2 + a_3)(t^i - T) + \varepsilon^i$$

So, calculating the limit, we have

$$\lim_{s \to 0} E[Y | t = T + s] = a_0 + a_1$$

Finally,

$$\text{ATE} = \lim_{s \to 0} E[Y | t = T + s] - \lim_{s \to 0} E[Y | t = T - s] = a_1$$

So, the ATE is nothing more than the coefficient a_1, as shown in figure 11.7.

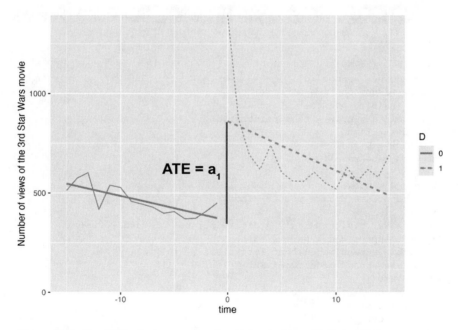

Figure 11.7   The ATE is the jump at time 0, which coincides with the coefficient a_1 of the estimated linear model.

To run a linear regression, we use the `lm` R function and the `statsmodels` Python package as in previous chapters. As in the previous section, we try a time window ranging from 10 to 4. (Less than 4 doesn't work because in linear models, you need more data points than parameters.) For each time window, we calculate the effect as the difference of means.

Listing 11.7   (R) Linear regression method with varying time window

```r
results <- data.frame()
time_windows <- 10:4
for(time_window in time_windows){
  ind <- abs(time_points) < time_window
  time_points_window <- time_points[ind]
  Y_window <- Y[ind]
  D_window <- D[ind]
  model <- lm(Y_window~D_window*time_points_window)
  res_stats <- cbind(
    time_window = time_window,
    t(coef(model)['D_window']),
    t(confint(model)[2, ]))
  results <- rbind(res_stats, results)
}
results
```

Listing 11.8   (Python) Linear regression method with varying time window

```python
d_coefs = []
lower_cis = []
upper_cis = []
time_windows = arange(10, 3, -1)
for time_window in time_windows:
  ind = abs(time_points) < time_window
  time_points_window = time_points[ind]
  Y_window = Y[ind]
  D_window = D[ind]
  df = pd.DataFrame({
    'y': Y_window,
    'd': D_window,
    'time_points': time_points_window
  })
  model = smf.ols(formula='y ~ d*time_points', data=df).fit()
  d_coefs.append(model.params['d'])
  lower_cis.append(model.conf_int().loc['d'][0])
  upper_cis.append(model.conf_int().loc['d'][1])
pd.DataFrame({
  'time_window': time_windows,
  'd': d_coefs,
  '2.5%': lower_cis,
  '97.5%': upper_cis
})
```

We show the results in figure 11.8. We have added the confidence intervals of the estimated coefficient (shaded region) directly provided by the results of the linear regression. The estimated coefficient decreases less with the time window than in the difference of means method explained earlier. So, there is less sensitivity to the time window parameter.

Again, the best estimate comes from the smallest time window, and its confidence interval contains the actual value of the effect (the horizontal line). The best estimate is calculated in the following listing, which gives us an effect of 785.02 (54.30, 1515.74), where the numbers in parentheses are the (2.5%, 97.5%) confidence interval of the estimation.

Listing 11.9   (R) Effect for time window 4

```
results[results$time_window==4, ]
```

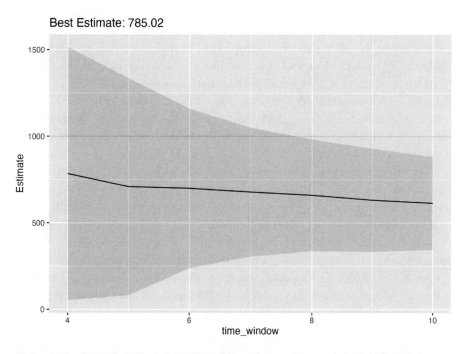

Figure 11.8   Estimated effect with different time windows. The _x_ axis is the different time windows we have used. The _y_ axis is the estimated effect of the algorithm. The horizontal line depicts the real effect. The darker gray area shows a confidence interval for the estimated effect. The best estimate is with time window 4, but we can only know that because we are using synthetic data.

Limitations of the linear approach to RDD

This method has two problems:

- The interval _w_ strongly affects the estimated intercepts and slopes of the model. For a larger _w_, the same slope and intercept must fit more data. So, the model is highly sensitive to the choice of _w_.
- It cannot deal with nonlinearities in data.

NONLINEAR MODELS

In practice, you have the option to use linear models, as discussed in the previous section. But it is recommended that you use nonlinear models because they can fit the data better. In particular, they can be more accurate in the vicinity of time event T, which is what we are interested in.

So, can we use machine learning to estimate the effect in an RDD approach? Yes. You should fit a separate model with your favorite supervised learning technique (random forests, boosting, deep learning, and so on) for each region, using the data before and after T. To determine the best models and their parameters, use cross-validation. Then make a prediction with each model separately on time T, and calculate the difference between the two predictions. You will obtain a valid estimator of the ATE at the timepoint T.

However, there's room for improvement in the estimation process. Interestingly, instead of machine learning, we can use an old statistical technique called *local linear regression* (LLR) (or local polynomial regression [LPR]). The reason is that supervised learning techniques in machine learning tend to be black boxes that are difficult to analyze. On the other hand, LLR provides explicit formulas, and we can better understand its behavior and make it more accurate than its machine learning counterparts.

We will estimate the ATE for RDD with the `rdrobust` package (https://rdpackages .github.io/rdrobust/). This package belongs to `rdpackages` (https://rdpackages .github.io/), a set of packages devoted to different approaches to RDD. The function `rdplot` gives a hint of the effect in figure 11.9.

To obtain the result (with the default library configuration), we use the function `rdrobust`, which tells us that the estimated effect is 770.05 (–11.42, 1551.52); in parentheses is the (2.5%, 97.5%) confidence interval of the estimation. The problem with this interval is that it contains a negative value, so we are not confident about whether the effect is even positive!

Listing 11.10   (R) Nonlinear estimation with the `rdrobust` function.

```
summary(rdrobust(Y, time_points))
```

Listing 11.11   (Python) Nonlinear estimation with the `rdrobust` function.

```
rdrobust(Y, time_points)
```

The results from the `rdrobust` method may seem worse than those from the linear model because the best approximation gave better confidence intervals (no negative numbers). However, we cheated a little, because we found the best approximation keeping in mind the actual solution. In practice, it would have been more difficult to determine the best approximation among different time windows.

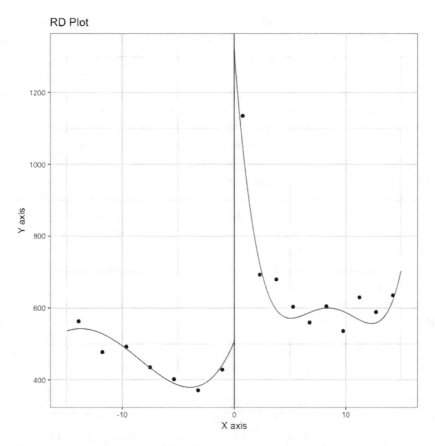

Figure 11.9   Exploratory plot of the effect with the rdplot function

HOW THE RDROBUST FUNCTION WORKS

If you're curious about the rdrobust estimation, this section explains the technical details of nonlinear estimation based on the LLR technique. Let's first revisit how linear regression works, and from there we can delve into LLR.

Suppose you want to run a linear regression only using the dataset before T: that is, the data falling in the interval $[T - w, T]$. The objective of the regression is to find an intercept (a_0) and slope (a_1) using the model $Y(t) = a_0 + a_1 (t-T) + \varepsilon^i$ that fits the data as well as possible. Such coefficients are found by minimizing the following *objective function* known as the *sum of squared residuals*:

$$\sum_t [Y(t) - (a_0 + a_1(t - T))]^2$$

where the residuals are the error terms $Y(t) - (a_0 + a_1(t - T))$. So, to find the intercept and slope, we need to run a method called ordinary least squares (OLS) that finds such minimizers (see chapter 6 for a review of linear regression).

LLR works differently. Instead of running a single optimization problem that finds one model used for the whole time period $[t - w, T]$, LLR runs an optimization program for each timepoint that we want to predict, as explained next.

Take a timepoint t_0 in which we want to make the prediction. Such a prediction will be made using a linear model that only works locally. One way to do this is to run the regression only on the points near the selected time t_0. That is, we will pick a parameter $h > 0$ called the *bandwidth* (how to choose it will be explained shortly) and run a regression only with the data around t_0—in other words, the data that falls in the interval $[t_0 - h, t_0 + h]$.

But following this logic, it makes more sense to weigh the observations: the observations closer to t_0 should contribute more to the linear coefficients than those far away. To achieve this, we can adjust the weights of the residuals during the minimization process. By assigning higher weights to the residuals near t_0 and lower weights to those farther away, the minimization process will prioritize reducing errors in points near t_0. This is because an error in a point close to t_0 will have a more significant effect on the overall objective function.

In mathematical terms, we introduce a weighting factor for the residuals in the objective function. This is achieved by multiplying each residual by a function known as the kernel, K_h:

$$\sum_t K_h(t - t_0)[Y(t) - (a_0 + a_1(t - t_0))]^2$$

Typical kernel functions include the uniform and triangular functions:

- *Uniform*—$K(z) = 1$ if $|z| < 1$ and 0 otherwise, as shown in figure 11.10
- *Triangular*—$K(z) = 1 - |z|$ if $|z| < 1$ and 0 otherwise, as shown in figure 11.11

Once we have defined the kernel, we apply the following transformation:

$$K_h(t - t_0) = K\left(\frac{t - t_0}{h}\right)$$

This transformation centers the kernel at t_0 and rescales it by h:

- *Uniform*—$K_h(t - t_0) = 1$ if $|t - t_0| < h$ and 0 otherwise
- *Triangular*—$K(z) = 1 - |t - t_0|/h$ if $|t - t_0| < h$ and 0 otherwise

Notice that now the kernel (for the uniform and triangular cases) is always 0 for timepoints farther from t_0 more than h: that is whenever $|t - t_0| > h$. So, the bandwidth h effectively controls which observations are included in the regression and which are not.

So, how do we choose the bandwidth h? Intuitively, we can run a cross-validation with different values of h and choose the one that gives a smaller predicting error. However, there are more elaborate ways to find the optimal h. From a practical perspective, the functions `rdplot` and `rdrobust` that are responsible for plotting and estimating the ATE use a method by default, and I suggest you use it. But if you want to better understand the details of the methods used for choosing h, I recommend starting with the rdrobust package documentation at https://mng.bz/Aamo (and the updated version at https://mng.bz/ZVDR) and following the references therein.

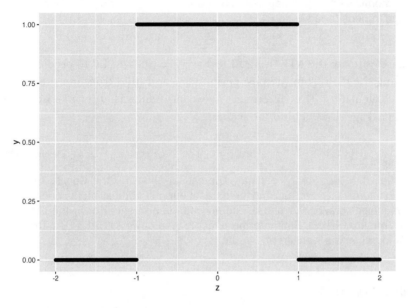

Figure 11.10   Uniform kernel

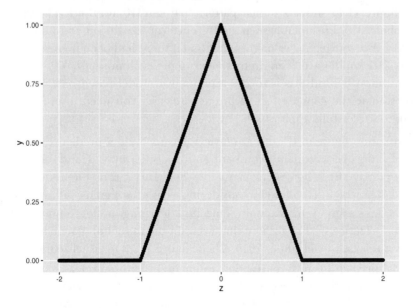

Figure 11.11   Triangular kernel

Using local polynomial regression

So far, we have seen the local linear regression method. Such a method can be generalized using polynomials instead of lines, as is the case of linear regression. You can also use polynomials in the `rdrobust` package. However, it is recommended to use polynomials only up to degree 2. For more details, you can read the paper by Gelman and Imbens (see section 11.7).

How can we estimate the ATE using LLR? Easy! We run an LLR to predict the value at T, first using the data from the post-period $t > T$ and then from the pre-period $t < T$, and then calculating the difference between them. That is precisely what the `rdrobust` package does behind the scenes.

Exercise 11.1

Using the `rdrobust` library, estimate the causal effect for the Google Trends data shown in figure 11.1. You can find the dataset gtrends_rdd.csv on the book's website (www.manning.com/books/causal-inference-for-data-science) or in the GitHub repo (https://mng.bz/RNOZ). Estimate the effect for the day "2015-12-18". The solution can be found on the website and in the repo.

11.3 Synthetic controls

The SCs method is capable of estimating what would have happened with the old *Star Wars* movie if there had been no new movie released. For instance, the Google Trends search in figure 11.12 shows a similar pattern between III and the *LoTR* saga, except for December 2015. Presumably such a difference can be attributed to the release of the new *Star Wars* movie. So, we might think that if there had been no new release, the evolution of III would have been pretty similar to the evolution of *LoTR*.

The intuition behind SCs is to use a predictive model based on the *LoTR* time series to estimate the causal effect of the new release. You need to understand two basic steps to successfully apply SCs:

1 Correlation between III and *LoTR* views lets us build a predictive model. Various factors like seasonality, competition from other movies, and socioeconomic factors may affect how many views they get. This means theoretically, we can predict how well III will do by considering what's happening with *LoTR*.

  So, let's assume that we train a machine learning model to predict III views from *LoTR* views. Also suppose that we train the model on data before the new movie release in December 2015. Check figure 11.13 to visualize the process.

2 Model predictions post-release date estimate the without-release counterfactual scenario. Imagine that we are confident that although the new release has an effect on III's views, it doesn't affect *LoTR* views. Then our model's forecasts on

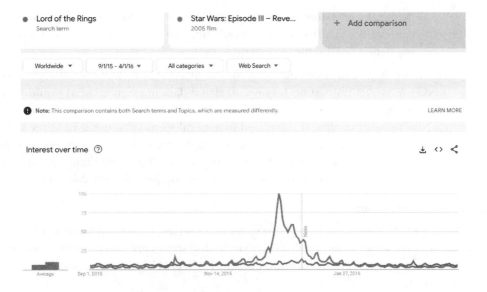

Figure 11.12 Comparison of interest in III and the *LoTR* saga. Although there seems to be an effect on III from the release of the new movie, *LoTR* seems to be unaffected by it. Source: Google Trends.

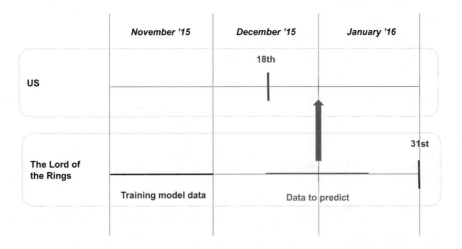

Figure 11.13 We can train a model with the data before the new release and predict after the release. These new predictions tell us what would have happened if there were no release. The effect of the release can be estimated by the difference between the real values and the predicted ones.

the post-release period (18 December 2015 to 18 January 2016) are likely to fail. The reason is that III lives in a "with-release" context, whereas *LoTR* lives in a "without-release" context. In summary, we find ourselves attempting to predict "with-release" behavior based on observations derived from a "without-release" context. So, we are essentially predicting the counterfactual of what would have happened to III if there were no VII release.

These two steps constitute the basis for the SCs method. The overall idea is to use a predictive model trained on highly correlated data to estimate what would have happened if the movie were not released.

Now we want to state this method in general so you can use it in other situations. First we will introduce the terminology for each time series. Then we will describe the steps of the algorithm so we can estimate the causal effect. And finally, we will state the assumptions we are making so that the SCs method provides reliable estimates.

11.3.1 Data simulation

To apply SCs, we need to add two more times series. They must be correlated with the main time series under analysis. The following scripts are based on the code from the previous section and incorporate variable Y, affected by the event, and correlated time series X_1, X_2.

Listing 11.12   (R) Creating Y and correlated time series X_1, X_2

```r
library(ggplot2)
library(CausalImpact)
set.seed(1234)
periods_n <- 15
impact <- 1000
time_points <- seq(-periods_n, periods_n)
n <- length(time_points)
seasonality <- -cos(time_points/(2*pi))
D <- as.numeric(time_points >= 0)
Y_0 <- 500 + 100*seasonality + rnorm(n, sd=50)
Y_1 <- Y_0 + impact * D / (abs(time_points) + 1)
Y <- D*Y_1 + (1-D)*Y_0
X_1 <- 400 + 100*seasonality + rnorm(n, sd=20)
X_2 <- 700 + 80*seasonality + rnorm(n, sd=60)
df <- data.frame(Y, X_1, X_2, time=time_points)
```

Listing 11.13   (Python) Creating Y and correlated time series X_1, X_2

```python
from numpy.random import normal, seed
from numpy import cos, mean, pi, arange, abs
import pandas as pd
import causalimpact
seed(1234)
periods_n = 15
impact = 1000
time_points = arange(-periods_n, periods_n + 1)
n = len(time_points)
seasonality = -cos(time_points / (2 * pi))
D = (time_points >= 0).astype(int)
Y_0 = 500 + 100 * seasonality + normal(size=n, scale=50)
```

```
Y_1 = Y_0 + impact * D / (abs(time_points) + 1)
Y = D * Y_1 + (1 - D) * Y_0
X_1 = 400 + 100 * seasonality + normal(size=n, scale=20)
X_2 = 700 + 80 * seasonality + normal(size=n, scale=60)
df = pd.DataFrame({
  "Y": Y, "X_1": X_1,
  "X_2": X_2, "time": time_points
})
```

You can see the time evolution of the three different time series in figure 11.14.

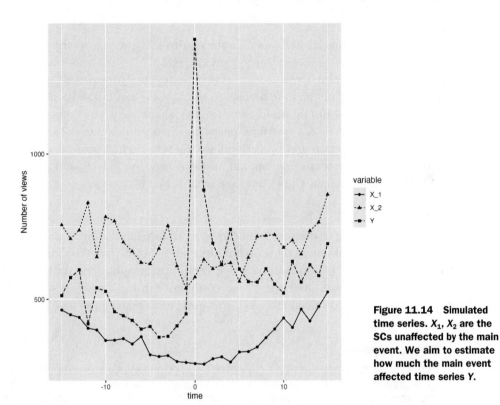

Figure 11.14 Simulated time series. X_1, X_2 are the SCs unaffected by the main event. We aim to estimate how much the main event affected time series Y.

11.3.2 *Synthetic controls terminology*

Let's name the SC ingredients. We want to understand the effect of such an event on the *outcome time series*, which we denote $Y(t)$. Variable t indexes time, and for each timepoint t, we have a value of the outcome $Y(t)$. In our example, the outcome variable is the daily number of movie views of III.

The second element is the *controls*, denoted by $X(t)$, which in our example is *LoTR* views. In this case, we may have more time series, one for each movie in the *LoTR* saga. They can be denoted by $X^i(t)$, so $X(t)$ corresponds to the vector $(X^1(t), ..., X^M(t))$, where M is the total number of controls we are using. In our example, $M = 3$ because in December 2015, there were three *LoTR* movies.

> **Controls only need to be predictive time series**
>
> In general, controls' time series don't have to be of the same nature as the outcome times series! This is a huge advantage of this method. For instance, in our example, the controls' time series $X(t)$ may contain socioeconomic information such as inflation rates, population average salaries, and weather forecasts.
>
> They do not need to be information about other movies! As long as controls $X(t)$ are highly correlated with the outcome and not affected by the event of interest (in our example, the release of the new movie), anything will do.

Finally, the predictions created based on the controls $X(t)$ to predict the outcome $Y(t)$ are denoted by $\hat{Y}(t)$.

Because we are going to train a predictive model and subsequently generate forecasts, we need to define the time periods in which these two tasks will take place. The training time interval should occur prior to time T, and we will refer to it as pretreatment period P_b. The forecasting time period is when we evaluate the counterfactual scenario. It should occur after time T, and we will refer to it as post-treatment P_a; usually it contains more than one timepoint. Both time periods P_b and P_a should be selected based on domain knowledge (see section 11.3.6).

11.3.3 Assumptions

SCs work well as long as their assumptions hold. Before employing SCs, it's important to assess the reasonability of these assumptions and your capacity to explain and support them to others. It's worth noting that even if the assumptions are true, a lack of confidence in them can undermine your confidence in the analysis results and deter you from using your own conclusions for your decision-making process.

> **SC assumptions**
>
> Suppose we have an outcome time series $Y(t)$ and a candidate event happening at $t = T$. Suppose also that we have another time series $X(t)$ that will act as controls. It's important to note that these control variables don't necessarily have to be the same type of data as the outcomes. They can be any kind of data as long as they meet the following conditions.
>
> We will assume that
> - $X(t)$ can be used to create a predictive model for $Y(t)$ with data before T.
> - The event at time T has no effect whatsoever on the controls time series $X(t)$.
> - A consistent relationship exists between outcomes and controls: no events near time T besides the main event distort the relationship between the time series $Y(t)$, $X(t)$.

Let's provide insight into these assumptions. The candidate event must not exert any influence on the control variables $X(t)$. If such control variables are affected by the event, their effectiveness as controls is compromised. This is because any predictions made after the occurrence of the event using these variables will no longer accurately reflect the counterfactual scenario in the absence of the event.

We're also considering the stability of the connection between outcomes and controls. But what if this stability is disrupted? Let's take an example where a new service provider emerges and offers the *Star Wars* saga but not the *LoTR* saga, coinciding with the release of a new *Star Wars* movie. This change will have a negative effect on the model's predictions, as the relationship between *Star Wars* and *LoTR* movie views has shifted. Consequently, our estimates of what may have happened differently (counterfactual estimates) can end up being biased.

More generally, let's say something else happens around time t apart from our main event. This occurrence affects the relationship between the time series. In such cases, we can't confidently attribute the differences between actual outcomes and predicted counterfactuals solely to the main event's effect. This uncertainty arises because changes in the relationship between the two time series can also be contributing factors.

11.3.4 *Effect estimation*

With SCs, we typically estimate the prolonged effect over time of our decision: that is, how much different the outcome would be after the main event if we had decided differently at time T. So, we will choose a timepoint range P_a. Check out section 11.3.6 for more details on how to choose such a range.

We cannot know the values of the outcome if we had decided differently. So, we approximate the difference between this quantity and what happened in reality by the difference between the prediction of the model and the factual outcome $\hat{Y}(t) - Y(t)$. And we average these differences of the period of time P_a

$$\text{ATET} = \frac{1}{|P_a|} \sum_{t \varepsilon P_a} \hat{Y}_t - Y_t \tag{11.2}$$

where $|P_a|$ is the number of time periods selected for the evaluation. The result is interpreted as what the treated group would have experienced in the absence of receiving the treatment. So we are essentially calculating the average treatment effect on the treated (ATET).

11.3.5 *Synthetic controls in practice*

Let's describe the four steps involved in applying the SC method:

1. Select time periods. Choose the time intervals for training P_b and predicting P_a.
2. Create a forecasting model. Train a predictive model to predict the outcome $Y(t)$ from the inputs $X(t)$ only using data in time period P_b, before time T. Such a predictive model can be created using standard supervised learning techniques: you can use boosting, linear regression, and so on, and hyperparameter tuning and model selection can be done using cross-validation.

3 Make predictions. Use the previous model to predict outcomes $\hat{Y}_t$ on time period P_a at times later than T. The selected timepoints to predict (there can be more than one) are determined by the analyst based on their domain knowledge (see the following section).

4 Evaluate the effect. calculate the average difference between the predicted and real outcomes (ATET) provided by equation 11.2.

NOTE The original paper on SCs by Abadie and Gardeazabal (see section 11.7) didn't use machine learning techniques but rather a variation of linear regression. Subsequent literature also does not use machine learning. However, I decided to explain the general version that can use machine learning instead of the classical one. It is closer in style to data science, making it easier for data scientists to understand, and it provides a more flexible approach.

11.3.6 *Selecting training and predicting time periods*

Selecting which data is used to train the model and which data to run the predictions on must be done based on domain knowledge: analysts need to deal with a set of trade-offs that involve sample sizes and causal effects.

Define the endpoints for the pretreatment period

$$P_b = [P_b^{\text{start}}, P_b^{\text{end}}]$$

and post-treatment period

$$P_a = [P_a^{\text{start}}, P_a^{\text{end}}]$$

So, they are ordered in time as

$$P_b^{\text{start}} < P_b^{\text{end}} < T < P_a^{\text{start}} < P_a^{\text{end}}$$

Let's now give some hints about how to choose these endpoints:

- The pretreatment beginning P_b^{start} should be chosen to maximize the predictive capacity. Generally speaking, we want the relationship between $Y(t)$ and $X(t)$ to be as consistent as possible during the pre-event period $t < T$. Such stability can be compromised if any of the time series is influenced by a distinct context. Consequently, as the time endpoint P_b^{start} moves farther away from the event time T, the probability of their correlation weakening increases, which in turn reduces the model's predictive capacity.

  However, keeping P_b^{start} close to time event T also reduces the sample size of the training datasets. Such reduction is translated into higher variances in our estimations.

  So, a basic approach would be trying different values of P_b^{start}, running a cross-validation for each to estimate the predictive capability of the model, and choosing the one with the lowest predictive error.

- In general, we can set the value of the pretreatment ending P_b^{end} just before the time of the main event. However, as in the earlier example, such a choice is not always correct.

  In our example, despite the fact that the new movie is scheduled for release on 18 December, figure 11.1 suggests that its influence on the viewership of older movies begins a few days earlier. This effect can be explained by people anticipating the new release and catching up on older movies. Given that our predictive model is designed to simulate the nonrelease counterfactual, it would not be advisable to incorporate data that is influenced by the release in the training dataset. Consequently, if we are being cautious, we can argue against incorporating any December 2015 data into the training set.

  So, the endpoint P_b^{end} should be earlier than T whenever there are anticipation effects. However, it's important to acknowledge that an earlier P_b^{end} leads to a reduction in sample size and potentially higher variance.

- Once the main event at time T has passed, we need to choose the evaluation period. In general, the beginning of the evaluation P_a^{start} can be chosen immediately after the main event at T. However, if the effect of the main event is delayed, it makes more sense to choose P_a^{start} farther from T.

  Consider a scenario where your organization initiates a marketing campaign targeting a specific segment of loyal customers. In this campaign, these chosen customers are given branded T-shirts and encouraged to post pictures wearing them on social media along with your company's tag. A competition is set up, promising a product discount to the post with the most shares. The effectiveness of this campaign is measured by the total number of mentions your company receives across popular social media platforms.

  However, because of the time required for transportation, it's not feasible to measure the campaign's effect immediately after its launch. There's a waiting period for the T-shirts to be delivered to customers. As a result, the value of P_a^{start} needs to be a certain number of days after the main event, which, in this instance, is the launch of the campaign.

- In some cases, the event produces a "novelty" effect in which the effect dilutes shortly after the event. In others, the event under study produces a sustained effect in time. Ultimately, we must choose whether we want to understand the short-term, medium-term, or long-term effects of the main event. This choice involves selecting the point in time P_a^{start} closer to or distant from time T. Such a decision depends on the objective of the analysis. But it's important to note that the farther P_a^{start} is from T, the more likely it is that the conditions surrounding the outcome $Y(t)$ and the control time series $X(t)$ will change, causing the predictive model to lose accuracy.

  Furthermore, in this scenario, we're navigating blind. Unlike during the training phase, where we can run cross-validations to assess the model's accuracy, in the post-treatment phase, the model predicts a scenario that didn't actually happen. This means we lack data to verify the correctness of our predictions. As a result, you'll need to rely on your expertise in the field to ensure that the relationship between the outcome $Y(t)$ and the controls $X(t)$ remains stable during the evaluation period.

Table 11.3 presents a summary of the advantages and disadvantages associated with selecting timepoints that are more distant from time T. Note that when choosing timepoints closer to T, the implications mentioned in the table are reversed.

Table 11.3 Consequences of choosing endpoints farther from time event T. The Direction arrow shows how the timepoints move with respect to T.

P_b^{start}	P_b^{end}	T	P_a^{start}	P_a^{end}
← Direction Training data window • More sample size • Potentially less accuracy due to context change	← Direction Event anticipation • Smaller sample size • Potentially more accuracy with less context change		→ Direction Delayed effects • Less data to evaluate the impact • Potentially less accuracy due to context change	→ Direction Long-term impact evaluation • More data to evaluate the impact • Potentially less accuracy due to context change

USING THE CAUSALIMPACT LIBRARY

Let's use the `CausalImpact` library to estimate the effect at time $T = 0$ on the synthetic dataset. For Python, we use the implementation `tfp-causalimpact` (https://github.com/google/tfp-causalimpact/tree/main). To do so, we choose the periods before and after the treatment, which, for now, cover the entire duration of our data. Then we estimate the effect.

Listing 11.14   (R) Causal effect analysis on the whole period

```
pre.period <- c(-periods_n, -1) + periods_n + 1
post.period <- c(0, periods_n) + periods_n + 1
estimated_impact <- CausalImpact(df, pre.period, post.period)
estimated_impact
```

Listing 11.15   (Python) Causal effect analysis on the whole period

```
pre_period = [0, periods_n-1]
post_period = [periods_n, 2 * periods_n]
estimated_impact = causalimpact.fit_causalimpact(
  df, pre_period, post_period
)
print(causalimpact.summary(
  estimated_impact, output_format="summary"
))
```

The result (in R) from the `CausalImpact` function is shown in figure 11.15. There are two columns, Average and Cumulative, which refer to the selected post-treatment time period. The Actual value, as the name says, refers to the time series *Y*. The Prediction value is the counterfactual predicted value provided by the `CausalImpact` algorithm. The estimated impact is then the Absolute Effect or, in relative terms, the Relative Effect. Confidence intervals are also provided for all these quantities.

```
Posterior inference {CausalImpact}

                         Average          Cumulative
Actual                   675              10801
Prediction (s.d.)        232 (118)        3719 (1891)
95% CI                   [-24, 478]       [-392, 7649]

Absolute effect (s.d.)   443 (118)        7083 (1891)
95% CI                   [197, 700]       [3152, 11193]

Relative effect (s.d.)   38% (8485%)      38% (8485%)
95% CI                   [-740%, 1767%]   [-740%, 1767%]

Posterior tail-area probability p:    0.002
Posterior prob. of a causal effect:   99.7998%

For more details, type: summary(impact, "report")
```

Figure 11.15 Estimated results from the `CausalImpact` library

The estimated absolute effect is 443 (197, 700); in parentheses, we give the (2.5%, 97.5%) confidence interval of the estimation. The average effect can be calculated with the code in the following listings: 211.29, which falls into the confidence interval provided by the algorithm.

Listing 11.16   (R) Average effect over the time period [0, 15]

```
inds = D > 0
mean(impact * D[inds] / (abs(time_points[inds]) + 1))
```

Listing 11.17   (Python) Average effect over the time period [0, 15]

```
inds = D > 0
mean(impact * D[inds] / (abs(time_points[inds]) + 1))
```

Figure 11.16 shows a typical plot created by the `CausalImpact` library:

- The original plot shows the original data with the counterfactual prediction and its confidence interval.
- The pointwise plot shows the difference between the factual and counterfactual outcomes at each timepoint.

- The cumulative shows the accumulated differences from the previous plot since the time of the event.

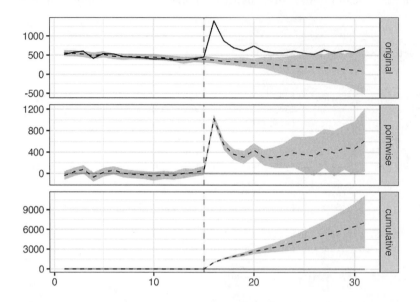

Figure 11.16   **The first plot shows the observed data versus the predicted counterfactual outcome. The second shows the pointwise difference. And the third one shows the accumulated difference between the real and counterfactual outcomes.**

To compare the SC method with RDD, we can run the algorithm taking only the post-treatment interval as the timepoint 0, the time of the event.

Listing 11.18   (R) Causal effect analysis only at the time of the event

```
pre.period <- c(-periods_n, -1) + periods_n + 1
post.period <- c(periods_n + 1, periods_n + 1)
estimated_impact <- CausalImpact(df, pre.period, post.period)
estimated_impact
```

Listing 11.19   (Python) Causal effect analysis only at the time of the event

```
pre_period = [0, periods_n-1]
post_period = [periods_n, periods_n]
estimated_impact = causalimpact.fit_causalimpact(
  df, pre_period, post_period
)
print(causalimpact.summary(
  estimated_impact, output_format="summary"
))
```

The result is shown in figure 11.17. Notice that in this case, the estimated effect is 1,024 (941, 1,102), which is much better than RDD.

```
Posterior inference {CausalImpact}

                          Average          Cumulative
Actual                    1394             1394
Prediction (s.d.)         370 (41)         370 (41)
95% CI                    [292, 453]       [292, 453]

Absolute effect (s.d.)    1024 (41)        1024 (41)
95% CI                    [941, 1102]      [941, 1102]

Relative effect (s.d.)    282% (44%)       282% (44%)
95% CI                    [208%, 377%]     [208%, 377%]

Posterior tail-area probability p:    0.001
Posterior prob. of a causal effect:   99.8999%

For more details, type: summary(impact, "report")
```

Figure 11.17 Estimated results from the `CausalImpact` **function when evaluating only at time 0.**

Exercise 11.2

Estimate the causal effect for the Google Trends data shown in figure 11.12 using the `CausalImpact` library. You can find the dataset gtrends_ sc.csv on the book's website (www.manning.com/books/causal-inference-for-data-science) or in the GitHub repo (https://mng.bz/RN0Z). Estimate the effect from the week "2015-12-20" until two weeks later. The solution can be found in the repo.

11.4   Differences in differences

What if instead of just estimating the effect of III, we want to understand how the release of VII affects all six previous *Star Wars* films? Furthermore, can we estimate the effect of all of them simultaneously? The last method, *difference in differences* (DiD), allows us to analyze groups of movies simultaneously. To do this, we need another group of movies that remain unaffected by the release of the new *Star Wars* film, to act as controls.

In this example, we aim to estimate the effect of the release of VII on the viewership of the previous six *Star Wars* films. We achieve this by comparing their viewership numbers with those of the three previously released *LoTR* movies. Figure 11.18 shows a simulated dataset. The group with $D = 1$ represents *Star Wars* movies, and the group with $D = 0$ represents the *LoTR* movies. We've added regression lines to help illustrate how the release of a new movie affects the number of views in other movies. Notice that in this case, we are dealing with panel data (many time series).

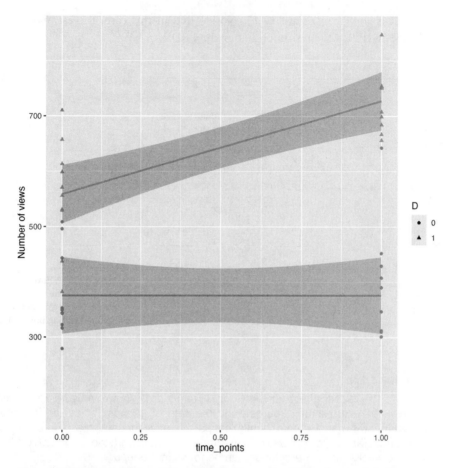

Figure 11.18   Simulated panel data example. The group with *D* = 1 represents *Star Wars* movies, and the group with *D* = 0 represents *LoTR* movies. Lines help us to visualize the change of trend due to the release of the new movie.

DiD essentially combines elements of the two previously mentioned techniques. It resembles RDD in that it estimates the effect by comparing changes in the period before and after the release. At the same time, it shares similarities with SCs in that it determines what might have occurred in the absence of the release by comparing the outcomes of the main group, called the *experimental group*, with another group of movies that remained unaffected, called the *control group*.

The informal intuition behind DiD is the following. Imagine that under normal circumstances, *Star Wars* movies are seen 100 times more than *LoTR* movies every week. But the week of the new release, *Star Wars* movies are seen 300 times more. We may think that the release is responsible for an increase of 200 times more movie views.

The DiD approach for estimating the effect of an event relies on the assumption that in the absence of the event, both the experimental and control groups *would have followed the same path of development.* Now we need to provide a formal approach to understand the limitations and capabilities of the DiD method.

11.4.1 Data simulation

In this example, we will sample some movie views from the *Star Wars* saga (assuming there were as many films as we wanted), identified as $D = 1$, and many others from *LoTR*, identified as $D = 0$. Unlike in the previous simulations, where the effect is 1,000, in this case, we've set the effect to only 200.

Listing 11.20   (R) Synthetic data creation

```r
library(did)
library(ggplot2)
set.seed(1234)
impact <- 200
n_group <- 10
time_points_base <- c(0, 1)
n <- length(time_points_base)
seasonality_base <- -cos(time_points_base/(2*pi))
time_points <- rep(time_points_base, 2*n_group)
seasonality <- rep(seasonality_base, 2*n_group)
D <- c(rep(0, 2*n_group), rep(1, 2*n_group))
id <- sort(rep(1:(2*n_group), 2))
Y_0 <- 500 + 200*D + 100*seasonality + rnorm(4*n_group, sd=100)
Y_1 <- Y_0 + D*time_points*impact
Y <- D*Y_1 + (1-D)*Y_0
df_observed <- data.frame(
  id, time_points, D, Y
)
```

Listing 11.21   (Python) Synthetic data creation

```python
from numpy.random import normal, seed
from numpy import cos, mean, pi, arange, hstack, array, floor
import statsmodels.formula.api as smf
import pandas as pd
from doubleml import DoubleMLData
from doubleml import DoubleMLDID
from sklearn.linear_model import LogisticRegression
from sklearn.linear_model import LinearRegression
seed(1234)
impact = 200
n_group = 10
time_points_base = arange(0, 2)
n = len(time_points_base)
seasonality_base = -cos(time_points_base / (2 * pi))
time_points = hstack((time_points_base,) * 2 * n_group)
seasonality = hstack((seasonality_base,) * 2 * n_group)
D = array([0] * (2 * n_group) + [1] * (2 * n_group))
id = list(range(1, 2 * n_group + 1)) * 2
id.sort()
Y_0 = 500 + 200 * D + 100 * seasonality + \
```

```
   normal(size=4 * n_group, scale=100)
Y_1 = Y_0 + D * time_points * impact
Y = D * Y_1 + (1 - D) * Y_0
df_observed = pd.DataFrame({
  "id": id, "time_points": time_points, "D": D, "Y": Y
})
```

The dataset `df_all` contains all the data related to the data generation process, which includes the full information about potential outcomes. In practice, we rarely have access to such information.

The dataset `df_observed` contains only the data we are supposed to obtain. In practice, we rarely have access to the full variables Y_0, Y_1 because they are the potential outcomes and are partially observed.

11.4.2 DiD terminology

Let's introduce some notation:

- Different individual items or units (depending on what you call them) are indexed by i, both experimental (the group to be studied) and control. In our example, index i denotes the movie to be considered (both *Star Wars* and *LoTR*) and ranges from 1 to 9 (six old *Star Wars* movies and three old *LoTR* movies). We also use the variable t to talk about time, and the main event we're interested in happens at time T. To make the notation lighter, let's assume T is 1, so we're mainly looking at the time interval [0, 1], which is right around the main event.
- The variable D^i denotes whether individual i is treated (a value of 0 means no, and 1 means yes). In our example, a treatment can be defined as releasing a new movie in the same saga.
- The outcome to be analyzed of individual i is denoted $Y^i(t)$.
- We also have the two potential outcomes for each individual i at time t, $Y_0^i(t)$ and $Y_1^i(t)$, determining the outcome if they are not treated and if they are, respectively. In our examples, they represent the number of views if a new movie from the same saga is released. Notice that before the event, the event itself has no effect on the outcomes. So, the potential outcomes $Y_0^i(t) = Y_1^i(0)$ are exactly the same. In addition, they coincide with the observed outcome: thus, $Y_0^i(0) = Y_1^i(0) = Y^i(0)$.

This terminology has been applied to figure 11.19. For the points on the left, $t = 0$, we show the observed values (that coincide with the potential outcomes). For the points on the right, unobserved potential outcomes $Y_0^i(1)$ are drawn as empty circles. Expectation points (explained next) are drawn in black.

Let's practice using potential outcome notation with some quantities that will be useful later:

- When we write an expectation, such as $E[Y^i(0)]$, it means the average over all individuals. For instance, in this case, $E[Y^i(0)]$ is the average outcome of all individuals at time 0. Test your knowledge: how would it be written as the same quantity at time 1? In this case, both quantities can be calculated directly from data.

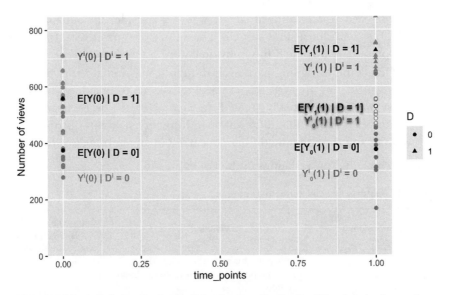

Figure 11.19   Data in terms of potential outcomes. For *D* = 0, all the data is observed. Unobserved potential outcomes are drawn as empty circles. Expectations are drawn in black. Counterfactual text labels have been shadowed.

- The quantities $E[Y_0^i(1)]$ and $E[Y_1^i(1)]$ are the average potential outcomes at time 1 if we treated all the individuals and if we did not, respectively. In "do" notation, we have $E[Y_0^i(1)] = E[Y^i(1)|do(D_1 = 0)]$ and $E[Y_1^i(1)] = E[Y^i(1)|do(D_1 = 1)]$.

  In our example, $E[Y_1^i(1)]$ would be the mean outcome if there was a new release for the *Star Wars* and also the *LoTR* sagas at the same time. Similarly, $E[Y_0^i(1)]$ would be the mean outcome if there was a new release for any saga. Test your knowledge: what are $E[Y_0^i(0)]$ and $E[Y_1^i(0)]$?

- The quantities $E[Y_0^i(0)]$ and $E[Y_1^i(0)]$ talk about potential outcomes at time 0. As explained earlier, at time zero, the potential outcomes coincide, so $E[Y_0^i(0)] = E[Y_1^i(0)] = E[Y^i(0)]$.

- The quantity $E[Y^i(0)|D^i = 0]$ is the average outcome at time 0 of those that are not treated. In our example, it would be the average number of views of the *LoTR* movies before the new release. Test your knowledge: what would be then the meaning of the expressions $E[Y^i(1)|D^i = 0]$, $E[Y^i(0)|D^i = 1]$, and $E[Y^i(1)|D^i = 1]$? Notice that these four quantities can be calculated from data.

- The quantity $E[Y_0^i(1)|D^i = 1]$ may sound a bit complex, but it's actually interesting. It's what we call a *counterfactual*, meaning it deals with a scenario that didn't happen but could have. Let's take it one step at a time and break it down to understand it better.

  First we're focusing on the group of treated individuals, which in our example are the *Star Wars* movies. We do this by conditioning or filtering the group so that $D^i = 1$, which means these movies were actually treated.

For each treated individual, we want to consider an outcome denoted as $Y_0^i(1)$, specifically at timepoint 1. The subscript 0 means we are interested in the potential outcome if this individual were not treated.

Here's the intriguing part: even though it may initially sound contradictory (are we treating them?), this expression asks us to imagine a scenario where those who were actually treated (a factual event) were hypothetically not treated (a scenario that didn't happen in reality, a counterfactual event). It's a way of exploring what might have occurred in an alternate world.

Table 11.4 lists the four variations of the last expression.

Table 11.4   Factuals and counterfactuals at time 1

Expression	Meaning	Can be calculated? With which formula?
$E[Y_0^i(1)\mid D^i = 1]$	Among the treated, what would be the outcome post-event if they had not been treated?	No
$E[Y_1^i(1)\mid D^i = 1]$	Among the treated, what would be the outcome post-event if they had been treated?	$E[Y^i(1)\mid D^i = 1]$
$E[Y_0^i(1)\mid D^i = 0]$	Among the nontreated, what would be the outcome post-event if they had not been treated?	$E[Y^i(1)\mid D^i = 0]$
$E[Y_1^i(1)\mid D^i = 0]$	Among the nontreated, what would be the outcome post-event if they had been treated?	No

On the other hand, at time 0, because the treatment does not affect the outcome (because it has not happened yet), we have

$$E\left[Y_0^i(0)|D^i = 1\right] = E\left[Y_1^i(0)|D^i = 1\right] = E\left[Y^i(0)|D^i = 1\right]$$
$$E\left[Y_0^i(0)|D^i = 0\right] = E\left[Y_1^i(0)|D^i = 0\right] = E\left[Y^i(0)|D^i = 0\right]$$

We can use the following notation to define our objective, which is the ATET:

$$\text{ATET} = E[Y_1^i(1) - Y_0^i(1)|D^i = 1]$$

In simpler terms, this represents the effect of releasing a new movie on the movies that received the treatment (in our example, *Star Wars* movies) compared to the case in which there was no release, as shown in figure 11.20.

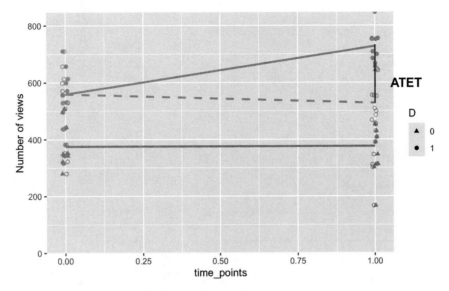

Figure 11.20 Visual representation of the ATET for the DiD setting

11.4.3 Assumptions

The main assumption in DiD is called *parallel paths* (or *common trend*). It assumes that if there were no treatment, the expected difference between groups before and after the time of the event would be the same. Let's write this expression mathematically:

- If there were no treatment, the outcome pre-event time would be $Y_0^i(0)$. So, the difference between groups before the event is

$$E\left[Y_0^i(0)|D^i = 1\right] - E\left[Y_0^i(0)|D^i = 0\right]$$

  Test your knowledge: what is the difference in the expected outcome between groups after the time of the event?

- The difference of the expected outcome between groups after the time of the event is

$$E\left[Y_1^i(1)|D^i = 1\right] - E\left[Y_1^i(1)|D^i = 0\right]$$

So, the parallel paths assumption can be expressed as

$$E\left[Y_0^i(0)|D^i = 1\right] - E\left[Y_0^i(0)|D^i = 0\right] = E\left[Y_0^i(1)|D^i = 1\right] - E\left[Y_0^i(1)|D^i = 0\right]$$

The parallel paths assumption is shown in figure 11.21, which states that the trends between the two groups $D = 0,1$ would have been parallel if there was no new release. The counterfactual path is drawn with a dashed line and is parallel to the line for the group $D = 0$.

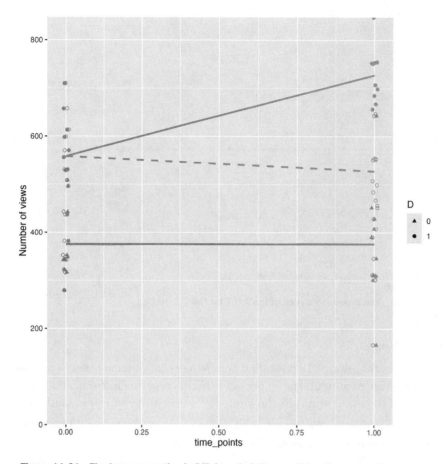

Figure 11.21   The key assumption in DiD is called the parallel paths assumption. It suggests that the trends between the two groups, *D* = 0 and *D* = 1, would have followed the same path if there had been no new release.

By rearranging terms, the parallel paths assumption can be expressed alternatively as

$$E\left[Y_0^i(0) - Y_0^i(1)|D^i = 1\right] = E\left[Y_0^i(0) - Y_0^i(1)|D^i = 0\right]$$

DiD assumptions

The main assumption in DiD is the so-called parallel paths assumption, which says that if there were no treatment, the expected difference between groups before and after the time of the event would be the same:

$$E\left[Y_0^i(0)|D^i = 1\right] - E\left[Y_0^i(0)|D^i = 0\right] = E\left[Y_0^i(1)|D^i = 1\right] - E\left[Y_0^i(1)|D^i = 0\right]$$

or, equivalently,

$$E\left[Y_0^i(0) - Y_0^i(1)|D^i = 1\right] = E\left[Y_0^i(0) - Y_0^i(1)|D^i = 0\right]$$

11.4.4 *Effect estimation*

The definition of the ATET is expressed in terms of potential outcomes. Remember that the potential outcomes are partially observed, so we don't have all the information necessary to calculate the ATET. To calculate the ATET from data, we would need to express the ATET only in terms of observed data, or equivalently a formula expressed in terms of the observed values $Y^i(t)$.

By combining the definition of the ATET with the parallel paths assumption, we can find a formula to calculate the ATET from data. Recall the definition of the ATET:

$$\text{ATET} = E\left[Y_1^i(1) - Y_0^i(1)|D^i = 1\right] = E\left[Y_1^i(1)|D^i = 1\right] - E\left[Y_0^i(1)|D^i = 1\right]$$

The potential outcome $Y_1^i(1)$ for those that have been treated, $D^i = 1$, is equal to the observed outcome $Y^i(1)$ because the potential outcome refers to what would happen if they were treated and the condition $D^i = 1$ tells you that they ended up being treated (this is known as the *consistency equation* of the potential outcomes framework; see chapter 10). So, the first term of the ATET can be calculated by averaging the outcomes post-treatment for those that are actually treated:

$$E\left[Y_1^i(0)|D^i = 1\right] = E\left[Y_1^i(0)|D^i = 1\right]$$

The second term $E[Y_0^i(1)|\ D^i = 1]$, as explained in section 11.4.2, is a nonobserved counterfactual. This term also appears in the parallel paths assumption. Thus, the idea is to work with the parallel paths expression to obtain an alternative formula for $E[Y_0^i(1)|D^i = 1]$ that can be calculated from data.

Remember that the parallel paths assumption is

$$E\left[Y_0^i(0)|D^i = 1\right] - E\left[Y_0^i(0)|D^i = 0\right] = E\left[Y_0^i(1)|D^i = 1\right] - E\left[Y_0^i(1)|D^i = 0\right]$$

Because at time $t = 0$, the event has no effect whatsoever, the following term can be calculated from data:

$$E\left[Y_0^i(0)|D^i = 1\right] - E\left[Y_0^i(0)|D^i = 0\right] = E\left[Y^i(0)|D^i = 1\right] - E\left[Y^i(0)|D^i = 0\right]$$

And for consistency of potential outcomes, the term $E[Y_0^i(1)|D^i = 0] = E[Y^i(1)|D^i = 0]$ can also be calculated from data. So we can isolate our term of interest:

$$E\left[Y^i(0)|D^i = 1\right] = E\left[Y^i(0)|D^i = 1\right] - E\left[Y^i(0)|D^i = 0\right] + E\left[Y^i(1)|D^i = 0\right]$$

Finally, combining all the terms, we have

$$\text{ATET} = E\left[Y^i(1)|D^i = 1\right] - \left(E\left[Y^i(0)|D^i = 1\right] - E\left[Y^i(0)|D^i = 0\right] + E\left[Y^i(1)|D^i = 0\right]\right)$$

which can be rearranged as

$$\text{ATET} = \Big(E\left[Y^i(1) - Y^i(0)|D^i = 1\right]\Big) - \Big(E\left[Y^i(1) - Y^i(0)|D^i = 0\right]\Big) \qquad \textbf{(11.3)}$$

Now you can guess where this technique got its name. The effect is calculated by the difference between two terms, in which each is also a difference:

- The difference for the treated before and after the event:

$$E\left[Y^i(1)|D^i = 1\right] - E\left[Y^i(0)|D^i = 1\right]$$

- The difference for the nontreated before and after the event:

$$E\left[Y^i(1)|D^i = 0\right] - E\left[Y^i(0)|D^i = 0\right]$$

11.4.5 *In practice*

As in the case of RDD, you will learn three methods. The first two are simpler, so you can use them as baselines. If you need a more sophisticated model, you can use the third, which incorporates additional covariates into the analysis.

DIRECT FORMULA

You can use equation 11.3 directly applied to data. Denote as I_1 the individuals i with $D^i = 1$ (and analogously for I_0), and as $n_{\sim}1$, $t_{\sim}$ the number of observations from I_1 at time t (and analogously for $n_{0,}t$). Then

$$\Delta(1) = \frac{1}{n_{1,1}} \sum_{i \varepsilon I_1} Y^i(1) - \frac{1}{n_{1,0}} \sum_{i \varepsilon I_1} Y^i(0)$$

$$\Delta(0) = \frac{1}{n_{0,1}} \sum_{i \varepsilon I_0} Y^i(1) - \frac{1}{n_{0,0}} \sum_{i \varepsilon I_0} Y^i(0)$$

$$\text{ATET} = \Delta_1 - \Delta_0$$

The code for calculating the ATET with this method is shown in the following listings, which give an estimation of the effect of 168.24; the actual value is 200.

Listing 11.22   (R) DiD ATE estimation with the direct method

```
diff_1 <- mean(df_observed[
  df_observed$time_points == 1 & df_observed$D == 1, 'Y'
]) - mean(df_observed[
  df_observed$time_points == 0 & df_observed$D == 1, 'Y'
])
diff_0 <- mean(df_observed[
  df_observed$time_points == 1 & df_observed$D == 0, 'Y'
]) -mean(df_observed[
```

```
    df_observed$time_points == 0 & df_observed$D == 0, 'Y'
])
diff_1 - diff_0
```

Listing 11.23   (Python) DiD ATE estimation with the direct method

```
diff_1 = mean(
  df_observed.loc[(df_observed.time_points == 1) & \
  (df_observed.D == 1), "Y"] \
) - mean(df_observed.loc[(df_observed.time_points == 0) & \
  (df_observed.D == 1), "Y"])
diff_0 = mean(
  df_observed.loc[(df_observed.time_points == 1) & \
  (df_observed.D == 0), "Y"] \
) - mean(df_observed.loc[(df_observed.time_points == 0) & \
  (df_observed.D == 0), "Y"])
diff_1 - diff_0
```

We can obtain confidence intervals using bootstrapping (explained in chapter 8) with the following steps:

- Resample your data. The sampling has to be done with replacement; otherwise, you will always get the same dataset, only in a different order.
- Calculate the ATET with equation 11.3.

Repeat the previous steps many times (typically between 1,000 and 10,000 times), and then calculate the a and $1 - a$ quantiles, where $0 < a < 1$. Typically, we use $a = 0.025$ for a 95% confidence interval, leading to the 2.5% and 97.5% quantiles.

LINEAR MODELS

An alternative is to use linear models. Even though they give the exact same estimates as equation 11.3, they have two advantages:

- They are implemented in standard packages such as the `lm` function in R and the `statmodels` library in Python.
- If you need to work with a variation of the DiD method, there's a good chance you can apply similar techniques using linear models, making your previous work reusable.

The linear model that provides the same estimates as equation 11.3 has the same flavor as the one discussed in the RDD section. We will use the model

$$Y^i(t) = a_0 + a_1 D^i + a_2 t^i + a_3 t^i D^i + \varepsilon_i(t)$$

where $E[\varepsilon^i(t)] = 0$ and the terms $\varepsilon^i(t)$ are independent of one another.

With this linear model specification, we let each group, $D = 0$ and $D = 1$, have its own intercept and slope. The reasoning is exactly the same as in the case of RDDs (if you don't remember, I suggest you re-read "Linear models" in section 11.2.5).

To understand what we should expect from applying the DiD approach in this model, we need to apply equation 11.3 (written again here for completeness) to the linear model chosen in this section:

$$\text{ATET} = E\left[Y^i(1) - Y^i(0)|D^i = 1\right] - E\left[Y^i(1) - Y^i(0)|D^i = 0\right]$$

Thus, to calculate the ATET, we need to calculate the four combinations of the form $E[Y^i(t)|D^i = d]$ for time variables $t = 0,1$ and decision variables $d = 0,1$. To do that, we only have to substitute the corresponding values of t and d in the linear formula. The error terms $\varepsilon^i(t)$ disappear because we apply expectations, and the error terms have zero expectation. The resulting calculations are shown in table 11.5.

Table 11.5   Values of the expression $E[Y^i(t)|D^i = d]$ for times $t = 0,1$ and decisions $d = 0,1$

	$t^i = 0$	$t^i = 1$
$D^i = 0$	a_0	$a_0 + a_2$
$D^i = 1$	$a_0 + a_1$	$a_0 + a_1 + a_2 + a_3$

So, we can find the ATET as

$$[(a_0 + a_1 + a_2 + a_3) - (a_0 + a_1)] - [(a_0 + a_2) - (a_0)] = [a_2 + a_3 - a_2] = a_3$$

That is, the ATET is just the coefficient a_3.

We can estimate the ATET with the code shown in the next two listings, which give the result 168.24 (49.4, 287.1). The estimated ATET is provided by the coefficient D:time_points. Notice that the point estimate 168.24 is exactly the same as in the case of directly applying equation 11.3. This relationship will always happen: the estimates from the linear model and equation 11.3 are always the same.

Listing 11.24   (R) DiD using linear regression; ATET estimated by `D:time_points`

```
model <- lm(Y~D*time_points, data=df_observed)
print(summary(model))
confint(model, level = 0.95)
```

Listing 11.25   (Python) DiD using linear regression; ATET estimated by `D:time_points`

```
model = smf.ols(formula="Y~D*time_points", data=df_observed).fit()
model.summary()
```

ADDITIONAL COVARIATES

The linear model can be further expanded by adding more timepoints or other covariates. For example, in our movie scenario, we can introduce another factor: the movie's age. This factor helps distinguish two groups among already released movies: older and newer films. To illustrate, we can classify *Star Wars* movies IV–VI, which were released in the 1970s–1980s, as older, whereas *Star Wars* I–III and all three *LoTR* movies (released between 1999 and 2005) are considered newer.

Additional covariates can encompass multiple factors, and they can take on continuous or discrete values. These factors have a direct influence on the outcome variable, $Y^i(t)$. For example, newer movies tend to be viewed more frequently than older ones, indicating that a movie's age affects the outcome variable, $Y^i(t)$.

Curiously enough, adding static covariates that do not depend on time or the decision variable has no effect on the DiD estimation. For example, consider the model

$$Y^i = a_0 + a_1 D^i + a_2 t^i + a_3 t^i D^i + b X^i + \varepsilon_i(t)$$

where X plays the role of the movie's age. When calculating the difference $E[Y^i(1) - Y^i(0)|D^i = 1]$ in equation 11.3, the term bX^i cancels and has no effect on the result. The same happens with the second difference in equation 11.3.

The following listings create a new dataset in which the outcome is affected by an age variable A. One-quarter of the nontreated are category $A = 1$, and one-half of the treated have that category.

Listing 11.26   (R) Generating a synthetic dataset with additional covariates

```
n_a <- floor(n_group/4)
A <- c(rep(1, n_a*2), rep(0, 2*(n_group - n_a)))
n_a <- floor(n_group/2)
A <- c(A, rep(1, n_a*2), rep(0, 2*(n_group - n_a)))
D <- c(rep(0, 2*n_group), rep(1, 2*n_group))
Y_0_age <- Y_0 - 50 * A
Y_1_age <- Y_1 - 50 * A
Y_age <- D*Y_1_age + (1-D)*Y_0_age
df_observed_age <- data.frame(
  id, time_points, D, Y=Y_age, A
)
```

Listing 11.27   (Python) Generating a synthetic dataset with additional covariates

```
n_a = int(floor(n_group / 4))
A = [1] * (n_a * 2) + [0] * (2 * (n_group - n_a))
n_a = int(floor(n_group / 2))
A = array(A + [1] * (n_a * 2) + [0] * (2 * (n_group - n_a)))
D = array([0] * (2 * n_group) + [1] * (2 * n_group))
Y_0_age = Y_0 - 50 * A
Y_1_age = Y_1 - 50 * A
Y_age = D * Y_1_age + (1 - D) * Y_0_age
df_observed_covariates = pd.DataFrame({
  "id": id, "time_points": time_points, "D": D, "Y": Y, "A": A
})
```

In the next two listings, using linear regression that includes A, we obtain the result 168.245 (93.12, 268.20). The estimated ATET is provided by the coefficient `D:time_points`. This result is the same point estimate as the estimation without the additional covariate.

Listing 11.28   (R) Estimating the ATET with linear models and additional covariates

```
model <- lm(Y~D*time_points + A, data=df_observed)
print(summary(model))
confint(model, level = 0.95)
```

Listing 11.29   (Python) Estimating the ATET with linear models and additional covariates

```
model = smf.ols(formula="Y~D*time_points + A", data=df_observed_covariates).fit()
model.summary()
```

Nonetheless, in general, adding more covariates with dependencies on time or other variables such as D can make the inference much harder. If you are interested, take a look at specialized literature about DiD.

DiD WITH THE DID AND DOUBLEML PACKAGES

You can calculate the ATET with the `DoubleML` package in Python or the `drdid` R package (https://cran.r-project.org/web/packages/DRDID). These packages are based on the paper "Doubly robust difference-in-differences estimators" by Pedro H.C. Sant'Anna and Jun Zhao. They can handle DiD with additional covariates with nonlinear relationships by using machine learning models, but in this section we will focus on their basic usage.

Listing 11.30   (R) DiD using the did R package

```
att_gt(
  yname='Y', tname = 'time_points', idname = 'id', gname = 'D',
  data = df_observed)
```

Here we apply the `att_gt` function, which gives us a result of 168.245 (61.23, 275.26)—pretty similar to the results obtained previously. As already mentioned, you can use these libraries for more complex situations in which there are additional covariates affecting the outcome and the decision variable D in a nonlinear way. These packages provide doubly robust estimates of the ATET.

In Python, we can use the `DoubleML` package to apply the DiD method. Notice that because `DoubleML` can deal with nonlinearities, we need to specify the type of machine learning models to use. For simplicity, we have chosen linear and logistic regressions. However, any machine learning algorithm compatible with the package can be used.

Listing 11.31 (Python) DiD using the `DoubleML` package

```
dml_data = DoubleMLData(
    df_observed_covariates, y_col="Y", d_cols="D", x_cols="A", \
    t_col="time_points" \
)
ml_g = LinearRegression()
ml_m = LogisticRegression(penalty=None)
dml_did = DoubleMLDID(
    dml_data,
    ml_g=ml_g,
    ml_m=ml_m,
    score="observational",
    in_sample_normalization=True,
    n_folds=5,
)
dml_did.fit()
print(dml_did)
```

11.5 Chapter quiz

As we conclude the chapter, it's important to ensure that you have a solid understanding of the key concepts. Here are the essential questions you should be able to answer clearly and concisely. If you can't, I suggest rereading the corresponding references:

1. What are the three kinds of data related to time?
   Answer in the introduction
2. Can you explain intuitively which is the assumption behind Regression Discontinuity Design that lets us estimate the causal effect?
   Answer in the sidebar "Why can we estimate the causal effect of RDD even when there are simultaneous factors?" in section 11.2
3. What common practical problem do the methods of difference in means and linear regression have when applied to RDD?
   Answer in the sidebars "Limitations of the difference in means approach" and "Limitations of the linear approach to RDD" in section 11.2.5
4. Can you intuitively explain the assumptions behind the SC approach?
   Answer in the sidebar "SC assumptions" in section 11.3.3
5. What are the trade-offs in choosing the time periods before and after the main event in the SC approach?
   Answer in table 11.3
6. From figure 11.19, which quantities expressed in the PO notation are observed? Which ones are calculated? And which ones are unobserved?

11.6 Method comparison

Table 11.6 gives a short summary of the methods discussed. The table shows the following:

- When we can apply the method, depending on the type of data and the assumptions

- What we are estimating with the method, in the Effect Estimation column

Table 11.6   Table showing when we can apply the method (Type of Data and Assumptions) and what estimates each method (Effect Estimation)

Method	Type of data	Assumptions	Effect estimation
RDD	Time series	$\lim_{s \to 0} E[Y_0(T - s)] = \lim_{s \to 0} E[Y_0(T + s)]$ and $\lim_{s \to 0} E[Y_1(T - s)] = \lim_{s \to 0} E[Y_1(T + s)]$	ATE at time T
SC	Time series	• $X(t)$ predict $Y(t)$ before T. • The main event at T has no effect on $X(t)$. • Consistent relationship between outcomes and controls.	Averaged ATET over a period of time post-event
DiD	Panel data	Parallel paths $E\left[Y_0^i(0) - Y_0^i(1)|D^i = 1\right] = E\left[Y_0^i(0) - Y_0^i(1)|D^i = 0\right]$	ATET at time T

Remember that in this chapter, we have seen the most basic formulations of each method. There are many variations for each one that work with different types of data, under different assumptions, and estimating different quantities. If you want to learn those variations, I suggest you read specialized literature on the topic.

11.7   References

- "Why high-order polynomials should not be used in regression discontinuity designs by Andrew Gelman and Guido Imbens (2018; https://mng.bz/DpXV)
- "The economic costs of conflict: a case study of the Basque country" by Alberto Abadie and Javier Gardeazabal (2003; https://mng.bz/lr6o)

Summary

- There are different types of time-related data: cross-sectional, time series, and panel data.
- We can use RDDs with time series data when there are no major, sudden changes from factors other than the main event.
- We can use SCs with time series data as long as we can correlate it with other time series.
- We can apply DiD with panel data to estimate the effect of an event on a group of elements.

appendix A
The math behind the
adjustment formula

In chapter 2, we introduced the adjustment formula from an intuitive point of view. If you're interested in a deeper dive into how this formula is formally developed using math, this section is for you. We'll clearly outline our assumptions, explain graphs using mathematical expressions, and work through some algebraic manipulations.

The main objective is the following. Assume we have data generated from figure A.1, which creates a probability distribution P:

1 The intervened graph, figure A.2, shows how we would like the data generated, which would create a probability distribution $P|do(T = A)$. For this proof, to improve the notation, we will use $P^{do(T = A)}$ to denote $P|do(T = A)$.

2 So, we want to calculate a quantity on the intervened graph: the recovery rate $P^{do(T = A)}$, but only using terms from the original graph with distribution P (it is the only information we have access to).

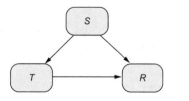

Figure A.1 Historical data generation process

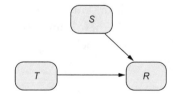

Figure A.2 How we would like the data to be generated

Each graph can be translated equivalently into a set of equations. Let's start with distribution P:

$$S := U_S$$
$$T := f_T(S, U_T)$$
$$R := f_R(S, T, U_R)$$

These equations form a *structural causal model* (SCM). Let's describe it in detail:

- The symbol := is the assignment operator, which is different than the equality (=) operator. The expression $x = Y$ means if we change x or y, the other will also change. In contrast, the expression $x := y$ means when y changes, x changes, but if you change x, y will not change. It models the intrinsic directionality of causality $y \to x$.
- The variables U_S, U_T, and U_R are exogenous variables: variables that collect all the context outside the model. We assume they are independent, but they have whatever distribution they need to have. These are the sources of variation in our system.
- Functions f_T and f_S are any type of function. We don't assume any functional form (examples of functional form are linear relationships and relationships described by a neural network).

This is a very general definition. However, we will see that these assumptions are enough, which is good because we can model a large range of situations. Let's write the set of equations for $P^{do(T=A)}$ (where the only difference is in the definition of T):

$$S := U_S$$
$$T := A$$
$$R := f_R(S, A, U_R)$$

If we assume these models, we can safely use the fact that variable S behaves the same way in both graphs and also that the relationship between R and variables S and T is the same. The only variable that behaves differently is T, which, of course, affects the values R will take (but not how they are calculated).

The idea we have expressed in words can also be expressed mathematically. That is, the fact that S behaves the same way means its distribution in both graphs is the same:

$$P(S) = P^{do(T=A)}(S)$$

In the same way, if we fix values $S = s$ and $T = A$ (we condition on these values), we will have

$$P(R = 1 | S = s, T = A) = P^{do(T=A)}(R = 1 | S = s, T = A)$$

We now have all the ingredients to derive the formula. We will use the variables from the kidney stone problem and their values, such as *Small* and Large, to make the formula simpler. However, it can be written in general with a little more work. Using the law of total probability (which works for all probability distributions and, in particular, for the intervened one), we have

$$P^{\text{do}(T=A)}(R = 1) =$$
$$P^{\text{do}(T=A)}(R = 1, S = \text{Small}) + P^{\text{do}(T=A)}(R = 1, L = \text{Large})$$

Now we develop each term by applying the definition of conditional probability:

$$P^{\text{do}(T=A)}(R = 1, S = \text{Small}) + P^{\text{do}(T=A)}(R = 1, L = \text{Large}) =$$
$$P^{\text{do}(T=A)}(R = 1|S = \text{Small})P^{\text{do}(T=A)}(S = \text{Small}) +$$
$$P^{\text{do}(T=A)}(R = 1|L = \text{Large})P^{\text{do}(T=A)}(L = \text{Large})$$

In the intervened graph, we can always condition on $T = A$ because we give treatment A to everyone, so we always have $T = A$. Remember, conditioning means selecting those cases; but in the intervened graph, the treatment always equals A, so we have

$$P^{\text{do}(T=A)}(R = 1|S = \text{Small}) =$$
$$P^{\text{do}(T=A)}(R = 1|S = \text{Small}, T = A)$$

Substituting these terms (and the analog for large stones), we get

$$P^{\text{do}(T=A)}(R = 1|S = \text{Small})P^{\text{do}(T=A)}(S = \text{Small}) +$$
$$P^{\text{do}(T=A)}(R = 1|L = \text{Large})$$
$$P^{\text{do}(T=A)}(L = \text{Large}) =$$
$$P^{\text{do}(T=A)}(R = 1|S = \text{Small}, T = A)P^{\text{do}(T=A)}(S = \text{Small}) +$$
$$P^{\text{do}(T=A)}(R = 1|L = \text{Large}, T = A)P^{\text{do}(T=A)}(L = \text{Large})$$

Now we can use the equivalences

$$P(S) = P^{\text{do}(T=A)}(S)$$

and

$$P(R = 1|S = s, T = A) = P^{\text{do}(T=A)}(R = 1|S = s, T = A)$$

and substitute them:

$$P^{\text{do}(T=A)}(R = 1|S = \text{Small}, T = A)P^{\text{do}(T=A)}(S = \text{Small}) +$$
$$P^{\text{do}(T=A)}(R = 1|L = \text{Large}, T = A)P^{\text{do}(T=A)}(L = \text{Large}) =$$
$$P(R = 1|S = \text{Small}, T = A)P(S = \text{Small}) +$$
$$P(R = 1|L = \text{Large}, T = A)P(L = \text{Large})$$

And that's it! We have expressed our quantity of interest in terms of quantities we can observe (the probability distribution P), obtaining the adjustment formula that we previously derived intuitively:

$$P^{\text{do}(T=A)}(R = 1) = P(R = 1|S = \text{Small}, T = A)P(S = \text{Small}) +$$
$$P(R = 1|L = \text{Large}, T = A)P(L = \text{Large})$$

appendix B
Solutions to exercises
in chapter 2

B.1 Solution to Simpson's paradox for treatment B

In Simpson's paradox, what would be the efficacy of treatment B if it were given to everyone? And which treatment would be better?

First let's decompose the recovery rate of treatment B. In this case, we have

$$81\% = 62\% \times 23\% + 87\% \times 77\%$$

If we apply treatment B, we update the calculation to

$$75\% = 62\% \times 49\% + 87\% \times 51\%$$

Recovery rates drop from 81% to 74%, as we would have a higher proportion of difficult (large) stones.

The difference between applying treatment A to everyone with a recovery rate of 83% and applying treatment B to everyone with an efficacy of 74% is 9 percentage points. This means A is better if the hospital is going to give it to everyone.

B.2 Observe and do are different things

Consider this simple example with $C\sim N(0,1)$ and $\varepsilon\sim N(0,1)$,

$$E := C + \varepsilon$$

That is, we have a very simple graph $C \to E$, and we describe the relationship using the mathematical formulas and probability distributions just explained. Note that we use the symbol :=, which means the relationship

$$E := C + \varepsilon$$

has to be read like code: once we have the value of C, we can calculate the value of E. But as in programming, if we change the value of E, the value of C doesn't change. As an exercise, calculate the distributions of the variables $E|C = c$, $E|do(C = c)$, $C|E = y$, and $C|do(E = y)$.

B.2.1   Solution

Because $C \rightarrow E$, intervening on C (remove all arrows incoming to C) doesn't change the graph, so intervening and observing are the same, so $E|do(C{=}c) = E|C = c$. But conditioning on $C = c$ (as we said in section 1.6.2 "A refresher on conditional probabilities and expectations" in chapter 1) when we have the exact dependency of E from C, we only have to substitute:

$$E = C + \varepsilon$$

Because the error term has a normal distribution, the distribution of E is also normal, and

$$E \sim N(c, 1)$$

Now, intervening on E doesn't affect C. This is because if A causes B, and we change B, the value of A will not change. This is intrinsic in causality. Analogously, if we do something with E, the value of C will not change. Thus the distribution of $C|do(E = y)$ is the same as C, so

$$C|do(E = y) \sim N(0, 1)$$

What remains is the distribution of $C|E = y$. This is read as follows. Both C and the error term have normal distributions, and the value of E is calculated from them. If we know that $E = y$, what is the distribution of C in this case?

$$y = C + \varepsilon$$

This requires a bit of math, but basically, we need to search for a reference for the distribution of a gaussian conditioned on its sum with another gaussian. The solution is that $C|E = y$ is also a gaussian with mean $y/2$ and variance the square root of $1/2$,

$$C|E = y \sim N\left(\frac{y}{2}, \frac{1}{2}^{0.5}\right)$$

B.3   What do we need to adjust?

The objective is to determine in each scenario which formula to use for calculating the ATE. Given the variables treatment T and outcome O, we'll walk through the following steps:

1 You need to check the structural equations and see how things change when you use different treatments in those equations. This means you have to calculate what happens in the equations when you change the treatment:

- Set the variable $T = 1$, regardless of the rest of the variables, and calculate the expected value of O (which, mathematically speaking, is $E[O|\text{do}(T=1)]$).
- Set the variable $T = 0$, and calculate the expected value of O (which, mathematically speaking, is $E[O|\text{do}(T=0)]$).
- Calculate the difference ATE $= E[O|\text{do}(T=1)] - E[O|\text{do}(T=0)]$.

2 Estimate the *difference in means* from data: that is, $E[O|T=1] - E[O|T=0]$.

3 Apply the adjustment formula to the dataset.

4 Answer the following question: among the difference in means and the adjustment formula, is there any unbiased estimator of the true ATE?

Thus, in each exercise, you need to complete table B.1, where adjustment(t) is the function that calculates the adjustment formula from data for treatment t.

Table B.1   Table to complete for each exercise

True ATE	
$E[O\|T = 1] - E[O\|T = 0]$	
adjustment(1) – adjustment(0)	
Estimation of ATE	

B.3.1   *RCT*

Fill table B.1 simulating the following case, with a sample size of 10,000, shown in figure B.1:

$$T := B(0.5)$$
$$R := B(0.3)T + B(0.5)(1 - T)$$

where $B(p)$ is drawn from Bernoulli distribution with expectation p.

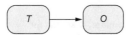

Figure B.1   RCT or A/B Test. *T* stands for Treatment and *O* for Outcome.

Listing B.1   (R) RCT example

```
set.seed(1234)
n <- 10000
treatment <- rbinom(n, 1, 0.5)
outcome <- rbinom(n, 1, 0.3)*treatment +
rbinom(n, 1, 0.5)*(1-treatment)
condition_prob_diff <- mean(outcome[treatment==1]) -
mean(outcome[treatment==0])
print(condition_prob_diff)
```

Listing B.2   (Python) RCT example (also importing for the next examples)

```
from numpy.random import binomial, normal, seed
from numpy import mean, unique
seed(1234)
n = 10000
treatment = binomial(1, 0.5, size=n)
outcome = binomial(1, 0.3, size=n)*treatment + \
binomial(1, 0.5, size=n)*(1-treatment)
condition_prob_diff = mean(outcome[treatment==1]) - \
mean(outcome[treatment==0])
print(condition_prob_diff)
```

Table B.2   Reported values come from the R code.

True ATE	-0.2
$E[O|T = 1] - E[O|T = 0]$	−0.200824
adjustment(1) − adjustment(0)	Doesn't apply
Estimation of ATE	−0.200824

B.3.2   Confounder

Fill table B.1 simulating the following case, with a sample size of 10,000, shown in figure B.2:

$$C := B(0.8)$$
$$T := B(0.6)\,C + B(0.2)(1 - C)$$
$$R := B(0.3)\,T + B(0.5)(1 - T) + C + \varepsilon$$

where $B(p)$ is drawn from Bernoulli distribution with expectation p, and $\varepsilon \sim N(0,1)$.

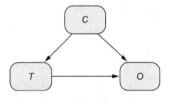

Figure B.2   Graph with a confounder. C stands for Confounder, T for Treatment, and O for Outcome.

Listing B.3   (R) Confounder example: data generation

```
set.seed(1234)
n <- 10000
confounder <- rbinom(n, 1, 0.8)
treatment <- rbinom(n, 1, 0.6)*confounder +
rbinom(n, 1, 0.2)*(1-confounder)
outcome <- rbinom(n, 1, 0.3)*treatment +
rbinom(n, 1, 0.5)*(1-treatment) + confounder + rnorm(n)
condition_prob_diff <- mean(outcome[treatment==1]) -
mean(outcome[treatment==0])
print(condition_prob_diff)
```

Listing B.4   (R) Adjustment formula

```r
adjustment <- function(t, o, z, t0){
    ind_t0 <- t == t0
    z_values <- unique(z)
    adjusted_prob <- 0
    for(z_ in z_values){
        ind_z_ <- z == z_
        ind <- ind_t0 & ind_z_
        adjusted_prob <- adjusted_prob +
        mean(o[ind])*mean(ind_z_)
    }
    return(adjusted_prob)
}
adj_result <- adjustment(treatment, outcome, confounder, 1) -
adjustment(treatment, outcome, confounder, 0)
print(adj_result)
```

Listing B.5   (Python) Confounder example: data generation

```python
seed(1234)
n = 10000
confounder = binomial(1, 0.8, size=n)
treatment = binomial(1, 0.6, size=n)*confounder + \
binomial(1, 0.2, size=n)*(1-confounder)
outcome = binomial(1, 0.3, size=n)*treatment + \
binomial(1, 0.5, size=n)*(1-treatment) + \
confounder + normal(size=n)
condition_prob_diff = mean(outcome[treatment==1]) - \
mean(outcome[treatment==0])
print(condition_prob_diff)
```

Listing B.6   (Python) Adjustment formula

```python
def adjustment(t, o, z, t0):
    ind_t0 = t == t0
    z_values = unique(z)
    adjusted_prob = 0
    for z_ in z_values:
        ind_z_ = z == z_
        ind = ind_t0 & ind_z_
        adjusted_prob = adjusted_prob + mean(o[ind])*mean(ind_z_)
    return(adjusted_prob)
adj_result = adjustment(treatment, outcome, confounder, 1) - \
adjustment(treatment, outcome, confounder, 0)
print(adj_result)
```

Table B.3   Reported values come from the R code.

True ATE	-0.2
$E[O\|T = 1] - E[O\|T = 0]$	0.0727654
adjustment(1) – adjustment(0)	–0.1729764
Estimation of ATE	–0.1729764

B.3.3   *Unobserved Confounder*

Fill table B.1 simulating the following case, with a sample size of 10,000, shown in figure B.3:

$$C := B(0.8)$$
$$T := B(0.6)\, C + B(0.2)(1 - C)$$
$$R := B(0.3)\, T + B(0.5)(1 - T) + C + \varepsilon$$

where $B(p)$ is drawn from Bernoulli distribution with expectation p, and $\varepsilon \sim N(0,1)$.

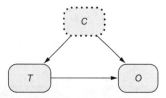

Figure B.3   Graph with an unobserved confounder (we don't have data about this variable). C stands for Confounder, T for Treatment and O for Outcome.

Listing B.7   (R) Unobserved confounder

```
set.seed(1234)
n <- 10000
confounder <- rbinom(n, 1, 0.8)
treatment <- rbinom(n, 1, 0.6)*confounder +
rbinom(n, 1, 0.2)*(1-confounder)
outcome <- rbinom(n, 1, 0.3)*treatment +
rbinom(n, 1, 0.5)*(1-treatment) + confounder + rnorm(n)
condition_prob_diff <- mean(outcome[treatment==1]) -
mean(outcome[treatment==0])
print(condition_prob_diff)
```

Listing B.8   (Python) Unobserved confounder

```
seed(1234)
n = 10000
confounder = binomial(1, 0.8, size=n)
treatment = binomial(1, 0.6, size=n)*confounder + \
binomial(1, 0.2, size=n)*(1-confounder)
outcome = binomial(1, 0.3, size=n)*treatment + \
binomial(1, 0.5, size=n)*(1-treatment) + \
confounder + normal(size=n)
condition_prob_diff = mean(outcome[treatment==1]) - \
mean(outcome[treatment==0])
print(condition_prob_diff)
```

Table B.4   Reported values come from the R code.

True ATE	−0.2
$E[O\|T = 1] - E[O\|T = 0]$	0.0727654
adjustment(1) − adjustment(0)	Cannot be calculated
Estimation of ATE	Cannot be calculated

B.3.4 Mediators

Fill table B.1 simulating the following case, with a sample size of 10,000, shown in figure B.4:

$$T := B(0.4)$$
$$M := B(0.6)\,T + B(0.2)(1 - T)$$
$$R := B(0.4)\,T + B(0.5)(1 - T) + M + \varepsilon$$

where $B(p)$ is drawn from Bernoulli distribution with expectation p, and $\varepsilon \sim N(0,1)$.

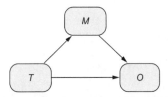

Figure B.4   Graph with a mediator. For example, post-treatment size is a mediator in the kidney stone example if once the treatment is given to patients, their kidney stone size may change. *M* stands for Mediator, *T* for Treatment, and *O* for Outcome.

Listing B.9   (R) Mediators

```
set.seed(1234)
n <- 10000
treatment <- rbinom(n, 1, 0.4)
mediator <- rbinom(n, 1, 0.6)*treatment +
rbinom(n, 1, 0.2)*(1-treatment)
outcome <- rbinom(n, 1, 0.4)*treatment +
rbinom(n, 1, 0.5)*(1-treatment) + mediator + rnorm(n)
condition_prob_diff <- mean(outcome[treatment==1]) -
mean(outcome[treatment==0])
print(condition_prob_diff)
adj_result <- adjustment(treatment, outcome, mediator, 1) -
adjustment(treatment, outcome, mediator, 0)
print(adj_result)
```

Listing B.10   (Python) Mediators

```
seed(1234)
n = 10000
treatment = binomial(1, 0.4, size=n)
mediator = binomial(1, 0.6, size=n)*treatment + \
binomial(1, 0.2, size=n)*(1-treatment)
outcome = binomial(1, 0.4, size=n)*treatment + \
binomial(1, 0.5, size=n)*(1-treatment) + \
mediator + normal(size=n)
condition_prob_diff = mean(outcome[treatment==1]) - \
mean(outcome[treatment==0])
print(condition_prob_diff)
adj_result = adjustment(treatment, outcome, mediator, 1) - \
adjustment(treatment, outcome, mediator, 0)
print(adj_result)
```

Table B.5   Reported values come from the R code.

True ATE	(0.6 + 0.4) - (0.2 + 0.5) = 0.3
$E[O\|T=1] - E[O\|T=0]$	0.2876732
adjustment(1) − adjustment(0)	−0.1170337
Estimation of ATE	0.2876732

B.3.5   *Outcome predictive variables*

Fill table B.1 simulating the following case, with a sample size of 10,000, shown in figure B.5:

$$T := B(0.4)$$
$$P := B(0.4)$$
$$O := B(0.4)\,T + B(0.5)(1-T) + P + \varepsilon$$

where $B(p)$ is drawn from Bernoulli distribution with expectation p, and $\varepsilon \sim N(0,1)$.

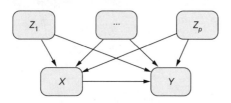

Figure B.5   A predictive outcome variable is a variable that predicts the outcome but not the treatment. In this case, there is no difference between applying the adjustment formula or just the difference of means from a bias point of view. However, adjusting for the predictive variable can be beneficial because it may decrease the variance of your estimations.

Listing B.11   (R) Predictor

```
set.seed(1234)
n <- 10000
treatment <- rbinom(n, 1, 0.4)
predictor <- rbinom(n, 1, 0.4)
outcome <- rbinom(n, 1, 0.4)*treatment +
rbinom(n, 1, 0.5)*(1-treatment) + predictor + rnorm(n)
condition_prob_diff <- mean(outcome[treatment==1]) -
mean(outcome[treatment==0])
print(condition_prob_diff)
adj_result <- adjustment(treatment, outcome, predictor, 1) -
adjustment(treatment, outcome, predictor, 0)
print(adj_result)
```

Listing B.12   (Python) Predictor

```
seed(1234)
n = 10000
treatment = binomial(1, 0.4, size=n)
predictor = binomial(1, 0.4, size=n)
outcome = binomial(1, 0.4, size=n)*treatment + \
```

```
binomial(1, 0.5, size=n)*(1-treatment) + \
predictor + normal(size=n)
condition_prob_diff = mean(outcome[treatment==1]) - \
mean(outcome[treatment==0])
print(condition_prob_diff)
adj_result = adjustment(treatment, outcome, predictor, 1) - \
adjustment(treatment, outcome, predictor, 0)
print(adj_result)
```

Table B.6   Reported values come from the R code.

True ATE	0.4 – 0.5 = –0.1
$E[O\|T = 1] - E[O\|T = 0]$	–0.0950824
adjustment(1) – adjustment(0)	–0.1011824
Estimation of ATE	Both are valid: –0.0950824 and –0.1011824

appendix C
Technical lemma for the propensity scores

In chapter 5, section 5.1.4, we learned that to find the ATE, we can group together all the patients who have the same propensity score. This works because with the same propensity score, the characteristics of the population are evenly distributed between the treated and control groups. In this appendix, we'll show the math that proves this is true. We will use conditional probabilities, so if necessary, review the definitions and concepts about conditioning described in chapter 1, section 1.6.2.

> **Objective**
> The objective of this appendix is to mathematically prove the following: given a propensity score, the distribution of population characteristics is the same in treated and control groups.

Let's start with an example. In figure C.1, we grouped together children and elderly people because their ratio (1 to 2) is consistent in both the treatment and control groups. Generally, when we group patients who share the same propensity score, the distribution of characteristics like age is the same between those receiving the treatment and those who do not.

We want to prove a general statement about propensity scores (that for a group with the same propensity score, the distribution of confounders is the same in both treated and control groups). To make the proof, we need to be able to describe this statement in abstract notation. Because abstract notation may be hard to follow, we will translate the example in figure C.1 into mathematical notation. Later, we will jump into the notation that describes the statement in general.

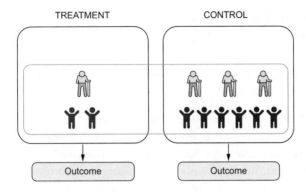

Figure C.1 In a group with the same propensity score, the age distribution is the same in the treated and control groups.

The group comprising children and older people is fully described by selecting patients with a propensity score of 1/4. This group, with a propensity score denoted by the variable S, is described mathematically this way: "conditioning on $S = 1/4$." Because the only confounder c we have is age, we can say that

$$P\left(c = \text{old}|S = \frac{1}{4}\right) = \frac{4}{12}$$

That is, the proportion of old people in the group with propensity score 1/4 is 4/12. We need to go one step further and talk about the proportion of old people in the group with a propensity score of 1/4 who are also treated. But adding another condition on the selection—being treated—is nothing more than also conditioning on treated patients. So, this is written as

$$P\left(c = \text{old}|S = \frac{1}{4}, T = 1\right) = \frac{1}{3}$$

because given three patients, only one is older (see figure C.2).

Figure C.2 Proportion of old people among the treated

So, we can conclude that the distribution of old people is the same in the treated $P(c = \text{old}|S = 1/4,\, T = 1)$ and control groups $P(c = \text{old}|S = 1/4,\, T = 0)$: that is,

$$P\left(c = \text{old}|S = \frac{1}{4}, T = 1\right) = P\left(c = \text{old}|S = \frac{1}{4}, T = 0\right)$$

With this example in mind, let's jump into the abstract notation of conditional probabilities and propensity scores. Pick some propensity score s (in the previous case, $1/4$), pick some confounder C (in our case, age), and pick a particular value of c (in our case, older patients). Saying that the distribution of C, among the group with propensity scores s, is the same in treated and control groups can be written as

$$P(C = c|t = 1, S = s) = P(C = c|t = 0, S = s)$$

or, with simplified notation,

$$P(c|t = 1, s) = P(c|t = 0, s)$$

Because the distribution of c in the subgroup $S = s$ is the same for $t = 1$ and $t = 0$, we are actually saying that $P(c|t, s)$ is independent of t. That is,

$$P(c|t, s) = P(c|s)$$

So, this last equation is the one we want to prove using mathematical techniques.

For simplicity, we will start by checking the case $T = 1$. By definition of conditional probability,

$$P(c|T = 1, s) = \frac{P(T = 1, c, s)}{P(T = 1, s)}$$

and applying the definition again,

$$P(c|T = 1, s) = \frac{P(T = 1|c, s)P(c, s)}{P(T = 1, s)}$$

Saying that we select patients with characteristic $C = c$ (in our example, older people) is more restrictive than saying $S = s$ (in our example, $S = 1/4$). So, the set of patients with $S = s$ and $C = c$ is exactly the same as the set of patients with $C = c$, and we can remove the s as follows:

$$P(T = 1|c, s) = P(T = 1|c)$$

At the same time, $P(T = 1|c)$ is precisely the definition of propensity score, so if s is the propensity score of the patients with characteristic $C = c$, $P(T = 1|c) = s$, and

$$P(T = 1|c, s) = s$$

On the other hand, by the definition of conditional probability,

$$P(T = 1, s) = P(T = 1|s)P(s)$$

To calculate the value of $P(T = 1|s)$, we need to understand what it means. If we read it, by definition, it means selecting those patients such that their probability of being treated is s, and calculating their probability of being treated—very recursive, but it is what it is. So, this probability is precisely s! Thus, $P(T = 1|s) = s$, and $P(T = 1, s) = sP(s)$.

Putting things together, we have

$$P(c|T = 1, s) = \frac{P(T = 1|c, s)P(c, s)}{P(T = 1, s)} =$$

$$\frac{sP(c, s)}{P(T = 1, s)} = \frac{sP(c, s)}{sP(s)} = \frac{P(c, s)}{P(s)} = P(c|s)$$

where we again use the definition of conditional probability.

appendix D
Proof for doubly
robust $\widehat{\text{ATE}}_{aipw}$ estimator

In chapter 8, we introduced the $\widehat{\text{ATE}}_{aipw}$ estimator and saw that it is doubly robust. If you are curious about why $\widehat{\text{ATE}}_{aipw}$ is doubly robust, you can find the proof here. We need to check the two following conditions:

- If the models from the T-learner are unbiased, $f_0(c) = E[Y|c,\ T = 0]$ and $f_1(c) = E[Y|c,\ T = 1]$, then $\widehat{\text{ATE}}_{aipw}$ is also unbiased: that is, $E[\widehat{\text{ATE}}_{aipw}] = \text{ATE}$.
- If the propensity score is unbiased, $s(c) = P(T = 1|c)$, then $\widehat{\text{ATE}}_{aipw}$ is also unbiased: that is, $E[\widehat{\text{ATE}}_{aipw}] = \text{ATE}$.

D.1 DR property with respect to the T-learner

We will first check the DR property for the T-learner. Assume that the models from the T-learner are unbiased. First, notice that $\widehat{\text{ATE}}_{aipw}$ can be expressed in terms of the T-learner estimator $\widehat{\text{ATE}}_t$. Consider the random variables T_i, C_i, and Y_i. Then

$$\widehat{\text{ATE}}_{aipw} = \frac{1}{n}\left[\sum_i f_1(C_i) - f_0(C_i)\right] +$$

$$\frac{1}{n}\left[\sum_i \frac{(Y_i - f_1(C_i))T_i}{s(C_i)} - \frac{(Y_i - f_0(C_i))(1 - T_i)}{1 - s(C_i)}\right] =$$

$$\widehat{\text{ATE}}_t + \widehat{\text{RES}}_t$$

If we can see that the residual has expectation zero, $E[\widehat{\text{RES}}_t] = 0$, we are done, because in that case,

$$E\left[\widehat{\text{ATE}}_t\right] = E\left[\widehat{\text{ATE}}_t\right] + E\left[\widehat{\text{RES}}_t\right] = \text{ATE}$$

354

Let's see that $E[\widehat{RES_t}] = 0$. For simplicity, we will drop the index i and calculate the expectation for only one term of the summand. Using the total law of expectation, we get

$$E\left[\widehat{RES_t}\right] = E_{C,T}\left[E_Y\left[\frac{(Y - f_1(C))T}{s(C)} - \frac{(Y - f_0(C))(1-T)}{1-s(C)}\bigg|C,T\right]\right] \tag{D.1}$$

Let's start with the first term:

$$E_Y\left[\frac{(Y - f_1(C))T}{s(C)}\bigg|C,T\right]$$

When $T = 0$, the term cancels because T is multiplying. Assume now that $T = 1$.

When we condition on C and $T = 1$, those variables become fixed. So, we can T with 1 and pull the terms with C out of the conditional expectation $E_Y|C$, $T = 1$. Thus,

$$E_Y\left[\frac{(Y - f_1(C))T}{s(C)}\bigg|C,T=1\right] = \frac{E_Y[(Y - f_1(C))|C,T=1]}{s(C)} =$$

$$\frac{E_Y[Y|C,T=1] - f_1(C)}{s(C)} = 0$$

because $f_1(c) = E[Y|\ C,\ T=1]$, by the hypothesis that the T-learner models are unbiased. We can reason similarly with the second term in equation D.1 and safely conclude that $E[\widehat{RES_t}] = 0$.

D.2   Doubly robust property with respect to inverse probability weighting

Let's check the doubly robust property with respect to inverse probability weighting (IPW). Suppose that $s(c) = P(T = 1|c)$. We want to see that $E[\widehat{ATE}_{aipw}] = ATE$. We will follow reasoning similar to the previous case.

First we need to rearrange the terms of $\widehat{ATE}_{aipw}$ to relate it to $\widehat{ATE}_{aipw}$. Notice that

$$f_1(C_i) + \frac{(Y_i - f_1(C_i))T_i}{s(C_i)} =$$
$$\frac{Y_i T_i}{s(C_i)} + \frac{f_1(C_i)(s(C_i) - T_i)}{s(C_i)}$$

And analogously for the term with f_0:

$$f_0(C_i) + \frac{(Y_i - f_0(C_i))(1 - T_i)}{1 - s(C_i)} =$$
$$\frac{Y_i(1 - T_i)}{1 - s(C_i)} + \frac{f_0(C_i)((1 - s(C_i)) - (1 - T_i))}{1 - s(C_i)}$$

So, we obtain the following relationship between $\widehat{\mathrm{ATE}}_{aipw}$ and $\widehat{\mathrm{ATE}}_{aipw}$:

$$\widehat{\mathrm{ATE}}_{aipw} = \frac{1}{n}\left[\sum_i f_1(C_i) - f_0(C_i)\right] +$$

$$\frac{1}{n}\left[\sum_i \frac{(Y_i - f_1(C_i))T_i}{s(C_i)} - \frac{(Y_i - f_0(C_i))(1 - T_i)}{1 - s(C_i)}\right] =$$

$$\frac{1}{n}\left[\sum_i \frac{Y_iT_i}{s(C_i)} - \frac{Y_i(1 - T_i)}{1 - s(C_i)}\right] +$$

$$\frac{1}{n}\left[\sum_i \frac{f_1(C_i)(s(C_i) - T_i)}{s(C_i)} - \frac{f_0(C_i)((1 - s(C_i)) - (1 - T_i))}{1 - s(C_i)}\right] =$$

$$\widehat{\mathrm{ATE}}_{ipw} + \widehat{\mathrm{RES}}_{ipw}$$

It remains to see that $E[\widehat{\mathrm{RES}}_{ipw}] = 0$. As in the case of the T-learner, we have this expectation for the residual with IPW:

$$E[\widehat{\mathrm{RES}}_{ipw}] =$$

$$E_C\left[E_T\left[\frac{f_1(C)(s(C) - T)}{s(C)} - \frac{f_0(C)((1 - s(C)) - (1 - T))}{1 - s(C)}\Big|C\right]\right]$$

Now,

$$E_T\left[\frac{f_1(C)(s(C) - T)}{s(C)}\Big|C\right] = \frac{f_1(C)E_T[(s(C) - T)|C]}{s(C)} = 0$$

because $E_T[(s(C) - T)|C] = s(C) - E_T[t|C] = 0$, by the hypothesis that $s(C)$ is unbiased. Using the same reasoning with the remaining term of the residual IPW, we can conclude that $E[\widehat{\mathrm{RES}}_{ipw}] = 0$.

appendix E
Technical lemma for the alternative instrumental variable estimator

In chapter 9, we provided an alternative formulation to the instrumental variable (IV) estimator in equation 9.2, which relies on the following technical result: if R is a binary variable, then for any variable Q,

$$\text{cov}(Q, R) = (E[Q|R = 1] - E[Q|R = 0])P(R = 1)P(R = 0)$$

That is,

$$\text{cov}(Q, R) = E[QR] - E[Q]E[R] =$$
$$E[Q|R = 1]\,P(R = 1) - (E[Q|R = 1]P(R = 1) + E[Q|R = 0]P(R = 0))P(R = 1) =$$
$$(E[Q|R = 1] - E[Q|R = 0])P(R = 1)P(R = 0)$$

appendix F
Proof of the instrumental variable formula for imperfect compliance

In this appendix, we will prove the instrumental variable (IV) formula for imperfect compliance from chapter 10. Assume that the instrument Z and decision D are binary, and that $P(D = 1|Z = 0) = 0$. Then the effect of D on the outcome Y is

$$\text{ATET} = \frac{E[Y|Z = 1] - E[Y|Z = 0]}{E[D|Z = 1]}$$

We will start with a technical result that will help us later in deriving the IV estimator. Given three random variables X, Y, Z with X and Z being binary, then for any value $x = 0, 1$, we have

$$E[Y|X = x] = E[Y|X = x, Z = 1]P(Z = 1|X = x) + E[Y|X = x, Z = 0]P(Z = 0|X = x)$$

Let's get the intuition with a simpler case, where all variables are binary and $x = 1$. We will mostly use the definition of conditional probability:

$$E[Y|X = 1] = P(Y = 1|X = 1) = \frac{P(Y = 1, X = 1)}{P(X = 1)} =$$

$$\frac{P(Y = 1, X = 1, Z = 1) + P(Y = 1, X = 1, Z = 0)}{P(X = 1)} =$$

$$\frac{P(Y = 1|X = 1, Z = 1)P(X = 1, Z = 1)}{P(X = 1)} +$$

$$\frac{P(Y = 1|X = 1, Z = 0)P(X = 1, Z = 0)}{P(X = 1)} =$$

$$\frac{P(Y = 1|X = 1, Z = 1)P(Z = 1|X = 1)P(X = 1)}{P(X = 1)} +$$
$$\frac{P(Y = 1|X = 1, Z = 0)P(Z = 0|X = 1)P(X = 1)}{P(X = 1)} =$$
$$P(Y = 1|X = 1, Z = 1)P(Z = 1|X = 1) + P(Y = 1|X = 1, Z = 0)P(Z = 0|X = 1) =$$
$$E[Y|X = 1, Z = 1]P(Z = 1|X = 1) + E[Y|X = 1, Z = 0]P(Z = 0|X = 1)$$

Assume we are in the IV scenario of the DAG in figure F.1 (repeated here from chapter 10 for simplicity). Also remember the consistency equation explained in chapter 10 and repeated here for convenience:

$$Y(i) = Y_0(i)(1 - T(i)) + Y_1(i)T(i) \tag{F.1}$$

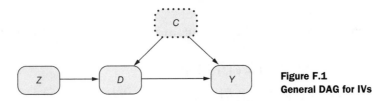

Figure F.1
General DAG for IVs

In addition, we have that there are no customers using the chatbot in the control group $P(D = 1|Z = 0) = 0$ (mainly because they don't have access to it). Now we want to see that

$$\text{ATET} = \frac{E[Y|Z = 1] - E[Y|Z = 0]}{E[D|Z = 1]}$$

To prove this result, we need some other intermediate calculations:

- Equation F.1 can be rearranged as follows:

$$Y = Y_0(1 - T) + Y_1 T = Y_0 + T(Y_1 - Y_0)$$

- The fact that $P(D = 1|Z = 0) = 0$ implies that of those who used the chatbot, all must be in the experimental group: $P(Z = 0|D = 1) = 0$ and $P(Z = 1|D = 1) = 1$.
- By the previous technical result, we have that

$$E[Y_1 - Y_0|D = 1] = E[Y_1 - Y_0|D = 1, Z = 1]P(Z = 1|D = 1) +$$
$$E[Y_1 - Y_0|D = 1, Z = 0]P(Z = 0|D = 1) = E[Y_1 - Y_0|D = 1, Z = 1]$$

- Because Z is unconfounded with Y, the potential outcomes Y_1, Y_0 are independent of Z. In particular, $E[Y_t|Z = 1] = E[Y_t]$.

- Because the variable D takes only values 0 and 1,

$$E[Y_1 D|Z = 1] = E[Y_1 \times 1|Z = 1, D = 1]P(D = 1|Z = 1) +$$
$$E[Y_1 \times 0|Z = 1, D = 1]P(D = 0|Z = 1) = E[Y1|Z = 1, D = 1]P(D = 1|Z = 1)$$

Now,

$$E[Y|Z = 1] = E[Y_0|Z = 1] + E[(Y_1 - Y_0)D|Z = 1] = E[Y_0] + E[(Y_1 - Y_0)D|Z = 1] =$$
$$E[Y_0] + E[Y_1 - Y_0|Z = 1, D = 1]P(D = 1|Z = 1) =$$
$$E[Y_0] + E[Y_1 - Y_0|D = 1]P(D = 1|Z = 1)$$

Analogously, we have that

$$E[Y|Z = 0] = E[Y_0] + E[Y_1 - Y_0|D = 1, Z = 0]P(D = 1|Z = 0) = E[Y_0]$$

because $P(D = 1|Z = 0) = 0$.

Finally, we can put together all the calculations, taking into account that by definition,

$$\text{ATET} = E[Y_1 - Y_0|D = 1]$$

$$E[Y|Z = 1] - E[Y|Z = 0] = E[Y_1 - Y_0|D = 1]P(D = 1|Z = 1)$$

So,

$$\text{ATET} = \frac{E[Y|Z = 1] - E[Y|Z = 0]}{P(D = 1|Z = 1)} = \frac{E[Y|Z = 1] - E[Y|Z = 0]}{E[D|Z = 1]}$$

index

A

A/B, limitiations of 16
adjustment formula 1, 7, 20, 31, 38, 42–44, 87
  average treatment effect (ATE) 44
  for outcomes with many values 43–44
  math behind 337–340
  propensity scores in 140–147
  when to apply 53
  with potential outcomes 282–285
AIPW (augmented inverse probability
  weighting) 243–245
assignment operator 48, 338
ATC (average treatment effect on the
  control) 139
ATEs (average treatment effects) 15, 31, 44, 174,
  277
  calculating from propensity scores
  140–147
ATT (average treatment effect on the
  treated) 139, 143
AUC (area under the curve) 133

B

back-door criterion 182, 201–207
  importance of 205–207
  relationship between ignorability and 287
Berkson's paradox 193
bootstrapping 240–241
  in DoubleML 241

C

CATE (conditional average treatment
  effect) 238
causal discovery 74
causal dynamics, through linear models
  165–176
  analogy of gas flowing through pipes 165
  calculating causation and correlation from
  arrows' coefficients 171–172
  collider correlation 169–170
  confounder correlation 167–168
  correlation and causation comparison 170
  correlation flowing through graphs 166–170
  do operator 173–176
  mediator correlation 168–169
causal effects, calculating causation and correlation from arrows' coefficients 172
causal graphs, do-calculus 218–219
causal inference 1, 67–84, 86
  estimating causal effect with IVs 256–261
  estimating causal effects with linear models
  153–164
  graphs 181–201
  machine learning and 114–116
  mathematical proof of ATE 350–353
  observing vs. intervening 341–342
  recommender systems 83
  Simpson's paradox, solution to 341
  steps in process of 5–8
  steps to formulate problem using graphs
  70–78

causal inference *(continued)*
  time-related events, synthetic controls
    310–321
  when to use graphs in analysis 68–70
causal models, breaking into independent
    modules 185–188
CausalImpact library 318–321
causality 3–29
  causal models vs. predictive models of
    machine learning 8–10
  chapter quiz 28
  experimental studies 10–16
  further reading 27–28
  observational studies 16–21
  statistics 21–27
chains 189–190
Chatbot Usage variable 253
clone method 270
CLT (central limit theorem) 232
colliders 192–194
  collider correlation 169–170
  collider effects 163–164
conditional expectations 25–27
conditional independence 182–201
  arrival time example of 183
  mathematical example of 183–185
  role of graphs in 184–185
conditional intervention 60–61
conditional probabilities 21, 23–27
conditioning 24, 36, 41
confidence intervals 8, 222, 239–243
  analytical formulas for 241–242
  in DoubleML 242–243
confounders 1, 7, 20–21
  confounder correlation 167–168
  confounder effects 161–163
  interventions and RCTs 46–47
  Simpson's paradox 32–38
  structural approach 47–53
confounding
  bias 20
consistency equation 329
control group 14, 322
controlling for variables 173
controls, good and bad 207–210
  bad controls 209–210
  good controls 208
  neutral controls 209
correlations 17
  calculating causation and correlation from
    arrows' coefficients 171–172

counterfactual 274, 280–282, 325
cross-fitting 108–112, 235
cyclic graphs 74–75

D

d-separation 195–199
  defining 199–201
DAGs (directed acyclic graphs) 8–9, 63
data-generating distributions 22–23
data-generating processes 40
data-generation process 22
descendants 200
df datasets 324
DiD (difference in differences) 234, 290,
    321–334
  additional covariates 333–334
  and DoubleML packages 334
  assumptions 327–328
  direct formula 330–331
  effect estimation 329–330
  linear models 331–332
  terminology 324–326
difference in means 31
direct effects 76, 152, 159–164
  collider effects 163–164
  confounder effects 161–163
  direct and indirect effects in practice using
    regression 160–161
  mediator effects 163
  summary of types of effects and which linear
    regressions to use in each case 164
  with linear models 150–177
DML (double machine learning) 222, 224–239
  efficiency of DML estimator 231–233
  FWL theorem 225–231
  heterogeneous treatment effects 238–239
  partially linear model 229
do 41
  linear models and 173–176
do-calculus 218–219
DoubleML library 117
  bootstrapping in 241
  confidence intervals 239–243
  double machine learning 224–239
  DR (doubly robust) estimators 223,
    243–245
DoubleML package 268–270, 334
DoubleMLIIVM class 270
DoubleMLPLR class 234, 236

DR (doubly robust)
estimators 243–245
techniques 223
drdid R package 334

E

efficient controls 211–218
adjusting for income 216–217
including variables in model 216
linear models 217–218
propensity scores 215
empirical distributions 22–23
endogenous variables 185
Engagement variable 253
estimating causal effects with simulating pricing
problem
drawing graph 154
effect of distance 157–159
effect of price 155–157
generating data 154
exchangeability 283
exclusion assumption 254
exogeneity assumption 254
exogenous variables 185, 338
expectations 21, 23–27
conditional expectations 25–27
conditional probabilities 23–25
experimental data 5
experimental group 322
experimental studies 10–16
A/B testing 12–13
randomized controlled trials 14–16

F

factorizing probability distributions 189–194
forks 191–192
FWL (Frisch, Waugh, and Lovell) theorem
225–231

G

Glivenko–Cantelli theorem 22
graphs 178–220
altering correlation between two variables
conditioning on third one 182–201
back-door criterion 201–207
calculating causation and correlation from
arrows' coefficients 171–172
collider correlation 169–170

conditional independence, role of graphs
in 184–185
confounder correlation 167–168
correlation and causation comparison 170
correlation flowing through 166–170
describing problem with 39
drawing 154
efficient controls 211–218
good, bad, and neutral controls 207–210
mediator correlation 168–169
resources for further reading 219
steps to formulate problem using 70–78
when to use in causal inference analysis
68–70

H

heterogeneous treatment effects 238–239
homogeneous treatment effects 286
hyperparameter tuning 236–237

I

ignorability assumption 283
imperfect compliance 286
indirect effects 76, 152, 159–164
collider effects 163–164
confounder effects 161–163
direct and indirect effects in practice using
regression 160–161
mediator effects 163
summary of types of effects and which linear
regressions to use in each case 164
with linear models 150–177
instrument, defined 249
interventions 40–47
in structural approach 51–53
observing vs. intervening 341–342
inverse probability weighting 140, 146–147
IRM (interactive regression model) 234, 244
ITT (intention to treat) 255
IVs (instrumental variables) 234, 249–270
assumptions of 254–255
estimating causal effect with 256–261
in RCTs 255
with potential outcomes 285–287

K

kidney stone example, simulating 49–50
kNN (k-nearest neighbors) 143–144

L

law of total probability 339
linear models 150, 217–218
    applying IVs with 256–258
    causal dynamics through 165–176
    estimating causal effects with 153–164
linear regression 150

M

matching 142–146
mediators
    mediator correlation 168–169
    mediator effects 163
(ML) machine learning, causal inference and
    93–100

N

noncompliant RCTs 255
nuisance function 235

O

observational data 5
observational studies 16–21
    causal effects under confounding 20–21
    simulating synthetic data 18–20
orthogonalization 234
outcome, defined 21

P

p-values 15
parallel paths 327–328
partially linear models, applying IVs for
    258–260
path analysis 166
per protocol 255
PLM (partially linear model) 224, 229
PLR (partially linear regression) 234
POs (potential outcomes) 8, 272–273
    framework, adjustment formula with
        282–285
    framework, assumptions of 287
    framework, DAGs and 287
    IVs with 285–287
positivity assumption 45–46, 77–78, 131
post-treatment variable 210
pretreatment variable 210

propensity scores 119–149, 215
    basic notions of 127–131
    developing intuition about 121–127

R

RCTs (randomized controlled trials) 10, 14–16,
    31, 46–47, 128
    analysis 15
    execution 14
    hypothesis and experiment design 14
    IVs (instrumental variables) 255
RDD (regression discontinuity design) 290
recommender systems 78–80
regression, direct and indirect effects in prac-
    tice using 160–161
relevance assumption 254
RHC (right-heart catheterization) dataset
    245

S

SCM (structural causal model) 188, 338
score function 234
SCs (synthetic controls) 290, 310–321
    assumptions 314–315
    data simulation 312–313
    effect estimation 315
    selecting training and predicting time
        periods 316–321
    terminology 313–314
selection bias 209
Simpson's paradox 32–38
    developing intuition 35–36
    problem with 33–35
    solution to 341
    solving 36–38
simultaneous factors 290
splines 239
spurious correlation 18
strong ignorability 283
structural approach 47–53
    interventions in 51–53
summary function 243
supervised learning 86
SVMs (support vector machines) 8
synthetic data 18–20

T

time series-related techniques 7

time-related events 288–336
   difference in differences 321–334
   method comparison 335–336
   synthetic controls 310–321
total effect 76
treatment variable 21
two-stage least squares (2SLS) algorithm
   263–264
type III error 76

W

walrus operator 48
weak instruments 265–268
Wright's method 176

Z

z-specific effect 60

RELATED MANNING TITLES

Causal AI
by Robert Osazuwa Ness

ISBN 9781633439917
500 pages (estimated), $59.99
December 2024 (estimated)

Experimentation for Engineers
by David Sweet

ISBN 9781617298158
248 pages, $59.99
January 2023

Data Without Labels
by Vaibhav Verdhan

ISBN 9781617298721
250 pages (estimated), $59.99
Spring 2025 (estimated)

Machine Learning Algorithms in Depth
by Vadim Smolyakov

ISBN 9781633439214
328 pages, $79.99
July 2024

For ordering information, go to www.manning.com